PRACTICAL CRIMINAL PROCEDURE

A Constitutional Manual

FOURTH EDITION

PRACTICAL CRIMINAL PROCEDURE

A Constitutional Manual

FOURTH EDITION

Brent E. Newton

Of Counsel,
Gerger, Hennessy & McFarlane
and
Adjunct Professor of Law,
American and Georgetown Universities

NATIONAL INSTITUTE FOR TRIAL ADVOCACY

Address inquiries to:

Reprint Permission
National Institute for Trial Advocacy
325 W. South Boulder Rd., Ste. 1
Louisville, CO 80027-1130
Phone: (800) 225-6482
Fax: (720) 890-7069
Email: permissions@nita.org

ISBN: 978-1-60156-928-8
FBA 1928
eISBN: 978-1-60156-929-5
eFBA 1929

Library of Congress Cataloging-in-Publication Data
Names: Newton, Brent E., 1967- author.
Title: Practical criminal procedure : a constitutional manual / Brent E. Newton, Of Counsel, Gerger, Hennessy & McFarlane and Adjunct Professor of Law, American and Georgetown Universities.
Description: Fourth Edition. | Boulder, CO : National Institute for Trial Advocacy, 2021. | Includes index.
Identifiers: LCCN 2021012399 (print) | LCCN 2021012400 (ebook) | ISBN 9781601569288 (paperback) | ISBN 9781601569295 (kindle edition) | ISBN 9781601569295 (mobi)
Subjects: LCSH: Criminal procedure–United States. | Civil rights–United States.
Classification: LCC KF9625 .N49 2021 (print) | LCC KF9625 (ebook) | DDC 345.73/05–dc23
LC record available at https://lccn.loc.gov/2021012399
LC ebook record available at https://lccn.loc.gov/2021012400

Printed in the United States.

Official co-publisher of NITA.
WKLegaledu.com/NITA

Certified Chain of Custody
Promoting Sustainable Forestry

www.sfiprogram.org

Dedicated to my late father, Wesley Phillips Newton.

CONTENTS

Contents

PREFACE

As both a criminal defense attorney (formerly a public defender and now a private practitioner) and a long-time, albeit part-time, law professor specializing in constitutional criminal procedure, I believe that I have a rare perspective on the subject of criminal procedure. I've worked well over a thousand criminal cases—ranging from misdemeanors and all types of noncapital felonies (both "white collar" and "blue collar" cases) to capital murders for which the prosecution sought the death penalty. I've represented clients in trial courts as well as handled direct appeals and postconviction habeas corpus litigation, in both state and federal courts, including the Supreme Court of the United States. On the other hand, as a legal academic who has taught several dozens of criminal procedure courses during the past two decades, I have enjoyed the luxury of stepping back from the heat of battle and looking at the legal landscape of constitutional criminal procedure in a more detached manner.

From this dual perspective, I have written this book for two primary audiences: practicing criminal lawyers (both defense counsel and prosecutors) looking for a relatively short yet comprehensive book of the constitutional rules of criminal procedure; and law students who wish to supplement a traditional academic casebook on criminal procedure with a shorter, "practical" perspective on the constitutional rules of criminal procedure.

There are many fine academic works—both casebooks and hornbooks—on criminal procedure.[1] In my opinion, however, none of them serves the purpose of this book, which is to provide a comprehensive yet easily accessible manual of the constitutional rules of criminal procedure. Academic books on criminal procedure, like academic books on virtually any law-related topic, tend to be just that—"academic"—and thus often fail to deal with the practical side of law practice. Virtually all lawyers who consult secondary sources in their area of practice want to cut to the chase. They want to understand complex legal issues "in context," i.e., they want to understand how legal issues commonly arise in real-world litigation. This book was written with those practicing lawyers in mind. Similarly, my experience teaching both substantive and advocacy courses at a law school has shown me that most law students want to learn about a particular legal subject from a practical perspective, not wade through lengthy excerpts of judicial opinions in order to separate the wheat from the chaff.

---

1. *See, e.g.,* YALE KAMISAR ET AL., MODERN CRIMINAL PROCEDURE (15th ed. 2018) (casebook); WAYNE R. LAFAVE ET AL., CRIMINAL PROCEDURE (6th ed. 2017) (hornbook).

Although I am a criminal defense lawyer, this book was not written exclusively for defense lawyers. Rather, it provides a neutral, objective overview of the rules of criminal procedure that will also be useful to prosecutors. The very nature of the subject matter lends itself primarily to a discussion of the rights of criminal defendants and the corresponding obligations of police officers and prosecutors. After all, the Bill of Rights protections that constitute the core of criminal procedure are just that—a collection of rights afforded to persons accused of crimes as opposed to rights that benefit the prosecution, law enforcement officers, or crime victims.[2]

In view of the limited length of this single volume, many topics cannot be discussed in great depth. Nonetheless, my goal when writing this book was to touch on every major topic in constitutional criminal procedure and to include at least a brief reference to every significant U.S. Supreme Court decision affecting constitutional criminal procedure. At the end of each chapter, I include a list of citations to, and brief summaries of, the "leading" Supreme Court cases (mentioned in the chapter) that every practitioner and law student who is serious about criminal procedure should know. Throughout the book, I also discuss the many important issues of constitutional criminal procedure not yet addressed by the Supreme Court, but that have been given extensive treatment by the lower state and federal courts (often resulting in a division or "split" among the lower courts, which sooner or later leads the Supreme Court to address the issue).

I would greatly appreciate input from judges, practitioners, and legal scholars. In view of the relatively short length of this book, annual supplements will not be published. Instead, I will attempt to update the entire book periodically to reflect changes in the law.

B.E.N.

Washington, D.C.

February 2021

---

2. *See, e.g.*, United States v. Dent, 984 F.2d 1453, 1466 (7th Cir. 1993) (Easterbrook, J., concurring) ("[T]he confrontation clause of the sixth amendment protects defendants, not prosecutors . . . .").

ACKNOWLEDGMENTS

First and foremost, I wish to thank my wonderful wife, Tirza Noelle Bartels. Not only has she strongly supported my dual career as a practicing lawyer and law professor, she has done so under what at times have been extremely difficult circumstances. She courageously battled cancer twice since 2000 and underwent an unimaginable litany of tests and treatments—including a stem cell transplant—all the while maintaining unwavering support for my career generally and this book in particular. (In 2009, we received the wonderful news that she finally had been cured.) Tirza also lent her grammarian talents, honed during her years as a middle-school English teacher, and line-edited this book. I also acknowledge the patience of my two daughters, Anna and Georgia, who endured many evenings, weekend days, and holidays when their dad was at the computer instead of with them. Finally, I wish to thank my long-time prior bosses—Roland E. Dahlin II and Marjorie A. Meyers, the former and current Federal Public Defenders for the Southern District of Texas. Both encouraged my academic career, including the writing of the first edition of this book, even if occasionally it detracted from my "day job" as a public defender.

This book is dedicated to my late father, Wesley Phillips Newton, PhD, an outstanding example of the "greatest generation." After coming home from World War II—where he fought in the Battle of the Bulge, was seriously injured, and served five months as a POW in Germany—he obtained a PhD in history and became a distinguished history professor. He authored several scholarly books and articles. Together with my mother, Merlin Owen Newton (also a retired professor of history and author), he instilled in me a strong belief in fairness, justice, and equality—the very foundations of our legal system.

INTRODUCTION

There are myriad provisions in the U.S. Constitution that govern the procedures that apply in a criminal prosecution. In addition to the Fifth and Fourteenth Amendments' guarantees that all persons are entitled to "due process" and the "equal protection" of the laws, and a few guarantees in Article I of the Constitution,[1] there are seventeen specific provisions in the Bill of Rights that affect the criminal process: 1) the First Amendment's Free Exercise Clause; 2) the First Amendment's Establishment Clause; 3) the Fourth Amendment's "warrant" and "probable cause" requirements, as well as its general prohibition against "unreasonable" searches and seizures; 4) the Fifth Amendment's Grand Jury Clause; 5) the Fifth Amendment's Double Jeopardy Clause; 6) the Fifth Amendment's prohibition against compelled self-incrimination; 7) the Sixth Amendment's right to a "speedy" trial; 8) the Sixth Amendment's right to a "public" trial; 9) the Sixth Amendment's right to an "impartial" jury; 10) the Sixth Amendment's "vicinage"[2] requirement; 11) the Sixth Amendment's right to be informed of the "nature and cause of the accusation"; 12) the Sixth Amendment's Confrontation Clause; 13) the Sixth Amendment's Compulsory Process Clause; 14) the Sixth Amendment's guarantee of the assistance of counsel; 15) the Eighth Amendment's prohibition against excessive bail; 16) the Eighth Amendment's prohibition against excessive fines; and 17) the Eighth Amendment's prohibition against cruel and unusual punishments.

Since the days of the Warren Court,[3] when the "criminal procedure revolution" began in earnest, almost all significant constitutional rules of criminal procedure found in the Bill of Rights have been "incorporated" via the Due Process Clause of the Fourteenth Amendment and applied to the states.[4] Thus, with the notable exception of the Grand Jury Clause of the Fifth Amendment (which has not been incorporated), the vast majority of the constitutional rules of criminal procedure apply equally in state and federal criminal prosecutions.[5]

---

1. *See* U.S. CONST. art. I, §§ 9 (prohibiting federal ex post facto laws and prohibiting the suspension of the writ of habeas corpus in peacetime) and 10 (prohibiting state ex post facto laws).

2. Although the Sixth Amendment does not use the term "vicinage," that common-law concept is what the Amendment refers to when it provides that juries in criminal prosecutions must be selected from persons in the "State and district wherein the crime shall have been committed." *See* Williams v. Florida, 399 U.S. 78, 93–95 (1970); *cf.* U.S. CONST. art. III, § 2 (addressing the related concept of venue in federal criminal prosecutions).

3. October 5, 1953 to June 23, 1969.

4. *See, e.g.*, Planned Parenthood v. Casey, 505 U.S. 833, 847 (1992) (plurality).

5. The Grand Jury Clause of the Fifth Amendment is discussed in chapter one. The Supreme Court has never been required to rule on whether two provisions—the Sixth Amendment vicinage clause and the Eighth Amendment's prohibition against excessive bail—are incorporated by the Fourteenth

This book addresses the many topics in constitutional criminal procedure in a chronological or linear manner—from the initial probable cause determination through pretrial and trial (or guilty plea) proceedings, to sentencing hearings and motions for a new trial, and concluding with direct and collateral appeals. This format helps the reader appreciate the practical side of criminal procedure.

For the most part, this book focuses on federal constitutional rules of criminal procedure that apply equally to state and federal prosecutions in the United States. A few of the rules discussed are quasi-constitutional in nature. Although the Supreme Court has never held that such rules are mandated by the Constitution, their long-standing and widespread application in every jurisdiction in the United States makes them tantamount to constitutionally based rules. Two good examples are: 1) preliminary hearings, at which the prosecution must establish probable cause to "bind over" defendants; and 2) lesser included offense instructions in noncapital cases, which provide a basis for juries to acquit defendants of a "greater" offense, but convict them of a "lesser" charge instead.

With the exception of federal habeas corpus review—discussed in the final chapter[6]—this book does not address particular statutes or court rules governing procedure, which often provide greater protections for criminal defendants (and correspondingly greater limitations on prosecutors and law enforcement officers) than the Constitution requires.[7] Nor does it address state constitutional rules of criminal

---

Amendment's Due Process Clause. The vast majority of lower courts have held that the vicinage requirement is not incorporated. Stevenson v. Lewis, 384 F.3d 1069, 1071 (9th Cir. 2004) (citing cases). The Court has assumed that the excessive bail clause is incorporated. Schilb v. Kuebel, 404 U.S. 357, 365 (1971).

6. This book gives federal habeas corpus review special treatment because, at least since the mid-1950s, it has been a significant mechanism for enforcing federal constitutional rights in state and federal criminal cases. *See* Rose v. Mitchell, 443 U.S. 545, 579–80 & n.1 (1979) (Powell, J., concurring) (discussing the history of the modern federal writ of habeas corpus). Even after the Antiterrorism and Effective Death Penalty Act of 1996—which somewhat limited the efficacy of the federal writ of habeas corpus in capital and noncapital cases alike—it continues to be an important vehicle for enforcing constitutional protections in criminal cases. *See, e.g.*, Brewer v. Quarterman, 550 U.S. 286 (2007) (granting federal habeas corpus relief to a state death row inmate). This book, therefore, devotes a separate chapter to discussing the statutory and judge-made rules of procedure governing federal habeas corpus appeals.

7. *See, e.g.*, FED. R. CRIM. P. 26.2 (requiring the prosecution to disclose witness statements to defense counsel after the witness has testified, irrespective of whether those prior statements are inconsistent with the witness's testimony); *see also* Jencks v. United States, 353 U.S. 657 (1957) (judicial decision antedating Rule 26.2 requiring disclosure of witness statements, but not as a federal constitutional requirement).

procedure[8] or federal "supervisory authority" rules of criminal procedure[9]—both of which likewise often provide greater protections for criminal defendants.

Needless to say, criminal practitioners and law students who intend to become criminal practitioners should master these other sources of criminal procedure that apply to prosecutions in their particular jurisdictions. However, because the bulk of defendants' rights (and police officers' and prosecutors' corresponding obligations) in criminal prosecutions are rooted in the U.S. Constitution, this book primarily focuses on federal constitutional rules of criminal procedure.

Understanding the constitutional rules of criminal procedure requires an appreciation that the Supreme Court, in formulating such rules, has been willing to tolerate a certain degree of imperfection and error—perhaps in recognition of the realities of an overburdened criminal justice system and a society in which crime rates are chronically high. The Court repeatedly has said that "due process does not require that every conceivable step be taken . . . to eliminate" the arrest and conviction of an innocent person[10] and also that a criminal defendant is entitled to "a fair trial, not a perfect one."[11] Thus, as discussed below, the Court's constitutional rules of criminal procedure at times have intentionally tolerated an appreciable amount of error.[12]

Understanding the rules of criminal procedure and applying them in practice requires a basic understanding of the process in a typical prosecution. A brief "flow chart" of the stages of a typical felony case in state or federal court appears on the following page.

There are variations in the stages of a criminal prosecution, depending on the jurisdiction. At least in felony cases, however, criminal prosecutions in most jurisdictions include these different stages.

---

8. *See, e.g.*, State v. Askerooth, 681 N.W.2d 353, 361–62 (Minn. 2004) (interpreting state constitutional provision against unreasonable searches and seizures in a broader manner than the U.S. Supreme Court's interpretation of the Fourth Amendment).

9. The Supreme Court and federal courts of appeals possess a general supervisory authority in federal criminal prosecutions to create rules of criminal procedure that are not constitutionally mandated nor applicable to state prosecutions. *See, e.g.*, McNabb v. United States, 318 U.S. 332, 340–41 (1943).

10. *See, e.g.*, Baker v. McCollan, 443 U.S. 137, 145 (1979) (internal citations omitted).

11. *See, e.g.*, Delaware v. Van Arsdall, 475 U.S. 673, 681 (1986) (citations and internal quotation marks omitted).

12. Strickland v. Washington, 466 U.S. 668 (1984) (even clearly incompetent conduct by a criminal defense attorney will not result in a reversal of a defendant's conviction unless there is a reasonable probability that, but for the lawyer's incompetence, the result of the trial would have been different).

FLOW CHART OF A TYPICAL CRIMINAL PROSECUTION

Events constituting the alleged crime

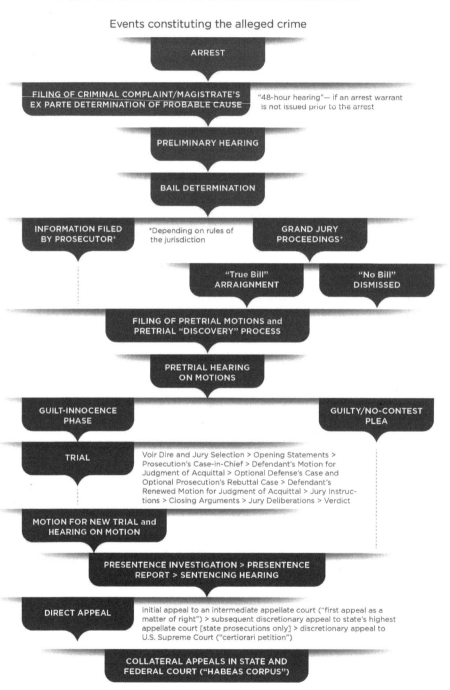

ARREST

FILING OF CRIMINAL COMPLAINT/MAGISTRATE'S EX PARTE DETERMINATION OF PROBABLE CAUSE — "48-hour hearing"— if an arrest warrant is not issued prior to the arrest

PRELIMINARY HEARING

BAIL DETERMINATION

INFORMATION FILED BY PROSECUTOR* — *Depending on rules of the jurisdiction — **GRAND JURY PROCEEDINGS***

"True Bill" ARRAIGNMENT — **"No Bill" DISMISSED**

FILING OF PRETRIAL MOTIONS and PRETRIAL "DISCOVERY" PROCESS

PRETRIAL HEARING ON MOTIONS

GUILT-INNOCENCE PHASE — **GUILTY/NO-CONTEST PLEA**

TRIAL — Voir Dire and Jury Selection > Opening Statements > Prosecution's Case-in-Chief > Defendant's Motion for Judgment of Acquittal > Optional Defense's Case and Optional Prosecution's Rebuttal Case > Defendant's Renewed Motion for Judgment of Acquittal > Jury Instructions > Closing Arguments > Jury Deliberations > Verdict

MOTION FOR NEW TRIAL and HEARING ON MOTION

PRESENTENCE INVESTIGATION > PRESENTENCE REPORT > SENTENCING HEARING

DIRECT APPEAL — Initial appeal to an intermediate appellate court ("first appeal as a matter of right") > subsequent discretionary appeal to state's highest appellate court [state prosecutions only] > discretionary appeal to U.S. Supreme Court ("certiorari petition")

COLLATERAL APPEALS IN STATE AND FEDERAL COURT ("HABEAS CORPUS")

CHAPTER ONE

PROBABLE CAUSE DETERMINATIONS BY JUDGES AND GRAND JURIES

In many jurisdictions, there are three points in the early part of a criminal prosecution at which it is determined whether "probable cause" exists—the first two by a magistrate or judge and the third by a grand jury. Although arguably duplicative, each probable cause determination is intended to assure that the prosecution has sufficient proof of its allegations to justify putting a criminal defendant on trial.

The Supreme Court has elusively defined the quantum of proof of "probable cause" in the following manner:

> The substance of all the definitions of probable cause is a reasonable ground for belief of guilt. . . . And this means less than evidence which would justify . . . conviction. . . . [I]t . . . mean[s] more than bare suspicion[.] Probable cause exists where the facts and circumstances within [a person's] knowledge and of which [he or she] had reasonably trustworthy information [are] sufficient in themselves to warrant a man of reasonable caution in the belief that an offense has been . . . committed [and that the defendant committed it].[1]

Probable cause is thus a lesser quantum of proof than a "preponderance" of the evidence, "clear and convincing" evidence, and "proof beyond a reasonable doubt."[2] It is, however, greater than the quantum of "reasonable suspicion" required for "*Terry* stops" and similar law enforcement encounters governed by less than probable cause.[3]

In criminal procedure, "probable cause" is used in at least four contexts (the first is addressed later in chapter five): 1) the quantum of proof required for a police officer to arrest a person for an offense without an arrest warrant or to engage in a warrantless search for or seizure of contraband or incriminating evidence, which is

---

1. Brinegar v. United States, 338 U.S. 160, 175–76 (1949) (citations and internal quotation marks omitted); *see also* District of Columbia v. Wesby, 138 S. Ct. 577, 586 (2018); Florida v. Harris, 568 U.S. 237, 242–45 (2013); Maryland v. Pringle, 540 U.S. 366, 371 (2003); Illinois v. Gates, 462 U.S. 213, 235–36 (1983).
2. United States v. Limares, 269 F.3d 794, 798 (7th Cir. 2001); *see also Pringle*, 540 U.S. at 371.
3. *See* Terry v. Ohio, 392 U.S. 1 (1968), discussed in chapter five.

the same standard governing a magistrate or judge who issues an arrest warrant or search warrant;[4] 2) the quantum of proof required for a magistrate or judge to sustain a warrantless arrest at an ex parte "*Gerstein*[5] hearing"; 3) the quantum of proof required for a magistrate or judge to "bind over" a defendant at the conclusion of a preliminary hearing; and 4) the quantum of proof required for a grand jury to return an indictment. Although theoretically the four types of probable cause mean the same thing, in reality they each mean something slightly different.

The most demanding variant of probable cause appears to be the quantum of proof that a magistrate or a judge requires to bind over a defendant at the conclusion of a preliminary hearing.[6] Logically, the quantum of proof governing a grand jury should be the most demanding,[7] considering that the dismissal of charges at a preliminary hearing for lack of probable cause does not bar a subsequent indictment by a grand jury. However, it is widely believed that the vast majority of grand juries do not actually apply the probable cause standard in any meaningful way— hence the adage, "a grand jury will indict a ham sandwich."[8]

1.1   *Gerstein* Hearings

In *Gerstein v. Pugh*,[9] the Supreme Court held that a law enforcement officer who arrests a defendant without an arrest warrant, an indictment, or other type of charging instrument that had been previously issued by a judge or magistrate, must take the arrested person before "a neutral and detached" magistrate or judge for a "prompt" determination of whether probable cause exists. Such determinations are typically referred to as "48-hour hearings" or "*Gerstein* hearings," and usually occur at or before a defendant's initial appearance in court. It is called a "48-hour" hearing because the Supreme Court in *County of Riverside v. McLaughlin*[10] held that under the Fourth Amendment, such a proceeding generally must occur within

---

4. *See* Whiteley v. Warden, 401 U.S. 560, 566 (1971) (probable cause standard governing police officers who engage in a warrantless search or seizure is the same as the standard governing a judicial official who issues a search or arrest warrant).

5. Gerstein v. Pugh, 420 U.S. 103 (1975).

6. *See* Williams v. Kobel, 789 F.2d 463, 468–69 (7th Cir. 1986); Hunter v. District Court, 543 P.2d 1265, 1269–71 (Colo. 1975) (Erickson, J., dissenting) (citing cases and Model Code of Prearraignment P.); Myers v. Commonwealth, 298 N.E.2d 819, 823–24 (Mass. 1973); *see also* Yale Kamisar et al., Modern Criminal Procedure 933 (15th ed. 2018).

7. Indeed, the standard instructions given to many federal grand juries actually define probable cause as being akin to the preponderance of the evidence standard. *See, e.g.*, Federal District Judges' Bench Book [S.D. Tex.]: Grand Jury Selection & Instructions, § 7.04, at 9 (defining probable cause as "evidence [that] persuades you [grand jurors] that a crime has probably been committed by the person or persons accused")

8. *See* People v. Carter, 566 N.E.2d 119, 124 (N.Y. 1990) (Titone, J., dissenting).

9. 420 U.S. 103 (1975).

10. 500 U.S. 44 (1991).

forty-eight hours of the arrest to be constitutionally reasonable (exclusive of weekend days and holidays).

Such a hearing is usually held as an ex parte proceeding rather than as an adversary hearing; i.e., the defendant is not represented by counsel at that juncture, and the "hearing" is typically nothing more than a magistrate's or judge's cursory review of an affidavit or a sworn oral statement of an arresting officer to determine whether probable cause exists to support the warrantless arrest. In the overwhelming majority of cases, probable cause is found to exist at a *Gerstein* hearing.

An open question—in terms of the Supreme Court's Fourth Amendment jurisprudence—is whether there is any remedy in criminal cases for a *Gerstein/McLaughlin* violation.[11] Both *Gerstein* and *McLaughlin* were civil rights actions rather than criminal prosecutions and thus did not require the Court to decide whether a criminal defendant has a remedy for a Fourth Amendment violation of this type. The most common remedial issue in a criminal prosecution is whether a court should suppress a defendant's confession obtained by police after the time that the defendant should have been taken before a magistrate.[12] The lower courts are divided on this issue, which curiously has not been litigated in many cases.[13]

1.2 Preliminary Hearings

Once a defendant is arrested (with or without a warrant) or is required to appear in court pursuant to a summons, they are entitled to a preliminary hearing, also commonly referred to as a "preliminary examination" or a "probable cause hearing."[14] The preliminary hearing is independent of, and occurs after, a *Gerstein* hearing. In most jurisdictions, the right to a preliminary hearing expires once a

---

11. Powell v. Nevada, 511 U.S. 79, 85 n.* (1994) (reserving the question for a future case).

12. The Fourth Amendment remedial issue should be distinguished from a nonconstitutional remedial issue concerning whether an "unreasonable" delay in bringing a federal defendant before a federal magistrate after arrest—*see* 18 U.S.C. § 3501(c) and FED. R. CRIM. P. 5(a)—constitutes a basis to suppress a confession given during a period of unreasonable delay. In Corley v. United States, 556 U.S. 303 (2009), the Supreme Court held that a confession made during a period of time that violates Rule 5(a)'s prompt presentation requirement is generally inadmissible in federal criminal cases. That suppression remedy is not a constitutional command and, thus, does not apply to criminal cases in the state courts.

13. *Compare, e.g.,* Anderson v. Caldern, 232 F.3d 1053, 1070–77 (9th Cir. 2000) (holding that evidence obtained as a result of a *Gerstein/McLaughlin* violation should be suppressed unless the taint from the violation is "attenuated"), *with* Lawhorn v. Allen, 519 F.3d 1272, 1292 (11th Cir. 2008) (refusing to adopt a per se rule of suppression based on a *Gerstein/McLaughlin* violation and, instead, primarily focusing on whether a defendant's confession obtained after the time when the defendant should have been taken before a magistrate was voluntary); United States v. Terrell, 483 F. App'x 161, 165 (6th Cir. 2012) (same).

14. *See, e.g.,* FED R. CRIM. P. 5.1; CALIF. PENAL CODE § 872; TEX. CODE CRIM. PROC. ANN. art. 16.01.

grand jury has returned an indictment. Furthermore, dismissal of the charges at a preliminary hearing does not bar the grand jury from returning an indictment.[15]

A preliminary hearing is an adversary proceeding in which the prosecution has the burden to establish probable cause that the defendant committed the charged offense. If the magistrate or judge who conducts a preliminary hearing determines that there is such probable cause, then the charges remain and the defendant is "bound over" (i.e., is detained without bond or released on bond) pending the grand jury's hearing of the case or disposition of the charges by a guilty plea (in the event the defendant waives the right to a grand jury).[16]

A preliminary hearing is not required by the U.S. Constitution,[17] although the right is afforded by statute or court rule in every jurisdiction in the United States. In federal court, defendants charged with felonies and nonpetty misdemeanors have a statutory right to a preliminary hearing;[18] in many state courts, only defendants charged with felonies have a statutory right to a preliminary hearing.[19] Although not required by the Constitution, a preliminary hearing is nonetheless a "critical stage" of the proceedings, at which a defendant is entitled to the assistance of counsel and other procedural protections.[20] In some jurisdictions, preliminary hearings rarely occur—most defendants waive them or are indicted expeditiously by a grand jury before a preliminary hearing can be conducted. In other jurisdictions, such as California and the federal system, preliminary hearings are much more commonplace.

To a degree even greater than the ex parte *Gerstein* hearing, the preliminary hearing serves a "screening" function. That is, its primary function is "to discover whether or not there are substantial grounds upon which a prosecution may be based."[21] The preliminary hearing has secondary purposes as well, including the preservation of testimony (for subsequent impeachment of the witness at trial or for admission as substantive evidence at trial in the event the witness later becomes unavailable) and pretrial discovery of the prosecution's evidence by the defense.[22]

In the vast majority of jurisdictions, a magistrate or judge is not constrained by the Fourth or Fifth Amendment's exclusionary rules concerning physical evidence and confessions when determining probable cause at a preliminary hearing.[23] That

---

15. *See* Jaben v. United States, 381 U.S. 214, 220 (1965); United States v. Dobbs, 506 F.2d 445 (5th Cir. 1975); Bowens v. Superior Court, 820 P.2d 600 (Cal. 1991).

16. *See* KAMISAR ET AL., *supra* n.6, at 929.

17. United States v. Coley, 441 F.2d 1299, 1301 (5th Cir. 1971).

18. FED. R. CRIM. P. 5.1(a).

19. *See, e.g.*, People v. Reno, 272 N.W.2d 144 (Mich. Ct. App. 1978).

20. *See, e.g.*, Coleman v. Alabama, 399 U.S. 1 (1970) (providing for right to counsel at preliminary hearing). The right to counsel under the Sixth Amendment is discussed in Chapter Three.

21. Thies v. State, 189 N.W. 539, 541 (Wis. 1922).

22. KAMISAR ET AL., *supra* n.6, at 924-26, 939-42.

23. *See* FED. R. CRIM. P. 5.1(e); *see also* State v. Kane, 588 A.2d 179, 184 (Conn. 1991).

is, illegally seized evidence or an illegally obtained confession (e.g., one obtained without *Miranda* warnings) is admissible at a preliminary hearing. However, the jurisdictions are divided over whether the rules of evidence (including the general rule against hearsay) apply at a preliminary hearing, although most jurisdictions permit probable cause determinations to be based on hearsay.[24] In virtually all jurisdictions, a defendant is not permitted to defeat a finding of probable cause by presenting evidence of an affirmative defense to the charges (such as insanity or entrapment) and instead is only permitted to offer truly "exculpatory" evidence that negates an essential element of the charged offense.[25]

In most jurisdictions, magistrates or judges who preside over preliminary hearings are generally permitted to make only limited credibility determinations about the evidence, even when the defense introduces competing evidence to rebut the prosecution's evidence.[26] Generally, the court should not make credibility determinations or weigh competing evidence when determining probable cause; the charges may be dismissed based on credibility determinations only if the magistrate or judge reasonably concludes that the prosecution's evidence or witnesses are incredible as a matter of law.[27] Furthermore, many courts have stressed that a preliminary hearing is not a "mini-trial" and, thus, a magistrate or judge presiding over the proceeding should not permit the defense a full-fledged opportunity to rebut the prosecution's case—an opportunity that is afforded to the defendant at a subsequent trial.[28] Therefore, if, after a reasonable yet limited opportunity for the defense to cross-examine the prosecution's witnesses and offer exculpatory evidence in rebuttal, the evidence viewed in a light most favorable to the prosecution establishes probable cause, then the defendant will be bound over.[29] In the vast majority of cases, the court finds probable cause and the defendant is bound over for trial.[30]

1.3   Grand Jury Proceedings

Although the vast majority of the rules of criminal procedure enshrined in the Bill of Rights have been "incorporated" by the Due Process Clause of the Fourteenth Amendment and thus made applicable to the states (in addition to the federal government), the Fifth Amendment's requirement that a grand jury issue an

---

24. *Compare* FED. R. EVID. 1101(d)(3) (rules of evidence inapplicable at federal preliminary hearing), with TEX. CODE CRIM. PROC. ANN. art. 16.07 (rules of evidence applicable at Texas preliminary hearing).

25. KAMISAR ET AL., *supra* n.6, at 944.

26. *See, e.g.*, Desper v. State, 318 S.E.2d 437 (W. Va. 1984); Myers v. Commonwealth, 298 N.E.2d 819 (Mass. 1973).

27. *See, e.g., Hunter*, 543 P.2d 1265.

28. *See, e.g.*, Coleman v. Burnett, 477 F.2d 1187, 1201 (D.C. Cir. 1973)

29. *See Williams*, 789 F.2d at 468–69; *see also* State v. Clark, 20 P.3d 300 (Utah 2001); People v. Hall, 999 P.2d 207 (Colo. 2000); State v. Bockert, 893 P.2d 832 (Kan. 1995).

30. The specific percentages vary by jurisdiction, but on average only a very small percentage of cases are dismissed at the conclusion of a preliminary hearing. *See* KAMISAR ET AL., *supra* n.6, at 954.

indictment in all felony cases has not been so incorporated.[31] Therefore, a state is free to dispense with the traditional requirement of a grand jury and allow charges to be filed directly by a prosecutor[32]—typically in a charging instrument called an "information." The only federal constitutional requirement that applies to the states is that a "neutral and detached" magistrate or judge find probable cause that the defendant committed the charged offense at a *Gerstein* hearing.[33] Although not constitutionally compelled to do so, eighteen states, however, require grand juries to issue indictments in felony cases as a matter of state constitutional law or state statute, and almost all of the remainder provide for grand juries as an available option for prosecutors.[34]

As discussed below, extremely limited constitutional remedies[35] are available for criminal defendants who challenge indictments on the ground that alleged procedural irregularities or prosecutorial misconduct occurred during the grand jury's deliberations, which are ex parte and secret in nature. Such challenges are made in the form of a pretrial motion to dismiss an indictment or on direct or postconviction appeal of a conviction following a trial (where the alleged irregularities or misconduct were discovered only after the trial).

As an initial matter, there are virtually no constitutional limits on the type of evidence or information that a grand jury can consider in returning an indictment. In *Costello v. United States*,[36] the Supreme Court rejected a federal defendant's claim that an indictment was invalid because it was based solely on hearsay. In *Costello*, the Supreme Court refused to require judicial review of the legal or factual sufficiency of the evidence relied on to return an indictment[37]—in contrast to the judicial review required when a criminal defendant challenges the sufficiency of the evidence supporting a guilty verdict.[38] Similarly, constitutional "exclusionary rules"—based on *Miranda* violations or unconstitutional searches or seizures of evidence—do not apply to grand jury proceedings.[39]

---

31. Beck v. Washington, 369 U.S. 541, 545 (1962) (discussing Hurtado v. California, 110 U.S. 516 (1884)).

32. *Id.*

33. *See* Cooksey v. Delo, 94 F.3d 1214, 1217 (8th Cir. 1996).

34. KAMISAR ET AL., *supra* n.6, at 946.

35. Federal courts traditionally have been more willing to dismiss indictments for nonconstitutional irregularities—under their "supervisory authority," *see, e.g.*, United States v. Maceo, 873 F.2d 1, 3–4 (1st Cir. 1989)—yet such irregularities or misconduct must be significant. *See, e.g.*, United States v. Breslin, 916 F. Supp. 438 (E.D. Pa. 1996) (listing numerous instances of prosecutorial misconduct during the grand jury proceedings).

36. 350 U.S. 359 (1956).

37. *Id.* at 362 ("[N]either the Fifth Amendment nor any other constitutional provision prescribes the kind of evidence upon which grand juries must act.").

38. *See* Jackson v. Virginia, 443 U.S. 307 (1979). Such judicial review of a petit jury's guilty verdict is discussed in Chapter Nine.

39. *See, e.g.*, United States v. Calandra, 414 U.S. 338 (1974).

There also are few constitutional limitations on prosecutorial or police misconduct before a grand jury. In *United States v. Williams*,[40] the Supreme Court held that prior to the return of an indictment, the prosecution has no duty to disclose exculpatory evidence in its possession to the defendant or to grand jurors—in contrast to such a prosecutorial duty of disclosure after a defendant has been charged.[41] The fact that a prosecutor or a member of the prosecution team knowingly presents perjured testimony to the grand jury also does not necessarily vitiate an indictment. Most courts hold that so long as there was sufficient independent, nonperjured evidence presented to grand jurors to support a finding of probable cause, the indictment is constitutionally valid notwithstanding the perjury.[42]

In the rare instance where misconduct or irregularities during grand jury proceedings rise to the level of a constitutional violation, whether there is a remedy available will usually depend on timing,[43] i.e., when the error is discovered by the defense and called to the trial court's attention.[44] If such constitutional error is discovered before a petit jury returns a guilty verdict, a district court often will dismiss the indictment, although the prosecution is permitted to seek another indictment as long as the error is not repeated.[45] However, if a constitutional error during the grand jury proceedings is not discovered until after a petit jury has returned a guilty verdict, then generally no remedy will be available because the petit jury's guilty verdict (which was based on a higher standard of proof)[46] will be deemed to have rendered any error in the grand jury's earlier proceedings harmless.[47]

---

40. United States v. Williams, 504 U.S. 36, 47 (1992).

41. *See* Brady v. Maryland, 373 U.S. 83 (1963). The "*Brady* doctrine" is discussed in Chapter Thirteen.

42. *See, e.g.,* United States v. Claiborne, 765 F.2d 784, 791 (9th Cir. 1985); United States v. Liciardello, 93 F. Supp. 3d 365, 369–70 (E.D. Pa. 2015).

43. *See* United States v. Martinez, 710 F. Supp. 415, 417 (D.P.R. 1989) (discussing the "timing" issue). If a defendant pleaded guilty, any claim of constitutional error in the grand jury process is waived (regardless of when the defendant discovered the error). *See* Tollett v. Henderson, 411 U.S. 258 (1973).

44. With the exception addressing discrimination claims in the context of grand jury selection and the nonapplicability of the *Brady* doctrine to grand jury proceedings, the Supreme Court has not addressed the availability of remedies, if any, for constitutional violations occurring during the grand jury process and instead only has addressed nonconstitutional claims (*e.g.,* a grand jury witness testified in the presence of another grand jury witness in violation of Fed. R. Crim. P. 6(d)). *See, e.g.,* Bank of Nova Scotia v. United States, 487 U.S. 250 (1988); United States v. Mechanik, 475 U.S. 66 (1986). Both *Bank of Nova Scotia* and *Mechanik* held that there is no remedy for nonconstitutional errors that did not prejudice the defendant. Most lower courts have assumed that a similar rule is applicable to constitutional errors (other than discrimination claims). *See, e.g.,* United States v. Navarro, 608 F.3d 529, 538–40 (9th Cir. 2010).

45. *See Martinez,* 710 F. Supp. at 417.

46. A petit jury can return a guilty verdict only if it finds beyond a reasonable doubt that the defendant is guilty; conversely, a grand jury can return an indictment if it finds probable cause. *See Mechanik,* 475 U.S. at 70.

47. *See* United States v. Reyes-Echevarria, 345 F.3d 1, 4 (1st Cir. 2003).

There is an important exception to this general rule of harmless error based on a jury's guilty verdict. If "the structural protections of the grand jury have been so compromised as to render the proceedings fundamentally unfair,"[48] then the indictment is invalid (and any conviction resulting from such indictment will be reversed) without any inquiry into whether such error was harmless.[49] Such a class of "structural" error appears to be limited to racial, ethnic, or gender discrimination in the selection of grand jurors.[50]

Just as there are significant limits on judicial review of indictments based on defects in the grand jury proceedings, the Bill of Rights affords very limited protections to grand jury witnesses, including unindicted suspects who are "targets" of the grand jury. A grand jury witness has no right to the assistance of counsel, retained or appointed, when she testifies before a grand jury.[51] It is customary that the witness may, however, take breaks during their testimony and consult with counsel outside of the grand jury's deliberation room.[52] Although the Supreme Court has held that a grand jury witness need not be read *Miranda* warnings prior to being compelled to testify (even if the grand jury is seeking to elicit incriminating testimony),[53] a grand jury witness may invoke the right to silence under the Fifth Amendment if they have a reasonable basis to fear incrimination.[54] However, a court can compel such a witness's testimony by granting "derivative use" or "transactional" immunity and, if the witness thereafter still refuses to testify, hold the witness in contempt of court and imprison them until they decide to testify.[55]

The Supreme Court also has held that a grand jury subpoena (including a subpoena duces tecum) does not amount to a "seizure" of the subpoenaed witness or the item sought by the subpoena duces tecum under the Fourth Amendment and thus probable cause is not required to enforce a subpoena.[56] The Court has recognized only a very limited Fourth Amendment protection that prohibits "overbroad"

---

48. *See* Bank of Nova Scotia, 487 U.S. at 256–57. The concept of "structural error" is discussed in chapter fourteen.

49. United States v. Nelson-Rodriguez, 319 F.3d 12, 29–30 (1st Cir. 2003).

50. *See, e.g.*, Vasquez v. Hillery, 474 U.S. 254 (1986); Campbell v. Louisiana, 523 U.S. 392 (1998).

51. United States v. Mandujano, 425 U.S. 564, 581 (1976).

52. *Id.* The Supreme Court has left open the question of whether the Constitution gives a grand jury witness a right to consult with counsel outside of the jury room. Connecticut v. Gabbert, 526 U.S. 286, 292 (1999).

53. *Mandujano*, 425 U.S. at 580.

54. *Id.* at 574.

55. *Id.* at 575; *see also* United States v. Hubbell, 530 U.S. 27, 38–39 (2000) (discussing such immunity). A high-profile example of such a use of the contempt power involved Susan McDougall, who refused to testify before a grand jury investigating former President Bill Clinton. In re Grand Jury Subpoena, 97 F.3d 1090 (8th Cir. 1996). The various types of immunity are discussed in chapter four.

56. United States v. Dionisio, 410 U.S. 1, 9–10 (1973).

National Institute for Trial Advocacy

subpoenas,[57] although courts tend to be very deferential to grand juries in terms of their subpoena power and apply a vague "reasonableness" standard.[58] However, when the "act of production" of some item of physical evidence (e.g., a diary) itself amounts to a "testimonial" act (e.g., bringing a copy of one's personal diary to the grand jury, thereby authenticating it[59]), the Supreme Court has held that the subject of the subpoena may refuse to comply with the subpoena duces tecum on Fifth Amendment right-to-silence grounds.[60] The only manner in which the subpoena duces tecum can be enforced in such a situation is through a grant of "derivative use" or "transactional" immunity.[61]

1.4 Leading Supreme Court Decisions Concerning Preliminary Hearings and Grand Juries

- *Coleman v. Alabama*, 399 U.S. 1 (1970) (although preliminary hearings are not constitutionally required, if a jurisdiction provides for one, it then constitutes a "critical stage" of the proceedings under the Sixth Amendment, and a defendant is entitled to the right to counsel at the preliminary hearing).

- *Gerstein v. Pugh*, 420 U.S. 103 (1975) (under the Fourth Amendment, criminal defendants arrested without a warrant or indictment having been issued are entitled to a "prompt" determination of whether probable cause exists by a neutral and detached judicial official; such a determination need not be made at an adversary preliminary hearing and, instead, may be made ex parte by a magistrate or judge based on the sworn allegations of a law enforcement officer).

- *County of Riverside v. McLaughlin*, 500 U.S. 44 (1991) (a delay in excess of forty-eight hours between a warrantless arrest and a "*Gerstein* hearing" is presumptively unreasonable under the Fourth Amendment).

- *Hurtado v. California*, 110 U.S. 516 (1884) (Fifth Amendment's Grand Jury Clause is not "incorporated" via the Due Process Clause of the Fourteenth Amendment; the states are not constitutionally obligated to use

---

57. *See, e.g.*, Donovan v. Lone Steer, Inc., 464 U.S. 408, 415 (1984); Okla. Press Pub. Co. v. Walling, 327 U.S. 186, 209 (1946).
58. *See, e.g.*, United States v. Judicial Watch, Inc., 371 F.3d 824, 833 (D.C. Cir. 2004); *see also* United States v. R. Enterprises, 498 U.S. 292 (1991) (affording deference to grand juries with respect to their subpoena power; distinguishing trial subpoenas in this regard).
59. *See, e.g.*, In re Kave, 760 F.2d 343, 358 (1st Cir. 1985).
60. United States v. Doe, 465 U.S. 605 (1984); Fisher v. United States, 425 U.S. 391, 410 (1976).
61. *Doe*, 465 U.S. at 614–15; *see also* Kastigar v. United States, 406 U.S. 441 (1972) (discussing the type of immunity required to compel a witness to testify).

grand juries even though the federal government is required to do so in felony cases).

- *Costello v. United States*, 350 U.S. 359 (1956) (a grand jury's indictment may be based solely on hearsay; no judicial review of the sufficiency of the evidence supporting an indictment).

- *United States v. Dionisio*, 410 U.S. 1 (1973) (enforcing compliance with a grand jury subpoena does not amount to a "seizure" under the Fourth Amendment; probable cause thus is not required for issuance or enforcement of a grand jury subpoena).

- *United States v. Mandujano*, 425 U.S. 564 (1976) (*Miranda* warnings need not be given to a grand jury witness, even if a witness is a "target" of the grand jury, although such a witness may invoke the Fifth Amendment privilege against self-incrimination).

- *United States v. Doe*, 465 U.S. 605 (1984) (under certain circumstances, a grand jury witness's "act of production" in response to a grand jury subpoena duces tecum constitutes self-incrimination, and the witness may refuse to comply by invoking the privilege against self-incrimination).

- *Vasquez v. Hillery*, 474 U.S. 254 (1986) (invidious discrimination in the selection of members of a state or federal grand jury violates the Equal Protection Clause and constitutes "structural" error requiring reversal of a conviction based on such a grand jury's indictment without any showing of harm to the defendant).

- *United States v. Mechanik*, 475 U.S. 66 (1986) (ordinarily, nonstructural errors that occurred during the grand jury process are automatically rendered harmless by a petit jury's subsequent guilty verdict on the charge contained in the indictment).

- *Bank of Nova Scotia v. United States*, 487 U.S. 250 (1988) (if a defendant discovers a nonstructural error that occurred in the grand jury process before a petit jury returns a guilty verdict, dismissal of the indictment is not required unless the defendant shows that the error influenced the grand jury in a manner that prejudiced the defendant).

- *United States v. Williams*, 504 U.S. 36 (1992) (prosecutor's duties under *Brady v. Maryland*, 373 U.S. 83 (1963), are not applicable to grand jury proceedings; thus, an indictment will not be dismissed if a member of the prosecution team suppressed material, exculpatory evidence during the grand jury proceedings).

CHAPTER TWO

BAIL PRACTICES

2.1   Bail Practices Generally

Bail (or "bond") practices vary widely in the many different jurisdictions in the United States. In most states, bail theoretically is available in the vast majority of noncapital cases[1] (with typical exceptions for defendants with serious prior criminal records and defendants already released on bond in a prior case who committed a new offense while on bond). In reality, though, while bail is set in the vast majority of state cases, defendants often do not secure release because they are unable to "make bail," even when it has been set.[2] In most jurisdictions, bail is typically granted or denied at the same time the preliminary hearing is held.

Bail determinations in many states are informal and often involve negotiations between prosecutors and defense counsel over the amount of bail and other conditions of release. Although many state courts are permitted to consider a defendant's general "dangerousness" in setting the bail amount and restrictive conditions of release (e.g., home detention with an ankle monitor), they usually cannot deny bail outright based on a finding that a defendant is a danger to the community, even in cases charging violent offenses.[3] In addition, bail practices in many states—unlike bail practice in the federal system—rely heavily on bail bondsmen (also referred to as "corporate sureties").[4]

Defendants typically secure release by paying a private bondsman a nonrefundable percentage of the bail amount (usually 10 percent) in exchange for the bondsman posting the bail. In situations where the defendant and prosecutor do not agree to a particular bail amount, bail amounts are often determined by a schedule that sets amounts for particular offenses.[5]

---

1. In all jurisdictions, bail in capital cases is either prohibited or virtually impossible to obtain. *See, e.g.,* Simpson v. Owens, 85 P.3d 478, 486 n.13 (Ariz. Ct. App. 2004).
2. *See generally* John A. Chamberlin, *Note, Bounty Hunters: Can the Criminal Justice System Live Without Them?*, 1998 U. ILL. L. REV. 1175 (1998) (discussing bail practices in the United States).
3. *See, e.g.,* Ex parte Colbert, 805 So. 2d 687 (Ala. 2001).
4. Despite the Supreme Court's extremely critical view of bail bondsmen, *see* Schilb v. Kuebel, 404 U.S. 357, 359–60, 373–74 (Douglas, J., dissenting); 381–82 & n.1 (Stewart, J., dissenting, joined by Brennan, J.), state bail systems that primarily utilize bail bondsmen have never been ruled per se unconstitutional.
5. *See Chamberlin, supra* n.2.

Bail practices in federal court are dramatically different from traditional state court bail practices.[6] In federal court, the granting of bail is not essentially automatic in noncapital cases, as it is in many state courts, because in the federal system a defendant's "dangerousness" may in many cases be sufficient in itself to deny bail.[7] Furthermore, a federal court's ruling on whether bail should be granted often occurs only after a formal adversary hearing, referred to as a "detention hearing."[8] In cases involving federal defendants without serious prior criminal records and not involving alleged crimes of violence or drug-trafficking offenses, bail in federal court usually is set at a defendant's initial appearance in court without the need for a detention hearing. However, in many types of federal cases—especially those involving crimes of violence and federal drug-trafficking offenses—bail is granted or denied only after a formal detention hearing.[9]

2.2 Federal Constitutional Issues Concerning Bail

Relatively few federal constitutional issues have arisen in connection with bail in criminal cases.[10] In both state and federal criminal cases, there is no constitutional right to bail under the Eighth Amendment.[11] Rather, the Eighth Amendment provides that if bail is authorized under the law of a jurisdiction, it cannot be set in an "excessive" amount. As the Supreme Court has stated:

> [Since] the passage of the Judiciary Act of 1789 . . . federal law has [provided for] bail. This traditional right to freedom before conviction permits the unhampered preparation of a defense, and serves to prevent the infliction of punishment prior to conviction. Unless this right to bail before trial is preserved, the presumption of innocence, secured only after centuries of struggle, would lose its meaning.
>
> The right to release before trial is conditioned upon the accused's giving adequate assurance that he will stand trial and submit to sentence if found guilty . . . . Bail set at a figure higher than an amount reasonably calculated to fulfill this purpose is "excessive" under the Eighth Amendment.[12]

---

6. *See* 18 U.S.C. §§ 3141, *et seq.* (Federal Bail Reform Act of 1984).

7. United States v. Salerno, 481 U.S. 739 (1987).

8. United States v. Byrd, 969 F.2d 106 (5th Cir. 1992).

9. *See generally* Hon. Bruce D. Pringle, *Bail and Detention in Federal Criminal Proceedings*, 22 COLO. LAW. 913 (May 1993).

10. Depending on the jurisdiction, there are myriad statutory and state constitutional issues that arise concerning bail. *See, e.g., Byrd*, 969 F.2d at 109 (interpreting provisions of the Federal Bail Reform Act).

11. Carlson v. Landon, 342 U.S. 524, 546 (1952). The Eighth Amendment provides: "Excessive bail shall not be required, nor excessive fines imposed, nor cruel and unusual punishments inflicted." U.S. CONST. amend. VIII.

12. Stack v. Boyle, 342 U.S. 1, 4–5 (1951) (internal citations omitted).

Successful challenges to bail as "excessive" are not uncommon. Every case turns on its own facts and circumstances—such as the gravity of the crime, the defendant's income and net worth, their ties to the community, and the potential danger posed to witnesses and victims if the defendant were to be released.[13] There are no bright lines under the Eighth Amendment's excessive bail clause. However, in the modern era, appellate courts in most jurisdictions consider bail exceeding one million dollars to be constitutionally excessive in cases not involving the most serious types of offenses (such as murder and large-scale drug trafficking offenses).[14]

Because bail is not constitutionally required, it does not violate the Constitution to deny bail outright to a defendant on the ground that even if they have offered sufficient proof "that [they] will stand trial and submit to sentence if found guilty" if released on bail,[15] the defendant poses a substantial danger to the community.[16] In *United States v. Salerno*, the Supreme Court held that it does not violate either due process or the Eighth Amendment's cruel and unusual punishment clause to deny bail if there is clear and convincing evidence that a criminal defendant (not yet convicted), if released on bail, would pose such a danger, even if the danger has nothing to do with the crime with which the defendant is charged.[17] Such "preventive detention" is now a regular occurrence in the federal court system and some states.[18]

There are two other potential constitutional limitations on the denial of bail (or the setting of bail in an amount that the defendant cannot meet). First, the Equal Protection Clause imposes some limited restraints on a jurisdiction's bail scheme. The Supreme Court has been deferential to states when reviewing the states' bail systems, applying only "rational basis" scrutiny to claims that a state's bail system discriminates between rich and poor persons.[19] However, if a jurisdiction's bail system entirely fails to take into account a particular defendant's financial resources

---

13. *See* Jones v. Grimes, 134 S.E.2d 790, 792 (Ga. 1964).

14. *See, e.g.*, DePena v. State, 56 S.W.3d 926, 928 (Tex. App. 2001); Alvarez v. Crowder, 645 So. 2d 63, 64 (Fla. Dist. Ct. App. 1994); State v. Borras, 399 So. 2d 212, 212–13 (La. 1981). In a 2004 noncapital case, a trial court set bail at one billion dollars, which predictably was reversed on appeal. Ex parte Durst, 148 S.W.3d 496 (Tex. App. 2004). It should be noted that federal courts, while they have jurisdiction to entertain federal habeas corpus actions challenging a state trial court's setting bail at an allegedly excessive level, are extremely deferential toward the state trial court's decision and will intervene only to correct an arbitrary amount. *See, e.g.*, United States ex rel. Garcia v. O'Grady, 812 F.2d 347 (7th Cir. 1987). Therefore, state appellate courts provide the most efficacious remedy for state defendants wishing to challenge trial courts' bail amounts as excessive.

15. *Stack*, 342 U.S. at 4–5.

16. *Salerno*, 481 U.S. at 755.

17. *Id.* at 745–55.

18. *See, e.g.*, 18 U.S.C. §§ 3141, *et seq.*; MASS. GEN. LAWS Ch. 276 § 58A.

19. *See* Schilb v. Kuebal, 404 U.S. 357, 365–66 (1971) (upholding Illinois's system whereby a defendant unable to post the full bond amount with the court, which was refundable at the conclusion of the case, was charged a 1 percent administrative fee for posting less than the full amount, while wealthier persons able to post the full bond amount with the court were not charged any fee).

(e.g., by establishing fixed schedules whereby set amounts of bail are established irrespective of a particular defendant's financial ability to make bail) and a court has no authority to release an indigent defendant on personal recognizance in an appropriate case, such a bail system arguably violates the constitutional principle of equal protection by discriminating against the defendant based on economic status.[20] Second, in rare cases, a defendant arguably has a due process right to be released on bail—at least temporarily and under restrictive conditions[21]—to permit the defendant to assist defense counsel in preparing for trial.[22]

2.3 Leading Supreme Court Decisions Regarding Bail

- *Stack v. Boyle*, 342 U.S. 1 (1951) (bail that is set in an amount higher than is "reasonably calculated" to assure the appearance of the defendant at trial violates the Eighth Amendment's prohibition against "excessive" bail).

- *Carlson v. Landon*, 342 U.S. 524 (1952) (the Eighth Amendment does not give a right to bail in every case but instead merely prohibits "excessive" bail in cases in which bail is made available under a jurisdiction's law).

- *Schilb v. Kuebal*, 404 U.S. 357 (1971) (it violates equal protection for a bail statute to discriminate against poor defendants without any rational basis for doing so).

- *United States v. Salerno*, 481 U.S. 739 (1987) (upholding the facial constitutionality of the "preventive detention" provision of the federal Bail Reform Act of 1984; a defendant's dangerousness, if proved by clear and convincing evidence, is a legitimate basis to deny bail outright to a defendant, even if their dangerousness has no direct relation to the crime with which they are charged).

---

20. *See, e.g.*, Pugh v. Rainwater, 572 F.2d 1053 (5th Cir. 1978) (en banc); Ackies v. Purdy, 322 F. Supp. 38 (S.D. Fla. 1970); *see also* Rodriguez v. Providence Cmty. Corr., Inc., 155 F. Supp. 3d 758, 768 (M.D. Tenn. 2015) ("A slew of recent district court cases have aptly and appropriately applied *Pugh* to invalidate bond systems that have the effect of imprisoning indigent individuals where [similarly situated defendants] with financial resources would go free."); O'Donnell v. Harris County, Texas, 321 F. Supp. 3d 763 (S.D. Tex. 2018) (preliminarily enjoining Harris County, Texas, courts' existing use of monetary bail in misdemeanor cases).
21. *See, e.g.*, United States v. Reese, 463 F.2d 830 (D.C. Cir. 1972).
22. *See, e.g.*, United States v. Pomeroy, 485 F.2d 272, 274 (9th Cir. 1973) (discussing *Kinney v. Lenon*, 425 F.2d 209 (9th Cir. 1970)). Such a rare case typically involves a detained defendant who knows potential defense witnesses by sight only and not by name—thus requiring the defendant's temporary release to assist his defense counsel in locating such defense witnesses. *See, e.g.*, *Kinney*, 425 F.2d 209.

Chapter Three

The Sixth Amendment Right to Counsel and Associated Rights

3.1 The Sixth Amendment Right to the Assistance of Counsel

At a criminal defendant's initial appearance in court on a criminal charge, the issue of whether they have a right to the assistance of counsel typically arises. At the outset, the Sixth Amendment right to counsel should be distinguished from the Fifth Amendment right to counsel. The former is expressly provided in the Sixth Amendment and applies to all "critical stages" of a prosecution; the latter was read into the Fifth Amendment by the Supreme Court in *Miranda v. Arizona*[1] as part of its "prophylactic" rule to assure the voluntariness of criminal defendants' confessions.[2] The Fifth Amendment right to counsel, which is concerned exclusively with a confession or other incriminating statement given by a defendant, is discussed in Chapter Six.[3] Furthermore, issues related to whether an attorney denied a criminal defendant the "effective" assistance of counsel under the Sixth Amendment is discussed in Chapter Thirteen.

The Supreme Court has repeatedly described the Sixth Amendment right to counsel as a "bedrock" rule of criminal procedure[4]—an "essential" right that is "basic to a fair trial"[5] and, "[o]f all the rights that an accused person has, . . [the one that is] by far the most pervasive, for it affects his ability to assert any other rights he may have."[6] The right to the assistance of counsel, the Court has recognized, "is indispensable to the fair administration of our adversarial system of criminal justice" because that right "safeguards the other rights deemed essential for the fair

---

1. Miranda v. Arizona, 384 U.S. 436 (1966).
2. *See* McNeil v. Wisconsin, 501 U.S. 171, 176–77 (1991).
3. This discusses the Sixth Amendment right to assistance of counsel at "critical stages" of the prosecution, but does not address the related issue of whether a confession must be suppressed because of a Sixth Amendment violation. That Sixth Amendment issue is addressed in Chapter Six.
4. *See* O'Dell v. Netherland, 521 U.S. 151, 167 (1997).
5. Penson v. Ohio, 488 U.S. 75, 88 (1988).
6. *Id.* at 84 (citation and internal quotation marks omitted).

prosecution of a criminal proceeding."[7] The Court has further explained the relationship between vindicating the right to counsel and our adversary system:

> The paramount importance of vigorous representation follows from the nature of our adversarial system of justice. This system is premised on the well-tested principle that truth—as well as fairness—is best discovered by powerful statements on both sides of the [case].[8]

Since the landmark decision of *Gideon v. Wainwright*,[9] the right to counsel has been guaranteed at all critical stages of felony criminal prosecutions in state and federal courts. "Critical stages" are "those links in the prosecutorial chain of events in which the potential for incrimination inheres or at which the opportunity for effective defense must be seized or foregone."[10] Critical stages include important pretrial proceedings where substantive rights and defenses are asserted or waived,[11] plea bargaining and guilty pleas,[12] the trial itself,[13] and sentencing.[14] However, the Sixth Amendment right to counsel does not apply to any stage of a case before prosecution formally commences; a mere arrest is insufficient to trigger the Sixth Amendment right to counsel.[15] This is not to say that an accused person cannot retain a lawyer to represent them (at their own expense) before charges are filed. It simply means that the Sixth Amendment does not require the assistance of counsel at that juncture.

---

7. Maine v. Moulton, 474 U.S. 159, 168–69 (1985).

8. *Penson*, 488 U.S. at 84 (citations and internal quotation marks omitted).

9. Gideon v. Wainwright, 372 U.S. 335 (1963).

10. Yohn v. Love, 76 F.3d 508, 522 (3d Cir. 1996) (citation and internal quotation marks omitted).

11. *See, e.g.*, Coleman v. Alabama, 399 U.S. 1 (1970) (right to counsel at the preliminary hearing).

12. Missouri v. Frye, 566 U.S. 134 (2012); Lafler v. Cooper, 566 U.S. 156 (2012); *see also* Childress v. Johnson, 103 F.3d 1221 (5th Cir. 1997) (plea bargaining and guilty plea proceedings are "critical stages").

13. The right extends only to those critical portions of a trial, such as the presentation of evidence or arguments to a jury. *See, e.g.*, Herring v. New York, 422 U.S. 853 (1975) (closing arguments are a critical stage); Burdine v. Johnson, 262 F.3d 336 (5th Cir. 2001) (en banc) (prosecution's presentation of testimony and evidence during trial deemed a critical stage).

14. Mempa v. Rhay, 389 U.S. 128 (1967).

15. *See* Kirby v. Illinois, 406 U.S. 682, 688 (1972) (right to counsel under Sixth Amendment "attaches" at the point of "adversary judicial proceedings," whether by way of formal charge, indictment, information, or commencement of preliminary hearing); *see also* United States v. Moody, 206 F.3d 609 (6th Cir. 2000) (holding that there was no right to the assistance of counsel during precharge plea bargaining process even though plea bargaining process clearly is a critical stage once a prosecution commences). A mere warrantless arrest—before the filing of any type of charging instrument—does not activate the right to counsel. United States v. Gouveia, 467 U.S. 180, 190 (1984). The arrest of a defendant pursuant to a pre-indictment criminal complaint (i.e., one filed by a police officer alone without prosecutorial involvement) is sufficient to trigger the Sixth Amendment right to counsel once the defendant appears in court to face the charges, even if a prosecutor had no role in the filing of the complaint. Rothgery v. Gillespie County, Tex., 554 U.S. 191 (2008). Lower courts have held that the mere filing of a criminal complaint and arrest of a defendant—without presenting the defendant to a court on the charges—does not cause the Sixth Amendment right to counsel to attach. *See, e.g.*, United States v. Boskic, 545 F.3d 69, 83 (1st Cir. 2008).

Although the right to counsel applies to all felony cases, regardless of the type of punishment the defendant receives, the right to counsel in misdemeanor cases depends on the type of punishment imposed. In order for the right to attach, the defendant must have received at least one day of actual incarceration—or a suspended jail sentence—to activate the right to counsel in a misdemeanor case; a fine-only misdemeanor sentence does not activate the right to counsel.[16] It is worth noting that although there is no right to counsel under any circumstances in a fine-only misdemeanor case, the Supreme Court has held that in very limited situations there is a constitutional right to appointed counsel in a civil proceeding (in particular, cases in which an indigent civil litigant could be incarcerated for contempt of court and where other circumstances exist).[17]

Although the Sixth Amendment speaks only of the right to "the assistance of counsel" for a defendant's "defen[s]e,"[18] the Supreme Court has held that state and federal courts must appoint counsel—at no cost—for defendants who are entitled to the assistance of counsel, but who are unable to afford their own lawyers.[19] The vast majority of criminal defendants in the state and federal systems are indigent and require the appointment of counsel.[20] Those defendants who can afford to retain their own counsel have a constitutional right to "counsel of their choice."[21] The only limitation to this rule is that the retained attorney must be properly licensed (or otherwise admitted to practice) in the relevant jurisdiction and may not have an impermissible conflict of interest.[22] A trial court's violation of a defendant's right

---

16. Alabama v. Shelton, 535 U.S. 654 (2002) (suspended jail sentence, right to counsel attached); Scott v. Illinois, 440 U.S. 367 (1979) (fine-only sentence, no right to counsel); Argersinger v. Hamlin, 407 U.S. 25 (1972) (sentence of actual imprisonment; right to counsel). The Supreme Court has not yet addressed whether a sentence of "stand-alone" probation—untethered to a suspended jail sentence—activates the right to counsel. *Compare* United States v. Pollard, 389 F.3d 101, 104–05 (4th Cir. 2004) (holding that sentence of probation without any suspended sentence attached to it does not trigger the right to counsel in a misdemeanor case), *with id.* at 106 (Titus, J., dissenting) (contending that a sentence of probation without a suspended sentence does trigger the right to counsel in a misdemeanor case).

17. Turner v. Rogers, 564 U.S. 431, 448–49 (2011).

18. U.S. CONST. amend. VI.

19. Kitchens v. Smith, 401 U.S. 847 (1971) (per curiam) (defendant's uncontroverted testimony that he "couldn't afford a lawyer" was sufficient to require the appointment of counsel). A defendant need not be entirely indigent, or be considered a "pauper," to qualify for appointed counsel. United States v. Brockman, 183 F.3d 891, 897 (8th Cir. 1999). "[I]t suffices if [a] defendant lacks financial resources on a practical basis to retain counsel." People v. Ellis, 722 N.E.2d 254, 257 (Ill. App. Ct. 1999).

20. Abbe Smith, *The Difference in Criminal Defense and the Difference It Makes*, 11 WASH. J.L. & POL. 83, 110 & n.143 (2003) (citing statistics from various jurisdictions).

21. Chandler v. Fretag, 348 U.S. 3, 9 (1954).

22. The subject of a defense attorney's conflict of interest is discussed in Chapter Thirteen. Although a defendant may waive the right to a conflict-free counsel, a trial court has discretion to refuse to honor such a waiver and require the defendant to obtain new, conflict-free counsel. Wheat v. United States, 486 U.S. 153, 162 (1988) (permitting a trial court to refuse a retained attorney to represent a defendant if the attorney has a conflict of interest). Although a trial court may refuse an

to retained counsel of their choice is a "structural" error that requires automatic reversal of the defendant's conviction on appeal—even if a subsequent attorney provided competent representation.[23] An indigent defendant has no constitutional right to appointed counsel of their choice.[24] Indeed, an indigent defendant has no constitutional right to a "meaningful relationship" with appointed counsel[25] as long as appointed counsel does not provide "ineffective assistance of counsel."[26]

The Supreme Court has also addressed the situation when the government seeks to freeze the assets of a criminal defendant, thereby interfering with their right to retain counsel of their choice.[27] The Court has held that tainted assets may be frozen before trial, while untainted assets may not be.[28] "Tainted" assets include funds or property "connected to" or "traceable to" a criminal offense.[29]

3.2   Waiver of the Right to Counsel and Right to Proceed Pro Se

Although the Supreme Court has held that the Sixth Amendment requires counsel be appointed for indigent defendants who are unable to retain counsel, the Court has also permitted defendants to waive that right as long as "the right [to counsel] is competently and intelligently waived."[30] In numerous cases since *Gideon*, the Court has elaborated on what it means to "knowingly and voluntarily" waive the right to counsel. Such a valid waiver means that the defendant understands "the significance and consequences" of the decision to proceed pro se.[31]

For a defendant to understand the consequences of waiving the right to counsel, the defendant must be aware of the "dangers and disadvantages of self-representation" so that the defendant "knows what he is doing and his choice is made with eyes open."[32] However, if a defendant is waiving their right to counsel at a guilty plea proceeding, the Supreme Court has held that a valid waiver ordinarily will occur when the presiding judge simply advises the defendant of their right to the

---

attorney's request to appear pro hac vice if the attorney's limited admission would disrupt or delay the proceedings, the right to counsel includes a general right to representation by an attorney not licensed in a particular jurisdiction, but who is licensed elsewhere and otherwise qualified. *See, e.g.,* United States v. Walters, 309 F.3d 589, 592 (9th Cir. 2002).

23. United States v. Gonzalez-Lopez, 548 U.S. 140 (2006).

24. Caplin & Drysdale v. United States, 491 U.S. 617, 624 (1989).

25. Morris v. Slappy, 461 U.S. 1 (1983).

26. Strickland v. Washington, 466 U.S. 668 (1984). Ineffective assistance issues are discussed in Chapter Thirteen.

27. Luis v. United States, 136 S. Ct. 1083 (2016).

28. *Luis*, 136 S. Ct. at 1088–90.

29. *Id.* at 1088.

30. Gideon v. Wainwright, 372 U.S. 335, 340 & n.3 (1963).

31. *See, e.g.,* Godinez v. Moran, 509 U.S. 389, 400–01 & n.12 (1993).

32. Faretta v. California, 422 U.S. 806, 835 (1975); Adams v. United States ex rel. McCann, 317 U.S. 269, 279 (1942).

assistance of counsel, including appointed counsel,[33] and the defendant voluntarily relinquishes that right.[34] A valid waiver will not be presumed from a silent record, and courts must "indulge every reasonable presumption against waiver."[35]

What constitutes a valid waiver of the right to counsel depends on the facts of each case, including the age, intelligence, education, background, and experience of the defendant.[36] As noted, the Supreme Court has required a more extensive waiver colloquy between a judge and defendant in trial cases than in cases where a pro se defendant enters a guilty plea.[37] The seriousness and complexity of the charges will also be taken into account when assessing the validity of the defendant's waiver— the more serious or complex the charges, the more substantial the colloquy required.[38] Thus, a pro se defendant pleading guilty to misdemeanor DWI charges may validly waive their right to counsel in a short colloquy with the trial judge, while a judge eliciting a waiver of counsel from a pro se defendant facing serious felony charges must engage in lengthier colloquy that assures that the defendant fully appreciates how counsel could assist in defending against such serious charges.[39]

The foregoing waiver requirements only apply to in-court waivers. Waivers of the Sixth Amendment right to counsel that occur outside the courtroom—usually involving police officers' interrogation of an indicted defendant who has not yet made a court appearance or retained counsel—only require the equivalent of a waiver simpliciter of *Miranda* rights and do not require judicial involvement.[40] Such waivers are discussed in Chapter Six.

A defendant may ordinarily choose to waive their right to counsel and proceed pro se in pleading guilty or in defending themself at a trial. Indeed, the defendant has a constitutional right to do so, and their conviction generally will be reversed if their right to proceed pro se was violated.[41] The sole exception to this general rule is if a trial court makes a factual finding that a pro se defendant's mental illness renders them incompetent to represent themselves at a trial, even if the defendant

---

33. A court "must affirmatively inform the defendant that it has a duty to appoint counsel for him if he [qualifies for free counsel]." Elsperman v. Wainwright, 358 F.2d 259, 260 (5th Cir. 1966); *see also* Smith v. Lane, 426 F.2d 767, 769 (7th Cir. 1970).

34. Iowa v. Tovar, 541 U.S. 77 (2004).

35. Johnson v. Zerbst, 304 U.S. 458, 464 (1938); *see also* Carnley v. Cochran, 369 U.S. 506, 516 (1962).

36. United States v. Scott, 909 F.2d 488, 490 (11th Cir. 1990).

37. *Tovar*, 541 U.S. 77.

38. *See* Von Moltke v. Gillies, 332 U.S. 708, 721–22 (1948) (plurality); *id.* at 727–28 (Frankfurter, J., concurring, joined by Jackson, J.).

39. *Compare Tovar*, 541 U.S. 77 (approving of a waiver simpliciter in a misdemeanor DUI case), *with Von Moltke*, 332 U.S. 708 (reversing the defendant's conviction after concluding that the trial judge engaged in an inadequate colloquy with the defendant who had pleaded guilty to a serious felony offense).

40. Patterson v. Illinois, 487 U.S. 285 (1988).

41. Faretta v. California, 422 U.S. 806 (1975). The right to proceed pro se does not extend to appeal. *See* Martinez v. Court of Appeal of California, 528 U.S. 152 (2000).

is mentally competent to stand trial.[42] After securing a valid waiver from a pro se defendant, a trial court nonetheless has discretion to appoint "stand-by counsel," even over the defendant's objection. Appointment of stand-by counsel does not constitute reversible error as long as such counsel does not interfere with the pro se defendant's self-representation.[43] A pro se defendant is not, however, entitled to "hybrid representation"—that is, both the assistance of counsel to represent them (in a stand-by capacity or outright) and the right to proceed pro se at the same time.[44] If a defendant accepts appointed counsel (other than in a stand-by capacity), the defendant cannot later complain that the lawyer refused to accede to defendant's demands about such things like what witnesses to call or what strategies to pursue—unless the lawyer's refusal to do so amounted to ineffective assistance of counsel under the standard discussed in Chapter Thirteen.[45]

3.3   Violation of the Right to Counsel

The Sixth Amendment right to counsel may be violated in four different ways: 1) an outright denial of the assistance of counsel (whether by way of a court's refusal to appoint counsel when constitutionally required to do so or by a pro se defendant's invalid waiver of the right to counsel) during a critical stage of the proceedings; 2) admission into evidence of a confession or other type of incriminating statement obtained in violation of the Sixth Amendment right to counsel; 3) ineffective assistance of counsel during a critical stage; and 4) government interference with the attorney-client relationship.

The first type of violation is discussed immediately above and is further discussed below. The second[46] and third[47] types are discussed in other chapters. The fourth type of Sixth Amendment violation typically occurs in one of two ways: 1) when the prosecution or police purposely intrude into or impede the attorney-client relationship;[48] and 2) when the trial court unduly interferes with the attorney-client

---

42. Indiana v. Edwards, 554 U.S. 164 (2008).

43. McKaskle v. Wiggins, 465 U.S. 168 (1984).

44. *Id.* at 183.

45. Under widely accepted rules of legal ethics, a criminal defense lawyer has the right to make ultimate decisions (after consultation with their client) about most matters during the course of a criminal prosecution (such as what motions to file and what witnesses to subpoena). Most courts have held that a defendant has an absolute right to make the decision only about three things: 1) whether to plead guilty or not guilty; 2) whether to testify on their own behalf at trial; and 3) whether to waive a jury trial. *See, e.g.,* State v. Rivera, 83 P.3d 169, 175 (Kan. 2004). The Supreme Court has not yet addressed what rights (other than the right to counsel), if any, a criminal defendant must personally waive for the waiver to be valid. *See* Gonzalez v. United States, 128 S. Ct. 1765, 1773–74 (2008) (Scalia, J., concurring in the judgment).

46. *See* Chapter Six.

47. *See* Chapter Thirteen.

48. *See, e.g.,* Shillinger v. Haworth, 70 F.3d 1132, 1142 (10th Cir. 1995).

relationship.[49] The prosecution or police violate the Sixth Amendment when they either engage in impermissible eavesdropping during a confidential attorney-client meeting (e.g., having a codefendant who is secretly cooperating with the prosecution attend a joint defense meeting where defense strategy is discussed)[50] or otherwise interfere with the attorney-client relationship.[51] A trial court violates the Sixth Amendment's right to counsel when it orders a defendant to have no communication with defense counsel during a substantial portion of a critical stage of the proceedings[52] or otherwise substantially interferes with a defense counsel's ability to offer meaningful assistance to their client.[53]

3.4 Challenging Uncounseled Convictions

Litigation over the Sixth Amendment right to counsel occurs either on a direct or habeas corpus appeal of an uncounseled conviction or in a collateral challenge[54] to

---

49. *See, e.g.*, Geders v. United States, 425 U.S. 80 (1976).

50. *Shillinger*, 70 F.3d at 1142; *see also* Weatherford v. Bursey, 429 U.S. 545, 558 (1977) (assuming without deciding that a prosecutorial agent's intentional intrusion into the attorney-client relationship and "communication of defense strategy to the prosecutor" would violate the Sixth Amendment).

51. *See* United States v. Stein, 541 F.3d 130 (2d Cir. 2008) (right to counsel violated where prosecutors improperly caused corporation to discontinue paying its employees' attorney fees in white-collar prosecution; affirming district court's dismissal of indictment as remedy); United States v. Amlani, 111 F.3d 705, 711 (9th Cir. 1997) (right to counsel is violated when members of the prosecution team intentionally undermined the defendant's confidence in his attorney and prejudice resulted); *see also* United States v. Morrison, 449 U.S. 361 (1981) (assuming without deciding that such prosecutorial interference with the attorney-client relationship was a Sixth Amendment violation, but holding that a remedy was not required unless the defendant could establish prejudice as a result of the violation).

52. *Geders*, 425 U.S. at 88–92 (trial court's order that defendant and defense have no communication during overnight recess between defendant's direct examination and cross-examination unduly infringed on the right to counsel); *but cf.* Perry v. Leeke, 488 U.S. 272 (1989) (distinguishing *Geders* and permitting such an order when there was only a fifteen-minute recess between the defendant's direct examination and cross-examination).

53. *See, e.g.*, Brooks v. Tennessee, 406 U.S. 605, 612–13 (1972) (requirement that defendant could testify on their own behalf only if they went first among all the defense witnesses violated the Sixth Amendment right to counsel by interfering with defense counsel's ability to advise their client whether or not the defendant should testify).

54. As used in this context, a "collateral" challenge to a prior conviction is made during a subsequent prosecution (usually at the sentencing phase when the prosecution seeks to enhance a defendant's sentence with the prior conviction). *See* Custis v. United States, 511 U.S. 485 (1994). Postconviction habeas corpus appeals also are referred to as "collateral" proceedings, yet the use of the term "collateral" in that context refers to a different type of challenge to a conviction or sentence. *See* Chapter Fifteen. The Supreme Court repeatedly has held that because vindication of the Sixth Amendment right to the assistance of counsel is so critical to a just conviction, a defendant can collaterally attack a prior conviction in a subsequent case on that ground. United States v. Tucker, 404 U.S. 443 (1972); Burgett v. Texas, 389 U.S. 109 (1967). Conversely, even if some other significant constitutional violation can be proven (such as an involuntary guilty plea) with respect to the prior conviction, the defendant cannot collaterally challenge their prior conviction in the subsequent case except on right-to-counsel grounds. *Custis*, 511 U.S. at 493–98.

a prior conviction in a subsequent case where the prior conviction is being used to enhance the defendant's punishment. Each type of litigation involves an allegation that a defendant was either not afforded the opportunity to exercise their right to counsel or did not validly waive the right to counsel when so afforded.

On direct appeals and habeas corpus appeals, the burden is on the prosecution to prove that a defendant's uncounseled conviction is constitutionally valid.[55] Typically, such a burden requires the prosecution to prove that the defendant's waiver of the right to counsel was executed in a knowing and voluntary manner.[56]

The burden shifts to the defense in a collateral challenge to the prior uncounseled conviction made in a subsequent prosecution.[57] The Supreme Court has placed both the initial burden of production and ultimate burden of persuasion on a defendant who seeks to collaterally challenge a prior uncounseled conviction.[58] Typically, this means defense counsel must locate the court file in the prior case and determine whether a court reporter recorded the relevant proceedings (e.g., the defendant's guilty plea hearing in the prior case where they waived their right to counsel) and also determine whether relevant documents (e.g., written waiver forms) are available. If no transcription or recording of the relevant proceeding is available, defense counsel will be forced to recreate the record with affidavits or testimony, assuming witnesses to the prior proceeding are available.

The Supreme Court has assumed, without actually deciding,[59] that a defendant may collaterally challenge a prior misdemeanor conviction—even though the Court in *Argersinger v. Hamlin* only spoke of a prohibition against incarcerating misdemeanants who did not have the assistance of counsel or did not validly waive their right to counsel.[60]

---

55. *See* Brewer v. Williams, 430 U.S. 387, 404 (1977); Henderson v. Frank, 155 F.3d 159, 166 (3d Cir. 1998); Garcia v. State, 909 S.W.2d 563, 566 (Tex. App. 1995); *but see* Moore v. Michigan, 355 U.S. 155 (1957) (in a direct appeal, placing the burden on the defendant to show the invalidity of their waiver of counsel). The court in Evans v. Raines, 534 F. Supp. 791, 800 n.17 (D. Ariz. 1982), noted the apparent conflict between the Supreme Court's decisions in *Moore* and *Brewer*.

56. *Brewer*, 430 U.S. 387.

57. *See Tovar*, 541 U.S. at 92; *see also Garcia*, 909 S.W.2d at 566.

58. *See Tovar*, 541 U.S. at 92 (burden of persuasion); Parke v. Raley, 506 U.S. 20 (1992) (burden of production).

59. *Tovar*, 54 U.S. at 88 n.10; Nichols v. United States, 511 U.S. 738, 748–49 (1994); *see also* State v. Von Ferguson, 169 P.3d 423, 428–29 (Utah 2007) (violation of right to counsel in misdemeanor case prevents use of underlying conviction for enhancement purposes in a subsequent case); *but see* United States v. Jackson, 493 F.3d 1179 (10th Cir. 2007) (holding that a collateral challenge to a misdemeanor conviction was not permitted since the right to counsel in misdemeanor cases is limited to situations where jail sentences are imposed; even if the right to counsel was violated as a result of a jail sentence being imposed on an uncounseled misdemeanant, the underlying conviction is nonetheless valid and may be used to enhance the defendant's sentence in a subsequent prosecution).

60. Argersinger v. Hamlin, 407 U.S. 25, 40 (1972).

3.5   Rights Associated with the Assistance of Counsel

In addition to affording criminal defendants the constitutional right to the assistance of counsel in the vast majority of criminal cases, the Supreme Court has also afforded defendants other types of defense resources that serve as adjuncts to the right to counsel. A defendant appealing their conviction or sentence who is unable to pay the cost of filing fees, a court reporter's transcripts of the relevant proceedings in the trial court, or other requirements for a direct appeal ordinarily is entitled to these things free of cost.[61] Likewise, a defendant is entitled to transcripts of a pretrial hearing or transcripts of a prior trial when such transcripts are necessary to enable effective cross-examination of a prosecution witness at trial.[62]

Furthermore, in trial proceedings, an expert witness whose testimony will serve as a "basic tool of an adequate defense" must be provided free of cost for an indigent defendant on a sufficient showing of the expert's necessity (i.e., that the expert witness is needed to rebut a prosecution expert witness or otherwise address a scientific or technical issue that will be a "significant factor at trial").[63] The expert assistance provided to an indigent defendant must be "sufficiently available to the defense and independent from the prosecution to effectively assist in evaluation, preparation, and presentation of the defense."[64] In *McWilliams*, the Supreme Court specifically left open the question of whether the Constitution requires the appointment of "right to an expert [entirely] independent from the prosecution," that is, as a member of the "defense team"—an issue which divides the lower courts.[65]

Such rights associated with the right to counsel are rooted in due process and equal protection guarantees rather than arising from the Sixth Amendment.[66]

3.6   Leading Supreme Court Decisions Concerning the Sixth Amendment Right to Counsel and Associated Rights

- *Johnson v. Zerbst*, 304 U.S. 458 (1938) (holding that there is a constitutional right to appointed counsel for indigent defendants in all federal cases; waiver of this right must be "knowing, voluntary, and intelligent," and "courts indulge every reasonable presumption" against waiver of the right).

---

61. Burns v. Ohio, 360 U.S. 252 (1959); Griffin v. Illinois, 351 U.S. 12 (1956).
62. Roberts v. LaVallee, 389 U.S. 40 (1967); *see also* Britt v. North Carolina, 404 U.S. 226, 227–28 (1971).
63. Ake v. Oklahoma, 470 U.S. 68, 76 (1985).
64. McWilliams v. Dunn, 137 S. Ct. 1790, 1799 (2017).
65. *Id.* at 1800; *see also id.* at 1801 (Alito, J., dissenting).
66. *Id.* at 77–83. Although *Ake* dealt only with a psychiatric expert witness, most lower courts have either held or assumed that *Ake*'s logic extends to necessary nonpsychiatric witnesses as well. *See, e.g.,* Rey v. State, 897 S.W.2d 333 (Tex. Crim. App. 1995). *Ake* is further discussed in Chapter Four.

- *Chandler v. Fretag*, 348 U.S. 3 (1954) (constitutional right to retain "counsel of one's choice" unless the attorney is not licensed in the jurisdiction or has an impermissible conflict of interest).

- *Griffin v. Illinois*, 351 U.S. 12 (1956) (constitutional right to free transcripts or adequate substitute thereof as well as waiver of other costs of an appeal for indigent criminal defendants who appeal their convictions or sentences).

- *Gideon v. Wainwright*, 372 U.S. 335 (1963) (constitutional right to appointed counsel for indigent state defendants in all felony cases; automatic reversal on appeal if this right is denied without a showing of any harm to the defendant).

- *Burgett v. Texas*, 389 U.S. 109 (1967) (prior, uncounseled conviction cannot be used to enhance punishment in a subsequent prosecution when defendant possessed constitutional right to counsel in the prior case and did not validly waive that right; defendant may collaterally challenge use of the prior, uncounseled conviction during proceedings in the subsequent case).

- *Kirby v. Illinois*, 406 U.S. 682 (1972) (Sixth Amendment right to counsel attaches at the initiation of adversary criminal proceedings by way of "formal charge, preliminary hearing, indictment, information, or arraignment").

- *Argersinger v. Hamlin*, 407 U.S. 25 (1972) (constitutional right to appointed counsel in state or federal misdemeanor cases in which a defendant is sentenced to any amount of jail time).

- *Faretta v. California*, 422 U.S. 806 (1975) (providing for the constitutional right to proceed pro se in criminal prosecution; waiver of right to counsel at a trial must be "knowing, voluntary, and intelligent," and trial judge must warn defendant of the "dangers and disadvantages" of proceeding pro se for waiver to be valid).

- *Scott v. Illinois*, 440 U.S. 367 (1979) (no right to counsel in a misdemeanor case in which a fine-only sentence is imposed).

- *United States v. Gouveia*, 467 U.S. 180 (1984) (mere arrest by itself does not cause the Sixth Amendment right to counsel to attach).

- *Ake v. Oklahoma*, 470 U.S. 68 (1985) (an indigent defendant has the constitutional right to an expert witness, such as a psychiatrist, without costs if such an expert is a "necessary tool" for the defense and the defendant makes an adequate showing of the need for such an expert in their case).

- *Wheat v. United States*, 486 U.S. 153 (1988) (although a defendant may waive their constitutional right to a defense counsel unburdened by a conflict of interest, a trial court has the discretion not to accept a defendant's waiver of the right to conflict-free counsel and thus may remove a conflicted attorney).

- *Alabama v. Shelton*, 535 U.S. 654 (2002) (the right to counsel in a misdemeanor case exists under *Argersinger* when a suspended jail sentence is imposed, even if the defendant serves no actual time in jail).

- *Iowa v. Tovar*, 541 U.S. 77 (2004) (pro se defendant's waiver of right to counsel in a case in which the defendant pleads guilty ordinarily requires less judicial involvement than a case in which a defendant waives the right to counsel at trial; *Faretta's* prophylactic requirement that a judge warn a defendant of the dangers and disadvantages of proceeding pro se ordinarily is inapplicable in a case in which a pro se defendant pleads guilty).

- *United States v. Gonzalez-Lopez*, 548 U.S. 140 (2006) (violation of Sixth Amendment right to counsel of choice is structural error requiring automatic reversal of defendant's conviction on appeal).

- *Indiana v. Edwards*, 554 U.S. 164 (2008) (trial court possesses authority to veto a pro se defendant's right to waive the right to counsel and represent themself at trial if the court finds that the defendant is not mentally competent to represent themselves at a trial, even if the defendant is otherwise mentally competent to stand trial).

- *Rothgery v. Gillespie County, TX*, 554 U.S. 191 (2008) (Sixth Amendment right to counsel attaches upon a law enforcement officer's filing of a criminal complaint against a defendant and presentation of defendant in court to face the charges, even if an attorney for the prosecution had no role in the filing of the complaint).

- *Luis v. United States*, 136 S. Ct. 1083 (2016) (government may not freeze defendant's untainted assets before trial in a manner that deprives the defendant of the ability to retain counsel of their choice).

CHAPTER FOUR

PRETRIAL MOTIONS (NONSUPPRESSION)

4.1   Introduction to Pretrial Motions

Both the prosecution and the defense regularly file pretrial motions in criminal cases, although defense lawyers typically file the bulk of such motions. As discussed at the outset, the concern of this book is constitutional criminal procedure. Therefore, the discussion that follows will be limited to pretrial motions that implicate constitutional issues.[1]

It is helpful to divide pretrial motions into two primary classes: "suppression" motions (e.g., a motion to suppress evidence based on an unconstitutional search or seizure[2] or a motion to suppress a defendant's confession as illegally obtained[3]), and "nonsuppression" motions (e.g., a motion to dismiss the indictment based on a violation of the Double Jeopardy Clause).[4] It is further helpful to categorize defense motions as "dispositive" or "nondispositive." A dispositive motion is one that, if granted, actually or effectively dismisses the case. A quintessential dispositive motion is a motion to dismiss an indictment based on a constitutional challenge to the underlying criminal statute (e.g., a claim that a penal statute violates the First Amendment because it criminalizes constitutionally protected conduct).[5] Although nondispositive in their nature, certain other motions can effectively be dispositive—such as a motion to suppress a defendant's confession. In many cases, without the evidence of a defendant's confession, the prosecution will not have sufficient remaining evidence to proceed to trial, and as a result of the motion being granted, the prosecution will very likely dismiss the case.

---

1. There are countless types of pretrial motions that do not implicate the U.S. Constitution. A good discussion of many such nonconstitutional pretrial motions is found in Federal Defenders of San Diego, Inc., DEFENDING A FEDERAL CRIMINAL CASE, Ch. 6 ("Motions Practice"), §§ 6–281, *et seq.* (2010). The two most common nonconstitutional pretrial motions are motions for discovery and motions in limine based on the rules of evidence. The former seeks pretrial disclosure of evidence (*see, e.g.,* FED. R. CRIM. P. 16), and the latter usually seeks a definitive or conditional pretrial ruling on the admissibility vel non of particular evidence before the trial starts.

2. *See, e.g.,* Arizona v. Hicks, 480 U.S. 321 (1987).

3. *See, e.g.,* Miranda v. Arizona, 384 U.S. 436 (1966).

4. Harris v. Oklahoma, 433 U.S. 682 (1977).

5. *See, e.g.,* United States v. Reidel, 402 U.S. 351 (1971).

Some motions (e.g., a motion to dismiss the indictment based on a facially unconstitutional statute) do not require an evidentiary hearing because there are no factual disputes or no need for further factual development. However, other motions (e.g., a motion to suppress a defendant's confession) typically require an evidentiary hearing, unless all the relevant facts are undisputed, which is rare. A motion must make specific enough allegations to create a "genuine dispute as to any material fact"[6] to avoid summary denial by the court without an evidentiary hearing.[7] Put another way, the allegations must be "sufficiently definite, clear, and specific to enable the trial court to conclude that contested issues of fact exist,"[8] thus requiring an evidentiary hearing.

The two chapters that follow address motions to suppress evidence (including a defendant's confession). This chapter addresses the most common types of nonsuppression motions filed by the defense:

1. motion for change of venue;

2. motion to sever a codefendant;

3. motion for mental competency determination;

4. motion to dismiss the indictment based on an unconstitutional penal statute;

5. motion to dismiss the indictment based on a violation of the defendant's constitutional right to a speedy trial or pre-indictment delay;

6. motion to dismiss the indictment based on an ex post facto violation;

7. motion to dismiss the indictment based on a double jeopardy violation;

8. motion to dismiss an indictment as being "duplicitous" or "multiplicitous";

9. motion to dismiss the indictment or exclude evidence because the prosecution or police have destroyed or failed to preserve potentially exculpatory evidence;

10. ex parte motion for a subpoena;

11. ex parte motion for appointment of an expert witness when the defendant is indigent;

---

6. *Cf.* Fed. R. Civ. P. 56(a) (the standard for avoiding summary judgment in civil cases).
7. *See, e.g.*, United States v. Harrelson, 705 F.2d 733, 737 (5th Cir. 1983); *cf.* Procunier v. Atchley, 400 U.S. 446 (1971).
8. United States v. Ramirez-Garcia, 269 F.3d 945, 947 (9th Cir. 2001).

12. motion to dismiss the indictment based on discrimination in the selection of the grand jury or its foreperson;[9]

13. motion to recuse the prosecutor or trial judge because of bias;

14. motion to dismiss a charge based on a vindictive prosecution;

15. motion to dismiss the indictment under *Kastigar*;[10]

16. motion to suppress eyewitness identification based on an impermissibly suggestive pretrial identification procedure;[11]

17. motion to dismiss an indictment based on an unconstitutional prior administrative adjudication that serves as an element of the charged offense; and

18. motion to disclose confidential informant.

In addition, this chapter addresses the following types of pretrial motions implicating constitutional issues that are commonly filed by the prosecution:

1. motion to forcibly medicate an incompetent defendant;

2. motion to exclude evidence or a defense witness based on noncompliance with the discovery rules;

3. motion to disqualify defense counsel based on a conflict of interest;

4. motion to close the courtroom to the public or for a "gag" order; and

5. motion for a handwriting or voice exemplar from the defendant or physical specimen from the defendant.

4.2 Defense Motions

4.2.1 Change of Venue

The Supreme Court has held that in extreme situations, excessive pretrial publicity about a criminal case may render a fair trial by an impartial jury impossible.[12] Similarly, even where there is not such excessive pretrial publicity by the media,

---

9. A motion to dismiss the indictment because of other types of defects or irregularities in the grand jury proceedings is discussed in Chapter One.

10. Kastigar v. United States, 406 U.S. 441 (1972).

11. Although this final defense motion is a "suppression" motion, it is not discussed in the two chapters that follow because it does not concern the Fourth Amendment's limits on searches or seizures, the Fifth Amendment's right to silence (and *Miranda*), or the Sixth Amendment right to counsel. Rather, it is rooted in the Due Process Clause, as discussed herein.

12. *See, e.g.*, Murphy v. Florida, 421 U.S. 794 (1975).

a change of venue may be necessary where the alleged crime occurred in a small community in which virtually every prospective juror is aware of the allegations and knows the defendant or the victim.[13]

Older decisions of the Supreme Court concluded that prejudice to a defendant must be presumed (and thus a change of venue must occur) when a sufficiently large percentage of prospective jurors admit to having formed an opinion about the defendant's guilt based on pretrial publicity.[14] The Supreme Court's more recent cases strongly suggest that even if there is a great deal of pretrial publicity and many, if not most, prospective jurors have preexisting opinions about the defendant's guilt, a change of venue is not necessarily required. The Court has held that as long as the trial judge extensively questions prospective jurors and selects a jury of persons who swore under oath that they would render a verdict solely based on the evidence presented at trial and were capable of setting aside their preexisting knowledge and opinions about the case, a change of venue is not required.[15] For that reason, motions for change of venue are rarely granted in the modern era.[16]

In those exceptional cases involving a tremendous amount of pretrial publicity, the lower courts are divided over the standard that must be applied in determining whether to presume prejudice and thus require a change of venue. A majority of the lower courts require a showing of a "reasonable likelihood" or a "substantial likelihood" of prejudice to the defendant in the absence of a change of venue, although a minority of lower courts require a defendant to show by "clear and convincing" evidence that they will be prejudiced.[17]

4.2.2   Sever a Codefendant

With one important exception, it is very difficult for a defendant to show that a joint trial with a codefendant would violate the defendant's constitutional rights. The main exception to the general rule of nonseverance is when a codefendant has given an out-of-court statement implicating the defendant in the alleged offense (which the prosecution intends to offer against the codefendant) and the

---

13. *Cf.* Woods v. Dugger, 923 F.2d 1454, 1461 & n.14 (11th Cir. 1991) (defendant, who allegedly murdered a prison guard was denied a fair trial when his trial occurred in the small rural community in which the prison was located).

14. *See* Irvin v. Dowd, 366 U.S. 717 (1961); Rideau v. Louisiana, 373 U.S. 723 (1963).

15. *See* Skilling v. United States, 561 U.S. 358 (2010); *Murphy*, 421 U.S. at 800–03; Patton v. Yount, 467 U.S. 1025, 1031–40 (1984).

16. *See, e.g.*, United States v. Campa, 459 F.3d 1121 (11th Cir. 2006) (en banc) (upholding district court's refusal to change venue from Miami in a high-profile prosecution of defendants as being Cuban spies); *see also* Stephen Jones & Holly Hillerman, *McVeigh, McJustice, McMedia*, 1998 U. Chi. Legal F. 53, 56 n.16 (1998).

17. *See* Brecheen v. Oklahoma, 485 U.S. 909, 910–11 (1988) (Marshall, J., joined by Brennan, J., dissenting from denial of certiorari) (discussing the divergent approaches of the lower courts); *see also* Knapp v. Leonardo, 46 F.3d 170, 176 (2d Cir. 1995) (applying "clear and convincing" standard); State v. Gary, 550 A.2d 1259, 1263 (N.J. Sup. Ct. App. Div. 1988) (same).

codefendant intends to invoke their right to silence by not testifying at the joint trial.[18] The U.S. Supreme Court has held that in such a situation, the defendant's rights under the Confrontation Clause of the Sixth Amendment are violated when the nontestifying[19] codefendant's out-of-court statement implicating the defendant is admitted at a joint trial because the defendant cannot cross-examine the codefendant.[20] The Court has further held that a limiting instruction to jurors—that they may not consider the codefendant's confession against the defendant—would be insufficient to overcome the potential "spillover" prejudice to the defendant.[21]

Therefore, the Supreme Court has given prosecutors a choice of whether to have a joint trial (and, if so, exclude the nontestifying codefendant's confession or redact it to exclude any reference to the defendant) or agree to a severance (to use the codefendant's confession at their separate trial). If a prosecutor chooses to redact the nontestifying codefendant's confession to make it available at a joint trial, the redaction must effectively eliminate any reference to the defendant. Thus, substituting a symbol, blank, or the phrase "another person" for the defendant's name is sufficient only if it does not obviously refer to the defendant.[22] The Supreme Court's decision in *Gray v. Maryland*, while making it more difficult for prosecutors to effectively redact a confession to avoid a *Bruton* problem, did not fully resolve what type of redactions are proper.[23] It is likely the Supreme Court will further address redactions in a future case.

Other than a "*Bruton* motion" for severance, it is extremely difficult for a defendant to prevail on a motion to sever on constitutional grounds. Generally, the mere fact that defendants possess "antagonistic defenses" (e.g., the codefendant blames the defendant for the alleged offense) is not a basis to sever the defendant's trial.[24] A possible exception to this rule is if one of the codefendants seeks to blame another codefendant for the offense and, in so doing, comments on that codefendant's silence at trial.[25] Another potentially meritorious ground for a severance is when one codefendant wishes to call another codefendant as a defense witness; if the latter

---

18. Bruton v. United States, 391 U.S. 123 (1968); *see also* Gray v. Maryland, 523 U.S. 185 (1998).

19. The *Bruton* rule, which is rooted in the Confrontation Clause, does not apply if the codefendant takes the stand and testifies at a joint trial; in such a situation, the defendant is able to cross-examine the codefendant, even if the codefendant denies having made the confession. *See* Nelson v. O'Neil, 402 U.S. 622 (1971).

20. *Gray*, 523 U.S. at 189–90.

21. *Bruton*, 391 U.S. 135–36.

22. *Gray*, 523 U.S. at 193–97; *see also* United States v. Gonzalez, 183 F.3d 1315, 1322–23 (11th Cir. 1999); United States v. Peterson, 140 F.3d 819, 822 (9th Cir. 1998).

23. *See* Bryant M. Richardson, *Hypothetical Fact-Pattern Casting Light on the Gray Area: An Analysis of the Use of Neutral Pronouns in Non-Testifying Codefendant Redacted Confessions Under* Bruton, Richardson, *and* Gray, 55 U. Miami L. Rev. 825 (2001).

24. *See* Zafiro v. United States, 506 U.S. 534 (1993).

25. De Luna v. United States, 308 F.2d 140, 154–55 (5th Cir. 1962) (requiring a severance under those specific circumstances); *but see* United States v. Pirro, 76 F. Supp. 2d 478, 487 (S.D.N.Y. 1999) (disagreeing with *De Luna* and refusing to grant a severance under those circumstances).

codefendant can provide favorable exculpatory testimony for the former codefendant, but will not do so at a joint trial, many—if not most—courts would grant a severance to permit the codefendant's testimony (after they have been separately tried).[26]

Even in capital cases, a joint sentencing phase—in which one codefendant offers mitigating evidence that, at the same time, functions as aggravating evidence against the other codefendant—is not a constitutional violation except perhaps in an extreme case.[27]

4.2.3   Mental Competency Determination

It violates due process to convict a mentally incompetent criminal defendant—either at a trial or through a guilty plea.[28] The Supreme Court has defined "competency" as meaning a defendant's "sufficient present ability to consult with his lawyer with a reasonable degree of rational understanding" and also a "rational as well as factual understanding" of both the charges against them and the judicial proceedings.[29]

Although theoretically a prosecutor or trial judge (acting sua sponte) has a duty to make inquiries about a criminal defendant's mental competency,[30] usually it is defense counsel (who is in the best position to know their client's mental condition) who raises the issue by filing a motion for an evidentiary hearing to determine the defendant's competency. Due process is not violated by placing the burden on the defense to prove the defendant's incompetency by a preponderance of the evidence,[31] but imposing a burden to prove their competency by clear and convincing evidence is unconstitutional.[32] It is unclear whether the question of mental

---

26. *See, e.g.,* United States v. Cobb, 185 F.3d 1193, 1197–98 (11th Cir. 1998). In a related line of cases, some courts will grant a severance of multiple charges against a single defendant where the defendant wishes to testify on their own behalf about one of the charges, but wishes to invoke their constitutional right to silence concerning other charges. *See, e.g.,* Baker v. United States, 401 F.2d 958 (D.C. Cir. 1968).

27. *See, e.g.,* Kansas v. Carr, 136 S. Ct. 633, 644–46 (2016) (finding that a joint capital sentencing hearing in which one codefendant offered mitigating evidence that portrayed the other codefendant as a "corrupting" influence on the first defendant did not violate either the Eighth Amendment or the Due Process Clause because the totality of the aggravating evidence strongly supported death sentences for both codefendants).

28. Pate v. Robinson, 383 U.S. 375, 378 (1966); *see also* Godinez v. Moran, 509 U.S. 389 (1993).

29. Dusky v. United States, 362 U.S. 402, 402 (1960) (per curiam).

30. Drope v. Missouri, 420 U.S. 162 (1975) (trial judge has a constitutional duty to conduct a competency hearing if there is a serious question about the defendant's competency).

31. Medina v. California, 505 U.S. 437 (1992). In federal cases, it is unclear whether the defendant or the prosecution has the burden regarding a competency motion. The circuit courts are split regarding which party has the burden. *See* United States v. Whittington, 586 F.3d 613, 617–18 (8th Cir. 2009) (citing cases).

32. Cooper v. Oklahoma, 517 U.S. 348 (1996).

competency is a factual determination (subject to deferential appellate review) or a mixed question of law and fact (subject to de novo review on appeal).[33]

4.2.4 *Dismiss the Indictment Based on an Unconstitutional Penal Statute*

A defendant may move to dismiss the indictment or other charging instrument on the ground that the penal statute—which the defendant is accused of violating—is unconstitutional in some manner. Such a legal challenge typically contends that the statute is vague, overbroad, violates the defendant's constitutional right to privacy, or—in federal cases—exceeds Congress's authority under the Commerce Clause or some other provision of Article I of the Constitution.

The doctrines of vagueness and overbreadth are related, yet distinct.[34] A criminal law is unconstitutionally vague when its language is so unclear or standardless "that it leaves the public uncertain as to the conduct it prohibits."[35] The vagueness doctrine is rooted in the Due Process Clause, which requires "fair notice" to the public in terms of what the law prohibits and also prohibits laws that are so standardless that they risk arbitrary or discriminatory enforcement by police officers.[36] A defendant challenging a penal statute on vagueness grounds need not prove that the statute is vague in all of its potential applications.[37] The vagueness doctrine applies not only to vague elements of a criminal offense, but also to vague statutes that increase the statutory penalty range that a defendant faces.[38]

---

33. In *Drope*, the Court stated that although "factual" in nature, the issue of a defendant's mental competency was nevertheless a constitutional matter to be reviewed with some degree of independence by the Court. 420 U.S. at 174–75 & n.10. However, in two subsequent per curiam decisions, decided in federal habeas corpus cases, the Court appeared to ignore its prior holding in *Drope*. In Maggio v. Fulford, 462 U.S. 111, 117 (1983) (per curiam), the Supreme Court appeared to hold that a trial court's ruling on a defendant's mental competency is a factual issue subject to great deference on appeal. In a separate opinion concurring in the judgment, Justice White stated that the Court's prior cases treated the issue as a "mixed question" of law and fact subject to de novo review on appeal. *Id.* at 118–19 (White, J., concurring in judgment); *see also* Demosthenes v. Baal, 495 U.S. 731 (1990) (per curiam). Since *Maggio* and *Demosthenes*, the lower courts have observed this uncertainty in the Court's mental competency jurisprudence. *See, e.g.,* Washington v. Johnson, 90 F.3d 945, 951 & n.4 (5th Cir. 1996); Cremeans v. Chapleau, 62 F.3d 167, 169–70 (6th Cir. 1995).
34. Kolender v. Lawson, 461 U.S. 352, 358 n.8 (1983).
35. City of Chicago v. Morales, 527 U.S. 41, 56 (1999) (citation and internal quotation marks omitted).
36. *See Morales*, 527 U.S. at 56–58; *see also* Posters 'N' Things v. United States, 511 U.S. 513, 525 (1994) ("[T]he void-for-vagueness doctrine requires that a penal statute define the criminal offense with sufficient definiteness that ordinary people can understand what conduct is prohibited and in a manner that does not encourage arbitrary and discriminatory enforcement.").
37. Johnson v. United States, 576 U.S. 591, 602-03 (2015).
38. *Id.* at 596.

The overbreadth doctrine is rooted in the First Amendment rather than the Due Process Clause.[39] A penal statute is "facially overbroad" if it unconstitutionally chills or prohibits a "substantial" amount of constitutionally protected speech.[40] A defendant may raise such a challenge even if their own alleged criminal conduct was not such protected speech; indeed, such challenges are "third-party" challenges in nature.[41] A statute is also facially unconstitutional under the First Amendment if it violates the First Amendment in all of its applications (including the defendant's conduct as well as that of third parties).[42] An unconstitutional law can be both vague and overbroad if it sweeps so broadly that it fails to establish minimum guidelines for its enforcement and it substantially impacts constitutionally protected speech of third parties not before the court.[43]

A penal statute may be unconstitutional because it violates a defendant's Fifth Amendment privilege against self-incrimination[44] or their constitutional right to privacy or some other substantive due process right.[45] In federal cases, a federal penal statute also may be unconstitutional if it exceeds Congress's authority to enact legislation pursuant to some enumerated power in Article I of the Constitution. The most common example of such a constitutional challenge to a federal statute is an argument that Congress has no authority to regulate certain intrastate conduct under the Interstate Commerce Clause.[46]

---

39. *See, e.g.*, Virginia v. Hicks, 539 U.S. 113, 118–19 (2003) (discussing the "overbreadth" doctrine).

40. Broadrick v. Oklahoma, 413 U.S. 601, 615 (1973); *see also* United States v. Hicks, 980 F.2d 963, 969–70 (5th Cir. 1992).

41. *Broadrick*, 413 U.S. at 611–12. Of course, if a defendant's own conduct or speech is arguably constitutionally protected under the First Amendment, then they can make an "as-applied"—as opposed to, or in addition to, a "facial"—challenge in a pretrial motion. *See Hicks*, 980 F.2d at 970–72 (discussing the difference between a "facial overbreadth" challenge and an "as-applied" First Amendment challenge). It should be noted, however, that some courts have refused to entertain "as applied" challenges in a pretrial motion. Such courts reason that "as-applied" challenges necessarily are based on the specific facts of the case and that such facts must be developed at the trial (and thus such challenges must be made after the facts are developed at trial). *See, e.g.*, United States v. Caputo, 288 F. Supp. 2d 912, 917 (N.D. Ill. 2003).

42. *See, e.g.*, United States v. Eichman, 496 U.S. 310 (1990) (invalidating the federal penal statute that outlawed flag-burning under the First Amendment).

43. *See, e.g.*, Gooding v. Wilson, 405 U.S. 518 (1972) (invalidating a Georgia criminal statute on both vagueness and overbreadth grounds). An appellate court can interpret what would otherwise be vague or overbroad statutory language in a manner that obviates the constitutional defect. *See* Osborne v. Ohio, 495 U.S. 103, 114–16 (1990).

44. *See, e.g.*, Leary v. United States, 395 U.S. 6 (1969); Haynes v. United States, 390 U.S. 85 (1968).

45. *See* Lawrence v. Texas, 539 U.S. 558 (2003) (striking down Texas's homosexual sodomy statute as violating the constitutional right to privacy); *cf.* Robinson v. California, 370 U.S. 660 (1962) (striking down California statute that criminalized being a drug addict as violating Eighth Amendment).

46. *See, e.g.*, United States v. Lopez, 514 U.S. 549 (1995) (striking down the former version of 18 U.S.C. § 922(q), which criminalized the possession of a firearm within a certain distance of a school as being beyond Congress's authority under the Commerce Clause).

4.2.5 Dismiss the Indictment Based on a Violation of the Constitutional Right to a Speedy Trial or Pre-Indictment Delay

The Sixth Amendment provides that a criminal defendant is entitled to a speedy trial.[47] This constitutional guarantee should be distinguished from statutory speedy trial requirements, which typically impose more stringent time limits on bringing a case to trial in a prompt manner.[48]

The constitutional speedy trial clock begins to run once a defendant is arrested or a defendant is "officially accused"[49]—contrasted with the Sixth Amendment right to counsel, which attaches only after formal charges are filed and not on a mere arrest.[50] If the defendant is not put to trial in a timely manner, they can move to dismiss the indictment or other charging instrument with prejudice.

The Supreme Court has set forth four criteria with respect to a speedy trial claim: 1) length of the delay; 2) reason for the delay; 3) defendant's assertion, or lack thereof, of the right during the period of delay; and 4) prejudice.[51] There is no "bright line" that determines when a speedy trial violation occurs; each case must be analyzed based on its own facts.[52] Although the Supreme Court has never articulated a minimum amount of delay that would trigger a speedy trial analysis, most lower courts appear to require a minimum period of delay of at least one year to make out a prima facie claim of a speedy trial violation.[53] If the delay is extraordinary (i.e., over five years) and the defendant is not responsible for it, then courts will presume prejudice and require the prosecution to "affirmatively prove that the delay left [the defendant's] ability to defend himself unimpaired."[54] If a lesser delay occurs (i.e., between one and five years), a defendant typically must establish actual prejudice—either in the form of prejudice to a defense at trial or in some other sense (e.g., unusual stress or anxiety).[55] The Court has held that the prosecution's good-faith dismissal of the indictment without prejudice will toll the speedy trial clock.[56]

---

47. Klopfer v. North Carolina, 386 U.S. 213 (1967); Barker v. Wingo, 407 U.S. 514 (1972).
48. *See, e.g.*, 18 U.S.C. §§ 3161, *et seq.*
49. United States v. MacDonald, 456 U.S. 1, 6–7 (1982).
50. The Sixth Amendment right to counsel is discussed in Chapter Three.
51. *Barker*, 407 U.S. at 530. Delays attributable to defense counsel—including court-appointed counsel—ordinarily are excluded from the legal analysis of a speedy trial claim. *See* Vermont v. Brillon, 556 U.S. 81 (2009).
52. United States v. Frye, 372 F.3d 729, 736 (5th Cir. 2004) (speedy trial claims analyzed under the *Barker* test are "fact specific").
53. *See* Doggett v. United States, 505 U.S. 647, 652 n.1 (1992); *see also* United States v. Velasquez, 749 F.3d 161, 174 (3d Cir. 2014).
54. *Doggett*, 505 U.S. at 657–58 & n.4; *see also* United States v. Serna-Villarreal, 352 F.3d 225, 232 (5th Cir. 2003) (citing cases from various courts that tend to draw the line at five years for such presumptive prejudice); Hartfield v. State, 516 S.W.3d 57, 70 (Tex. App. 2017) (presuming prejudice under *Doggett* based on an "astronomical" thirty-two-year delay).
55. *See* Strunk v. United States, 412 U.S. 434 (1973); Moore v. Arizona, 414 U.S. 25 (1973).
56. *MacDonald*, 456 U.S. at 8–10 & n.12.

In *United States v. Lovasco*,[57] the Supreme Court refused to extend the Sixth Amendment's speedy trial guarantee to pre-indictment delay (i.e., a delay between the date of the alleged crime and the indictment), but it did hold that the Due Process Clause may require dismissal of an indictment where the defendant was actually prejudiced by such a delay and the prosecution was culpable in some manner in delaying the indictment.[58] The Court did not define what it meant by the prosecution's culpability in this regard, and state and federal lower courts are divided over whether actual bad faith (as opposed to some lesser degree of culpability such as gross negligence) by the prosecution is required.[59]

4.2.6 Dismiss the Indictment Based on an Ex Post Facto Violation[60]

Under Article I, §§ 9 and 10 of the Constitution, neither Congress nor state legislatures may enact ex post facto laws. The Supreme Court has categorized four types of laws as impermissible ex post facto laws:

> [1] Every law that makes an action done before the passing of the law, and which was *innocent* when done, criminal; and punishes such action. [2] Every law that *aggravates a crime*, or makes it *greater* than it was, when committed. [3] Every law that *changes the punishment*, and inflicts a *greater punishment*, than the law annexed to the crime, when committed. [4] Every law that alters the *legal* rules of *evidence*, and receives less, or different, testimony, than the law required at the time of the commission of the offen[s]e, *in order to convict the offender*.[61]

With respect to the first category, the Court has also held that the retroactive abolition of an available defense to a crime or retroactive limitation on the availability of such a defense is an impermissible ex post facto law.[62] With respect to the third category, the Court has held that retroactive application of sentencing guidelines that increase a defendant's guideline sentencing range would violate the Ex Post Facto Clause.[63]

---

57. 431 U.S. 783 (1977).

58. *Id.* at 790.

59. *See* Commonwealth v. Scher, 803 A.2d 1204, 1216–20 (Pa. 2002) (discussing the division among the lower courts); *see also* Hoo v. United States, 484 U.S. 1035, 1035 (1988) (White, J., dissenting from denial of certiorari) (discussing the split among federal circuits on the issue).

60. A pretrial motion to dismiss the indictment or other charging instrument based on an ex post facto violation would only be appropriate where the law charges a new offense (or a greater degree of a preexisting offense) that did not exist at the time of the alleged crime. If a law is ex post facto with respect to the authorized punishment or the type of evidence that may be used to convict at a trial, then objections should be lodged at the relevant point in the proceedings once the ex post facto violation becomes apparent. Ex post facto sentencing laws are discussed in Chapter Twelve.

61. Carmell v. Texas, 529 U.S. 513, 522 (2000) (quoting from Calder v. Bull, 3 U.S. (3 Dall.) 386, 390 (1798)) (italics in original); *see also* Stogner v. California, 539 U.S. 607 (2003).

62. Collins v. Youngblood, 497 U.S. 37, 49–50 (1990).

63. Miller v. Florida, 482 U.S. 423 (1987) (holding that retroactive application of more severe

The prohibition against ex post facto laws only applies to criminal laws and does not apply to civil laws, even ones that result in incarceration of a citizen (e.g., civil commitment laws for sexual predators with mental illness).[64] In addition, the constitutional prohibition against ex post facto laws applies only to statutes; it does not apply either to judicial decisions that retroactively abolish substantive rights or defenses (created by prior judicial decisions) or to judicial decisions interpreting the scope of penal statutes.[65] Nonetheless, the Supreme Court has applied a less demanding limitation with respect to such retroactively applied judicial decisions, although the Court has done so solely as a matter of due process (which requires fair notice to the public of the penal law's requirements).[66] The Court has refused to incorporate its ex post facto jurisprudence in its entirety in the context of retroactive abolition of judicial decisions that hitherto were favorable to criminal defendants. Rather, the Court has limited retroactive abolition of judicial decisions only when such abolition was "unexpected and indefensible by reference to the law which had been expressed prior to the conduct at issue."[67]

4.2.7 Dismiss the Indictment Based on a Double Jeopardy Violation

The right to be free of double jeopardy attaches when the petit jury is sworn at the beginning of a jury trial or when the first witness is sworn at a bench trial.[68] Although the Supreme Court has not yet directly addressed the issue, most lower courts have held that jeopardy also attaches when a court accepts a defendant's guilty plea (where the defendant waived their right to a trial).[69] Double jeopardy protections only apply to criminal jeopardy; civil penalties (such as property forfeitures or taxes) do not implicate the Double Jeopardy Clause unless the legislature intended them as punitive.[70]

There are two primary species of double jeopardy violations. The first, to which the bulk of the Supreme Court's double jeopardy jurisprudence is devoted, is referred to as an impermissible "multiple prosecution" by the same sovereign. The second is referred to as "multiple punishments." The former involves successive prosecutions (i.e., different proceedings in which a defendant's guilt or innocence

---

"presumptive" guidelines violated Ex Post Facto Clause); *see also* Peugh v. United States, 569 U.S. 530, 544 (2013) (holding same, regarding "advisory" guidelines that serve as a "lodestone of sentencing").

64. Kansas v. Hendricks, 521 U.S. 346 (1997).

65. Rogers v. Tennessee, 532 U.S. 451 (2001) (refusing to apply Ex Post Facto Clause to the Tennessee Supreme Court's retroactive abolition of the common-law "year-and-a-day" rule in murder cases).

66. *Id.* at 459.

67. *Id.* at 461 (citation and internal quotation marks omitted).

68. Martinez v. Illinois, 572 U.S. 833, 839 (2014); Crist v. Bretz, 437 U.S. 28, 37–38 & n.15 (1978).

69. *See, e.g.,* Morris v. Reynolds, 264 F.3d 38 (2d Cir. 2001).

70. See Hudson v. United States, 522 U.S. 93 (1997); United States v. Ursery, 518 U.S. 267 (1996).

is adjudicated). The latter involves multiple punishments (resulting from multiple convictions) in the same proceeding,[71] and is discussed further in this chapter and in Chapter Twelve. If the former type of double jeopardy violation is at issue, a defendant typically will raise the issue by filing a pretrial motion to dismiss the indictment or other charging instrument in the second prosecution. A defendant waives a double jeopardy objection to a successive prosecution by successfully moving to sever multiple charges that qualify as the "same offense," even if they were acquitted of one of the offenses at the first trial.[72]

A prerequisite for either type of double jeopardy violation is that the second prosecution or second punishment be for the "same offen[s]e."[73] The Court has defined "same offense" by reference to the elements of the first and second charged offenses.[74] "Elements" are the components of a crime—almost always including both mens rea and actus reus elements.[75] For double jeopardy purposes, one offense is the same as another if both offenses share all the same elements and do not have at least one element not present in the other offense.[76] For example, aggravated assault with a deadly weapon and simple assault (of the same victim) are the same offense for double jeopardy purposes because all the elements of simple assault are contained in aggravated assault and simple assault has no additional element not also contained in aggravated assault.[77]

When determining whether two crimes constitute the same offense for double jeopardy purposes, courts often must decide whether one of the offenses is a lesser included offense of the other.[78] A "lesser included offense" is a crime whose elements comprise a complete subset of another ("greater") offense.[79] If there is a conviction or acquittal on a lesser offense in the first proceeding, it bars a second prosecution on the greater offense.[80] Likewise, a conviction or acquittal on a greater offense bars a second prosecution on the lesser offense.[81]

If two offenses are not the same offense for double jeopardy purposes, it is generally irrelevant whether the two offenses concern the same conduct by the defendant

---

71. *See generally* Ohio v. Johnson, 467 U.S. 493, 498–99 (1984) (discussing the two species of double jeopardy claims). The Court has noted that the "multiple prosecution" species has two subspecies: a successive prosecution following a conviction and a successive prosecution following an acquittal. *Id.*

72. Courier v. Virginia, 138 S. Ct. 2144 (2018).

73. U.S. Const. amend. V; *see also* United States v. Dixon, 509 U.S. 688 (1993).

74. *See* Blockburger v. United States, 284 U.S. 299 (1932).

75. *See* United States v. Gaudin, 515 U.S. 506, 510–12 (1995).

76. *Dixon*, 509 U.S. at 696.

77. *See, e.g.*, Manigault v. State, 486 A.2d 240, 246 & n.2 (Md. Ct. Spec. App. 1985).

78. *See* Harris v. Oklahoma, 433 U.S. 682 (1977) (per curiam); Brown v. Ohio, 432 U.S. 161 (1977).

79. Schmuck v. United States, 489 U.S. 705, 716–17 (1989).

80. *Brown*, 432 U.S. at 169–70.

81. *Harris*, 433 U.S. at 682–83.

or are proven with the same evidence.[82] The exception here is if a defendant was acquitted at their initial trial and the prosecution then seeks to try the defendant on a different charge based on the same alleged criminal transaction. If the acquittal was based on a determination that a particular fact was not proven beyond a reasonable doubt, then under the collateral estoppel variation of the double jeopardy principle, the prosecution is precluded from attempting to prove that same fact at a subsequent trial, even if the new charge is not the same offense.[83]

Under the dual sovereignty rule, there is no double jeopardy violation if a different sovereign within the United States prosecutes the defendant for the same offense.[84] For example, the federal government can prosecute a defendant for bank robbery after a state has prosecuted the same defendant (successfully or unsuccessfully) for the same alleged bank robbery, or vice-versa.[85]

If a trial court grants the prosecution's motion for a mistrial or the court sua sponte declares a mistrial after jeopardy has attached, but prior to a verdict, and the defendant objects to the mistrial, double jeopardy bars a retrial on the same offense unless there was a manifest necessity for declaring the mistrial.[86]

---

82. *Dixon*, 509 U.S. at 703–05 (overruling Grady v. Corbin, 495 U.S. 508 (1990)).
83. Ashe v. Swenson, 397 U.S. 436 (1970) (where first robbery trial ended in an acquittal based on jury's reasonable doubt that the defendant was the masked robber who had robbed six men playing poker, the prosecution was collaterally estopped from trying same defendant for robbery of another of the poker players who had not been a complainant at the initial trial); *see also* Yeager v. United States, 557 U.S. 110 (2009) (applying *Ashe* test to a case in which the jury acquitted on some counts, but failed to reach a verdict on other counts in a manner that was logically inconsistent with the acquittals because the same essential elements existed as to all of the counts; holding that the acquittals barred retrial on the counts on which the jury could not reach a verdict). Note that if a jury reaches a verdict with factually inconsistent results—an acquittal on one count and a conviction on another count, with the conviction being factually inconsistent with the acquittal—a subsequent appellate reversal of the conviction on a ground unrelated to the inconsistency will not bar a retrial of the defendant on the reversed count. *See* Bravo-Fernandez v. United States, 137 S. Ct. 352 (2016).
84. *See* Gamble v. United States, 139 S. Ct. 1960 (2019) (by a 7-2 vote, reaffirming the doctrine after granting certiorari to reconsider it); Heath v. Alabama, 474 U.S. 82 (1985) (successive prosecution in Alabama state court after conviction for same offense in Georgia state court did not violate double jeopardy); Bartkus v. Illinois, 359 U.S. 121 (1959) (successive prosecution in Illinois state court after prosecution in federal court for same offense did not violate double jeopardy); Abbate v. United States, 359 U.S. 187 (1959) (successive prosecution in federal court after prosecution in state court for same offense did not violate double jeopardy). An exception to the "dual sovereignty" rule exists if one sovereign was the "tool" of the other sovereign in the former's prosecution. *Bartkus*, 359 U.S. at 123–24. The Supreme Court has held that successive prosecutions regarding the "same offense" in different state courts within the same state (e.g., a prosecution for felony assault in a county's court after a prosecution for the lesser included misdemeanor offense of simple assault in municipal court) would be improper under the Double Jeopardy Clause. *See* Waller v. Florida, 397 U.S. 387 (1970).
85. *See* United States v. Sewell, 252 F.3d 647, 651 (2d Cir. 2001).
86. Illinois v. Somerville, 410 U.S. 458 (1973).

A "manifest necessity" means a high degree of necessity,[87] such as a trial judge's reasonable conclusion that a jury is hopelessly deadlocked after a good-faith attempt at deliberations.[88] Whether there is a manifest necessity generally depends on the specific facts and circumstances of each case.[89]

If the defense moves for a mistrial or does not oppose a prosecutor's motion for a mistrial (or a judge's sua sponte declaration of a mistrial), then the defendant generally has no double jeopardy claim.[90] An exception exists if the prosecutor intentionally goaded the defense into moving for a mistrial because the prosecutor feared losing the trial; if that occurs, then a retrial after the mistrial would be barred.[91]

Occasionally, at the end of a jury trial, the court will grant a motion for judgment of acquittal or for a directed verdict. These motions ask the court to take the case away from the jury and enter a judgment of acquittal based on a ruling that the evidence is legally insufficient to support a guilty verdict by a rational jury.[92] As long as such a judgment of acquittal is entered before the jury returns a guilty verdict, the trial court's ruling is tantamount to a jury's not guilty verdict for double jeopardy purposes—meaning that the prosecution cannot retry the defendant or appeal the trial court's ruling to an appellate court.[93] This bar applies even if the trial judge clearly erred in finding insufficient evidence to support a rational jury's guilty verdict; right or wrong, the judge's judgment of acquittal bars a retrial or an appeal by the prosecution.[94] Conversely, if the trial court enters a judgment of acquittal after the jury has returned a guilty verdict, the prosecution may appeal on the ground that the evidence supported the jury's guilty verdict and that the trial court erred in its post-verdict ruling.[95] An appellate court that disagrees with the trial court's ruling in such a case will reinstate the jury's guilty verdict, which does not require a retrial and thus does not place the defendant in jeopardy for a second time.[96]

Sometimes, after jeopardy attaches, a trial court will dismiss a case prior to the jury's deliberations or after a hung jury but will not explicitly grant a judgment of acquittal. In such a case, the Double Jeopardy Clause does not bar a retrial if the trial court's ruling is unrelated to the defendant's guilt or innocence (e.g., a ruling

---

87. Arizona v. Washington, 434 U.S. 497, 506 (1978); *see also* Downum v. United States, 372 U.S. 734, 736 (1963).
88. *See, e.g.,* In re Ford, 987 F.2d 334 (6th Cir. 1992).
89. *See* United States v. Stevens, 177 F.3d 579, 584 (6th Cir. 1999).
90. Oregon v. Kennedy, 456 U.S. 667, 673 (1982).
91. *Id.* at 676.
92. *See, e.g.,* FED. R. CRIM. P. 29. Motions for judgment of acquittal are discussed in Chapter Nine.
93. United States v. Martin Linen Supply Co., 430 U.S. 564 (1977); Martinez v. Illinois, 134 S. Ct. 2070 (2014) (per curiam). Likewise, a trial court's not guilty verdict at a bench trial bars a retrial or appeal by the prosecution. Smalis v. Pennsylvania, 476 U.S. 140 (1986).
94. Sanabria v. United States, 437 U.S. 54 (1978); *see also* Evans v. Michigan, 568 U.S. 1069 (2013); Smith v. Massachusetts, 543 U.S. 462 (2005).
95. United States v. Wilson, 420 U.S. 332 (1975).
96. *See id.*

that the indictment was legally defective because it failed to charge all of the elements of the offense).[97] However, the fact that the trial court does not label its ruling an acquittal is not dispositive. For example, if, after jeopardy has attached, the trial court effectively finds there is insufficient evidence supporting a guilty verdict or that the defendant has established an affirmative defense to the charges (e.g., insanity), the lack of an acquittal label is irrelevant and a retrial is barred.[98]

4.2.8   Dismiss the Indictment as "Duplicitous" or "Multiplicitous"

An indictment or other charging instrument that contains more than one distinct criminal charge in a single count is considered "duplicitous." Conversely, an indictment that charges a single offense in more than one count (whether or not the offense is codified in more than one statutory provision) is considered "multiplicitous."[99]

A duplicitous count of an indictment has the potential of violating the constitutional principle that a jury's guilty verdict must be unanimous (in a federal case) or reflect the views of at least nine of twelve jurors (in a state case) as to each and every element of the charged offense.[100] The most common type of duplicitous charge involves allegations of an offense against multiple victims in a single count. For example, in a case in which a single count of the indictment charged the defendant with defrauding numerous financial institutions on separate dates, the court held that the charge was duplicitous and required the prosecution to elect a single allegation of fraud involving just one financial institution.[101]

A multiplicitous indictment implicates the Double Jeopardy Clause because a defendant could be subjected to unconstitutional multiple punishments for the same offense.[102] In determining whether multiple counts of an indictment are multiplicitous, courts must apply the *Blockburger* test—namely, whether the offenses charged in each count contain at least one element that the other counts do not; and, if they do not, whether the legislature intended there to be multiple punishments for multiple convictions based on offenses involving the same elements.[103] For example, an

---

97. United States v. Scott, 437 U.S. 82 (1978).

98. United States v. Jorn, 400 U.S. 470, 478 n.7 (1971).

99. *See, e.g.*, United States v. Conley, 291 F.3d 464, 469–70 & n.4 (7th Cir. 2002) (discussing the difference between "duplicity" and "multiplicity"); State v. Via, 704 P.2d 238, 245–46 (Ariz. 1985) (same).

100. *See, e.g.*, United States v. Verrecchia, 196 F.3d 294, 297 (1st Cir. 1999); United States v. Pleasant, 125 F. Supp. 2d 173, 174–75 (E.D. Va. 2000); *see also* Richardson v. United States, 526 U.S. 813, 817 (1999); Schad v. Arizona, 501 U.S. 624, 631–32 (1991) (plurality). This constitutional principle is discussed in Chapter Ten.

101. United States v. Hinton, 127 F. Supp. 2d 548 (D.N.J. 2000).

102. *See, e.g.*, United States v. Tucker, 345 F.3d 320, 337 (5th Cir. 2003).

103. *See, e.g.*, United States v. Vargas-Castillo, 329 F.3d 715, 719 (9th Cir. 2003) (citing Blockburger v. United States, 284 U.S. 299 (1932)); United States v. Brechtel, 997 F.2d 1108, 1112 (5th Cir. 1993) (citing Missouri v. Hunter, 459 U.S. 359 (1983)).

indictment that charged a defendant with two counts, each referencing a different penal statute, but each concerning the same conduct—one count alleging that the defendant made a false statement relating to an application for citizenship and the other count alleging that they attempted to procure citizenship contrary to law (namely, by lying on the application)—was multiplicitous because the two alleged offenses contained the same elements.[104]

4.2.9 Dismiss the Indictment or Exclude Evidence Because the Prosecution or Police Have Destroyed or Failed to Preserve Potentially Exculpatory Evidence

The *Brady*[105] doctrine is discussed in Chapter Thirteen. Under *Brady* and its progeny, the prosecution has an affirmative duty under the Due Process Clause to disclose to the defense, before trial, material exculpatory evidence and evidence that impeaches the prosecution's witnesses.[106] *Brady* issues typically arise after a defendant is convicted and discovers such evidence; the remedy for a meritorious *Brady* claim is a new trial.[107] A related due process claim arises when the prosecution (including law enforcement officers) destroyed or failed to preserve potentially exculpatory or impeachment evidence.

As discussed elsewhere, to win a new trial under *Brady*, the defendant must demonstrate that there was a "reasonable probability" that but for the nondisclosure of the evidence in question, the defendant would have been acquitted rather than convicted at trial.[108] Such an analysis is counterfactual in nature—meaning that a reviewing court must ask how a rational jury would have voted if the suppressed evidence had been disclosed to the defense prior to the trial and presented to jurors.

But what if evidence in the possession of the prosecution team was destroyed—by act or omission—before it could be disclosed to the defense? For instance, what if, in a rape or murder case, police officers accidentally discarded a DNA sample (i.e., bodily fluid or hair) found at the crime scene before it could be tested? In such a situation—where no one will ever know whether the destroyed evidence would have proven to be exculpatory—the defendant is not entitled any remedy under the Constitution[109] unless they can show the potentially exculpatory evidence was

---

104. United States v. Rogers, 898 F. Supp. 219, 221–22 (S.D.N.Y. 1995).

105. Brady v. Maryland, 373 U.S. 83 (1963).

106. Kyles v. Whitley, 514 U.S. 419 (1995).

107. *Id.*

108. *Id.* at 434.

109. While not constitutionally mandated, some courts have required the submission of "spoliation instructions" to juries when the prosecution or police have negligently destroyed potentially exculpatory evidence. *See, e.g.,* State v. Fulminante, 975 P.2d 75, 93 (Ariz. 1999). Such instructions permit jurors to draw adverse inferences against the prosecution that the destroyed evidence would have been favorable to the defendant's case. *Id.*

National Institute for Trial Advocacy

destroyed in bad faith.[110] "Bad faith" is shown when "the police themselves by their conduct indicate that the evidence could [have] form[ed] a basis for exonerating the defendant."[111] Merely being negligent in allowing potentially exculpatory evidence to be destroyed is not tantamount to bad faith.[112] Nor is the fact that the defense had filed a discovery motion requesting access to the evidence at the time of its destruction automatically a basis for finding bad faith.[113] The requirement that actual bad faith be shown erects a high hurdle for defendants; few defendants actually have prevailed in making this type of claim.[114]

If a defendant can show bad faith, a court must decide on the appropriate remedy. In some situations, an outright dismissal of the charges may be the only equitable remedy where the bad-faith destruction of potentially exculpatory evidence entirely undermined the defendant's ability to mount a defense; in other cases, rather than dismiss the charges, courts will simply suppress evidence that the prosecution wishes to offer, but that cannot be fairly rebutted by the defense because of the destruction of other evidence in the prosecution's possession.[115]

A related issue arises when the government deports foreign witnesses before the defense has the opportunity to interview them. This issue is usually in the context of federal immigration prosecutions for alien smuggling.[116] If the witnesses were deported before being interviewed by agents of the government—and, thus, what the witnesses had to say is unknown—then the *Youngblood/Trombetta* standard applies and bad faith must be shown.[117] However, if the witnesses were interviewed before being deported (usually by immigration officials) and a record of their statements exists, a court should dismiss the indictment if there is a reasonable probability (within the meaning of the *Brady* doctrine) that the deported witnesses' testimony would have resulted in an acquittal at trial.[118] The lower courts are divided on whether bad faith must be shown in addition to a reasonable probability that the deported aliens' testimony would have exculpated the defendant at trial.[119] In view of the Supreme Court's repeated statement that bad faith need not be shown in the

---

110. Arizona v. Youngblood, 488 U.S. 51 (1988); California v. Trombetta, 467 U.S. 479 (1984).

111. *Youngblood*, 488 U.S. at 58.

112. *Id.* at 57–58.

113. Illinois v. Fisher, 540 U.S. 544 (2004) (per curiam).

114. *See* Teresa N. Chen, *The* Youngblood *Success Stories: Overcoming the "Bad Faith" Destruction of Evidence Standard*, 109 W. Va. L. Rev. 421 (Winter 2007) (noting the paucity of cases in which relief has been granted).

115. *See Trombetta*, 467 U.S. at 487; *see also* United States v. Elliott, 83 F. Supp. 2d 637, 649 (E.D. Va. 1999).

116. United States v. Valenzuela-Bernal, 458 U.S. 858 (1982).

117. United States v. Ramirez-Lopez, 315 F.3d 1143, 1165 & n.6 (9th Cir.) (Kozinski, J., dissenting), *vacated, opinion withdrawn,* and *appeal dismissed*, 327 F.3d 829 (9th Cir. 2003).

118. *Valenzuela-Bernal*, 458 U.S. at 873–74.

119. *Compare* United States v. Barajas-Chavez, 358 F.3d 1263, 1267–68 (10th Cir. 2004) ("bad faith" must be shown) *with* United States v. Dring, 930 F.2d 687, 694 n.7 (9th Cir. 1991) (bad faith irrelevant when deported aliens' testimony would have been favorable and material).

Brady context, it would appear that bad faith need not be shown when there is such a reasonable probability.[120] In other words, in such a situation, the constitutional question is more akin to a classic *Brady* issue than a *Youngblood/Trombetta* issue; bad faith appears to be relevant only in the latter context.

4.2.10   Ex Parte Motion for a Subpoena

The Compulsory Process Clause in the Sixth Amendment requires trial courts to issue—and, if necessary, enforce[121]—subpoenas (including subpoenas duces tecum) for defense witnesses whose testimony will be "favorable" to the defense and "necessary" for a fair trial.[122] If a witness is in the custody of a state or federal jail or prison, the defendant may request the trial court issue a "writ of habeas corpus ad testificandum," which is tantamount to a subpoena, but directed to the warden of the institution to bring the inmate to court to testify.[123] In addition, where defendants are indigent and thus unable to afford witness fees and other costs associated with subpoenas (including a witness's travel expenses and copying expenses in the case of a subpoena duces tecum), the constitutional principle of equal protection requires courts to pay for such expenses when a subpoena is otherwise required to be issued and enforced.[124]

Although the Supreme Court has stated that a defendant must show that a witness or evidence will be "material" as well as "favorable" for the Compulsory Process Clause to require a subpoena to issue,[125] the Court has not addressed the issue of whether the *Brady* doctrine's somewhat demanding materiality standard applies in the subpoena context—as it does in the special situation involving the deportation of potential defense witnesses before the defense has a chance to subpoena them.[126]

---

120. *See* Ramirez-Lopez, 315 F.3d at 1165 & n.6 (Kozinski, J., dissenting).

121. *See, e.g.*, United States v. Hegwood, 562 F.2d 946, 952 (5th Cir. 1977). When an indigent defendant applies for issuance of a subpoena and payment of witness fees and expenses by the court, the defendant ordinarily may file the application in an ex parte manner and the trial court ordinarily should order the clerk of the court to seal the subpoena application and corresponding order issuing the subpoena. Requiring an indigent defendant to file an unsealed application and serve it on the prosecution would place them at a disadvantage (based on their poverty) because it would provide the prosecution with pretrial discovery of the defendant's trial strategy (which must be explained in the application). *See, e.g.*, United States v. Hang, 75 F.3d 1275, 1281 (8th Cir. 1996). Equal protection of the laws is promoted by such an ex parte procedure because nonindigent defendants need not apply for issuance of a subpoena (without costs) from the court.

122. Washington v. Texas, 388 U.S. 14, 16 (1967); *see also* Taylor v. Illinois, 484 U.S. 400 (1988).

123. United States v. Cruz-Jiminez, 977 F.2d 95, 100 (3d Cir. 1992).

124. A subpoena may be enforced by a court through issuance of a bench warrant ordering the arrest of a witness who has been properly served with a subpoena, but who refuses to comply with it. It also may be enforced through the trial court's contempt power. *See, e.g.*, Commonwealth v. Ferguson, 552 A.2d 1075, 1089 (Pa. Super. Ct. 1988).

125. *Washington*, 388 U.S. at 16–18.

126. *See* Valenzuela-Bernal, 458 U.S. at 873 & n.9.

The lower courts are divided on the type of materiality required in the subpoena context.[127] Most appear to apply a materiality standard for subpoenas that is more akin to a traditional relevancy test—namely, that a defendant's subpoena application makes a plausible showing that the requested evidence or testimony is "relevant to any issue" and that the allegations in the subpoena application are not "incredible on their face."[128]

A related issue arises when a defendant seeks to subpoena records in the possession of a government agency that is obliged under a statute to keep the record confidential (e.g., Child Protective Services) and the agency seeks to quash the subpoena. In *Pennsylvania v. Ritchie*,[129] the Supreme Court held that when the defendant has shown that the records in question might be favorable material at trial, due process requires the trial court to examine the confidential records in chambers and determine whether any of the records are material within the meaning of the *Brady* doctrine.[130] The Court in *Ritchie* held its decision was rooted in the Due Process Clause rather than in the Compulsory Process Clause because the defendant's subpoena was not aimed at specified evidence, but was more exploratory in nature.[131] It is an open question—which has divided the lower courts—whether *Ritchie* applies to privileged information possessed by nongovernmental third parties.[132] The apparent consensus among the lower courts is that *Ritchie* does not apply to the attorney-client privilege, an "absolute" privilege.[133] Whether *Ritchie* extends to other absolute (as opposed to "qualified") privileges (e.g., psychotherapist-patient privilege) has divided the lower courts.[134]

4.2.11 Ex Parte Motion for Appointment of an Expert Witness When the Defendant Is Indigent

As discussed above in the context of free transcripts for indigent defendants,[135] constitutional principles of equal protection and due process may require courts to provide indigent defendants with "adjuncts" to the right to counsel that a

---

127. *Compare*, e.g., Richmond v. Embry, 122 F.3d 866, 873 & n.5 (10th Cir. 1997) (applying the *Brady* type "materiality" standard), *with id.* at 876–77 (Henry, J., concurring) (applying a more "traditional relevancy" standard of materiality); Arizona v. Carlos, 17 P.3d 118, 123 (Ariz. 2001) (same).

128. *See, e.g.*, United States v. Sims, 637 F.2d 625, 627–28 (9th Cir. 1980) (citing cases).

129. 480 U.S. 39 (1987).

130. *Id.* at 58.

131. *Id.* at 56–57.

132. *Compare*, e.g., People v. Webb, 862 P.2d 779, 794 (Cal. 1993) (*Ritchie* not applicable to private third parties) *with* State v. Rehkop, 908 A.2d 488, 495 (Vt. 2006) (*Ritchie* applicable to nongovernmental entities).

133. *See, e.g.*, People v. Gurule, 51 P.3d 224, 250 (Cal. 2002).

134. *See* Commonwealth v. Barroso, 122 S.W.3d 554, 561–62 (Ky. 2003) (citing conflicting cases from various jurisdictions).

135. *See* Chapter Three.

nonindigent defendant could afford. In *Ake v. Oklahoma*,[136] the Supreme Court held that an indigent defendant is entitled to the state-funded assistance of a psychiatric expert witness when their mental state is a "significant factor" at the trial (e.g., when they raise an insanity defense).[137] In *Ake*, the Court spoke in general terms of the need to provide indigent defendants with "the basic tools" for an "adequate defense" when they demonstrate a need for such basic tools in addition to the assistance of counsel.[138] Although the Court has not had occasion to apply its holding in *Ake* to nonpsychiatric expert witnesses (e.g., ballistics experts, fingerprint experts, medical forensic experts),[139] many lower courts have held that (or assumed arguendo that) *Ake* applies to nonpsychiatric experts.[140] The Supreme Court has held that an indigent defendant's right to an expert under *Ake* means an expert "who is sufficiently available to the defense and independent from the prosecution to effectively assist in evaluation, preparation, and presentation of the defense."[141] The court did not go so far as to hold that such an expert must be an actual "member of the defense team."[142] The lower courts remain divided on that issue.[143]

If a defendant files an *Ake* motion, it customarily has been filed in an ex parte manner and under seal, much in the same way indigent defendants' ex parte subpoena motions are filed. Requiring a defendant to reveal the contents of the pretrial *Ake* motion to the prosecutor prior to trial would put the defendant in an unfair position—it would require them to reveal confidential defense matters that a nonindigent defendant (able to employ their own expert) would not have to reveal until they actually designate the expert as a witness.[144]

---

136. Ake v. Oklahoma, 470 U.S. 68 (1985).

137. *Id.* at 83.

138. *Id.* at 77.

139. In Caldwell v. Mississippi, 472 U.S. 320 (1985), the Court was asked to extend *Ake* to nonpsychiatric experts—in particular, fingerprint and ballistic experts—but refused to address the issue in that case because the defendant never offered any specific reasons why he needed such court-afforded assistance. *Id.* at 323 n.1; *see also* Johnson v. Oklahoma, 484 U.S. 878, 880 (1987) (Marshall, J., dissenting from denial of certiorari, joined by Brennan, J.) (noting the issue was left open in *Caldwell*).

140. *See, e.g.*, State v. Wong, 92 A.3d 220, 235–36 & n.15 (Conn. 2014); Husske v. Commonwealth, 476 S.E.2d 920, 925 (Va. 1996); Rey v. State, 897 S.W.2d 333 (Tex. Crim. App. 1995); Little v. Armontrout, 835 F.2d 1240 (8th Cir. 1987). The Fifth Circuit has held that to qualify for a nonpsychiatric expert, a defendant must demonstrate that the prosecutor's contrary expert—whose testimony a defense expert would have rebutted—was "critical" to the conviction. Moore v. Johnson, 225 F.3d 495, 502 (5th Cir. 2000). Such a stringent standard appears more demanding than *Ake* requires.

141. McWilliams v. Dunn, 137 S. Ct. 1790, 1799 (2017) (citation and internal quotation marks omitted).

142. *See id.* at 1799–1800; *see also id.* at 1801–02 (Alito, J. dissenting).

143. *Id.* at 1801–02 (Alito, J., dissenting); *see also* Danica Bird, *Indigent Criminal Defendants Are Entitled to a Defense Team Mental Health Expert*, 22 J. GENDER RACE & JUST. 351, 361–66 (2019) (discussing the division among the lower courts).

144. *See* Williams v. State, 958 S.W.2d 186, 192–93 (Tex. Crim. App. 1997) (discussing *Ake*, 470 U.S. at 82–83).

4.2.12   Dismiss the Indictment Based on Discrimination in the Selection of the Grand Jury or Its Foreperson

Invidious discrimination in the selection of grand jurors based on race, national origin, ethnicity, or gender is an equal protection violation and requires dismissal of the indictment returned by such a tainted grand jury.[145] Any defendant, regardless of race, ethnicity, country of origin, or gender, has standing to file such a motion.[146]

The Supreme Court's jurisprudence concerning equal protection challenges of grand jury selection is quite similar to its jurisprudence concerning equal protection challenges to the selection of the venire from which the petit jury is selected. Indeed, some cases involve challenges to the discriminatory manner in which both the grand jury and petit jury were selected.[147] The key difference is that a challenge to the venire is in the form of a motion to strike the tainted venire (also called an "array"),[148] whereas a challenge to the grand jury is in the form of a motion to dismiss (or "quash") the indictment.[149] Such challenges to the petit jury venire are discussed in Chapter Seven.

To prevail on such a motion to dismiss the indictment, a criminal defendant—much like a civil plaintiff in an employment discrimination case[150]—first must make out a "prima facie case" of systematic exclusion or substantial underrepresentation of a protected class of citizens. A prima facie case is sufficient enough proof to permit a court to infer a probability of intentional discrimination in the selection of grand jurors.[151] The Supreme Court has required three things to be shown to make out a prima facie case: 1) the group of persons excluded or substantially underrepresented is a protected class under the Equal Protection Clause;[152]

---

145. *See, e.g.*, Campbell v. Louisiana, 523 U.S. 392 (1998); Vasquez v. Hillery, 474 U.S. 254 (1986); Whitus v. Georgia, 385 U.S. 545 (1967). The Court has recognized a related due process challenge to such an improperly selected grand jury, yet such a separate claim appears to offer no more ammunition to a defendant. *See* Mosley v. Dretke, 370 F.3d 467, 474–78 (5th Cir. 2004) (discussing the two types of claims).

146. *Campbell*, 523 U.S. at 401–02.

147. *See, e.g.*, Peters v. Kiff, 407 U.S. 493 (1972); Jones v. Georgia, 389 U.S. 24 (1967) (per curiam).

148. *See, e.g.*, Avery v. Georgia, 345 U.S. 559 (1953).

149. *See, e.g.*, Whitus, 385 U.S. at 553. The dismissal of the indictment as a remedy is "without prejudice"—meaning that the prosecutor may seek another indictment from a properly selected grand jury. *See id.*

150. *See, e.g.*, Int'l Brotherhood of Teamsters v. United States, 431 U.S. 324, 339 (1977).

151. Rose v. Mitchell, 443 U.S. 545, 565 (1979); Alexander v. Louisiana, 405 U.S. 625, 629–33 (1972); *see also Mosley*, 370 F.3d at 475.

152. A related claim is that a "distinctive group" has been excluded or is significantly underrepresented in grand juries in violation of the implied "fair cross-section" requirement of the Sixth Amendment. In federal prosecutions, the Sixth Amendment's "fair cross-section" requirement is applicable to grand juries as well as petit juries. *See, e.g.*, United States v. Ovalle, 136 F.3d 1092, 1099 (6th Cir. 1998). An open question, which has divided the lower courts, is whether state grand juries (as well as petit juries) are subject to the Sixth Amendment's implied "fair cross-section" requirement. *Compare* Ford v. Seabold, 841 F.2d 677, 687–88 (6th Cir. 1988) (fair cross-section requirement only applies to state petit juries) *with* State v. Jenison, 405 A.2d 3, 6–8 (R.I. 1979) (fair-cross section requirement applies to both state grand juries and petit juries).

2) the degree of underrepresentation is calculable by comparing the proportion of the total percentage of the relevant class in the total population to those called to serve as grand jurors over a "significant period of time"; and 3) the procedure for selecting grand jurors is susceptible to abuse.[153] Usually the degree of underrepresentation is the dispositive issue that is litigated with respect to the threshold prima facie case issue. Such an issue turns on statistics.[154] Once a prima facie case has been established by the defendant, "the burden of proof shifts to the [prosecution] to rebut the presumption of unconstitutional action by showing that permissible racially neutral selection criteria and procedures have produced the monochromatic result."[155] If the prosecution fails to do so, then the trial court must dismiss the indictment.[156]

An issue that has not been fully resolved by the Supreme Court is whether proof of discrimination in the selection of a grand jury foreperson violates the Constitution and requires dismissal of an indictment.[157] At least in certain situations—such as when the foreperson is selected independently of the other members of the grand jury (as opposed to being selected from among the grand jurors previously empaneled) and has a role other than solely a "ministerial" one—there is no question that discriminatory selection of a foreperson is a basis to dismiss the indictment.[158] However, whether an equal protection claim is viable when a foreperson is selected from among existing grand jurors (who were selected in a valid manner) and when the role of the foreperson is purely ministerial remains an open question and continues to divide the lower courts.[159]

A "distinctive group" for purposes of the fair cross-section requirement theoretically need not also be a protected class under the Equal Protection Clause. In practice, though, in most cases, "distinctive" groups under the Sixth Amendment will be roughly equivalent to protected classes under the Equal Protection Clause. *See* Lockhart v. McCree, 476 U.S. 162, 175 (1986). Therefore, whether the fair cross-section applies to state grand juries is largely an academic matter in that sense. Nonetheless, because intentional discrimination need not be shown to prevail on a fair cross-section challenge— as opposed to a mere showing of "state action" resulting in a significant underrepresentation of a distinctive group, whether intentional or not (*see* State v. Rogers, 55 P.3d 488, 494 n.8 (Or. 2002))—the larger issue is not entirely academic. The "fair cross-section" requirement (as applied to the selection of petit jury venires) is discussed in Chapter Seven.

153. *Rose*, 443 U.S. at 565 (internal quotes and citations omitted).

154. A detailed discussion of the technical aspects of such statistical analysis is beyond the scope of this book. Suffice it to say that there must be proof that a cognizable group was underrepresented over a significant time period in a statistically significant manner. *See, e.g., Mosley*, 370 F.3d at 479 & n.6 (discussing the statistical issue; noting the difference between "absolute" statistical disparities and "comparative" statistical disparities); United States v. Royal, 174 F.3d 1, 3–10 (1st Cir. 1999) (same). For that reason, lawyers who litigate such issues typically employ statisticians as expert witnesses.

155. *Alexander*, 405 U.S. at 632.

156. *See id.*

157. *See* Campbell, 523 U.S. 392; Hobby v. United States, 468 U.S. 339 (1984).

158. *Campbell*, 523 U.S. at 402–03; *Mosley*, 370 F.3d at 474–79; *see also Rose*, 443 U.S. at 566–74.

159. *See, e.g.*, State v. Divers, 793 So. 2d 308 (La. App. 2001) (in a two-to-one decision, affirming order of trial court dismissing the indictment after finding that the prosecution failed to rebut the defendant's prima facie case when foreperson was chosen from existing grand jurors by trial court; dissenting judge argued that there was no equal protection violation because foreperson was chosen

Because most jurisdictions now derive lists of prospective grand jurors (as well as petit jurors) from the rolls of registered voters, property taxpayers, or persons with a driver's license,[160] challenges to grand juries on equal protection grounds have become infrequent compared to prior decades, when "the key man" system or another nonrandom method was used in which the potential for discrimination existed.[161] Challenges to the selection of grand jury forepersons are still relatively common though, because many jurisdictions still provide that forepersons are selected by a trial judge or in another nonrandom manner in which the potential for discrimination exists.[162]

4.2.13 Recuse the Prosecutor or Trial Judge Because of Bias

Occasionally, a trial judge or prosecutor has an interest in a criminal prosecution that transcends the ordinary interest to see that justice is done. Although there are statutes in most jurisdictions that require recusal of a trial judge or disqualification of a prosecutor for certain specific reasons[163] or when the appearance of bias exists (even when in fact there is no bias),[164] the Due Process Clause requires recusal of a judge or disqualification of a prosecutor under specific circumstances.

4.2.13.1 Recuse a Trial Judge

Due process requires "a neutral and detached judge"[165]—irrespective of and in addition to an impartial jury guaranteed by the Sixth and Fourteenth Amendments. Both are independently required in the adversary system.[166] At a jury trial, the judge is not a mere "moderator," but instead is the "governor" of the criminal

---

from existing grand jurors who were selected in a nondiscriminatory manner and further that the role of the foreperson was purely ministerial); Mosley v. State, 983 S.W.2d 249, 255 (Tex. Crim. App. 1998) (rejecting equal protection challenge to selection of foreperson because role of foreperson was purely ministerial and foreperson was chosen from existing grand jurors who had been properly selected).

160. *See, e.g.,* Dobyne v. State, 805 So. 2d 733, 747–48 (Ala. Crim. App. 2000); *see generally* Marjorie A. Shields, *Validity and Application of Computerized Jury Selection Practice & Procedure,* 110 A.L.R. 5th 329, § 5 (citing cases).

161. The "key man" system commonly used in the past—in which county officials would select a key man to recruit grand jurors—was widely challenged. *See, e.g.,* Castaneda v. Partida, 430 U.S. 482, 484–85, 497 (1977).

162. *See, e.g.,* Woodfox v. Cain, 772 F.3d 358 (5th Cir. 2014) (finding constitutional violation in selection of state grand jury foreperson).

163. *See, e.g.,* 28 U.S.C. § 455(b); Haw. Rev. Stat. Ann. § 601-7.

164. *See, e.g.,* Liteky v. United States, 510 U.S. 540, 545–47 (1994) (discussing 28 U.S.C. § 455(a)); People v. Lee, 93 P.3d 544, 548–49 (Colo. App. 2003) (discussing Colo. Rev. Stat. Ann. § 20-1-107(2)).

165. Ward v. Village of Monroeville, 409 U.S. 57, 61–62 (1972).

166. *See, e.g.,* United States v. Lanham, 416 F.2d 1140, 1144 (5th Cir. 1969) ("A fair and impartial trial is guaranteed to every defendant, and fundamentally means a trial before an impartial judge and by an impartial jury.") (citation and internal quotation marks omitted).

trial.[167] Even though the jury is the ultimate decision maker—in terms of a defendant's guilt or innocence—the trial judge plays a critical role in that process both before and during a jury trial.[168] Thus, due process requires an unbiased trial judge.

There are various types of judicial bias that may rise to the level of a due process violation. The most obvious types of bias are a judge with racial, ethnic, or religious bias against a defendant;[169] a judge with a direct or indirect financial interest in the result of a case;[170] a judge who previously was a witness to the alleged offense (in a capacity other than as a judge);[171] a judge who regularly accepted bribes from defendants to "fix" their cases;[172] a judge involved romantically with the prosecutor during the trial;[173] a judge who previously served as a prosecutor in the defendant's case;[174] and a judge in a contempt-of-court case who became "personally embroiled" with the contemnor (resulting in the allegedly contemptuous conduct).[175] When determining whether due process required a judge to recuse themselves from a criminal case, a reviewing court does not merely inquire whether actual bias existed, but also whether "objectively speaking, the probability of actual bias on the part of the judge or decisionmaker [was] too high to be constitutionally tolerable."[176]

---

167. Quercia v. United States, 289 U.S. 466, 469 (1933).

168. *See, e.g.*, State v. Mims, 235 N.W.2d 381, 387–88 (Minn. 1975) ("The trial judge, as the neutral factor in the interplay of our adversary system, is vested with the responsibility to ensure the integrity of all stages of the proceedings. This pervasive responsibility includes avoidance of both the reality and the appearance of any impropriety by so directing and guiding the proceedings as to afford the jury fair and independent opportunity to reach an impartial result on the issue of guilt.").

169. *See, e.g.*, United States v. Bakker, 925 F.2d 728, 740–41 (4th Cir. 1991) (finding that judge possessed religious bias against the defendant, a former minister convicted of defrauding people who donated money to his ministry); Berry v. United States, 283 F.2d 465, 467 (8th Cir. 1960) (finding that judge possessed racial prejudice against the defendant); Berger v. United States, 255 U.S. 22, 28 (1921) (finding that judge possessed ethnic prejudice against German-American defendant).

170. Tumey v. Ohio, 273 U.S. 510 (1927); *see also Ward*; Aetna Life Insur. Co. v. Lavoie, 475 U.S. 813 (1986) (civil case in which justice on state supreme court was found to have strong appearance of bias, thus requiring his recusal as a matter of due process, because an appellate decision in which he participated directly impacted a pending litigation in another case in which he was a party).

171. In re Murchison, 349 U.S. 133 (1955).

172. *See* Bracy v. Gramley, 520 U.S. 899, 905–06 (1997) (holding that due process would be violated if the capital defendant could establish the trial judge who presided over their capital case and who had taken bribes to "fix" other capital cases to spare those other defendants of the death penalty was biased against the defendant, who did not offer a bribe), *subsequent proceeding on remand, sub nom.* Bracey v. Schomig, 286 F.3d 406 (7th Cir. 2002) (en banc) (vacating death penalty based on judicial bias; defendant did not offer the judge a bribe and the court recognized that there was too great a risk that the corrupt judge engaged in "compensatory bias" in the defendant's case).

173. *See, e.g.*, United States v. Berman, 28 M.J. 615 (AFCMR 1989).

174. Williams v. Pennsylvania, 136 S. Ct. 1899 (2016) (holding that state supreme court justice violated Due Process Clause by ruling on the appeal of capital defendant in whose case the justice, in his prior job as district attorney, had authorized the death penalty).

175. Mayberry v. Pennsylvania, 400 U.S. 455 (1971).

176. Rippo v. Baker, 137 S. Ct. 905, 907 (2017) (per curiam).

In evaluating claims of judicial bias, courts employ the "extrajudicial bias" doctrine. This doctrine provides that as a general matter, alleged judicial bias that stems solely from the judge's opinions derived from the facts and circumstances of the case at bar—as opposed to some extrajudicial source—do not provide a basis for recusal.[177] An exception to this general rule exists if the judge's bias, although "intrajudicial," nonetheless reveals a "high degree of favoritism or antagonism" toward one of the parties in the case[178] or when such intrajudicial bias is "pervasive" in the case.[179]

4.2.13.2 Recuse the Prosecutor

Like a judge, a prosecutor also must be free of bias. However, the Supreme Court has recognized that because prosecutors are "necessarily permitted to be zealous in their enforcement of the law," they "may not necessarily be held to as stringent a standard of disinterest as judges."[180] The most frequent basis for disqualification of a prosecutor is that they possess an improper conflict of interest. Although "[t]he Due Process Clause is not a code of ethics for prosecutors,"[181] a prosecutor's violation of the ethical proscription against conflicts of interest may rise to the level of a due process violation.[182] Such unconstitutional conflicts may result from a prosecutor's serving in a case in which the defendant was a former client in a related case (when the prosecutor was formerly a defense lawyer);[183] prosecuting an individual with whom the prosecutor is embroiled in a civil action;[184] having a romantic or sexual affair with the trial judge during the prosecution;[185] and being paid by the victim or victim's family to prosecute the case as a "private prosecutor."[186] If sufficient proof of such prejudice were offered, presumably a prosecutor with racial, ethnic, or religious bias against a defendant also should be disqualified.[187]

---

177. Liteky v. United States, 510 U.S. 540, 545–47 (1994); United States v. Grinnell Corp., 384 U.S. 563, 580–83 (1966).

178. *Liteky*, 510 U.S. at 555.

179. *See, e.g.*, United States v. Phillips, 664 F.2d 971, 1002–03 (5th Cir. 1981); Parker v. State, 587 So. 2d 1072, 1097 (Ala. Crim. App. 1991).

180. Young v. United States ex rel. Vuitton et Fils, S.A., 481 U.S. 787, 807 (1987).

181. Mabry v. Johnson, 467 U.S. 504, 511 (1984).

182. *See, e.g.*, State v. Boyd, 560 S.W.2d 296 (Mo. Ct. App. 1977); *see also* United States v. Goot, 894 F.2d 231, 236 (7th Cir. 1990).

183. *See, e.g.*, State v. Chavez, 540 So. 2d 992, 995 (La. Ct. App. 1989) ("This guarantee [that a prosecutor not have formerly represented the defendant in a substantially related matter] lies at the very heart of a defendant's right to due process."); Ex parte Spain, 589 S.W.2d 132, 134 (Tex. Crim. App. 1979).

184. *See, e.g.*, Ganger v. Payton, 379 F.2d 709 (4th Cir. 1967).

185. *See, e.g.*, Berman, 28 M.J. 615.

186. *See, e.g.*, Adkins v. Commonwealth, 492 S.E.2d 833 (Va. Ct. App. 1997).

187. *See* Wayte v. United States, 470 U.S. 598, 608 (1985) (although a prosecutor has tremendous discretion in terms of bringing a criminal prosecution, such discretion cannot be affected by bigotry).

If a particular prosecutor—either an assistant or the head of the office—is disqualified, the rest of the office usually need not be disqualified as long as the basis for disqualification has not tainted the entire office.[188]

4.2.14 *Dismiss a Charge Based on a "Vindictive" Prosecution*

Related to the concept of prosecutorial bias is the constitutional rule that a criminal charge must be dismissed (even if supported by evidence) if it is the result of a vindictive prosecution.[189] The Supreme Court has recognized two types of "vindictive prosecution" claims.

The first, and the most difficult to prove, is "actual" vindictiveness. To prevail on such a claim, a defendant must rebut the law's presumption that a prosecutorial charging decision was legitimate and was not made to punish a defendant for exercising a certain right (such as filing a pretrial motion to suppress evidence).[190] Rebutting such a presumption is, of course, quite difficult to do, and, as a result, such actual vindictiveness claims are rare.[191]

The second type of claim, although more limited in its application, shifts the presumption to the prosecution and makes it easier for a defendant to prevail. When a defendant has filed a motion for a new trial or appealed a conviction to a higher court, the prosecutor generally is presumed to have acted vindictively—and in violation of due process—if they add an additional or greater charge based on the same conduct[192] that was the basis of the original charge and there appears to be a "reasonable likelihood" that the defendant is being punished for having challenged their original conviction.[193] Such a presumption of prosecutorial vindictiveness is rebuttable—meaning the prosecutor can come forward with a valid reason for filing the additional charges.[194] If a court accepts such an explanation, then the new charges will not be dismissed.[195]

---

188. *See, e.g.*, Commonwealth v. Miller, 422 A.2d 525 (Pa. Super. Ct. 1980).

189. Blackledge v. Perry, 417 U.S. 21 (1974); Thigpen v. Roberts, 468 U.S. 27 (1984).

190. United States v. Goodwin, 457 U.S. 368, 384 & n.19 (1982).

191. *Id.* at 384 n.19; *see also* United States v. Johnson, 171 F.3d 139, 140–41 (2d Cir. 1999) (holding that a showing of "actual" vindictiveness required "direct evidence," such as a statement by the prosecutor evincing such actual vindictiveness). One such case dismissing an indictment based on a finding of "actual" vindictiveness was United States v. Wilson, 120 F. Supp. 2d 550 (E.D.N.C. 2000).

192. If the new charge is based on different conduct than that covered in the original charge, then such a presumption is inapplicable. *See, e.g.*, State v. Williams, 677 N.W.2d 691, 703–04 (Wis. Ct. App. 2004).

193. Thigpen, 468 U.S. at 30–31 (discussing Blackledge, 417 U.S. 21).

194. Bragan v. Poindexter, 249 F.3d 476, 484–85 (6th Cir. 2001).

195. *See, e.g.*, Townsend v. State, 134 S.W.3d 545, 549–50 (Ark. 2003) (finding that the prosecution rebutted the presumption of vindictiveness).

The presumption of prosecutorial vindictiveness does not apply to the extremely common pretrial situation in which a prosecutor files a more serious charge after a defendant refuses to plead guilty to a lesser offense.[196] In such a situation, a defendant must establish actual vindictiveness, which, as previously noted, is extremely difficult to show.[197] The related doctrine of "judicial vindictiveness"—with respect to a trial court's sentencing decisions—is discussed in Chapter Twelve.

4.2.15 *Dismiss the Indictment under* Kastigar

If a prosecutor (whether acting with or without a grand jury) grants "derivative use immunity" to a witness as a precondition of the witness's testimony or unsworn statements made to a grand jury, petit jury, or law enforcement officials outside of the courtroom, then the Fifth Amendment's privilege against self-incrimination ordinarily prohibits the prosecution from using any such information against the witness, directly or indirectly.[198] Indirect, or derivative, use of any information provided by the witness would include locating incriminating evidence or other witnesses who would be able to inculpate the first witness based on the "immunized" information provided. By contrast, broader "transactional immunity" means that the prosecutor cannot prosecute the witness for any criminal offense admitted by the witness.[199]

Although the Supreme Court's seminal decision in *Kastigar* specifically concerned statutory "use immunity" afforded under 18 U.S.C. § 6002, the consensus among lower courts since *Kastigar* is that its holding equally applies to informal or nonstatutory use immunity agreements, which are commonly made part of plea agreements or "proffer letters" provided to cooperating defendants by prosecutors.[200] *Kastigar* also applies equally to federal and state prosecutors who provide use immunity to a witness.[201]

If the prosecutor offered a witness use immunity and subsequently indicted the witness for a criminal offense that had any possible relation to the subject

---

196. Goodwin, 457 U.S. at 372–84; *see also* Bordenkircher v. Hayes, 434 U.S. 357 (1978); Leonard v. Commonwealth, 571 S.E.2d 306, 311–12 (Va. Ct. App. 2002) (discussing "actual bias").

197. The doctrine of "prosecutorial vindictiveness" should be distinguished from the constitutional doctrine of "selective prosecution." The latter, which is much more difficult to prove, requires a defendant to show that they were arrested or prosecuted—while others who were similarly situated were not prosecuted—based on some impermissible factor such as race or religion. *See* United States v. Armstrong, 517 U.S. 456 (1996); McCleskey v. Kemp, 481 U.S. 279 (1987); *see also* Commonwealth v. Lora, 886 N.E.2d 688, 697–99 (Mass. 2008); Jones v. Sterling, 110 P.3d 1271 (Ariz. 2005).

198. Kastigar v. United States, 406 U.S. 441 (1972); *see also* United States v. Hubbell, 530 U.S. 27 (2000).

199. *See* United States v. McDaniel, 482 F.2d 305, 307–10 (8th Cir. 1973).

200. *See, e.g.*, United States v. Plummer, 941 F.2d 799 (9th Cir. 1991).

201. *See, e.g.*, State v. Beard, 507 S.E.2d 688 (W. Va. 1998); *cf.* Garrity v. New Jersey, 385 U.S. 493 (1967).

matter of the witness's immunized statements, then the defendant has the option of filing a "*Kastigar* motion" to dismiss the indictment and request a pretrial "*Kastigar* hearing." At such a hearing, the prosecution must by a preponderance of the evidence "prove a negative," namely, prove that each item of evidence and each witness it relied on in charging the defendant, as well as each item of evidence and witness that it intends to introduce at the trial,[202] was obtained wholly independently from the immunized information. If the prosecutor fails to do so, the indictment must be dismissed or any tainted witnesses or evidence will be excluded during the trial.[203]

If an informal use immunity agreement is at issue, there often will be a dispute over whether the agreement covers only direct use of information provided by the witness or includes indirect (or "derivative") use as well. Most lower courts have held that the term "use immunity" by itself implicitly includes derivative use unless the prosecution explicitly states in the agreement that use immunity does not include derivative use.[204] Another recurring dispute occurs when one prosecutor's office (state or federal) enters into a use immunity agreement with a defendant and subsequently another prosecutor's office (state or federal) in a different jurisdiction seeks to use the immunized information against the same defendant. In the majority of cases, the second prosecutor's office is permitted to use the immunized information because it was not a party to the agreement.[205] If the use immunity agreement does not apply to other prosecutor's offices, it is nonetheless arguable that depending on the circumstances, the statements given by the witness may rise to the level of an involuntary confession that cannot be used by any prosecutor in any subsequent prosecution.[206]

---

202. The prosecution's proof must proceed "witness-by-witness; . . line-by-line, and item-by-item" for each grand jury witness and prospective trial witness. United States v. North, 910 F.2d 843, 872, *opinion withdrawn and superseded in part on other grounds on rehearing*, 920 F.2d 940 (D.C. Cir. 1990).
203. *See, e.g.*, United States v. Garrett, 797 F.2d 656 (8th Cir. 1986).
204. *See, e.g.*, United States v. Kilroy, 27 F.3d 679 (D.C. Cir. 1994); *but see* United States v. Smallwood, 311 F. Supp. 2d 535, 542–44 & n.15 (E.D. Va. 2004).
205. *See, e.g.*, Taylor v. Singletary, 148 F.3d 1276 (11th Cir. 1998) (use immunity agreement between one U.S. Attorney's office and federal defendant did not prevent state prosecutor from using the immunized information in a subsequent state prosecution); State v. Bryant, 42 P.3d 1278, 1284–85 (Wash. 2002) (one county district attorney's use immunity agreement did not bind another county district attorney).
206. *See* Shotwell Manuf. Co. v. United States, 371 U.S. 341, 347 (1963) (in dicta stating that a confession following a promise of immunity is involuntary); *cf.* New Jersey v. Portash, 440 U.S. 450, 459 (1979) (testimony given following grant of legislative immunity is considered "involuntary" if subsequently used against that same defendant); *but see Taylor*, 148 F.3d at 1281–85 (rejecting such an involuntary confession claim). The issue of whether a defendant's statement to the authorities was involuntary under the Due Process Clause is discussed in Chapter Six.

4.2.16　Suppress an Eyewitness Identification Based on an Impermissibly Suggestive Pretrial Identification Procedure

After a suspect has been arrested, and if an eyewitness (often a victim) is available, law enforcement agencies sometimes will place the suspect in a live lineup, in which the suspect and a number of other persons with superficially similar characteristics (e.g., gender, age, race) stand next to each other and the witness is then asked to identify the perpetrator. Similarly, before or after arrests occur, photographic arrays are used, placing the suspect's photograph alongside photographs of other persons with the same general features. Less commonly, police officers will use a "show-up" as a means of identifying a suspect, i.e., the officers show witnesses a suspect who has just been arrested and ask the witnesses whether the suspect is the perpetrator (without using a lineup). When such pretrial identification procedures have been used, defense counsel frequently file pretrial motions to suppress or exclude the results of the procedures (when their clients have been identified) as well as a witness's subsequent in-court identification of the defendant. Such motions are rooted in the Due Process Clause and based on a line of Supreme Court decisions beginning with *Stovall v. Denno*.[207] In seeking to suppress or exclude an eyewitness's in-court identification, defense counsel will contend that a witness's identification of the defendant in the courtroom is "tainted fruit" of the earlier, allegedly invalid, pretrial identification procedure.

Determining whether evidence of a witness's pretrial identification of a suspect during such identification procedures—as well as the witness's subsequent in-court identification of the suspect—must be excluded during a trial requires an examination of two elements. First, a court must determine whether the pretrial identification procedure was "impermissibly suggestive."[208] The Supreme Court has held that a pretrial identification procedure is impermissibly suggestive if a suspect "is in some way emphasized"[209] from among the choices for the witness. For that reason, a show-up involving only the suspect has been condemned by the Court as impermissibly suggestive.[210]

If a court determines that a pretrial identification procedure was unduly suggestive, the court next must determine whether the procedure posed a "very substantial likelihood of irreparable misidentification."[211] If it did not, then the pretrial identification and in-court identification are permitted.[212] In addressing the second element, courts must engage in an evaluation of the "totality of the circumstances"

---

207. *See* Stovall v. Denno, 388 U.S. 293, 302 (1967); Simmons v. United States, 390 U.S. 377, 384 (1968); Foster v. California, 394 U.S. 440, 442–43 (1969); Neil v. Biggers, 409 U.S. 188 (1972); Manson v. Brathwaite, 432 U.S. 98 (1977).
208. *Simmons*, 390 U.S. at 384.
209. *Id.* at 383.
210. *Foster*, 394 U.S. at 443.
211. *Manson*, 432 U.S. at 106 n.8.
212. *Id.* at 113–14.

surrounding the witness's initial observation of the perpetrator of the crime and the witness's subsequent identification of the suspect.[213] Courts review the totality of the circumstances by considering five factors: 1) the witness's opportunity to view the accused at the time of the initial viewing; 2) the witness's degree of attention to the subject during the initial viewing; 3) the accuracy of the witness's description of the accused after the initial viewing; 4) the degree of certainty exhibited by the witness during the pretrial identification procedure;[214] and 5) the amount of time that elapsed between the crime and the pretrial identification.[215] The Supreme Court has stated that "[a]gainst these factors is to be weighed the corrupting effect of the suggestive identification itself."[216] The Court has held that to challenge a pretrial lineup or show-up procedure as a constitutional violation, the procedure must have been arranged by law enforcement.[217] The Court further held that the Constitution does not regulate impermissibly suggestive and unreliable identification procedures not orchestrated by state actors.[218]

It should be noted that there is a separate constitutional basis for excluding both a witness's pretrial identification and their subsequent in-court identification. If a live lineup or show-up (as opposed to photographic lineup) occurred after a defendant's right to counsel attached under the Sixth Amendment, the police should have afforded the defendant the right to have counsel present during the identification procedure.[219] If counsel was not made available and the defendant did not validly waive the right to counsel, then the pretrial identification procedure and possibly the witness's in-court identification during the trial must be excluded.[220] This is true even if the pretrial identification procedure was not impermissibly suggestive.[221]

---

213. *Simmons*, 390 U.S. at 382–83.

214. Notably, although the Supreme Court has never revisited the issue of a witness's degree of confidence, modern social scientists have demonstrated that this factor is not a valid indicator of the accuracy of a witness's identification. *See, e.g.*, Kevin Krug, *The Relationship Between Confidence and Accuracy: Current Thoughts of the Literature and a New Area of Research*, 3 Applied Psychology in Criminal Justice 7, 9 (2007) ("Despite the belief of those in the court system and public regarding the [confidence-accuracy] relationship, the majority of the research asserts that confidence is a poor indicator of memory accuracy.") (Citing numerous studies).

215. *Neil*, 409 U.S. at 199–200.

216. *Manson*, 432 U.S. at 114.

217. Perry v. New Hampshire, 565 U.S. 228 (2012) (finding no due process violation where, unknown to police officers, a witness had observed a suspect being arrested by a police officer and later identified him as the perpetrator; even if the witness had been influenced by seeing the suspect being arrested, the Court held, it was not the result of a lineup or show-up procedure intentionally orchestrated by the police officers).

218. *Id.* at 239–48.

219. United States v. Ash, 413 U.S. 300 (1973).

220. United States v. Wade, 388 U.S. 218 (1967); Gilbert v. California, 388 U.S. 263 (1967). The witness's in-court identification must be suppressed unless the prosecution proves by "clear and convincing evidence" that the in-court identification was not "tainted fruit" of the unconstitutional pretrial procedure. *Wade*, 388 U.S. at 240.

221. Kirby v. Illinois, 406 U.S. 682, 690–91 (1972).

Motions to suppress pretrial identifications and in-court identifications based on right-to-counsel violations are further discussed in Chapter Six.

4.2.17 Dismiss an Indictment Based on an Unconstitutional Prior Administrative Adjudication that Serves as an Element of the Charged Offense

Occasionally, an element of an offense depends on a prior adjudication concerning the defendant by an administrative agency or other administrative body (e.g., in a criminal prosecution of a defendant for driving with a suspended license, the prosecution must prove that a state administrative body had suspended the defendant's driver's license).[222] In *United States v. Mendoza-Lopez*,[223] the Supreme Court held that a criminal defendant has a limited right to collaterally attack such a prior administrative adjudication in a subsequent criminal prosecution if the defendant can establish: 1) that the result of the administrative proceeding was "fundamentally unfair" and, thus, violated due process; and 2) that the defendant was denied their right to judicial review of the administrative ruling at the time of the administrative adjudication.[224] With respect to the latter requirement, a defendant whose waiver of the right to judicial review was not "knowing and voluntary" is deemed to have been denied such judicial review, assuming such review was available.[225] Such a collateral attack of the administrative ruling is raised in a pretrial motion to dismiss the indictment.[226] In *Mendoza-Lopez*, the Supreme Court upheld a district court's dismissal of an indictment charging the defendant with illegally reentering the United States after a previous deportation order because the immigration agency's prior deportation of the defendant was fundamentally unfair and the defendant did not knowingly waive their right to judicial review of the deportation order.[227]

4.2.18 Disclosure of Confidential Informant

Many criminal prosecutions result from police investigations that began after incriminating information was provided by a "confidential informant." The Supreme Court has held that on request by the defendant, the prosecution generally must disclose the identity of the informant only if the informant participated in, was a witness to, or otherwise played a crucial role in the alleged offense.[228]

---

222. *See, e.g.*, State v. Lang, 463 N.W.2d 648 (N.D. 1990).
223. 481 U.S. 828 (1987).
224. *Id.* at 837–39 n.17.
225. *Id.* at 839–40 ("Because the waivers of their rights to appeal were not considered or intelligent, respondents were deprived of judicial review of their deportation proceeding").
226. *Id.* at 842.
227. *Id.*
228. Roviaro v. United States, 353 U.S. 53 (1957).

A trial court must balance the need of the defense to have access to the inform-ant—as a potential witness for the defense (e.g., to prove entrapment)—against the prosecution's interest in keeping the person's identity confidential.[229] The rule of *Rovario* appears to be constitutional in nature.[230] Where an informant was merely a "tipster" for police and did not participate in or witness the alleged offense, the Constitution generally does not require disclosure of the informant's identity.[231]

Although filed with somewhat less frequency than defense motions, pretrial mo-tions filed by the prosecution also can implicate constitutional issues of criminal procedure.

4.3   Prosecution Motions

4.3.1   *Forcibly Medicate an Incompetent Defendant*

As discussed above, defense counsel sometimes file motions to determine whether their clients are mentally competent. If a defendant is found to be incompetent and refuses to take medication aimed at restoring their competency, a prosecutor may file a motion to compel the defendant to submit to medication to restore the de-fendant's competency. In *Sell v. United States*, the Supreme Court held that in order for a trial court to grant such a motion, the criminal charges must be "serious"; the proposed medication must be "medically appropriate" and should not have side effects on the defendant that could undermine the trial's fairness; there must be no less intrusive alternatives available; and finally, the forced medication must significantly further important governmental interests.[232] Lower courts have inter-preted the Court's decision in *Sell* to require the prosecution to prove by clear and convincing evidence that the proposed involuntary medication will be effective.[233] The Court in *Sell* opined that it would be a "rare" occurrence for such a motion to be granted under this rigorous standard, at least in situations where an incompetent defendant does not pose a danger to themself or to others.[234]

---

229. *See id.* at 62.
230. *See* United States v. Valenzuela-Bernal, 458 U.S. 858, 870 (1982).
231. *See* McCray v. Illinois, 386 U.S. 300 (1967).
232. Sell v. United States, 539 U.S. 166, 179–81 (2003); *see also* Riggins v. Nevada, 504 U.S. 127 (1992).
233. *See, e.g.*, United States v. Reynolds, 553 F. Supp. 2d 788, 792 (S.D. Tex. 2008) (citing cases).
234. *Sell*, 539 U.S. at 180. Since *Sell*, most courts have denied such motions. *See, e.g.*, Warren v. State, 778 S.E.2d 749, 769 (Ga. 2015) (reversing trial court's granting of prosecution's motion after concluding that "the trial court's order was insufficient in numerous respects to justify Warren's involuntary medication for the sole purpose of making him mentally competent to stand trial . . ."); *Reynolds*, 553 F. Supp. 2d 788; United States v. Evans, 293 F. Supp. 2d 668 (W.D. Va. 2003). A different situation may arise in death penalty cases where a capital defendant is incompetent to be executed (under the rule articulated in Ford v. Wainwright, 477 U.S. 399 (1986)) and the prosecution seeks to forcibly medicate the defendant in order to restore their competency long enough to execute them. *See, e.g.*, Singleton v. Norris, 319 F.3d 1018 (8th Cir. 2003) (en banc). That issue is discussed in Chapter Twelve.

4.3.2 Exclude a Defense Witness or Evidence Based on Noncompliance with Discovery Rules

Although as a general manner a criminal defendant has a right to subpoena favorable defense witnesses to testify on their own behalf at trial[235] and has a more general constitutional right to present a defense,[236] the Supreme Court has held that the state has a legitimate interest in conditioning the presentation of certain types of defensive evidence on a reasonable pretrial disclosure of such a defense to the prosecution. For instance, the Court has upheld a state's rule of criminal procedure requiring a defendant to give timely pretrial notification of an alibi defense (including the names and addresses of the alibi witnesses).[237]

If a defendant or their attorney willfully refuse to comply with such pretrial discovery rules, then it is not a per se violation of the Constitution to exclude the defendant's witnesses or evidence.[238] The Court has held that a case-by-case approach is required and that with a sufficiently abusive violation of the discovery rules, the Constitution is not violated by exclusion of the defendant's witness or evidence sought to be introduced in violation of the discovery rules.[239] The Court also has held that if the prosecution is entitled to pretrial discovery from the defense, then due process requires that the prosecution similarly must provide equivalent pretrial discovery.[240]

4.3.3 Disqualify Defense Counsel Based on a Conflict of Interest

As discussed in Chapter Three, as a general matter, a defendant has a constitutional right to retained counsel of their choice.[241] Furthermore, when counsel is appointed to represent a criminal defendant, that attorney-client relationship ordinarily remains inviolate until the case is terminated.[242] However, a defendant will occasionally retain a lawyer or be appointed a lawyer who possesses a conflict of interest that may interfere with the lawyer's constitutional obligation to provide "effective" assistance of counsel under the Sixth Amendment.[243] In such

---

235. The Compulsory Process Clause is discussed in section 8.4.
236. Washington v. Texas, 388 U.S. 14, 19 (1967); *see also* Chambers v. Mississippi, 410 U.S. 284 (1973).
237. Williams v. Florida, 399 U.S. 78 (1970).
238. Michigan v. Lucas, 500 U.S. 145 (1991); Taylor v. Illinois, 484 U.S. 400 (1988); United States v. Nobles, 422 U.S. 225 (1975).
239. *Lucas*, 500 U.S. at 152–53.
240. Wardius v. Oregon, 412 U.S. 470 (1973).
241. *See* Chapter Three.
242. *See* Stearnes v. Clinton, 780 S.W.2d 216 (Tex. Crim. App. 1989) (once an attorney is appointed by the trial court to represent a criminal defendant, the attorney-client relationship is subject to the same protections from outside interference as the relationship between privately retained counsel and a criminal defendant).
243. The requirement of conflict-free "effective" assistance of counsel is discussed in Chapter Thirteen.

circumstances, a prosecutor may file a motion to disqualify defense counsel to prevent a conviction from being challenged based on the conflict at some later point in the proceedings.[244] In *Wheat v. United States*,[245] the Supreme Court held that a trial court has discretion to grant such a motion if there is either an "actual" or "serious potential" conflict of interest.[246] Even if a criminal defendant is willing to waive their constitutional right to conflict-free counsel in such circumstances, a trial court may refuse to honor the waiver.[247]

4.3.4 Close the Courtroom to the Public or for a "Gag" Order

The Sixth Amendment provides for "public" trials.[248] In two main situations, prosecutors have moved to close the courtroom from the public during judicial proceedings—first, when a witness (such as a child rape victim) must testify about an especially embarrassing or humiliating event; and second, when a prosecution witness (such as a confidential informant) wishes to maintain anonymity for safety reasons. Either the defendant or the media can oppose the motion. Often, however, defendants do not oppose such motions and occasionally even file their own motions to close the courtroom. If a defendant opposes a prosecutor's motion to close the courtroom, the Supreme Court has held that a trial court should not grant the motion without specific findings of an "overriding interest" for closing the courtroom and lesser alternatives have been considered, but found to be inadequate.[249] Furthermore, the closure can be no broader than necessary to protect the overriding interest.[250]

It is usually the media, however, that oppose the closing of the courtroom from the public. Although the media and public cannot invoke the defendant's Sixth Amendment's guarantee of a public trial,[251] the Supreme Court has held that the media (and the public generally) have a First Amendment right to access to the courtroom. Under the First Amendment, the trial court may close the courtroom only after making the type of specific findings required when a defendant objects

---

244. *See, e.g.*, United States v. Algee, 309 F.3d 1011 (7th Cir. 2002); State ex rel. Blake v. Hatcher, 624 S.E.2d 844 (W. Va. 2005). Some retained defense counsel who are the subject of such motions to disqualify have complained that the real motivation behind such motions is to remove a formidable adversary and thus weaken the defense. *See, e.g.*, United States v. Register, 182 F.3d 820, 833 (11th Cir. 1999).

245. 486 U.S. 153 (1988).

246. *Id.* at 164.

247. *Id.* at 162.

248. U.S. CONST. amend. VI ("the accused shall enjoy the right to a . . . public trial").

249. Waller v. Georgia, 467 U.S. 39 (1984); *see also* Presley v. Georgia, 130 S. Ct. 721 (2010) (per curiam).

250. *Waller*, 467 U.S. at 47–48.

251. Gannett Co. v. DePasquale, 443 U.S. 368 (1979) (Sixth Amendment right to a "public" trial belongs to a defendant alone).

and then must "narrowly tailor" the closure.[252] The two legal standards governing closure of the courtroom—one when the media object, the other when the defendant objects—are essentially identical.[253] A related issue arises when the prosecution files a motion to have an anonymous jury—typically in a criminal prosecution of a mobster or a high-profile case where jurors may fear harassment or retaliation because of their participation in the trial.[254] Although the U.S. Supreme Court has not yet addressed the propriety of empaneling jurors whose identities are not revealed to the public or the defense, the lower courts that have addressed the issue have sanctioned the practice when there is a substantial risk of jury intimidation or jury tampering.[255]

In certain high-profile prosecutions, the prosecution[256] may move the trial court for a gag order that limits the type of public comment that the parties or their counsel may make about the pending case or, more rarely, an order that limits the extent of the media's coverage of the case (prior to its completion).[257] The latter type of gag order—against the media—almost never is granted because it is considered impermissible "prior restraint" under the First Amendment.[258] However, the former type of gag order is more likely to be granted, at least where there is a "substantial likelihood" that public comment from the parties or the attorneys in a case will prejudice one or both parties' right to a fair trial.[259] Such a gag order, however, must be "narrowly tailored" and employ the "least restrictive means" (i.e., it cannot prohibit all public comment).[260]

4.3.5 Handwriting or Voice Exemplar or Physical Specimen from Defendant

In cases in which the prosecution has evidence in the form of handwriting or voice recordings, prosecutors can move the court to order a defendant to provide handwriting or voice exemplars when a defendant has refused to provide them

---

252. Richmond Newspapers, Inc. v. Virginia, 448 U.S. 555 (1980); Globe Newspaper Co. v. Superior Court, 457 U.S. 596 (1982); Press-Enterprise Co. v. Superior Court, 464 U.S. 501 (1984), later proceeding, 478 U.S. 1 (1986).
253. United States v. Edwards, 303 F.3d 606, 615–16 (5th Cir. 2002).
254. *See, e.g.,* United States v. Krout, 66 F.3d 1420, 1427–28 (5th Cir. 1995) (discussing cases from various lower courts).
255. *Id.*
256. The defense occasionally will file such a motion, *see, e.g.,* United States v. Walker, 890 F. Supp. 954 (D. Kan. 1995), and trial courts occasionally enter such gag orders sua sponte, *see, e.g.,* United States v. Brown, 218 F.3d 415 (5th Cir. 2000).
257. *See, e.g.,* United States v. Mandel, 408 F. Supp. 673 (D. Md. 1975).
258. *See* Nebraska Press Ass'n v. Stuart, 427 U.S. 539 (1976).
259. *Brown,* 218 F.3d at 426–28 (*citing* Gentile v. State Bar of Nevada, 501 U.S. 1030 (1991)); *but see* Karhani v. Meijer, 270 F. Supp. 2d 926, 933–34 & n.8 (E.D. Mich. 2003) (requiring a showing that there is a "clear and present danger" that the parties' or lawyers' public comments would prejudice the fairness of the trial).
260. *Brown,* 218 F.3d at 426–28.

voluntarily.[261] The Supreme Court has held that simple exemplars of this type—just like fingerprints—are not testimonial and thus not self-incriminating under the Fifth Amendment.[262] Therefore, such motions routinely are granted if the prosecution demonstrates that they are necessary. Similarly, prosecutors often file motions to compel unwilling defendants to provide physical specimens (e.g., a blood sample for a DNA test) when the case involves evidence of such a nature and a scientific comparison is necessary. Although extracting such a specimen involves a "search" and "seizure" under the Fourth Amendment, such motions will be granted so long as there is probable cause to believe that the defendant's specimen will be incriminating.[263]

4.4　Leading Supreme Court Decisions Concerning Constitutional Issues Raised in Pretrial Motions (Nonsuppression)

- *Ashe v. Swenson*, 397 U.S. 436 (1970) (recognizing the collateral estoppel principle under the Double Jeopardy Clause when the trial record in a prior case reveals that a defendant was acquitted based on a factfinder's conclusion that the prosecution failed to prove a certain fact beyond a reasonable doubt; prosecution is estopped from proving that fact in a subsequent case involving the same defendant, even if the charge in the subsequent case is different from the charge in the first case and even if the prosecution has new evidence to prove the fact).

- *Kastigar v. United States*, 406 U.S. 441 (1972) (when a defendant is offered derivative use immunity in exchange for their sworn testimony or unsworn statements to law enforcement, the prosecution may not introduce any evidence that was in any way derived from the defendant's immunized testimony or statements; the prosecution has the burden to prove that its evidence is not "tainted" in any way by the immunized testimony or statements).

---

261. If such exemplars are sought prior to an indictment being returned by a grand jury, prosecutors will obtain a grand jury subpoena and seek a trial court to enforce it by ordering a noncompliant defendant to be held in contempt. *See, e.g.*, In re Doe, 860 F.2d 40, 42 (2d Cir. 1988).

262. *See, e.g.*, United States v. Mara, 410 U.S. 19 (1973); United States v. Dionisio, 410 U.S. 1 (1973).

263. *Cf.* Schmerber v. California, 384 U.S. 757 (1966) (upholding warrantless extraction of blood under "exigent circumstances" so long as probable cause exists); *see also* State v. Hearns, 855 A.2d 549, 552–54 (N.H. 2004) (affirming trial court's order granting motion to require defendant to provide DNA sample where there was probable cause to believe their DNA would be incriminating evidence).

- *Barker v. Wingo*, 407 U.S. 514 (1972) (setting forth four-part standard governing motions to dismiss the indictment based on a violation of the Speedy Trial Clause of the Sixth Amendment).

- *Ward v. Village of Monroeville*, 409 U.S. 57 (1972) (due process requires an impartial judge in a criminal case).

- *Illinois v. Somerville*, 410 U.S. 458 (1973) (if a mistrial occurs at a trial after jeopardy has attached and the defense did not ask for or acquiesce in the mistrial, the prosecution may not seek to retry the defendant unless there was a manifest necessity justifying the mistrial).

- *Blackledge v. Perry*, 417 U.S. 21 (1974) (discussing the prosecutorial vindictiveness doctrine).

- *Drope v. Missouri*, 420 U.S. 162 (1975) (due process is violated by prosecution of mentally incompetent defendant; trial judge has duty to sua sponte raise competency issue if information known to the judge raises serious question of whether defendant is incompetent).

- *Murphy v. Florida*, 421 U.S. 794 (1975) (leading modern decision on whether prospective jurors' exposure to pretrial publicity requires a change of venue; discussion of how trial judge during voir dire can reduce potential prejudice to defendant).

- *Manson v. Brathwaite*, 432 U.S. 98 (1977) (leading decision on whether an eyewitness's in-court identification of a criminal defendant during a lineup or show-up was tainted by an "impermissibly suggestive" pretrial identification procedure; in order for trial court to suppress pretrial and in-court identifications, a defendant must establish that there was a "very substantial likelihood of irreparable misidentification" resulting from an impermissibly suggestive procedure).

- *Brown v. Ohio*, 432 U.S. 161 (1977) (holding that a conviction or acquittal on a lesser included offense bars a subsequent prosecution on a greater offense under the Double Jeopardy Clause and vice-versa).

- *Oregon v. Kennedy*, 456 U.S. 667 (1982) (although ordinarily a defendant who successfully moves for a mistrial after jeopardy has attached may be retried without violating the Double Jeopardy Clause, an exception exists where the prosecutor intentionally goaded the defense into moving for a mistrial).

- *United States v. Valenzuela-Bernal*, 458 U.S. 858 (1982) (dismissal of indictment required when government deported potential defense witness(es) before trial if there is a reasonable probability that the testimony of the deported witness(es) would have prevented a conviction; burden on defendant to establish materiality of unavailable testimony).

- *Waller v. Georgia*, 467 U.S. 39 (1984) (setting forth four-part standard that trial courts must apply in deciding whether to close the courtroom to the public over the objection of the defendant).

- *Ake v. Oklahoma*, 470 U.S. 68 (1985) (an indigent defendant has the constitutional right to an expert witness, such as a psychiatrist, without cost if the expert is a necessary tool for the defense and the defendant makes an adequate showing of the need for such expert).

- *Heath v. Alabama*, 474 U.S. 82 (1985) (discussing the dual sovereignty exception to the Double Jeopardy Clause).

- *Pennsylvania v. Ritchie*, 480 U.S. 39 (1987) (due process requires trial court to examine in camera confidential file in possession of a nonparty, such as a child protective services agency, that might include exculpatory or impeachment material for the defense at trial; due process requires trial court to reveal such information to the defense notwithstanding a jurisdiction's confidentiality laws if there is a reasonable probability that disclosure of such confidential information would prevent a conviction).

- *Young v. United States ex rel. Vuitton et Fils, S.A.*, 481 U.S. 787 (1987) (leading Supreme Court decision concerning the due process requirement that prosecutors be personally disinterested in criminal cases that they prosecute).

- *United States v. Mendoza-Lopez*, 481 U.S. 828 (1987) (indictment must be dismissed if prior administrative adjudication that is an element of a subsequent criminal prosecution was "fundamentally unfair," and also if the defendant was effectively denied meaningful judicial review of the administrative adjudication).

- *Taylor v. Illinois*, 484 U.S. 400 (1988) (leading modern decision on the Compulsory Process Clause; holding that Clause is not violated by a trial court's refusal to issue or enforce a defense subpoena if the defense willfully violated a procedural rule related to timely disclosure of the subpoenaed witness).

- *Wheat v. United States*, 486 U.S. 153 (1988) (trial court has the discretion not to accept a defendant's waiver of the right to conflict-free counsel and, thus, may grant the prosecution's motion to disqualify defense counsel who has a conflict of interest).

- *Arizona v. Youngblood*, 488 U.S. 51 (1988) (law enforcement's destruction of untested evidence that might have been exculpatory to the defense, such as DNA evidence, is not a basis to dismiss the indictment when defendant cannot show that the evidence in fact was exculpatory, unless law enforcement had a bad faith motive in destroying evidence).

- *Doggett v. United States*, 505 U.S. 647 (1992) (discussing right to a speedy trial; modifying *Barker* by presuming prejudice in cases of extraordinary post-indictment delay attributable to the prosecution).

- *United States v. Dixon*, 509 U.S. 688 (1993) (applying the "same elements" test of *Blockburger v. United States*, 284 U.S. 299 (1932), to "successive prosecution" double jeopardy claims and rejecting the "same evidence/same transaction" test).

- *Gray v. Maryland*, 523 U.S. 185 (1998) (leading modern decision discussing motions to sever nontestifying codefendant or, in the alternative, to exclude codefendant's unredacted confession, as required by *Bruton v. United States*, 391 U.S. 123 (1968); holding that a redaction of defendant's identity from codefendant's confession must sufficiently exclude implicit references to defendant as well as explicit references).

- *Campbell v. Louisiana*, 523 U.S. 392 (1998) (leading modern decision on motions to dismiss the indictment based on invidious discrimination in the selection of members of the grand jury, including the grand jury foreperson).

- *City of Chicago v. Morales*, 527 U.S. 41 (1999) (leading modern decision concerning unconstitutionally vague penal statutes).

- *Carmell v. Texas*, 529 U.S. 513 (2000) (leading modern decision concerning the Ex Post Facto Clause and the limits it imposes on the retroactive application of legislation in a criminal case to pre-enactment offenses).

- *Rogers v. Tennessee*, 532 U.S. 451 (2001) (holding that a judicial decision is not subject to the Ex Post Facto Clause, although due process may be violated in certain instances by retroactive application of judicial decisions to a defendant's predecision criminal conduct).

- *Virginia v. Hicks*, 539 U.S. 113 (2003) (leading modern decision on the First Amendment substantial overbreadth doctrine).

- *Sell v. United States*, 539 U.S. 166 (2003) (setting forth four-part standard governing when a trial court may order a mentally incompetent defendant to be forcibly medicated to restore their mental competency).

- *Perry v. New Hampshire*, 565 U.S. 228 (2012) (Due process not violated by unreliable pretrial lineup or show-up unless it was arranged by police officers; unreliable identifications by themselves do not violate Constitution).

- *McWilliams v. Dunn*, 137 S. Ct. 1790, 1799 (2017) (holding that an indigent defendant's right to expert assistance under *Ake* means an expert "who is sufficiently available to the defense and independent from the prosecution to effectively assist in evaluation, preparation, and presentation of the defense").

- *Gamble v. United States*, 139 S. Ct. 1960 (2019) (reaffirming the dual sovereignty doctrine concerning the Double Jeopardy Clause).

CHAPTER FIVE

MOTIONS TO SUPPRESS EVIDENCE UNDER THE FOURTH AMENDMENT

5.1 Introduction to Motions to Suppress

The most common type of pretrial motion in a criminal case is a motion to suppress (i.e., exclude) evidence,[1] including a defendant's confession, and thus prohibit its admission during the trial. There are two main categories of motions to suppress: 1) motions seeking to suppress evidence or a defendant's confession under the Fourth Amendment based on an unconstitutional "search" or "seizure" (the latter term encompassing seizure of property as well as the detention of a person); and 2) motions seeking to suppress a defendant's confession as involuntary under the Due Process Clause, having been obtained in violation of the Fifth Amendment "prophylactic" rule announced in *Miranda v. Arizona*[2] or having been obtained in violation of the Sixth Amendment right to counsel.

A trial judge generally must conduct an evidentiary hearing on a motion to suppress outside the presence of the jurors.[3] A defendant's testimony at such a pretrial

---

1. For purposes of this book, "evidence" refers to physical evidence or incriminating information other than a defendant's confession (confessions are discussed in the next chapter). Evidence includes not only contraband (e.g., illegal drugs), but also evidence or information that, although not illegal per se, may be used to prove the defendant's guilt (e.g., a piece of paper with names and numbers that is identified as a ledger used by a drug dealer). Evidence also includes a witness's testimony about physical evidence and information (e.g., a police officer's testimony that they found drugs in the defendant's pocket).
2. Miranda v. Arizona, 384 U.S. 436 (1966).
3. *See, e.g.*, Jackson v. Denno, 378 U.S. 368 (1964) (hearing on motion to suppress defendant's confession as involuntary); Simmons v. United States, 390 U.S. 377, 390–94 (1968) (hearing on motion to suppress evidence under Fourth Amendment where defendant testifies). In some jurisdictions, the defendant, if unsuccessful at the suppression hearing, may choose to relitigate a Fourth or Fifth Amendment suppression issue de novo in front of the jury without jurors knowing that the trial judge had previously denied the motion. *See, e.g.*, TEX. CODE CRIM. PROC. ANN. arts. 38.22, §§ 6–7 & 38.23. In most jurisdictions (including the federal system), however, a defendant may not relitigate any suppression issue in front of a jury other than whether a defendant's confession was involuntary. *See, e.g.*, 18 U.S.C. § 3501(a); *see also* Crane v. Kentucky, 476 U.S. 683 (1986) (holding that a criminal defendant is constitutionally entitled to challenge the voluntariness of their confession in front of the jury, including by offering expert testimony about their mental condition at the time of the confession).

suppression hearing is inadmissible at the subsequent trial as long as the defendant remains silent at the trial.[4] However, if a defendant testifies at the trial in a manner contrary to their prior testimony at the pretrial hearing, the prosecution may impeach the defendant with the prior inconsistent testimony.[5]

Motions to suppress evidence (other than a defendant's confession) under the Fourth Amendment are discussed in this chapter. Motions to suppress a defendant's confession under Fourth, Fifth, and Sixth Amendments are discussed in the following chapter. Although the two types of motions occasionally overlap in terms of the legal issues involved, to aid in understanding each, it is helpful to separate them.[6]

Motions to suppress evidence under the Fourth Amendment—based on an allegedly illegal search or seizure—have led to more constitutional criminal procedure decisions from the modern Supreme Court than any other constitutional provision. This chapter will address all of the major issues raised under the Fourth Amendment, although space constraints will limit the depth of the discussion of any particular issue. The reader—particularly a lawyer litigating a Fourth Amendment issue—would be wise to consult a more in-depth source.[7]

5.2 What Constitutes a Fourth Amendment "Search" or "Seizure" and Who Has "Standing" to File a Motion to Suppress?

More often than not, a police officer's search or seizure occurs without a warrant previously having been issued by a judge or magistrate. Contrary to popular belief, the Fourth Amendment does not flatly prohibit warrantless searches and seizures; instead, it only prohibits unreasonable warrantless searches and seizures.[8] Although

---

4. *Simmons*, 390 U.S. at 393–94.

5. Although the Supreme Court has not so held, the Court intimated that such impeachment would be proper in United States v. Salvucci, 448 U.S. 83, 93–94 & nn. 8 & 9 (1980), and the majority of lower courts have permitted such impeachment. *See, e.g.*, Reinert v. Larkins, 379 F.3d 76, 96 n.5 (3d Cir. 2004).

6. If physical evidence has been seized by law enforcement without a search warrant, the prosecution has the burden (by a preponderance of the evidence) at the suppression hearing to show that the evidence was seized in a constitutional manner. *See, e.g.*, United States v. Scheffer, 463 F.2d 567, 574 (5th Cir. 1972). If physical evidence was seized with a search warrant, a defendant has the burden (by a preponderance of the evidence) in seeking to suppress such physical evidence under the Fourth Amendment. *See, e.g.*, Franks v. Delaware, 438 U.S. 154, 155–56 (1978). If a defendant challenges the admissibility of their confession under the Fifth Amendment, the prosecution bears the burden (by a preponderance of the evidence). *See* Lego v. Twomey, 404 U.S. 477, 489 (1972).

7. One of the best secondary sources on the Fourth Amendment is the multivolume treatise, W. Lafave, Search and Seizure: A Treatise on the Fourth Amendment (4th ed. 2004). For a shorter primer on the Fourth Amendment, *see* Brent E. Newton, *The Real-World Fourth Amendment*, 43 Hastings Const. L. Quarterly 759 (2016).

8. "The right of the people to be secure in their persons, houses, papers, and effects, against unreasonable searches and seizures, shall not be violated, and no Warrants shall issue, except upon probable cause . . ." U.S. Const. amend. IV. A majority of the Supreme Court consistently has interpreted the prohibition of unreasonable searches and seizures and the requirement for a warrant

the Supreme Court has held that a search or seizure without a warrant is presumed to be unreasonable and thus unconstitutional, that presumption can be rebutted if the prosecution demonstrates that a warrantless search or seizure fell within an established exception to the Fourth Amendment's warrant requirement.[9] In the overwhelming majority of cases in which a warrant was previously obtained, a search or seizure specifically authorized by the warrant will withstand a constitutional challenge.[10] It is cases involving warrantless searches and seizures that typically require courts to determine whether a search or seizure was "unreasonable" under the Fourth Amendment. Since the days of the Warren Court, when the Fourth Amendment was enforced with the most vigor, a steady stream of exceptions to the warrant requirement has appeared to have overtaken the rule.[11]

The only types of searches or seizures regulated by the Fourth Amendment are those undertaken by a government official (federal, state, or local) or a private person working under the auspices of a government official (e.g., a confidential informant).[12] A search or seizure by a private party—without any "state action"—does not implicate the Fourth Amendment, even if the private party subsequently turned over incriminating evidence to the police.[13]

Generally speaking, the Supreme Court's Fourth Amendment jurisprudence draws a "firm line" between searches and seizures inside a person's residence (including a temporary residence such as a motel room) and areas outside of their residence.[14] This is not to say that all warrantless searches or seizures within the home will be invalidated; nor is it to say that all warrantless searches and seizures outside of the home will be deemed reasonable. Rather, because a person's expectation of privacy generally is the greatest in their home, the Fourth Amendment simply operates with its greatest force within the home.

---

based on probable cause as related yet independent clauses. While a warrant generally makes a search or seizure reasonable, a warrantless search or seizure is not necessarily unreasonable. *See, e.g.*, United States v. Rabinowitz, 339 U.S. 56, 60 (1950), *overruled on other grounds*, Chimel v. California, 395 U.S. 752 (1969). Justice Frankfurter contended that the two clauses are not independent and that a warrantless search or seizure is unreasonable except in the rarest of cases. *Id.* at 68–71 (Frankfurter, J., dissenting, joined by Jackson, J.). Justice Frankfurter's position has never been embraced by a majority of the Court.

9. Katz v. United States, 389 U.S. 347, 357 (1967).

10. This is not to say that the mere fact that a warrant was issued invariably renders a subsequent search or seizure reasonable under the Fourth Amendment. However, under the "good faith" doctrine, the vast majority of searches or seizures pursuant to a warrant are not subject to challenge. *See* section 5.5 (discussing the good faith doctrine).

11. Florida v. White, 526 U.S. 559, 569 (1999) (Stevens, J., dissenting, joined by Ginsburg, J.) ("the exceptions have all but swallowed the general rule").

12. United States v. Jacobsen, 466 U.S. 109 (1984).

13. *Id.* Some states' constitutions or statutes regulate "private" searches. *See, e.g.*, State v. Johnson, 939 S.W.2d 586, 587–88 (Tex. Crim. App. 1996) (interpreting Tex. Code Crim Proc. Ann. art. 38.23(a) to apply to private searches without any state action).

14. *See* Kyllo v. United States, 533 U.S. 27, 37–40 (2001).

Because the Supreme Court has "incorporated" the Fourth Amendment in the Due Process Clause of the Fourteenth Amendment and thus applied it equally to state and federal prosecutions,[15] an unconstitutional search or seizure by a state or local official prevents "tainted" evidence from being offered in a federal prosecution—and vice versa.[16] Likewise, as a general rule, evidence resulting from an unconstitutional search or seizure by one state's law enforcement official cannot be used in a prosecution in a different state.[17]

A particular search or seizure is constitutional or unconstitutional at its outset. The fact that officers establish probable cause during the course of what began as an unconstitutional search or seizure does not retroactively render the initial (invalid) search or seizure valid under the Fourth Amendment.[18] For that reason, the Fourth Amendment protects both the innocent and guilty from unreasonable searches and seizures.[19]

A defendant in a criminal case has "standing" to file a motion to suppress evidence searched or seized by a law enforcement official only if the defendant had a valid constitutional privacy or property interest in the subject of the search or seizure.[20]

5.2.1 What Constitutes a Fourth Amendment "Search"?

Because not all governmental intrusion into people's lives is regulated by the Fourth Amendment, the relevant inquiry is "whether or not a Fourth Amendment 'search' has occurred."[21] Whether official action constitutes an unreasonable "search" within the meaning of the Fourth Amendment is a highly fact-specific

---

15. Mapp v. Ohio, 367 U.S. 643 (1961).
16. Elkins v. United States, 364 U.S. 206 (1960) (evidence unconstitutionally seized by state law enforcement officials cannot be used in a federal prosecution); *see also* United States v. Janis, 428 U.S. 433, 456–57 (1976) (discussing "intersovereign" application of the Fourth Amendment's exclusionary rule); Reid v. Georgia, 448 U.S. 438 (1980) (per curiam) (in a state prosecution, suppressing evidence unconstitutionally seized by federal law enforcement agents).
17. *See* State v. Caron, 586 A.2d 1127, 1139 (Vt. 1990); United States ex rel. Krogness v. Gladden, 242 F. Supp. 499, 500 (D. Or. 1965); *but cf.* Thornton v. State, 145 S.W.3d 228 (Tex. Crim. App. 2004) (although agreeing as a general matter that the exclusionary rule applies to unconstitutional searches and seizures by another state's law enforcement officials, concluding that the taint of the Fourth Amendment violation in that case was sufficiently "attenuated" by the time of the second state's use of the first state's unconstitutionally obtained information).
18. Ker v. California, 374 U.S. 23, 41 n.12. (1963).
19. *Id.* at 33.
20. *See, e.g.*, Rakas v. Illinois, 439 U.S. 128 (1978) (passenger in car had no standing to file motion to suppress incriminating evidence found by police in the car where defendant asserted neither privacy or property interest in car or items within it); Brendlin v. California, 551 U.S. 249 (2007) (passenger in car had standing to challenge police officer's unreasonable warrantless stop of car, which led to incriminating evidence found on defendant's person, because defendant's person was seized during stop of car). Fourth Amendment standing is discussed further below.
21. *Kyllo*, 533 U.S. at 31.

issue that often turns on factual minutiae. The Supreme Court has recognized two doctrinally distinct types of searches—one that turns on a defendant's *privacy* interests and a second that turns on a defendant's *property* interests.

5.2.1.1   "Searches" that Implicate a Defendant's "Privacy" Interests

As a threshold matter, this type of search occurs when a governmental official discovers or inspects a person, a physical item, or a place "with his senses"[22]—by touching or handling, visually inspecting, hearing, or smelling, including "enhanced" sensual inspections (e.g., through the use of a thermal imaging device to detect heat inside a building). The key issue is whether a defendant had a reasonable expectation of privacy in the area or item being "sensed" in some manner by a law enforcement officer and, in addition, the officer lacked authority to engage in the search.[23] What constitutes a "reasonable expectation of privacy" is both a subjective and objective inquiry. A defendant subjectively must have had an expectation of privacy, and from an objective standpoint, that expectation of privacy must be one that society deems reasonable.[24]

As a general rule, when a police officer manipulates or moves a physical object to inspect it without a warrant—even if the movement is only a trivial amount and even if no damage results—a Fourth Amendment search has occurred if it exposes something previously hidden from perception.[25] However, if the owner of the property possessed it in a manner in which they should have reasonably expected the object to be moved or manipulated by members of the public without their permission, then an officer's handling of the object in such a manner does not constitute an unreasonable search.[26]

Olfactory searches that are challenged under the Fourth Amendment usually involve trained police canines searching for human scents or drugs. The Supreme Court has held that police "dog sniffs" of the airspace around luggage exposed to

---

22. Pledger v. State, 572 S.E.2d 348, 351 n.3 (Ga. Ct. App. 2002).

23. *Rakas*, 439 U.S. at 143; *see also* United States v. Knotts, 460 U.S. 276 (1983) (police officers' monitoring of warrantless electronic tracking device on a car is not a search because there is no reasonable expectation of privacy in movement of automobile on public roads); United States v. Karo, 468 U.S. 705, 714–19 (1984) (police officers' monitoring of warrantless electronic tracking device placed inside person's residence without consent of residents or consent of any other person entering the home with residents' permission constitutes an unconstitutional search).

24. California v. Ciraolo, 476 U.S. 207 (1986).

25. *See, e.g.,* Arizona v. Hicks, 480 U.S. 321, 324–25 (1987) (police officer's movement of a record player a few inches to have access to the serial number on it constituted a search under the Fourth Amendment); Bond v. United States, 529 U.S. 334 (2000) (police officer's manipulation of luggage in bin of public bus constituted a search).

26. *Cf.* New York v. Class, 475 U.S. 106 (1986) (police officer's reaching into defendant's car to move papers that obstructed the VIN of the car was not an unreasonable search because there is a strong governmental interest in having a car's VIN exposed for official inspection during a traffic stop).

the public (e.g., checked luggage on a plane) or dog sniffs of the exterior of an automobile in public do not constitute Fourth Amendment searches because the owner of such luggage or a car does not have any expectation of privacy in the airspace being smelled.[27] The lower courts are divided on whether (or in what circumstances) a dog sniff of a person constitutes a search,[28] and the Supreme Court has not yet addressed that issue. The results of human sniffs (i.e., by police officers) also have been suppressed when at the time the officer smelled something incriminating (e.g., marijuana smoke), the officer had no legal authority to be in the position to smell it.[29] If, however, the officer sensed the incriminating smell from a lawful vantage point, the sniff was a valid Fourth Amendment search.[30]

With respect to auditory "searches," the Supreme Court has held that police officers may not use a warrantless audio-monitoring or recording device to listen in on a conversation where each person involved in the conversation has a reasonable expectation of privacy.[31] However, a person who engages in what they believe to be a "private" conversation with an undercover officer or confidential informant working with the police cannot object under the Fourth Amendment to police officers' warrantless recording or monitoring of the conversation.[32] This is true because a person who speaks to another always runs the risk that the intended audience may be an undercover law enforcement agent or confidential informant.[33] An officer's warrantless use of an enhanced listening device—i.e., one that significantly enhances the "naked ear"—would appear to violate the Fourth Amendment, at least in situations where the speaker was not in fact speaking to a person working with law enforcement and otherwise was engaging in what was intended to be a private conversation.[34]

---

27. United States v. Place, 462 U.S. 696, 707 (1983) (luggage); *see also* Illinois v. Caballes, 543 U.S. 405 (2005) (exterior of automobile).

28. *Compare* B.C. v. Plumas Unified School District, 192 F.3d 1260 (9th Cir. 1999) ("close proximity" dog sniff of a person constituted a search), *with* United States v. Reyes, 349 F.3d 219 (5th Cir. 2003) ("non-contact" dog sniff of a person does not constitute a search).

29. *See, e.g.*, Strange v. State, 530 So. 2d 1336, 1340 (Miss. 1988) (officers' smelling of marijuana occurred only after they unconstitutionally entered the defendant's home and, thus, could not validate the initial search).

30. *See, e.g.*, Mazen v. Seidel, 940 P.2d 923, 929 (Ariz. 1997).

31. Katz v. United States, 389 U.S. 347 (1967) (defendant's private conversation with another private person from a public phone booth protected under Fourth Amendment; results of a warrantless "bug" on the pay telephone were suppressed). Under some circumstances, however, even private parties have no reasonable expectation of privacy in their conversation—such as a telephone call between a prison inmate and their spouse. *See* United States v. Madoch, 149 F.3d 596 (7th Cir. 1998). The Supreme Court has also held that a person does not have a reasonable expectation of privacy in the telephone company's records of what numbers were dialed from their telephone. Smith v. Maryland, 442 U.S. 735 (1979) (police officers do not need to obtain search warrants to use "pen registers").

32. *See* United States v. White, 401 U.S. 745 (1971); Lewis v. United States, 385 U.S. 206 (1966).

33. Hoffa v. United States, 385 U.S. 293, 303 (1966).

34. *See, e.g.*, State v. Benton, 521 A.2d 204, 206 (Conn. App. Ct. 1987).

National Institute for Trial Advocacy

In terms of visual surveillance by law enforcement, the Supreme Court has drawn a constitutional line between "open fields" and the "curtilage" of a home.[35] Simply put, it is not a Fourth Amendment search for officers to enter open fields or other publicly exposed areas around a person's residence; however, entering the curtilage of a residence is an unreasonable search when there is no warrant.[36] However, if police officers engage in a naked-eye visual inspection of the area inside the curtilage—even a fully enclosed curtilage (such as a fenced-in backyard)—from the vantage point of a person lawfully situated outside of the curtilage, a search has not occurred.[37]

Although some lower courts have held that technologically-enhanced visual inspections of areas within the curtilage of a person's residence (such as through a telescope or binoculars) constitute Fourth Amendment searches,[38] the U.S. Supreme Court appears to have drawn a line in this context between the inside and outside of a person's home for Fourth Amendment purposes.[39] In *Kyllo v. United States*,[40] the Court held that police officers' use of a thermal imaging device to scan heat being released from inside the defendant's home—which detected suspected marijuana growth inside the home—was a search because the heat could have come from an innocent source (e.g., hot water) and thus was not necessarily evidence of illegal activity. The Court was careful to note the difference between a search of the exterior and interior of a home.[41] With respect to the exterior of a home—even areas within the curtilage—the Court reaffirmed its prior cases upholding aerial observations of areas within the curtilage necessarily factored in the "technology enabling human flight," which obviously did not exist when the Fourth Amendment was adopted.[42]

---

35. Oliver v. United States, 466 U.S. 170, 180 (1984) (discussing "curtilage" and "open fields" doctrines). "Curtilage" is defined as: "The land or yard adjoining a house, usu[ally] within an enclosure." BLACK'S LAW DICTIONARY 411 (8th ed. 2004).

36. *See* United States v. Dunn, 480 U.S. 294 (1987) (defendant's barn not within the curtilage because of its significant distance from the defendant's home and nature of use of the barn, i.e., for drug manufacturing).

37. *See, e.g.*, Florida v. Riley, 488 U.S. 445 (1989) (aerial observation from 400 feet while in helicopter); California v. Ciraolo, 476 U.S. 207 (1986) (aerial observation from 1000 feet while in plane); United States v. Hatfield, 333 F.3d 1189, 1196 (10th Cir. 2003) (police officer's naked-eye visual inspection of defendant's enclosed backyard from neighboring lot was not a "search"). Both the plane in *Ciraolo* and the helicopter in *Riley* were within FAA-approved navigable airspace.

38. *See, e.g.,* Commonwealth v. Lemanski, 529 A.2d 1085 (Pa. Super. Ct. 1987); Bernstiel v. State, 416 So. 2d 827 (Fla. Dist. Ct. App. 1982).

39. In prior cases, the Court in dicta had held that the use of binoculars to enhance a police officer's vision of a defendant in a public place did not constitute an impermissible search. *See, e.g.*, On Lee v. United States, 343 U.S. 747, 754 (1952).

40. Kyllo v. United States, 533 U.S. 27 (2001).

41. *Id.* at 33–34; *see also* Karo, 468 U.S. at 714–19 (warrantless electronic tracking device placed in a defendant's home by police officers constitutes an invalid search, while warrantless tracking device placed in defendant's car driven on public roads does not).

42. *Kyllo*, 533 U.S. at 34; *see also* Dow Chemical Co. v. United States, 476 U.S. 227, 238–39 (1986) (holding that use of enhanced visual device to photograph the outside of a business did not constitute an impermissible search).

Thus, after *Kyllo*, it is arguable that there is no Fourth Amendment search if officers use sensory-enhancing devices to peer inside the curtilage (from the lawful vantage point of a neighbor or member of the public) as long as the device does not peer into or otherwise reveal possibly innocent activity *inside* the home.

In *Carpenter v. United States*[43] and *United States v. Jones*,[44] a majority of the Court held that the Fourth Amendment is violated by police officers' warrantless long-term tracking of a suspect's movements by use of GPS monitoring or by accessing phone company records of the cell towers to which the defendant's cell phone sent signals. The Court suggested that such monitoring must be at least seven days in length to violate the Fourth Amendment.[45] Therefore, in order to track a suspect using GPS monitoring or cell tower records for a period of seven days of more, police officers need to obtain a search warrant. The Court in *Carpenter* specifically addressed the Fourth Amendment "third-party doctrine," whereby officers ordinarily may obtain records about a defendant from a third-party business (such as bank records) without a warrant, and held that its holding was a "narrow" exception to that doctrine, which otherwise still applies.[46]

5.2.1.2 "Searches" that Implicate a Defendant's "Property" Interests

Beginning in 2012 with *United States v. Jones*,[47] the modern Supreme Court resurrected what was long thought to be an abandoned Fourth Amendment doctrine[48]—namely, a "search" that was unreasonable not because it violated a defendant's privacy interests, but instead because it violated a defendant's property interests. In *Jones*, the Court ruled that police officers' warrantless placement of a small GPS device on a defendant's car (which revealed incriminating information about the defendant's travels) was an unreasonable search because it would have constituted a "trespass of chattels" at the time that the Fourth Amendment was adopted (even though it would not constitute a trespass under modern tort law).[49]

In *Florida v. Jardines*,[50] the Court extended its new property-based search doctrine to a police officer's warrantless use of a police drug dog that entered the curtilage of the defendant's home and detected particles of illegal drugs coming from

---

43. Carpenter v. United States, 138 S. Ct. 2206 (2018) (maj. op. of Chief Justice Roberts).

44. United States v. Jones, 565 U.S. 400, 415 (2012) (Sotomayor, J., concurring); *id.* at 430 (Alito, J., concurring in the judgment, joined by Ginsburg, Breyer & Kagan, JJ.).

45. *Carpenter*, 138 S. Ct. at 2217 n.3.

46. *Id.* at 2220.

47. 565 U.S. 400, 402–13 (2012) (maj. op. of Scalia, J.).

48. In the famous case of Katz v. United States, 389 U.S. 347 (1967), the Court had rejected the property-based "trespass" requirement in Olmstead v. United States, 277 U.S. 438 (1928), and instead focused on a defendant's privacy interests. *See Katz*, 389 U.S. at 352–53.

49. *Jones*, 565 U.S. at 405–13.

50. Florida v. Jardines, 569 U.S. 1 (2013).

inside the defendant's home.[51] The Court reasoned that although under the law of trespass, homeowners extend an "implied license" to visitors (including police officers) to come into the curtilage and knock on the door for the purpose of engaging in a voluntary encounter with the residents, such a license does not extend to a police officer's use of drug dog within the curtilage.[52] Because the Court in *Jones* and *Jardines* concluded that the police officers violated by "physically intruding" onto the defendants' property interests, the Court did not need to address the separate question of whether the officers also violated the defendants' privacy interests.[53] Although the Court has not yet applied its what's-old-is-new-again property interest doctrine in any other cases within different factual scenarios, the lower courts have done so in several cases.[54] It is significant to note that the property doctrine only applies to the types of property mentioned in the Fourth Amendment ("persons, houses, papers, and effects").[55]

5.2.2 What Constitutes a Fourth Amendment "Seizure"?

There are two main categories of "seizures" under the Fourth Amendment—the seizure of property and the seizure of persons.[56] The latter is commonly referred to as an "arrest" or "detention" of a person.[57] Just as with searches, the Fourth Amendment's limits on seizures apply with greatest force within the home.[58]

5.2.2.1 Seizures of Property

"A 'seizure' of property . . . occurs when there is some meaningful interference with an individual's possessory interests in that property."[59] The Court's modern jurisprudence has held that the constitutional proscription against unreasonable seizures of property is not defined by arcane notions of property law.[60] Rather, warrantless seizures are unreasonable under the Fourth Amendment either when a person has a sufficient possessory interest in the seized property or when a person has a reasonable expectation of privacy in the seized property.[61] For that reason,

---

51. *Id.* at 1413–17.
52. *Id.* at 1416.
53. *Id.* at 1417 (*citing* Jones, 132 S. Ct. at 950–52).
54. *See, e.g.*, People v. Burns, 50 N.E.3d 610 (Ill. 2016) (applying *Jardines* to invalidate a warrantless search by police drug dog within the "landing area" inside defendant's apartment complex); State v. Rendon, 477 S.W.3d 805 (Tex. Crim. App. 2015) (same).
55. *Jones*, 565 U.S. at 404; *Jardines*, 133 S. Ct. at 1414 (noting that the curtilage around a house also is protected).
56. Payton v. New York, 445 U.S. 573, 589–90 (1980).
57. Terry v. Ohio, 392 U.S. 1 (1968).
58. *Payton*, 445 U.S. at 589–90.
59. Soldal v. Cook County, 506 U.S. 56, 61 (1992) (citation and internal quotes omitted).
60. Rawlings v. Kentucky, 448 U.S. 98, 105–06 (1980).
61. *Soldal*, 506 U.S. at 62–66 (the Fourth Amendment "protects property as well as privacy"); *see also* Rawlings, 448 U.S. at 104–05; Rakas v. Illinois, 439 U.S. 128 (1978). Although the Fourth

an unreasonable seizure can occur even if no search has occurred.[62] For instance, in *United States v. Place*,[63] the warrantless dog sniff of the airspace around the defendant's luggage was not a Fourth Amendment search because there was no reasonable expectation of privacy in it, but the police officers' ninety-minute warrantless detention of the luggage while awaiting the arrival of a narcotics dog was an unreasonable seizure.[64]

Seizures of voluntarily abandoned items of property are not protected by the Fourth Amendment.[65] However, a defendant's abandonment of property after an unconstitutional seizure does not foreclose a Fourth Amendment claim.[66]

5.2.2.2 Arrests and Detentions of Persons

A person is "seized" under the Fourth Amendment when from an objective standpoint, "a reasonable person [in his situation] would have believed that he was not free to leave" or was not "free to disregard the police and go about his business."[67] A suspect fleeing the police during a chase is not seized until physical contact occurs or until they submit to the police's show of authority.[68] This issue is similar, but distinct from the issue of whether a defendant is "in custody" for purposes of requiring *Miranda* warnings[69]—a matter that is discussed later.

Amendment's principal object is the protection of legitimate privacy rights, it also protects a person's property rights. *Soldal*, 506 U.S. at 64.

62. *Soldal*, 506 U.S. at 68–69.

63. 462 U.S. 696 (1983).

64. *Id*. at 708; *see also* Soldal, 506 U.S. at 63–64.

65. *See* California v. Hodari D., 499 U.S. 621 (1991) (drugs thrown away by defendant during chase by police officers were abandoned by the defendant; warrantless seizure of the drugs was not a "Fourth Amendment seizure"); California v. Greenwood, 486 U.S. 35 (1988) (officers may search trash left on curbside, outside curtilage, without a warrant because such garbage is deemed to be abandoned); United States v. Williams, 569 F.2d 823, 826 (5th Cir. 1978) (defendant who fled from his parked vehicle in a parking lot because he feared that police officers would discover incriminating evidence inside it "abandoned" it and, thus, no Fourth Amendment violation occurred when officers searched it without a warrant); *but cf*. Smith v. Ohio, 494 U.S. 541, 543–44 (1990) (per curiam) (a defendant who initially threw a paper bag that he was carrying on the hood of a car when police officers confronted him, but then attempted to reclaim the bag when officers approached it, did not abandon the bag).

66. *See, e.g.*, United States v. Beck, 602 F.2d 726, 729–30 (5th Cir. 1979); United States v. King, 990 F.2d 1552, 1564–65 & n.7 (10th Cir. 1993).

67. United States v. Mendenhall, 446 U.S. 544, 554–55 (1980) (plurality); *see also* Florida v. Royer, 460 U.S. 491 (1983); Florida v. Bostick, 501 U.S. 429, 434 (1991).

68. *Hodari D.*, 499 U.S. at 624–26.

69. *Miranda* warnings are required when a defendant "has been taken into custody or otherwise deprived of [their] freedom of action in any significant way." Miranda v. Arizona, 384 U.S. 436, 444 (1966); *see also* Stansbury v. California, 511 U.S. 318, 322 (1994) (per curiam). *Miranda* "custody" may or may not occur during certain Fourth Amendment seizures. *See* Berkemer v. McCarty, 468 U.S. 420, 430–42 (1984) (holding that *Miranda* warnings are not ordinarily required during . . . routine traffic stops, even though such law enforcement encounters constitute seizures under the Fourth Amendment); *see also* United States v. Kim, 292 F.3d 969, 976 (9th Cir. 2002) ("whether

Whether a person has been seized depends on the totality of the circumstances of each case.[70] When a police officer approaches a person and asks to speak to him about suspected criminal activity, but does not otherwise restrain their movements (such as by keeping the individual's personal effects or by displaying weapons), courts generally will find that no seizure took place.[71] In other words, not every police-citizen encounter constitutes a seizure.[72] "Examples of circumstances that might indicate a seizure . . would be the threatening presence of several officers, the display of a weapon by an officer, some physical touching of the person of the citizen, or the use of language or tone of voice indicating that compliance with the officer's request might be compelled."[73] If a person is unconstitutionally seized, then any evidence discovered during a search as an incident of their detention (e.g., drugs found in a pocket during a pat down) or any evidence obtained from them (e.g., evidence of their fingerprints taken after an illegal arrest) must be suppressed.[74]

As discussed below, the Supreme Court has drawn a line between two different types of seizures of a person—a "full-fledged arrest" and a more limited "investigative detention."[75] Both are Fourth Amendment seizures of a human being, but the implications of the two types of seizures—in terms of the degree of physical searching and the length of the permissible detention—are significantly different, as explained below.

5.2.3 Fourth Amendment "Standing"

Traditionally, courts have required a defendant to possess "standing" to file a motion to suppress under the Fourth Amendment in a criminal case.[76] In *Rakas*

---

an individual . . . has been unreasonably seized for Fourth Amendment purposes and whether that individual is 'in custody' for *Miranda* purposes are two different issues"). Many times, a person is both seized for Fourth Amendment purposes and in custody for *Miranda* purposes; however, the two types of detentions do not necessarily overlap.

70. *Mendenhall,* 446 U.S. at 554–55.

71. *Id.*

72. *See, e.g.,* United States v. Drayton, 536 U.S. 194, 200–01 (2002) ("Law enforcement officers do not violate the Fourth Amendment[] . . . merely by approaching individuals . . . in public places and putting questions to them if they are willing to listen."). Courts consistently also have upheld "knock and talk" encounters—i.e., the practice of police officers knocking on a person's front door and asking the person to answer questions or consent to a search. *See, e.g.,* United States v. Gould, 364 F.3d 578, 590 (5th Cir. 2004) (en banc).

73. *Mendenhall,* 446 U.S. at 554.

74. *See, e.g.,* Davis v. Mississippi, 394 U.S. 721 (1969) (suppressing evidence of defendant's fingerprints obtained during the defendant's unlawful detention); Reid v. Georgia, 448 U.S. 438 (1980) (per curiam) (suppressing evidence of cocaine seized from defendant after he was illegally detained). As discussed below, in some circumstances a defendant's voluntary confession following an illegal detention must be suppressed under the Fourth Amendment. *See* Brown v. Illinois, 422 U.S. 590 (1975).

75. *See* section 5.3.3.4.

76. *See, e.g.,* Jones v. United States, 362 U.S. 257, 261 (1960).

v. Illinois,[77] the Supreme Court stated that the "standing label" is unhelpful in the Fourth Amendment context and a better way of describing the inquiry is whether the individual defendant claims to have had their Fourth Amendment rights violated.[78]

If so, the defendant may file a motion to suppress based on the asserted Fourth Amendment violation.[79] Since *Rakas*, the Court has rejected "third-party standing" arguments regarding Fourth Amendment claims. If a defendant does not allege that their Fourth Amendment rights have been violated by a search or seizure, then they lack a sufficient basis to file a motion to suppress under the Fourth Amendment.[80] Put another way, a person's Fourth Amendment rights are personal rights and cannot be asserted vicariously.[81] The traditional standing inquiry thus collapses into the substantive Fourth Amendment question of whether a challenged search or seizure infringed a legitimate possessory or privacy interest of the defendant.[82] Notwithstanding the Supreme Court's rejection of the "standing" nomenclature in *Rakas* in 1978, courts since then have continued to use the ersatz standing concept in the Fourth Amendment context.[83]

Because Fourth Amendment standing now merges into the substantive analysis of a Fourth Amendment claim, a defendant must assert a legitimate possessory or privacy interest to file a motion to suppress under the Fourth Amendment. Thus, for instance, the Supreme Court has held that an overnight guest inside a third party's home has a reasonable expectation of privacy that is violated by an unconstitutional search of the home,[84] but a purely commercial visitor (such as a person temporarily visiting another's home to sell or buy illegal drugs) does not have standing.[85] A person driving a rental car with the permission of the authorized driver—who was the only one on the rental contract—possesses standing to object to an unconstitutional seizure and search of the car even when that person was driving it alone (without the authorized driver).[86]

Another recurring issue involves public employees in their places of work. The Supreme Court has held that, depending on the circumstances, a public employee

---

77. Rakas v. Illinois, 439 U.S. 128 (1978).

78. *Id.* at 132–34.

79. *Id.*

80. United States v. Padilla, 508 U.S. 77 (1993) (per curiam).

81. *Rakas*, 439 U.S. at 132–34.

82. *See, e.g.*, Arizona v. Hicks, 480 U.S. 321 (1987); Rawlings v. Kentucky, 448 U.S. 98 (1980).

83. *See, e.g.*, Padilla, 508 U.S. at 81–82 (discussing the decision of the Ninth Circuit); Minnesota v. Carter, 525 U.S. 83, 87–88 (1998) (discussing the decisions of the Minnesota courts).

84. Minnesota v. Olson, 495 U.S. 91 (1990). Since *Olson*, most lower courts have extended the concept of an "overnight guest" to include social guests who are present in a residence for an appreciable amount of time, even if not overnight. *See, e.g.*, State v. Hess, 680 N.W.2d 314, 322 (S.D. 2004).

85. *Carter*, 525 U.S. at 87–89.

86. Byrd v. United States, 138 S. Ct. 1518 (2018).

may have standing to object to a search of their office area.[87] Finally, a defendant has no standing to challenge a police officer's warrantless search of third-party business records implicating the defendant (e.g., the defendant's bank records or telephone records).[88]

5.3 The Fourth Amendment's "Warrant Requirement" and Its Many Exceptions

5.3.1 Issues Concerning the Application for and Issuance of a Warrant

If law enforcement officials wish to apply for a warrant that authorizes a search or seizure of property or an arrest of a defendant, they must apply for one from a "neutral and detached" judge or magistrate.[89] Typically, the application is a written affidavit describing what the official believes is probable cause justifying issuance of a warrant. A warrant is void ab initio—and may not be used to uphold a search or seizure—if the magistrate or judge who issued it was not neutral and detached.[90] For instance, a warrant was void when the magistrate who issued it was paid per warrant issued (and who received no money if they refused to issue a warrant); the magistrate's financial conflict of interest was sufficient to find that they were not neutral and detached under those circumstances.[91] Another case held that a part-time magistrate was not neutral and detached where their full-time job was working as an administrator at the local jail.[92]

Arrest warrants and search warrants are governed by similar rules but are different in a key respect. Both, of course, can only be issued based on a finding of probable cause. An arrest warrant "is issued by a magistrate upon a showing that probable cause exists to believe that the subject of the warrant has committed an offense. . . ."[93] Search warrants, conversely, "may be issued to search *any* property, whether or not occupied by a[n] [innocent] third party, at which there is probable cause to believe

---

87. *See* O'Connor v. Ortega, 480 U.S. 709 (1987); City of Ontario v. Quon, 560 U.S. 746 (2010); *see also* United States v. Slanina, 283 F.3d 670, 676–80 (5th Cir.) *vacated on other grounds*, 537 U.S. 802 (2002).

88. *See* United States v. Miller, 425 U.S. 435 (1976). The business itself may have constitutional basis to demand a judicial determination of probable cause before turning over the records to police officers, *see* City of Los Angeles v. Patel, 576 U.S. 409, 421 (2015), but the customer ordinarily does not possess such a basis.

89. Shadwick v. City of Tampa, 407 U.S. 345, 350 (1972).

90. United States v. Parker, 373 F.3d 770 (6th Cir. 2004).

91. *See* Connally v. Georgia, 429 U.S. 245 (1977) (per curiam); *see also* Coolidge v. New Hampshire, 403 U.S. 443 (1971) (Attorney General not neutral and detached magistrate). Whether a magistrate is "neutral and detached" under the Fourth Amendment is similar to the issue of whether a judge is biased under the Due Process Clause. *See, e.g.*, Ward v. Village of Monroeville, 409 U.S. 57 (1972). The latter issue is discussed in Chapter Four.

92. *Parker*, 373 F.3d at 773–74.

93. Steagald v. United States, 451 U.S. 204, 213 (1981).

that fruits, instrumentalities, or evidence of a crime will be found."[94] "The right to search and the validity of the seizure are not dependent on the right to arrest."[95]

Both search and arrest warrants must not be overbroad in their scope and instead—in the words of the Fourth Amendment—must "particularly describe[] the place to be searched [or] the persons or things to be seized."[96] Even if a law enforcement officer's application for a warrant describes in sufficient detail the object of the warrant, a judicial officer's warrant that fails to do so is invalid unless it incorporates the application and the application is attached to the warrant when presented to the subject of the warrant at the time of its execution.[97]

A warrant is subject to two time constraints. The first time constraint is the one expressly stated in the warrant or required by the law of the relevant jurisdiction; most jurisdictions require a warrant (a search or arrest warrant) to be executed within a specific time period (e.g., three days). An expired warrant cannot be used to justify a search or seizure under the Fourth Amendment.[98] The second time constraint is that a search warrant, even if executed within the time permitted by the law of the jurisdiction, cannot be based on "stale" information.[99] Whether information contained in an application for a search warrant is stale "depends on the nature of the criminal activity, the length of the activity, and the nature of the property to be seized."[100] Modern courts have been quite generous to law enforcement in determining whether a warrant is based on stale information, especially in drug cases and child pornography cases. The courts have reasoned that drug dealers and persons possessing child pornography tend to keep their contraband and continue in their illegal activity over a long period of time. Thus, months' old information is generally not considered stale in such cases.[101] The converse of a stale warrant is an "anticipatory" warrant—that is, a warrant that is issued *before* the relevant criminal activity occurs (e.g., police seek a search warrant based on information that a suspect has ordered illegal contraband through the mail; the warrant authorizes a search of the suspect's residence only if the suspect accepts delivery of the contraband). The Supreme Court upheld such anticipatory warrants as long as

---

94. Zurcher v. Stanford Daily, 436 U.S. 547, 554 (1978).

95. *Id.* at 557 (citation and internal quotation marks omitted).

96. U.S. Const. Amend. IV; *see* Maryland v. Garrison, 480 U.S. 79, 84–85 (1987); Andresen v. Maryland, 427 U.S. 463, 480 (1976).

97. Groh v. Ramirez, 540 U.S. 551, 555–58 (2004); United States v. Tracey, 597 F.3d 140 (3d Cir. 2010); United States v. McGrew, 122 F.3d 847 (9th Cir. 1997).

98. *See, e.g.,* Jones v. United States, 357 U.S. 493 (1958) (evidence suppressed because warrant had expired).

99. Sgro v. United States, 287 U.S. 206, 210–11 (1932).

100. United States v. Harris, 369 F.3d 1157, 1165 (10th Cir. 2004) (citation and internal quotation marks omitted).

101. *See, e.g.,* United States v. Lacy, 119 F.3d 742 (9th Cir. 1997) (ten-month-old information not stale in a child pornography case); United States v. Valdovinos, 103 F. App'x 221 (9th Cir. 2004) (nine-month-old information in a drug case not stale).

probable cause exists that the future condition will occur and also that if the future condition in fact occurs, probable cause of a crime will then exist.[102]

A warrant is invalid under the Fourth Amendment if the application for the warrant contained material, affirmative falsehoods or factual omissions and if a law enforcement officer acted intentionally or in "reckless disregard" of the truth in submitting the application.[103] "Materiality" as used here means that, after the falsehoods are excised from the application or the omitted information is added, there is no longer probable cause supporting issuance of the warrant from an objective standpoint.[104] Similarly, if a warrant application contains information obtained from an illegal search or seizure, the warrant issued based on that application is valid only if after excising the "tainted" information from the application there still is a showing of probable cause.[105]

The Fourth Amendment requires that when officers execute a search or an arrest warrant at a residence or other building not open to the public, ordinarily they must knock on the door, announce their identity and purpose (e.g., "police officers—we have a warrant"), and then wait a reasonable amount of time for the occupants to open the door before proceeding to forcibly enter a locked door or open an unlocked door.[106] Failure to comply with this constitutional "knock and announce rule" formerly resulted in the suppression of the evidence seized during execution of an otherwise lawful warrant.[107] However, in 2006 in *Hudson v. Michigan*,[108] the Supreme Court held that the Fourth Amendment exclusionary rule does not apply to violations of the constitutional "knock and announce rule"; thus, the only remedy remaining for such a constitutional violation would be money damages in a civil rights action.

It is an open question in the Supreme Court's jurisprudence whether the Fourth Amendment requires, under any circumstances, officers who are executing a warrant to present a copy of the warrant to the occupants of the residence at some point during the search. The Court has said in dicta that officers need not invariably present a warrant at the outset of the search, but left open the issue of whether it

---

102. United States v. Grubbs, 547 U.S. 90 (2006).
103. Franks v. Delaware, 438 U.S. 154 (1978) (material misrepresentations); United States v. Carpenter, 360 F.3d 591 (6th Cir. 2004) (material omissions); United States v. Cronan, 937 F.2d 163 (5th Cir. 1991) (same).
104. *Franks*, 438 U.S. at 171–72.
105. *See, e.g.*, United States v. Herrold, 962 F.2d 1131, 1137–38 (3d Cir. 1992) (citing cases).
106. Richards v. Wisconsin, 520 U.S. 385 (1997); Wilson v. Arkansas, 514 U.S. 927 (1995). The Supreme Court has held that police officers' opening an unlocked door is equivalent to forcibly breaking into a locked door under the Fourth Amendment. *See* Sabbath v. United States, 391 U.S. 585, 590–91 (1968).
107. *See, e.g.*, United States v. Cantu, 230 F.3d 148 (5th Cir. 2000).
108. 547 U.S. 586 (2006).

would be unreasonable not to do so when asked for a copy by occupants who pose no danger to the officers.[109]

5.3.2 Exceptions to the Search Warrant Requirement

There are myriad recognized exceptions to the Fourth Amendment's general requirement that a search warrant must be obtained before a place is searched or an item is seized. As a general rule, if officers discover contraband or incriminating evidence during a valid warrantless search in accordance with one of the recognized exceptions, such evidence is admissible against the defendant under the Fourth Amendment. Although there are many such exceptions (discussed below), if a search or seizure does not fall within one of them, then the fruits of the search or seizure must be suppressed—no matter how guilty the defendant may be, and no matter how serious their crime.[110]

5.3.2.1 Plain View, Plain Feel, and Plain Smell Exceptions

Perhaps the most common exception is that officers may seize contraband or incriminating evidence without a warrant if it is in "plain view," the officer is lawfully in the position to observe the item, and the illegal or evidentiary nature of the object is "immediately apparent" to the officer.[111] Typically, the exception applies when an officer is executing a search or arrest warrant concerning one crime and discovers evidence of another crime that falls outside the scope of the warrant (e.g., an officer executing a search warrant for drugs discovers illegal firearms in the immediate presence of the drugs).[112] The contraband or evidence must truly be in "plain view," and its incriminating nature or evidentiary value must be immediately apparent without any additional search or seizure. For example, police officers who lawfully were inside a person's residence investigating a suspected shooting engaged in an unconstitutional search of a suspected stolen stereo component when they moved it only a few inches to expose its serial number (which, when checked,

---

109. Groh v. Ramirez, 540 U.S. 551, 562 n.5 (2004). The lower courts have held either that there is no "presentment" requirement imposed by the Fourth Amendment, *see, e.g.*, People v. Ellison, 773 N.Y.S.2d 860, 867–68 & n.5 (N.Y. Sup. Ct. 2004), *rev'd on other grounds*, 46 A.D.3d 1341 (N.Y. App. Div. 2007), or that the Fourth Amendment exclusionary rule does not apply to violations of a constitutional presentment requirement, *see, e.g.*, United States v. Hector, 474 F.3d 1150, 1154 (9th Cir. 2007).

110. *See* Flippo v. West Virginia, 528 U.S. 11 (1999) (per curiam) (no "murder scene" exception to the Fourth Amendment, where no established exception otherwise applies); *see also* Ker v. California, 374 U.S. 23, 33 (1963) (Fourth Amendment protects the innocent as well as the guilty from unreasonable searches and seizures).

111. Warden v. Hayden, 387 U.S. 294 (1967); Texas v. Brown, 460 U.S. 730 (1983) (plurality); Horton v. California, 496 U.S. 128 (1990).

112. *See, e.g.*, United States v. Simpson, 10 F.3d 645 (9th Cir. 1993), *vacated on other grounds*, 513 U.S. 983 (1994).

showed the item was stolen).[113] The stolen status of the stereo component was not "immediately apparent"—and thus probable cause to seize it did not exist—from the officer's initial, lawful vantage point. The officer had to move it a few inches, which constituted an impermissible warrantless search, to reveal its serial number. Therefore, the "plain view" exception did not apply in that case.[114]

The Supreme Court has applied the same logic to situations when an officer is legally touching a person—such as a lawful pat down of a suspect—and the incriminating nature of something inside the person's clothing is "immediately apparent," thus supplying probable cause (e.g., an illegal concealed weapon inside a person's pants pocket).[115] If the incriminating nature of an object inside a person's clothing is not "immediately apparent" without further searching, then the "plain feel" exception does not apply. For instance, if an officer who is legally patting down a person feels a small container in the defendant's pocket and then proceeds to open it (revealing drugs), the officer's warrantless opening of the container is unconstitutional because there was not probable cause to believe that drugs were inside the closed container.[116] Many lower courts also have extended the plain view doctrine to situations involving "plain smells" that provide probable cause of illegal activity, such as the smell of burnt marijuana.[117]

5.3.2.2 Exigent Circumstances and the Community Caretaker Exceptions

The Supreme Court has long recognized that an emergency situation or "exigent circumstances" can render a warrantless search or seizure of property reasonable under the Fourth Amendment.[118] Thus, for example, police officers can enter a building (including a private residence) without a warrant if they are in "hot pursuit" of a fleeing felony suspect and have a reasonable basis to believe that the suspect has entered the building.[119] Any incriminating evidence or contraband discovered in plain view inside the building is admissible under the Fourth Amendment; in addition, officers also may engage in a warrantless search of the house for any dangerous weapons that the suspect carried into the house.[120] Another variation of the exigent circumstances exception permits officers to seize "evanescent" evidence or

---

113. Arizona v. Hicks, 480 U.S. 321 (1987).
114. *Id.*
115. *See* Minnesota v. Dickerson, 508 U.S. 366 (1993).
116. *Id.* at 378–79.
117. *See, e.g.*, United States v. Ryles, 988 F.2d 13 (5th Cir. 1993) (police officer who legally stopped car and who legally placed head within interior of car, exposing him to the smell of burning marijuana, had a right to search the car without a warrant); *but cf.* Strange v. State, 530 So. 2d 1336, 1340 (Miss. 1988) (officers' smelling of marijuana occurred only after they unconstitutionally entered the defendant's home and, thus, could not validate the initial unconstitutional search).
118. Payton v. New York, 445 U.S. 573, 586–87 (1980).
119. Warden v. Hayden, 387 U.S. 294, 298–99 (1967).
120. *Id.*

contraband without a warrant if they reasonably believe that it will be destroyed or removed before a warrant can be obtained.[121]

Note that the exigent circumstances exception does not apply, however, when the law enforcement officers themselves created the exigency in a manner that could have been avoided.[122] Merely knocking on a suspect's front door and announcing "police officers"—knowing that such action may cause the suspect to attempt to destroy incriminating evidence inside the house—does not unreasonably create the exigency.[123] Only if officers "gain entry into premises by means of actual or threatened violation of the Fourth Amendment" would they unreasonably create the exigency.[124]

A related exception to the warrant requirement is the "community caretaker" exception, which permits a warrantless search or seizure when it initially was motivated by "no claim of criminal liability [and is] . . . totally divorced from the detection, investigation, or acquisition of evidence relating to" a suspected criminal violation.[125] Application of such a community caretaker exception is most common—and most likely to be upheld—in the context of automobiles[126] (for example, police officers stop a car because they believed that the driver might be physically ill and discover that the driver is intoxicated).[127] It is much more controversial when applied to warrantless entries into private homes (for example, without consent or a warrant, officers enter a private home because they have a suspicion that the elderly homeowner may be ill and, once inside, discover illegal drugs being used by the homeowner's grandson).[128] In its cases decided so far, the Supreme Court has limited this exception to the warrant requirement to situations where police officers have an "objectively reasonable basis for believing" that a

---

121. *See, e.g.,* Cupp v. Murphy, 412 U.S. 291 (1973) (warrantless fingernail scrapings upheld when police had probable cause and defendant could have easily cleaned his hands and removed evidence before warrant could be obtained); Schmerber v. California, 384 U.S. 757, 770 (1966) (warrantless taking of blood/alcohol sample upheld when police had probable cause to believe that the defendant had committed a serious vehicular accident while driving under the influence of alcohol). Note that the Court has recently held that a warrantless extraction of blood from a DUI suspect is not automatically justified in a routine DUI case. Rather, the totality of the circumstances must be determined in each case to assess whether a search warrant could have been obtained. See Missouri v. McNeely, 569 U.S. 141 (2013). However, if the officers possess probable cause to believe that an unconscious driver is intoxicated, exigent circumstances "almost always" exist to take the unconscious driver's blood without a warrant. *See* Mitchell v. Wisconsin, 139 S. Ct. 2525, 2531 (2019).
122. *See* Kentucky v. King, 563 U.S. 452, 462 (2011).
123. *Id.* at 467–69.
124. *Id.* at 469.
125. Cady v. Dombrowski, 413 U.S. 433, 441 (1973).
126. *See* United States v. Newbourn, 600 F.2d 452 (4th Cir. 1979).
127. *See, e.g.,* Wright v. State, 7 S.W.3d 148, 151–52 (Tex. Crim. App. 1999).
128. The broader community caretaker doctrine should be distinguished from the narrower "emergency aid" exception to the warrant requirement. The Supreme Court has recognized that officers' reasonable belief (based on particularized information) that a person inside a home is seriously injured and in need of immediate medical aid justifies a warrantless entry. Mincey v. Arizona, 437 U.S. 385, 392–93 (1978); *see also* Laney v. State, 117 S.W.3d 854, 862–63 (Tex. Crim. App. 2003).

person inside a residence is seriously injured or is facing "imminent injury" or death and requires "emergency aid."[129]

5.3.2.3 Searches "Incident to Arrest"

Perhaps the most common type of warrantless search occurs after a police officer validly arrests a person (whether with or without an arrest warrant). The Supreme Court has held that once an officer validly arrests a person, the officer may search not only that person's clothing and property (including closed containers like a wallet or purse) in their immediate possession, but also the immediate area around the arrested person (including closets).[130] Such warrantless searches are permitted without any probable cause or reasonable suspicion to believe that the arrested person has any evidence of a crime or dangerous weapons in their possession or in their immediate area.[131] Rather, a search "incident to arrest" is justified as a "preventative" (or "prophylactic") search based on two premises—officer safety and the need to prevent destruction of any evidence that may exist.[132]

There are certain limits on such warrantless searches. For example, an arresting officer may not search the digital data on an arrestee's cellular phone as an "incident to arrest."[133] An officer who has arrested a suspect for driving while intoxicated may not draw blood (for a blood-alcohol test) as an incident to arrest, although the officer may require the arrestee to take a breathalyzer test as an incident to arrest.[134]

5.3.2.4 The "Automobile Exception" and Related Exceptions Involving Automobiles, Drivers, and Passengers

5.3.2.4.1 *The "Automobile Exception"*

If, as a general rule, people's homes receive the greatest protection under the Fourth Amendment, people's automobiles receive the least protection. For that reason, another commonly applied exception to the warrant requirement is the

---

129. Brigham City, Utah, v. Stuart, 547 U.S. 398, 403–05 (2006); *see also* Michigan v. Fisher, 558 U.S. 45 (2009) (per curiam).
130. Chimel v. California, 395 U.S. 752 (1969); *see also* Maryland v. Buie, 494 U.S. 325, 334 (1990) (regarding police officers who entered a defendant's home to arrest him pursuant to an arrest warrant, the Court stated: "We . . hold that as an incident to the arrest the officers could, as a precautionary matter and without probable cause or reasonable suspicion, look in closets and other spaces immediately adjoining the place of arrest from which an attack could be immediately launched. Beyond that, however, we hold that there must be articulable facts which, taken together with the rational inferences from those facts, would warrant a reasonably prudent officer in believing that the area to be swept harbors an individual posing a danger to those on the arrest scene.").
131. *Chimel*, 395 U.S. at 762–63.
132. *Id.*
133. Riley v. California, 573 U.S. 373 (2014).
134. Birchfield v. North Dakota, 136 S. Ct. 2160 (2016).

"automobile exception," which provides that any time law enforcement officers have probable cause to believe that an automobile contains incriminating evidence or contraband, a warrantless search of the car and seizure of such items are permitted under the Fourth Amendment.[135] Officers need not believe that there are exigent circumstances justifying the warrantless search; the mere fact that they possess probable cause to believe that contraband or evidence is inside the vehicle is sufficient.[136] This exception has been extended to apply to mobile homes and boats, as long as such vehicles are "readily capable" of being made "movable."[137] Police officers' right to search vehicles without a warrant pursuant to the automobile exception does not cease once a vehicle has been impounded by the police.[138] Note one important limit to the application of the automobile exception: it generally does not apply to vehicles parked within the curtilage of a home.[139]

The scope of a warrantless search pursuant to the automobile exception is limited to areas in the car (including closed containers inside the car) for which there is probable cause to believe that incriminating evidence or contraband is present.[140] Such searches may extend to containers in the car belonging to a passenger (such as a purse) even when the driver is the only person being arrested, as long as the object of the search could be concealed in the passenger's container.[141]

5.3.2.4.2 *"Belton Searches" of Automobiles "Incident to Arrest"*

An equally sweeping exception, first recognized in *New York v. Belton*,[142] permitted officers who arrested a driver or passenger of a car (based on probable cause) to search the car's entire passenger compartment and any containers within the passenger compartment—including things such as glove compartments and consoles—without a warrant even if officers had no basis to believe any incriminating evidence, contraband, or weapons would be found there.[143] Such a search was deemed to be justified as a "contemporaneous incident" of arrest; however, the allowable search was limited in scope to the passenger compartment and could not be extended to the closed trunk of a car[144] (although it could be extended to a hatchback of a car).[145]

---

135. Maryland v. Dyson, 527 U.S. 465, 466–67 (1999) (per curiam); *see also* California v. Carney, 471 U.S. 386 (1985); Pennsylvania v. Labron, 518 U.S. 938 (1996) (per curiam).
136. Michigan v. Thomas, 458 U.S. 259 (1982).
137. *Carney*, 471 U.S. at 392–93; United States v. Lingenfelter, 997 F.2d 632, 640 (9th Cir. 1993).
138. Florida v. Meyers, 466 U.S. 380 (1984) (per curiam).
139. Collins v. Virginia, 138 S. Ct. 1663 (2018).
140. California v. Acevedo, 500 U.S. 565 (1991); *see also* United States v. Ross, 456 U.S. 798 (1982).
141. Wyoming v. Houghton, 526 U.S. 295 (1999).
142. New York v. Belton, 453 U.S. 454 (1981).
143. *Id.* at 460.
144. *Id.* at 460 & n.4.
145. United States v. Mayo, 394 F.3d 1271, 1277 (9th Cir. 2005).

In *Thornton v. United States*,[146] a majority of the Court extended *Belton* to "recent occupants" of parked cars—for example, a warrantless *Belton* search was permitted when police officers lawfully arrested a person who had parked their car and walked away from it.[147] An open question was how close a person had to be to their car—spatially and/or temporally—to qualify as a "recent occupant."[148] That issue was litigated in the lower courts in the wake of *Thornton*.[149]

In 2009, in *Arizona v. Gant*,[150] a closely divided Supreme Court limited the application of *Belton*'s "bright-line rule" by holding that officers may not engage in a warrantless search of a car if the driver and any occupants are first safely detained and not within "reaching distance" of the car's passenger compartment (and thus the officers at the scene are not in danger). The Court also stated that officers alternatively could search the car without a warrant (even if the driver and any occupants were safely detained) if it was "reasonable to believe" that incriminating evidence concerning the offense of arrest was inside the car.[151] *Gant* did not in any way affect the automobile exception, which allows officers to engage in a warrantless search of a car if they have probable cause to believe it contains evidence of *any* offense (even one unrelated to the driver's arrest).[152]

The *Belton* rule, as limited by *Gant*, applies to situations when officers have probable cause and proceed to arrest an occupant or recent occupant of a car for a felony or misdemeanor.[153] However, even if officers have probable cause to arrest, but instead choose to issue a citation rather than arrest the occupant or recent occupant of the car, then the rule does not apply.[154]

5.3.2.4.3 *Traffic Stops*

The Supreme Court has held that, consistent with the Fourth Amendment, a police officer may temporarily seize an automobile and detain its driver and passengers if the officer possesses probable cause to believe that the driver committed a violation of the traffic laws[155]—even if, under local law, the traffic offense is only subject to a fine and not any jail time.[156] The vast majority of lower courts have held that such warrantless traffic stops also are permitted if the officer had only

---

146. 541 U.S. 615 (2004).
147. *Id.* at 619–22.
148. *Id.* at 621 & n.2.
149. *See, e.g.*, State v. Rathbun, 101 P.3d 119 (Wash. App. 2004) (defendant who was arrested forty to sixty feet from car was not a "recent occupant" under *Thornton*).
150. Arizona v. Gant, 556 U.S. 332 (2009).
151. *Id.* at 341–51.
152. *See* United States v. Polanco, 634 F.3d 39, 42 (1st Cir. 2011).
153. *See, e.g.*, State v. Wheaton, 827 P.2d 1174 (Idaho Ct. App. 1991).
154. Knowles v. Iowa, 525 U.S. 113 (1998).
155. Maryland v. Wilson, 519 U.S. 408 (1997); Pennsylvania v. Mimms, 434 U.S. 106 (1977) (per curiam).
156. Atwater v. City of Lago Vista, 532 U.S. 318 (2001).

reasonable suspicion that the driver committed a traffic violation.[157] The officer may conduct a warrantless pat down of the driver and passengers and engage in a cursory "protective sweep" of the vehicle's passenger compartment as long as the officer has reasonable suspicion that they possess dangerous weapons, even if there is no basis to believe that any crime was committed (other than the driver's commission of a traffic violation).[158] All of these activities by law enforcement officers are constitutional, even if the police had an ulterior motive for pulling over the car (e.g., a hunch that the driver or passengers had drugs in the car, which does not amount to reasonable suspicion), as long as, objectively, the police possess probable cause that a traffic violation occurred.[159] If it turns out that an officer did not possess probable cause or reasonable suspicion that a traffic violation occurred, any incriminating evidence obtained during the traffic stop must be suppressed.[160] Both the driver and any passenger have standing to challenge such an illegal search or seizure.[161]

An issue that frequently arises in the context of traffic stops is whether police officers unconstitutionally extended the stop by questioning the driver or passengers about matters unrelated to the alleged traffic violation without reasonable suspicion or probable cause (such as questions aimed at determining whether the driver was engaged in drug trafficking) or by engaging in other activities (for example, running a narcotics dog around the outside of the car). With respect to dog sniffs, the Supreme Court approved a dog sniff of a vehicle that occurred during a traffic stop (meaning before the traffic stop was completed) because the Court "accept[ed] the state court's conclusion that the duration of the stop . . . was entirely justified by the traffic offense and the ordinary inquiries incident to such a stop."[162] Conversely, when a nonconsensual dog sniff occurred *after* a completed traffic stop, the evidence discovered after the drug dog alerted to inside the car had to be suppressed as a violation of the Fourth Amendment.[163] The Supreme Court held that officers may question the driver or passengers about matters unrelated to the traffic stop—during the stop—as long as they do not "measurably extend" the duration of the stop.[164] If a court determines that an officer developed reasonable suspicion or probable cause concerning another criminal offense only after extending the traffic stop, then the fruits of a search or seizure obtained thereafter will be suppressed.[165]

---

157. United States v. Stewart, 551 F.3d 187, 191–92 (2d Cir. 2009).

158. Arizona v. Johnson, 555 U.S. 323 (2009); Michigan v. Long, 463 U.S. 1032 (1983).

159. Wren v. United States, 517 U.S. 806 (1996).

160. *See, e.g.*, United States v. Gant, 412 F. Supp. 2d 451 (E.D. Pa. 2005); *see also* Stewart, 551 F.3d at 191–92.

161. Brendlin v. California, 551 U.S. 249 (2007); *see also* United States v. Mosley, 454 F.3d 249 (6th Cir. 2006).

162. Illinois v. Caballes, 543 U.S. 545 (2005).

163. Rodriguez v. United States, 575 U.S. 348 (2015).

164. *Johnson*, 555 U.S. at 333.

165. *See, e.g.*, United States v. Martin, 679 F. Supp. 2d 723 (W.D. La. 2010).

5.3.2.5 "Protective Sweeps" of Residences

Warrantless "protective sweeps" are also authorized as an incident to arrest with respect to an arrestee's person or residence. If a defendant is arrested in a residence, the officers may engage in a brief warrantless search of the area immediately in the defendant's control,[166] and further may search in a more in-depth manner (e.g., rooms in other parts of the house) if officers have a reasonable basis to believe that persons posing a danger to the officers may be hiding in such places.[167] Such searches may not be full-fledged evidentiary searches; rather, they must be limited in scope to searching for readily available weapons or other persons in the home who could present a danger to police.[168] Although the Supreme Court has not yet addressed the issue since *Maryland v. Buie*, the clear majority of lower courts have extended *Buie* to permit warrantless protective sweeps of the inside of an arrestee's residence when they were arrested outside the residence, but near to it.[169] The lower courts are divided over whether a protective sweep is permitted when officers engage in a warrantless "knock and talk" at a residence without reasonable suspicion that a criminal offense has been committed, but with reasonable suspicion that a weapon or other danger lurks inside the residence.[170]

5.3.2.6 "Inventory Searches" of Personal Effects and Automobiles

If a person has been lawfully arrested, as a general rule police officers may search the arrestee's personal effects (including things such as bags and purses that they were carrying) or their automobile (if arrested while driving or arrested after having parked their car in a public place) as part of an inventory of the arrestee's personal property.[171] For such "inventory searches" to be valid, they must be conducted pursuant to a preexisting policy of the relevant law enforcement agency (written or unwritten); if a purported inventory search occurs on an ad hoc basis and there is no established policy (written or unwritten), then under the Fourth

---

166. Chimel v. California, 395 U.S. 752 (1969).

167. Maryland v. Buie, 494 U.S. 325, 336 (1990) (to justify such a search, the officers must possess a "reasonable, articulable suspicion that the house is harboring a person posing a danger to those on the arrest scene").

168. *Id.* at 335.

169. *See, e.g.*, United States v. Wilson, 306 F.3d 231 (5th Cir. 2002); *but cf.* Vale v. Louisiana, 399 U.S. 30, 34 (1970) (prohibiting a warrantless search "incident to arrest" of the inside of a defendant's home when the defendant was arrested outside their home and near the entrance). At least in situations where officers have reasonable suspicion to believe a third person is inside the defendant's residence, *Vale* arguably is no longer good law in light of *Buie*, which was concerned with the danger posed by third persons as opposed to the defendant.

170. *Compare, e.g.*, United States v. Gould, 364 F.3d 578 (5th Cir. 2004) (en banc) (permitting protective sweep), *with* United States v. Torres-Castro, 470 F.3d 992, 997 (10th Cir. 2006) (not permitting it).

171. *See* Illinois v. Lafayette, 462 U.S. 640 (1983); South Dakota v. Opperman, 428 U.S. 364 (1976).

Amendment the court must suppress the fruits of the search.[172] Even if a law enforcement agency has an established inventory policy, the failure of such a policy to cover whether police may open closed containers as part of the inventory requires suppression of evidence discovered when officers opened closed containers during an inventory search.[173]

5.3.2.7 "Regulatory" Searches and Other "Special Circumstances" Searches

As a result of certain "special circumstances" that the framers of the Fourth Amendment could not have envisioned in the late 1700s, the modern Supreme Court has carved out certain categorical exceptions to the Fourth Amendment's warrant requirement in light of modern realities. In addition, in many of these cases, neither probable cause nor reasonable suspicion is required for such a search.[174]

For instance, the Court has held that "closely regulated businesses"—businesses traditionally subject to close governmental inspection, such as liquor stores or pawnshops that sell firearms—may be routinely searched without a warrant or probable cause if authorized by the legislature.[175]

Similarly, in other areas where there is a "special need" for governmental oversight and where "important non-law enforcement purposes" exist,[176] the Court has held that a warrant is unnecessary. For example, persons entering airports or public buildings may be searched without a warrant and without any level of suspicion, and K–12 public school students wishing to participate in extracurricular activities may be subjected to random drug tests.[177] Lower courts increasingly have upheld warrantless, suspicionless "terrorism" searches in public places like subways.[178] Even in the law enforcement context, there are certain areas where the Court has found special needs for searches without a warrant. For example, prisoners' persons and cells may be searched without a warrant,[179] and persons on probation or parole are subject to warrantless searches of their bodies and residences without probable cause (although reasonable suspicion is required for searches of probationers).[180] In other situations where there is a "law enforcement purpose"—even if other state interests exist as well—both probable cause and a warrant may be required absent exigent circumstances.[181]

---

172. Colorado v. Bertine, 479 U.S. 367 (1987).
173. Florida v. Wells, 495 U.S. 1, 4–5 (1990).
174. *See generally* United States v. Kincade, 379 F.3d 813, 822–24 (9th Cir. 2004) (en banc).
175. *See, e.g.*, New York v. Burger, 482 U.S. 691, 700–01 (1987).
176. *Kincade*, 379 F.3d at 823.
177. *Id.* at 822–23.
178. MacWade v. Kelly, 460 F.3d 260 (2d Cir. 2006).
179. *Kincade*, 379 F.3d at 822–23.
180. *See* Samson v. California, 547 U.S. 843 (2006) (parolees); United States v. Knights, 534 U.S. 112 (2001) (probationers).
181. *See, e.g.*, Roe v. Tex. Dep't of Protective and Regulatory Services, 299 F.3d 395, 406–08 (5th

5.3.2.8 Border Searches

In recent decades, the Supreme Court increasingly has been willing to allow law enforcement to engage in warrantless searches at or near the U.S. borders. At international borders leading into the United States,[182] federal immigration and customs officials may engage in warrantless searches and seizures of persons driving, flying, or walking into or out of the United States.[183] The degree of intrusiveness of such searches depends on the degree of suspicion that officials possess.[184]

For "routine" border searches (such as patting down a person, or searching their carryon luggage), officials need not articulate any reason at all; for "nonroutine" border searches (subjecting a person to an x-ray of their body or a body-cavity search, for example), officials need only articulate "reasonable suspicion" and do not need probable cause or a warrant.[185] The line between routine and non-routine searches is often a difficult one to draw. For instance, the Court has held that officials at the border who dismantled a car's gas tank (revealing marijuana hidden inside) engaged in a mere routine search that did not require reasonable suspicion as long as no permanent damage occurred to the car.[186]

In addition to allowing for such warrantless "border searches," the Court permits warrantless, suspicionless seizures of persons driving in relatively close proximity of the border who approach fixed immigration checkpoints.[187] However, such searches, unlike more sweeping border searches, must be brief and limited in scope and duration. Officials are limited to asking "a brief question or two" about the driver and passengers' immigration status and requesting documentation evidencing a right to be in the United States.[188] Without reasonable suspicion or probable cause, officials who go beyond such limited questioning while persons are still being seized at the checkpoint violate the Fourth Amendment; any evidence or incriminating statements obtained thereafter will be suppressed.[189] If officials wish to stop cars driving within a close proximity of the border (but not at a fixed checkpoint)

Cir. 2002) (probable cause and warrant required for a state social worker to strip-search a client where there were no exigent circumstances).

182. International airports located inside the United States are treated as the "functional equivalent" of an international border—thus subjecting incoming passengers to "border searches." United States v. De Gutierrez, 667 F.2d 16, 19 n.2 (5th Cir. 1982).

183. United States v. Odutayo, 406 F.3d 386 (5th Cir. 2005). For similar reasons, the Supreme Court has said that international mail—as opposed to domestic first-class mail—may be opened without a warrant and without any reasonable suspicion or probable cause. United States v. Ramsey, 431 U.S. 606 (1977).

184. *Gutierrez*, 667 F.2d at 19–20.

185. United States v. Flores-Montano, 541 U.S. 149 (2004); United States v. Montoya de Hernandez, 473 U.S. 531 (1985); *see also* Bradley v. United States, 299 F.3d 197, 203 (3d Cir. 2002).

186. *Flores-Montano*, 541 U.S. at 150–55.

187. United States v. Martinez-Fuerte, 428 U.S. 543 (1976).

188. *Id.* at 558.

189. *See, e.g.*, United States v. Portillo-Aguirre, 311 F.3d 647 (5th Cir. 2002).

and question the car's occupants, they must possess "reasonable suspicion" that the car contains illegal aliens or contraband or the driver or passengers otherwise have violated the law.[190]

5.3.2.9 Entries into Residences to Execute Arrest Warrants or in "Hot Pursuit" of Fleeing Felons

An officer is permitted to enter a defendant's residence to arrest the defendant pursuant to a felony or misdemeanor arrest warrant without a separate search warrant authorizing entry into the residence.[191] Any incriminating evidence or contraband in the residence that is in "plain view" and whose evidentiary value is "immediately apparent" may be seized by the arresting officer without a search warrant.[192] Conversely, an officer generally may not enter a third-party's house to execute an arrest warrant for a person who is in the third-party's home on a temporary basis without a separate search warrant.[193] The exception to this rule—as well as an exception to the rule that an officer may not enter a suspected felon's own home to arrest him without an arrest warrant—is that an officer may enter a home without a search warrant if the officer is in "hot pursuit" of a fleeing felon who has gone into the home.[194]

5.3.2.10 Consensual Searches

As a general rule, if a person voluntarily consents to a search or seizure, then no warrant (and no probable cause or reasonable suspicion) is required.[195] According to the Supreme Court, consent is valid if it is an "essentially free and unconstrained choice by its maker"; that is, the person who gives consent must not have their "will . . . overborne."[196] This is similar to the constitutional test applied to confessions in evaluating their voluntariness.[197] A defendant has standing to object that a third

---

190. Almeida-Sanchez v. United States, 413 U.S. 266 (1973); United States v. Brignoni-Ponce, 422 U.S. 873 (1975).

191. Payton v. New York, 445 U.S. 573, 603 (1980); *see also* United States v. Ray, 199 F. Supp. 2d 1104, 1112 (D. Kan. 2002) (*Payton*, although it discussed felony arrest warrants, applies equally to misdemeanor arrest warrants) (citing cases). If the officers have no arrest warrant, then they may not ordinarily enter the residence and any evidence seized within the home will be suppressed. *Payton*, 445 U.S. at 603.

192. *Payton*, 445 U.S. at 603.

193. Steagald v. United States, 451 U.S. 204 (1981).

194. Welsh v. Wisconsin, 466 U.S. 740 (1984). The Supreme Court in *Welsh* suggested—and most lower courts have agreed—that "hot pursuit" of a fleeing misdemeanant ordinarily would not justify a warrantless entry into a residence in which the defendant has entered. *Id.* at 750–53 & n.11; *see also* Patzner v. Burkett, 779 F.2d 1363 (8th Cir. 1985).

195. Schneckloth v. Bustamonte, 412 U.S. 218 (1973). Whether consent is voluntary is a factual finding made by a trial court that is entitled to deference on appeal. *Id.* at 248–49.

196. *Id.* at 225.

197. *Id.* at 225–27. The issue of whether a confession is voluntary is discussed in Chapter Six.

person's consent was involuntary if the defendant possessed a privacy or possessory interest in the place searched or item seized pursuant to the third-party's consent.[198]

Whether consent is voluntary requires a court to examine the totality of the circumstances—both the characteristics of the person who gave consent (his age, intelligence, education, prior experience with law enforcement, etc.) and whether the officer who obtained consent engaged in improper behavior (such as making threats or promises).[199] Every case is analyzed based on its own unique facts.[200] Consent is not rendered involuntary simply because the person giving consent was in custody, although the fact that a person was in custody when giving consent is a factor that militates in favor of finding that the consent was involuntary.[201] In addition, just because a suspect knew that a police officer's search would yield contraband or incriminating evidence does not render consent involuntary.[202]

One instance in which consent is rendered per se invalid is when police officers falsely claim that they possess a search warrant when in fact they do not.[203] That situation should be distinguished from one where a police officer states that they "will" or "could" obtain a warrant and that consent should be given to obviate the need for applying for a warrant. With respect to the latter scenario, lower courts have reached divergent results.[204]

The Supreme Court repeatedly has held that to be constitutionally valid, a person's consent need not be "knowing"; it only needs to be "voluntary." That is, the person giving consent need not know that they have a right to refuse consent with impunity.[205] Nonetheless, whether the person knew that they had a right to refuse consent is one of many factors considered by a court in assessing whether consent was voluntary.[206]

When a person gives consent to search, the officers' search is limited in scope to what a reasonable person would have anticipated in giving such consent.[207] Thus,

---

198. Bumper v. North Carolina, 391 U.S. 543, 548 n.11 (1968); *see also* Rakas v. Illinois, 439 U.S. 128, 136 (1978).

199. *Schneckloth*, 412 U.S. at 226–27.

200. *Id.* For an excellent primer on whether consent is valid, see Jimmie E. Tinsley, *Consent to Search Given Under Coercive Circumstances*, 26 Am. Jur. Proof of Facts 2d 465 (2004 update).

201. *See* United States v. Watson, 423 U.S. 411 (1976); *see also* United States v. Kelley, 981 F.2d 1464, 1470 (5th Cir. 1993).

202. Florida v. Bostick, 501 U.S. 429, 437–38 (1991).

203. *Bumper*, 391 U.S. at 549–550.

204. *See, e.g.*, United States v. Savage, 459 F.2d 60 (5th Cir. 1972) (holding that the officer's statement that he "probably" would be able to obtain a warrant did not render the consent invalid); Whitman v. State, 336 A.2d 515, 530–31 (Md. App. 1975) (police officer's statement that "we can get [a warrant]" rendered the defendant's consent invalid).

205. *Schneckloth*, 412 U.S. at 246; *see also* Ohio v. Robinette, 519 U.S. 33 (1996); United States v. Drayton, 536 U.S. 194 (2002).

206. *Schneckloth*, 412 U.S. at 226–27.

207. Florida v. Jimeno, 500 U.S. 248 (1991) (consent to search car for drugs includes consent to search closed containers that could contain drugs).

for example, a police officer who generally asked to search a person's car for drugs would, from an objective standpoint, exceed the reasonable scope of such consent by slashing open the spare tire.[208] When officers destroy property during a consensual search, they exceed the scope of consent that only was general in nature and did not specifically permit or anticipate property destruction from an objective standpoint.[209]

An issue that commonly arises regarding consensual searches is when a third person consents to a search that yields incriminating evidence against a defendant. The Supreme Court has held that whether a third person has authority to consent depends on the circumstances of each case.[210] Generally speaking, co-inhabitants with "common authority" over a residence or a car have authority to consent, while third persons such as landlords, hotel clerks, and babysitters do not.[211] Common authority means "mutual use of the property by persons generally having joint access or control for most purposes, so that it is reasonable to recognize that any of the co-inhabitants has the right to permit the inspection in their own right and that the others have assumed the risk that one of their number might permit the common area to be searched."[212] "Common authority is, of course, not to be implied from the mere property interest a third party has in the property. The authority which justifies the third-party consent does not rest upon the law of property, with its attendant historical and legal refinements . . ."[213] A person with an equal or superior interest in a particular property may veto a co-occupant's consent, thus preventing a warrantless search by officers,[214] but only if such a veto occurs *contemporaneously* with the co-occupant's purported consent and where the person objecting is physically present.[215]

A related issue is when a third party possesses "apparent authority"—but in fact lacks actual authority—to give consent.[216] The Supreme Court has held that such third-party consent is valid as long as the police officers who obtained the third-party consent had an objectively reasonable basis for believing that the third party possessed authority to consent.[217] However, the officer's belief must be an objectively reasonable one based on a factual (as opposed to legal) mistake.[218] Thus, if the officers reasonably, but mistakenly, believe that as a matter of law a third person

---

208. United States v. Strickland, 902 F.2d 937, 941–42 (11th Cir. 1990).

209. *See* United States v. Osage, 235 F.3d 518 (10th Cir. 2000).

210. United States v. Matlock, 415 U.S. 164 (1974).

211. *Id.* at 170–71.

212. *Id.* at 171 n.7.

213. *Id.*

214. Georgia v. Randolph, 547 U.S. 103 (2006).

215. Fernandez v. California, 571 U.S. 292, 303-05 (2014).

216. *See* Illinois v. Rodriguez, 497 U.S. 177 (1990).

217. *Id.* at 185–86.

218. *See, e.g.*, United States v. Welch, 4 F.3d 761, 764–65 (9th Cir. 1993); United States v. Whitfield, 939 F.2d 1071, 1074 (D.C. Cir. 1991).

has authority to consent when in fact the third person does not possess such authority (e.g., a minor babysitter who answers the door, identifies herself as such, and purports to give consent when she has no such legal authority), then the third-party consent is invalid.[219]

5.3.3 Exceptions to the Arrest Warrant Requirement

5.3.3.1 Felony Arrests in Public

The Supreme Court has held that a warrantless arrest of a person in public (as opposed to their residence) always is reasonable under the Fourth Amendment if the officers have probable cause to believe that the defendant is committing a felony offense or has committed a felony offense in the past.[220] "Public" includes a person's voluntary exposure of themself at the threshold of an open door of their residence (in response to police officers' knocking on the door).[221] The lower courts are divided over whether this rule applies if a defendant came to the door based on a ruse or subterfuge by police officers.[222]

With respect to warrantless misdemeanor arrests based on probable cause, the Court has held that such arrests can occur in public if the defendant is presently committing the misdemeanor offense; however, the Court has left open the question of whether police can arrest a defendant in public without a warrant for past misdemeanor offenses.[223] If the Court continues its current trend in Fourth Amendment cases toward adopting uniformly applied common-law rules concerning searches and seizures that existed at the time that the Fourth Amendment was promulgated,[224] it is likely that the Court will hold that warrantless arrests of persons for past misdemeanor offenses is unconstitutional even if an officer possessed probable cause.[225]

---

219. State v. Tonroy, 92 P.3d 1116, 1120 (Kan. App. 2004).
220. United States v. Watson, 423 U.S. 411 (1976).
221. United States v. Santana, 427 U.S. 38 (1976).
222. *See, e.g.*, United States v. Johnson, 626 F.2d 753 (9th Cir. 1980) (police officer who gets a defendant to open a door by a ruse or subterfuge cannot arrest defendant who opens the door without a warrant), *aff'd on other grounds*, 457 U.S. 537 (1982); People v. Fernandez, 599 N.Y.S.2d 405, 408–10 (N.Y. Super. Ct. 1993) (police officer may use "noncoercive subterfuge" to get person to come to door, but may not use a ruse that coerces a defendant to open the door).
223. Atwater v. City of Lago Vista, 532 U.S. 318, 340–41 n.11 (2001).
224. *See, e.g.*, Wilson v. Arkansas, 514 U.S. 927 (1995).
225. In *Atwater*, the Court cited myriad founding-era common law authorities for this proposition. *See Atwater*, 532 U.S. at 328–45; *see also* Snyder v. United States, 285 F. 1, 2 (4th Cir. 1922) ("That an officer may not make an arrest for a misdemeanor not committed in [their] presence, without a warrant, has been so frequently decided as not to require citation of authority."); *see also* William A. Schroeder, *Warrantless Misdemeanor Arrests and the Fourth Amendment*, 58 Mo. L. Rev. 771, 774 (Fall 1993). In dicta, the Court repeatedly has held that warrantless misdemeanor arrests are valid only when the defendant has committed the offense in the presence of the officer. *See, e.g.*, Maryland v. Pringle, 540 U.S. 366, 370 (2003) ("A warrantless arrest of an individual in a public place for

5.3.3.2 Temporary Detention of a Residence's Occupants During Application for, or Execution of, a Search Warrant

Police officers are permitted, without an arrest warrant, to temporarily detain a person and prohibit that person from entering their residence for a reasonable amount of time needed to apply for a search warrant when officers possess probable cause to believe that there is incriminating evidence or contraband inside the residence.[226]

When officers execute a search warrant for incriminating evidence or contraband in a residence, they also are permitted under the Fourth Amendment to temporarily detain all occupants inside and nearby the residence (without separate arrest warrants) for a reasonable amount of time pending the completion of the search.[227] However, officers cannot detain persons who are not in the immediate area of the residence in which a search warrant was being executed without a separate arrest warrant or other valid basis to detain them.[228] Although officers may detain all persons in or closely nearby the premises during the execution of a search warrant, the officers may not search the detained persons without a separate warrant; officers may, however, "pat down" anyone where there is "reasonable suspicion" to believe that the suspect is armed and poses a danger to police officers.[229]

5.3.3.3 Roadblocks

Outside of the international border context (discussed above), the Supreme Court has been less willing to permit "checkpoints" or "roadblocks" of cars for non-immigration purposes. Roadblocks for general "crime control"—e.g., roadblocks at which police officers are looking for evidence of drugs or illegal guns—are unconstitutional.[230] Roadblocks seeking to curtail drunk drivers or unlicensed drivers are the limited exception to this rule; they are constitutional as long as uniformed officers stop all motorists or a specific percentage of motorists (e.g., one in five) who approach the roadblock and as long as the duration of the stop is limited to determining whether motorists are licensed or under the influence of alcohol or drugs.[231]

However, police officers may not randomly stop motorists to check their licenses or determine whether they are driving under the influence without at least reasonable suspicion of a crime.[232] Roadblocks at which police officers briefly question

---

a felony, or a misdemeanor committed in the officer's presence, is consistent with the Fourth Amendment if the arrest is supported by probable cause.").

226. Illinois v. McArthur, 531 U.S. 326 (2001).
227. Michigan v. Summers, 452 U.S. 692 (1981).
228. *See* Bailey v. United States, 568 U.S. 186 (2013).
229. Ybarra v. Illinois, 444 U.S. 85, 94 (1979).
230. City of Indianapolis v. Edmond, 531 U.S. 32 (2000).
231. Michigan Dep't of State Police v. Sitz, 496 U.S. 444 (1990).
232. Delaware v. Prouse, 440 U.S. 648 (1979).

National Institute for Trial Advocacy

persons about whether they witnessed a crime that occurred in the area also pass constitutional muster so long as the stops are brief in duration.[233]

5.3.3.4   *Terry* "Stop and Frisk" Encounters and "Investigatory Detentions"

Perhaps the most sweeping exception to the Fourth Amendment's warrant and probable cause requirements was created in 1968 by the Supreme Court in *Terry v. Ohio*.[234] The Court in *Terry* held that under the Fourth Amendment it is "reasonable" for a law enforcement officer without a warrant to temporarily detain[235] and question a person when the officer has "reasonable suspicion" that the person is about to engage in or is engaging in criminal activity.[236] The Court has extended *Terry*'s holding to investigations of past, completed felonies, but has reserved judgment on whether a *Terry* stop and frisk is reasonable under the Fourth Amendment when an officer is investigating a past misdemeanor.[237] The lower courts are divided on that issue.[238]

For reasonable suspicion to exist, the "officer must be able to point to specific and articulable facts which, taken together with rational inferences from those facts," justify a brief detention and questioning.[239] This standard, which is less than probable cause, is an objective one—"would the facts available to the officer at the moment . . . 'warrant a man of reasonable caution in the belief' that the action taken was appropriate?"[240] Mere subjective "hunches" of an officer—even if possessed in good faith—are insufficient.[241] However, courts determining whether reasonable suspicion existed must afford some degree of deference to law enforcement officers in their inferences from the facts known to them.[242] *Terry*'s authorization of warrantless "investigative detentions" has been extended to a variety of situations

---

233. Illinois v. Lidster, 540 U.S. 419 (2004).

234. Terry v. Ohio, 392 U.S. 1 (1968).

235. The degree of restraint permitted during a *Terry* stop has divided the lower courts and has not yet been addressed with clarity by the Supreme Court. Some courts hold that officers' pointing guns and handcuffing a suspect during an investigatory detention does not transform the *Terry* stop into a full-fledged arrest (which would require probable cause and not merely reasonable suspicion). *See, e.g.*, United States v. Jacob, 377 F.3d 573, 579 (6th Cir. 2004); Thomas v. Commonwealth, 434 S.E.2d 319, 323 (Va. Ct. App. 1993). Other courts, however, have held that such actions by police officers ordinarily will exceed the limited bounds of a valid *Terry* stop. *See, e.g.*, United States v. Del Vizo, 918 F.2d 821, 825 (9th Cir. 1990).

236. *Terry*, 392 U.S. at 21–22; *but cf.* Dunaway v. New York, 442 U.S. 200 (1979) (*Terry* stops cannot extend to full-fledged custody for interrogation/investigation without probable cause).

237. United States v. Hensley, 469 U.S. 221, 229 (1985) ("We need not and do not decide today whether *Terry* stops to investigate all past crimes, however serious, are permitted. It is enough to say that, if police have a reasonable suspicion, grounded in specific and articulable facts, that a person they encounter was involved in or is wanted in connection with a completed felony, then a *Terry* stop may be made to investigate that suspicion.").

238. *See* United States v. Grigg, 498 F.3d 1070, 1075–79 (9th Cir. 2007) (citing conflicting cases).

239. *Terry*, 392 U.S. at 21.

240. *Id*. at 21–22.

241. *Id*. at 22.

242. United States v. Arvizu, 534 U.S. 266, 273–74 (2002).

by the Supreme Court in the past three decades, including temporary seizures of property as well as persons.[243] Because its standard is relatively low, "*Terry* accepts the risk that officers may stop innocent people."[244] What constitutes reasonable suspicion—and how it contrasts with probable cause—is discussed further below.

In addition to allowing such brief "stops" of suspicious persons, *Terry* also permits "frisks" of the detained persons' outer clothing where there is reasonable suspicion that the person is armed and dangerous.[245] "[G]eneral exploratory searches" for evidence are not permitted.[246] Any information or evidence that gives an officer probable cause that is discovered during such a limited stop-and-frisk will permit a full-fledged warrantless arrest and a warrantless seizure of incriminating evidence or contraband discovered in the course of a *Terry* frisk.[247]

At the time *Terry* was decided, only one justice—William O. Douglas, perhaps the most liberal member in the Court's history—dissented.[248] He contended that *Terry*'s stop-and-frisk rule violated the plain language of the Fourth Amendment, which spoke of "probable cause," as well as the historical understanding of the amendment.[249] Ironically, one of the Court's most conservative members, Justice Scalia, made a similar argument, at least regarding the "frisk" portion of *Terry*—i.e., that at the time of the amendment's adoption, all searches required probable cause and nothing less.[250] Whether *Terry*'s frisk rule will survive in an era when the Court increasingly defines the minimal constitutional protections afforded under the Bill of Rights by what the founding-era common law provided remains to be seen.

A common issue that arises in the context of *Terry* stops is whether information that rose to the level of probable cause (thus allowing for a full-fledged arrest) was developed during the course of a *Terry* stop or, instead, was developed after the stop should have ended.[251] The Supreme Court has held that police officers who engage in *Terry* stops must "diligently pursue[] a means of investigation that [is] likely to confirm or dispel their suspicions quickly"; a *Terry* stop thus may last only as long

---

243. *See, e.g.*, Arvizu, 534 U.S. 266; United States v. Sokolow, 490 U.S. 1 (1989); United States v. Sharpe, 470 U.S. 675 (1985); United States v. Cortez, 449 U.S. 411 (1981). In United States v. Place, 462 U.S. 696 (1983), the Court held that law enforcement officers have a right to temporarily seize property without a warrant for a reasonable amount of time upon mere reasonable suspicion. *Id.* at 702–07.

244. Illinois v. Wardlow, 528 U.S. 119, 126 (2000).

245. *Terry*, 392 U.S. at 24–29.

246. *Id.* at 30.

247. *Id.*

248. *Id.* at 35 (Douglas, J., dissenting).

249. *Id.* at 35–38 (Douglas, J., dissenting).

250. Minnesota v. Dickerson, 508 U.S. 366, 379–82 (1993) (Scalia, J., concurring) (noting that at the time the Fourth Amendment was adopted, the common law would not have permitted warrantless searches based on anything less than probable cause).

251. *See, e.g.*, United States v. Brigham, 382 F.3d 500 (5th Cir. 2004) (en banc).

National Institute for Trial Advocacy

as it is reasonably needed to effectuate the purpose of the stop.[252] Therefore, once an officer's suspicion is dispelled from an objective standpoint or it is clear that the suspect will not dispel or confirm the suspicion (as when the suspect refuses to talk to the officer), then any search or seizure thereafter violates the Fourth Amendment and any evidentiary fruits derived therefrom must be suppressed.[253] However, there are no bright lines in terms of how long a *Terry* stop may last in order to determine whether it was reasonable under the Fourth Amendment.[254] Each case must be judged based on its own unique set of facts.[255]

5.4 "Probable Cause" Versus "Reasonable Suspicion"

"Articulating precisely what 'reasonable suspicion' and 'probable cause' mean is not possible. They are commonsense, nontechnical conceptions that deal with the factual and practical considerations of everyday life on which reasonable and prudent [people], not legal technicians, act."[256] The Supreme Court has vaguely defined "probable cause" as existing "where the known facts and circumstances are sufficient to warrant a man of reasonable prudence in the belief" that a crime was committed by the defendant or contraband or other incriminating evidence is present in a particular place.[257] The standard for "reasonable suspicion" is equally vague, but even less demanding—"a particularized and objective basis for suspecting [a] person . . . of criminal activity."[258] Neither requires even a preponderance of the evidence.[259] Either probable cause or reasonable suspicion can be based on the "collective knowledge" of multiple police officers, at least when there is actual communication between the officers (e.g., one officer, who has probable cause to arrest the defendant, radios another officer, who knows only the defendant's identity, and asks that officer to arrest the defendant).[260]

Both probable cause and reasonable suspicion must be assessed based on a "totality of the circumstances" known to a police officer, and both are analyzed from an objective standpoint.[261] At least with respect to probable cause, an officer's

---

252. *Sharpe*, 470 U.S. at 686.
253. *See, e.g.*, United States v. Martin, 679 F. Supp. 2d 723 (W.D. La. 2010) (suppressing evidence obtained after *Terry* stop should have ended).
254. *Sharpe*, 470 U.S. at 685–86.
255. *Id.*
256. Ornelas v. United States, 517 U.S. 690, 695 (1996) (internal quotation marks and citations omitted).
257. *Id.* at 695–96.
258. *Id.* at 696.
259. *Pringle*, 540 U.S. at 371; *see also* Kansas v. Glover, 140 S. Ct. 1183, 1188 (2020) ("The reasonable suspicion inquiry 'falls considerably short' of 51% accuracy."); District of Columbia v. Wesby, 138 S. Ct. 577, 586 (2018) ("Probable cause is not a high bar.") (citation and internal quotation marks omitted).
260. *See, e.g.*, United States v. Pardue, 385 F.3d 101, 106–07 (1st Cir. 2004).
261. Illinois v. Gates, 462 U.S. 213, 230 (1983) (probable cause); *Arvizu*, 534 U.S. at 273 (reasonable suspicion).

subjective state of mind is irrelevant as long as objectively the facts known to the officer rise to the level of probable cause.[262] Often the determination of whether probable cause or reasonable suspicion existed turns on factual minutiae.[263]

The Supreme Court repeatedly held that the legal standards governing both probable cause and reasonable suspicion allow for certain types of reasonable mistakes of fact or law by police officers. In particular, probable cause or reasonable suspicion can be based on:

- a police officer's reasonable mistake of fact about the identity of a perpetrator of an alleged crime;[264]

- a police officer's reasonable mistake of fact about whether they were searching the specific premises named in the search warrant;[265]

- a police officer's reasonable mistake of law (for example, whether a driver of a car had violated a particular traffic law when the state of the law was not clear at the time of the traffic stop);[266] and

- a police officer's reasonable reliance on a penal statute, the defendant's violation of which resulted in a warrantless arrest and search incident to arrest, when the penal statute was only later declared invalid by a court.[267]

Although both probable cause and reasonable suspicion are "not finely tuned standards" and thus "not readily . . reduced to a neat set of legal rules,"[268] a few rules of general application may be derived from the Supreme Court's jurisprudence.

---

262. Whren v. United States, 517 U.S. 806, 811–19 (1996); *see also* Devenpeck v. Alford, 543 U.S. 146 (2004). The lower courts are divided over whether such a purely objective test applies to reasonable suspicion. *Compare* Cole v. State, 562 S.E.2d 720, 724 (Ga. App. 2002) (dissenting opinion's criticism of majority's purely "objective" test concerning reasonable suspicion without any consideration of whether officer subjectively possessed any suspicion), *with* State v. Lear, 722 A.2d 1266, 1267–68 (Me. 1998) ("The court must find that the officer actually entertained the suspicion" before such suspicion can be deemed reasonable from an objective standpoint.). In *Whren*, the Court held that "pretextual" searches and seizures are valid as long as probable cause existed from an objective standpoint. That is, as long as an objective reason for the stop rises to the level of probable cause (*e.g.*, the defendant ran a stop sign), then police may stop the defendant even if officer's actual motive is to investigate another offense where no reasonable suspicion or probable cause concerning that other offense exists. *Whren*, 517 U.S. at 811–19.
263. *E.g., compare* United States v. Person, 134 F. Supp. 2d 517 (E.D.N.Y. 2001) (finding no reasonable suspicion existed at the time of the *Terry* stop), *with* United States v. Valentine, 232 F.3d 350 (3d Cir. 2000) (finding that reasonable suspicion existed in a case with similar facts).
264. Hill v. California, 401 U.S. 797 (1971).
265. Maryland v. Garrison, 480 U.S. 79 (1987); *see also* Los Angeles Cnty. v. Rettele, 550 U.S. 609 (2007) (per curiam).
266. Heien v. North Carolina, 574 U.S. 54 (2014) (no Fourth Amendment violation).
267. Michigan v. DeFillippo, 443 U.S. 31 (1979).
268. *Ornelas*, 517 U.S. at 695–96 (citations and internal quotation marks omitted).

First, a person's mere presence near criminal activity or mere association with criminals by itself does not give rise to probable cause.[269] Although such presence or association (at least where close in proximity) may or may not permit an officer to engage in a brief *Terry* stop (to ask questions about the close association), it does not by itself justify a *Terry* frisk unless the officer had reasonable suspicion to believe that the associate is armed.[270] Additional facts beyond mere association are required to establish probable cause.[271]

Second, an "anonymous tip" to police officers (usually done via telephone) that a defendant possesses contraband such as a gun or drugs—without any corroboration or specific predictive information[272]—is not sufficient by itself to establish probable cause or reasonable suspicion.[273] An apparent exception to this rule is when a stranger gives a police officer a detailed tip face-to-face.[274] Information from a police "informant" (a known person who provides the police with information about alleged crimes), whose reliability is established and whose information is specific, is sufficient to provide reasonable suspicion[275] and usually probable cause.[276] Third,

---

269. United States v. Di Re, 332 U.S. 581, 593 (1948).

270. Ybarra v. Illinois, 444 U.S. 85, 91–93 (1979); Sibron v. New York, 392 U.S. 40, 62 (1968); *see also* Illinois v. Wardlow, 528 U.S. 119, 124 (2000) ("An individual's presence in an area of expected criminal activity, standing alone, is not enough to support a reasonable, particularized suspicion that the person is committing a crime."). Notwithstanding these cases, some lower courts have permitted *Terry* stops and frisks of companions of persons for whom there is probable cause to arrest or reasonable suspicion for a *Terry* stop and frisk. *See, e.g.*, United States v. Berryhill, 445 F.2d 1189, 1192–93 (9th Cir. 1971). Such cases appear to conflict with *Ybarra* and *Sibron*. *See* United States v. Bell, 762 F.2d 495, 498–99 (6th Cir. 1985).

271. Maryland v. Pringle, 540 U.S. 366, 373 (2003) (defendant's presence in car as a passenger along with two others at 3:16 a.m., when car contained a large amount of money and a large quantity of cocaine packaged for sale in a manner that was accessible to all three men, provided probable cause to arrest all three men); *see also id.* (distinguishing *Ybarra*, *Sibron*, and *Di Re* as involving mere association and nothing more).

272. *See* Alabama v. White, 496 U.S. 325 (1990) (anonymous tip that correctly predicted specific actions of defendant provided reasonable suspicion once the predictive information was proved to be correct; at that point, reliability of tipster was sufficiently established).

273. Florida v. J.L., 529 U.S. 266 (2000). In Navarette v. California, 572 U.S. 393 (2014), a divided Court found that reasonable suspicion existed when an anonymous caller called 911 and reported that a suspected drunk driver had just run the caller off the road. A police officer located the suspected driver at a point down the road that corresponded to the distance that the car would have traveled since the 911 call was made. *Id.* at 398–404.

274. *See, e.g.*, State v. Mann, 857 A.2d 329, 346–47 (Conn. 2004).

275. Adams v. Williams, 407 U.S. 143 (1972) (known informant, who had given reliable information previously, provided information that gave an officer the right to engage in a *Terry* stop and frisk).

276. Illinois v. Gates, 462 U.S. 213 (1983) (discussing when informants' allegations rise to the level of probable cause); *see also* Taylor v. Alabama, 457 U.S. 687 (1982) (finding informant's reliability not established and that their information was not detailed enough to establish probable cause). As a general rule, the prosecution is not constitutionally required to reveal the identity of a confidential informant during a pretrial hearing on a motion to suppress at which the reliability of the informant is challenged by the defense. McCray v. Illinois, 386 U.S. 300, 312–14 (1967); *but cf.* Roviaro v. United States, 353 U.S. 53 (1957) (in federal prosecutions, establishing the nonconstitutional rule

a person's unprovoked "flight" (as opposed to merely walking away) from a police officer—at least in a "high crime" area—by itself is sufficient to provide reasonable suspicion (but not probable cause).[277] An officer possesses reasonable suspicion that an unknown driver of an automobile is the registered owner—thus permitting a stop of the car when a police computer check of the car's license plate showed that the registered owner had their license suspended.[278] Finally, an "alert" by a trained and certified police dog provides probable cause that there is illegal contraband for which the dog has been trained in the area where the dog alerted.[279]

Probable cause and reasonable suspicion may be based on hearsay evidence as long as it is sufficiently reliable.[280] Probable cause and reasonable suspicion also may be based on a defendant's confession given in violation of *Miranda v. Arizona,*[281] thus permitting a defendant to be detained or searched (at least where probable cause exists) based on a confession that will not be admissible in court.[282]

5.5   The Fourth Amendment "Exclusionary Rule"[283]

If an officer engages in an unconstitutional search or seizure, under the exclusionary rule, "any evidence that was obtained as a result of the Fourth Amendment violation ordinarily must be 'suppressed' (i.e., excluded) at trial."[284] The exclusionary rule also applies to "derivative" evidence or information, including a defendant's confession. According to the Supreme Court, such derivative evidence is "tainted fruit of the poisonous tree."[285] Thus, for example, if a defendant is arrested in violation of the Fourth Amendment and pursuant to a search (incident to the invalid arrest) the arresting officer discovers a pawn ticket for a stereo (which is later determined to have been stolen and pawned by the defendant), then the pawn ticket, the officer's testimony that the defendant possessed the pawn ticket, and the stereo must be suppressed.[286]

---

that the identity of informer must be disclosed if they have potentially relevant information that could aid the defense).

277. Illinois v. Wardlow, 528 U.S. 119 (2000).

278. Kansas v. Glover, 140 S. Ct. 1183 (2020).

279. Florida v. Harris, 568 U.S. 237 (2013).

280. Jones v. United States, 362 U.S. 257 (1960).

281. Miranda v. Arizona, 384 U.S. 436 (1966).

282. *See, e.g.,* United States v. Patterson, 812 F.2d 1188, 1193 (9th Cir. 1987).

283. Similar exclusionary rules exist in the context of confessions obtained in violation of the Fifth and Sixth Amendments. *See* Chapter Six.

284. Weeks v. United States, 232 U.S. 383 (1914); Mapp v. Ohio, 367 U.S. 643 (1961). A violation of a state law governing searches and seizures that does not also independently violate the Fourth Amendment is not a constitutional violation requiring suppression of the evidence under the Fourth Amendment exclusionary rule. *See* Virginia v. Moore, 553 U.S. 164 (2008).

285. Wong Sun v. United States, 371 U.S. 471 (1963); Silverthorne Lumber Co. v. United States, 251 U.S. 385 (1920).

286. *See, e.g.,* United States v. Hawkins, 49 C.M.R. 57 (A.C.M.R. 1974).

This "derivative evidence" component of the exclusionary rule is subject to a "taint attenuation" analysis with respect to certain types of evidence. Under *Brown v. Illinois*, if a defendant is unconstitutionally arrested and then confesses or consents to a search (that results in the discovery of incriminating evidence), the confession or fruits of the consensual search must be suppressed unless the prosecution can establish that the taint of the illegal arrest had "dissipated" by the time of the defendant's confession or consent.[287] *Brown's* four factors are: 1) the "temporal proximity" between the illegal arrest and the defendant's confession or consent-to-search; 2) whether *Miranda* warnings were read to the defendant; 3) whether any "intervening circumstances" occurred (such as the defendant's consultation with an attorney); and 4) the " flagrancy" of the Fourth Amendment violation involved in the illegal arrest.[288] A court must balance the four factors in determining whether the taint was sufficiently attenuated.[289] Conversely, if a defendant confesses or consents to a search following an unconstitutional search or seizure of physical evidence—and does so only after learning of the results of the search or seizure—then there is no taint attenuation analysis if the defendant establishes that the antecedent search or seizure in any way "induced" their confession or consent.[290] Similarly, the Court has found that the taint of an unconstitutional seizure of a person is sufficiently attenuated when a police officer discovers that the seized person has a valid preexisting arrest warrant. Any evidence discovered as an incident of the arrest that ensued is not excluded under the Fourth Amendment.[291]

The Supreme Court also has held that the trial testimony of a voluntarily appearing witness, discovered as a result of an unconstitutional search or seizure, ordinarily cannot be suppressed because the witness's free will in choosing to testify is sufficient to attenuate the taint of the antecedent Fourth Amendment violation.[292]

The Supreme Court has further held that a criminal defendant's body (as opposed to items found on their person) cannot be suppressed as a result of an unconstitutional arrest—meaning that the prosecution will not be barred simply because the defendant's presence in court was the result of an illegal arrest.[293] The Fourth Amendment exclusionary rule is subject to other limitations as well. Although

---

287. Brown v. Illinois, 422 U.S. 590 (1975) (setting forth four-part test regarding confessions following an illegal arrest); United States v. Vega, 221 F.3d 789, 801 (5th Cir. 2000) (applying *Brown* to a defendant's consent to search following an illegal arrest).

288. *Brown*, 422 U.S. at 603–04.

289. *Id.*

290. Fahy v. Connecticut, 375 U.S. 85, 90–91 (1963) (remanding so that the defendant could have "a chance to show that his admissions were induced by being confronted with the illegally seized evidence"); *see also* State v. Hodges, 851 P.2d 352, 363 (Kan. 1993); State v. Abdouch, 434 N.W.2d 317, 328 (Neb. 1989); State v. Pinder, 489 A.2d 653, 657 (N.H. 1985); People v. Robbins, 369 N.E.2d 577 (Ill. App. Ct. 1977).

291. Utah v. Strieff, 136 S. Ct. 2056 (2016).

292. United States v. Ceccolini, 435 U.S. 268 (1978).

293. United States v. Crews, 445 U.S. 463, 474 (1980).

the prosecution cannot use tainted evidence during its case-in-chief at a trial and further cannot use such evidence to impeach defense witnesses (other than the defendant, who can be impeached with tainted evidence),[294] such unconstitutionally seized evidence can be used at sentencing hearings and hearings to revoke probation or parole.[295]

If the prosecution can establish by a preponderance of the evidence that unconstitutionally obtained evidence "inevitably" would have been discovered in a legal manner (even without the illegal search or seizure)[296] or was lawfully obtained through an "independent source,"[297] then the evidence will not be suppressed under the exclusionary rule. A majority of lower courts have held that a court may not apply the inevitable discovery doctrine to a situation where the police easily could have obtained a warrant based on probable cause antedating the warrantless search or seizure, but simply did not do so.[298] Perhaps the greatest limitation on the operation of the Fourth Amendment exclusionary rule is the "good-faith exception" to the warrant requirement.[299]

In *United States v. Leon*, the Supreme Court held that if a court issued a search or arrest warrant that was not based on probable cause, then the fruits of the subsequent search or seizure will be admitted into evidence as long as the officer who executed the warrant acted in an "objectively reasonable" manner in relying on the invalid warrant.[300] However, if the officer either obtained the warrant through deliberate material falsehoods or omissions in their application or based their application on illegally seized evidence or information gained during an illegal search that was material to the probable cause determination, then the fruits of the search or seizure will be suppressed.[301] Furthermore, a warrant that is based on a "facially

---

294. James v. Illinois, 493 U.S. 307 (1990) (impeachment of third-party witness with illegally seized evidence not permitted); Walder v. United States, 347 U.S. 62 (1954) (impeachment of defendant with illegally seized evidence permitted).

295. Pennsylvania Board of Probation & Parole v. Scott, 524 U.S. 357 (1998).

296. *See, e.g.*, Speight v. United States, 671 A.2d 442, 454 (D.C. 1996) (incriminating evidence illegally seized during *Terry* stop and frisk inevitably would have been discovered in a lawful manner as a result of an independent development of probable cause that occurred during the same time period; evidence inevitably would have been discovered during a search incident to a legal arrest that would have occurred following the development of such independent probable cause).

297. *See, e.g.*, Murray v. United States, 487 U.S. 533 (1988) ("independent source" doctrine applies if police officers who unconstitutionally seized evidence without a warrant then applied for a search warrant based solely on probable cause known to the officers before the warrantless seizure).

298. *See, e.g.*, United States v. Mejia, 69 F.3d 309, 320 (9th Cir. 1995); United States v. Johnson, 22 F.3d 674, 683 (6th Cir. 1994); State v. Pearson, 682 N.E.2d 1086, 1094 (Ohio App. 1996); *but see* United States v. Harding, 273 F. Supp. 2d 411, 421–23 (S.D.N.Y. 2003).

299. United States v. Leon, 468 U.S. 897 (1984).

300. *Id.* at 905–26. A related principle under the Court's Fourth Amendment jurisprudence is that an officer's subjective belief that they lacked probable cause—when in fact they possessed probable cause from an objective point of view—will not void a search or seizure. Whren v. United States, 517 U.S. 806, 813 (1996); *cf.* Scott v. United States, 436 U.S. 128 (1978).

301. *Leon*, 468 U.S. at 923.

invalid" application—that is, one that clearly does not establish probable cause or clearly does not comply with the Fourth Amendment's "particularity" requirement—forecloses application of the good-faith exception.[302] In addition, the good-faith exception does not apply to a warrant issued by a judicial officer who was not "detached and neutral."[303]

An open question in the Court's Fourth Amendment jurisprudence that has divided the lower courts is to what degree *Leon*'s good-faith exception is applicable to *warrantless* searches or seizures.[304] In pre-*Leon* cases, the Court repeatedly rejected the notion that an officer's subjective "good faith" in engaging in a warrantless search or seizure justified the officer's actions if they lacked probable cause from an objective standpoint,[305] save the situation when an officer acting in good faith mistakenly arrested the wrong person when they possessed probable cause to arrest the actual suspect.[306] The Supreme Court's 2009 decision in *Herring v. United States*[307] suggests that the modern Court may be taking a significantly different path. In *Herring*, a bare majority of the Court held that a police officer's "negligent" mistaken belief that an arrest warrant existed for a defendant did not require suppression of the fruits of the illegal arrest under the Fourth Amendment exclusionary rule.[308]

Whether other types of negligent, but nonetheless good faith, violations of the Fourth Amendment when no warrant existed—such as an officer's negligent, mistaken belief that (as a matter of law) they possessed reasonable suspicion to engage in a *Terry* stop-and-frisk when, objectively, the facts (although close) did not amount to reasonable suspicion—will preclude application of the exclusionary rule is an open question.[309]

Finally, in *Davis v. United States*,[310] the Court held that the good-faith exception applies to warrantless searches that at the time they occurred were authorized (as constitutional) by binding appellate precedent—even if subsequently that precedent

---

302. *Id.*

303. United States v. Parker, 373 F.3d 770 (6th Cir. 2004).

304. *Compare* United States v. De Leon-Reyna, 930 F.2d 396, 399 (5th Cir. 1991) (en banc) (*Leon*'s good-faith exception applicable to warrantless searches and seizures), *with* United States v. Winsor, 846 F.2d 1569 (9th Cir. 1988) (good-faith exception only applicable to searches or seizures pursuant to warrants); Commonwealth v. Censullo, 661 N.E.2d 936 (Mass. App. Ct. 1996) (same).

305. *See, e.g.,* Beck v. Ohio, 379 U.S. 89, 97 (1964).

306. *See* Hill v. California, 401 U.S. 797 (1971) (officer's reasonable yet mistaken arrest of wrong person when he had probable cause to arrest the actual suspect upheld); *see also* Maryland v. Garrison, 480 U.S. 79 (1987) (officer's reasonable yet mistaken execution of search warrant on wrong apartment based on vagueness of search warrant upheld).

307. 555 U.S. 135 (2009).

308. *Id.* at 147.

309. In the pre-*Herring* era, most lower courts refused to apply *Leon* to such "good faith" warrantless situations. *See, e.g.,* United States v. Herrera, 444 F.3d 1238, 1251 (10th Cir. 2006).

310. Davis v. United States, 564 U.S. 229 (2011).

was overruled.[311] Although the warrantless search turned out to be unconstitutional (based on the subsequent decision), the good-faith exception applies, and the evidence obtained during the warrantless search is admissible.[312]

5.6 Leading Supreme Court Decisions Concerning Fourth Amendment Issues Raised by Pretrial Motions to Suppress

- *Wong Sun v. United States*, 371 U.S. 471 (1963) (leading case discussing "tainted fruit of the poisonous tree" doctrine).

- *Fahy v. Connecticut*, 375 U.S. 85, 90–91 (1963) (holding that when a defendant confessed only after "being confronted with . . . illegally seized evidence," that confession must be suppressed as tainted fruit if the confrontation "induced" the confession).

- *Warden v. Hayden*, 387 U.S. 294 (1967) (discussing "exigent circumstances" exception to Fourth Amendment's warrant requirement).

- *Katz v. United States*, 389 U.S. 347 (1967) (generally holding that the Fourth Amendment protects a defendant from warrantless searches that violate the "reasonable expectation of privacy"; specifically holding that a defendant possesses a reasonable expectation of privacy during a telephone conversation while in a public phone booth and that law enforcement officers may not monitor such conversations without prior judicial authorization and probable cause).

- *Terry v. Ohio*, 392 U.S. 1 (1968) (permitting a warrantless "stop and frisk" based on "reasonable suspicion"; refusing to demand a greater showing of "probable cause" for such a "limited" search and seizure).

- *United States v. White*, 401 U.S. 745 (1971) (defendant has no "reasonable expectation of privacy" in private conversation with a person who turns out to be an undercover police officer).

- *Schneckloth v. Bustamonte*, 412 U.S. 218 (1973) (a defendant's consent to permit a law enforcement officer to engage in a warrantless search or seizure must be "voluntary" consent for evidentiary fruits of the consensual search to be admissible; voluntariness is a factual question that a court determines by examining the "totality of the circumstances").

---

311. *Id.* at 240–47.
312. *Id.*

- *Shadwick v. City of Tampa*, 407 U.S. 345 (1972) (Fourth Amendment requires that a judge or magistrate issuing a warrant be "detached and neutral").

- *Cady v. Dombrowski*, 413 U.S. 433 (1973) (discussing the "community caretaker" exception to the Fourth Amendment's warrant requirement).

- *United States v. Matlock*, 415 U.S. 164 (1974) (holding that a third party with "common authority" over place or object—along with the defendant—may consent to a search or seizure of it by police; defendant's consent is not required if voluntary third-party consent given).

- *Brown v. Illinois*, 422 U.S. 590 (1975) (setting forth four-part standard governing when a defendant's confession or fruits of a consensual search following an illegal arrest must be suppressed).

- *United States v. Brignoni-Ponce*, 422 U.S. 873 (1975) (discussing "roving border patrols"; holding that "reasonable suspicion" that a car possesses illegal aliens or its driver or passengers otherwise have broken the law is required for warrantless stop; refusing to treat such stops as border searches not subject to any level of suspicion because they do not occur at the border or at a fixed checkpoint near the border).

- *United States v. Watson*, 423 U.S. 411 (1976) (a warrantless arrest of a defendant "in public" is constitutional as long as a law enforcement officer possessed probable cause to believe that the defendant in the past had committed, or was then committing, a felony offense or was then committing a misdemeanor offense in the presence of the officer).

- *United States v. Santana*, 427 U.S. 38 (1976) ("public" warrantless arrests under *Watson* include an arrest of a defendant who voluntarily opened the door of their residence and exposed themself to public view at the threshold of their residence).

- *United States v. Martinez-Fuerte*, 428 U.S. 543 (1976) (temporary warrantless detention of a person or car at international border or a fixed checkpoint reasonably near the border by immigration officials is constitutional for the limited purpose of determining citizenship or immigration status of detained individuals; no level of suspicion required to temporarily detain for this limited purpose, although reasonable suspicion or probable cause required for more extended detentions).

- *United States v. Ceccolini*, 435 U.S. 268 (1978) (discussing when the testimony of a third-party witness discovered only as the result of an unconstitutional search or seizure may be suppressed; holding that as a general matter testimony of third-party witness will not be suppressed as tainted fruit as long as the testimony is an act of free will by the witness).

- *Zurcher v. Stanford Daily*, 436 U.S. 547 (1978) (search warrant may be directed at persons who are not accused of a crime).

- *Franks v. Delaware*, 438 U.S. 154 (1978) (when a police officer knowingly or recklessly included affirmative falsehoods or omitted relevant facts in an affidavit in support of a warrant, the fruits of the subsequent search or seizure must be suppressed if, without consideration of the falsehoods or with consideration of the omissions, there would not have been probable cause).

- *Rakas v. Illinois*, 439 U.S. 128 (1978) (disapproving the standing concept previously used to determine whether a defendant could assert a Fourth Amendment claim; holding instead that a defendant may assert a Fourth Amendment claim only if the defendant has a reasonable expectation of privacy in the object seized or the place searched or a sufficient possessory interest in property seized).

- *Ybarra v. Illinois*, 444 U.S. 85 (1979) (mere presence of a bystander in a public place where police officers are searching for contraband ordinarily will not provide reasonable suspicion or probable cause to search the mere bystander for either contraband or weapons; officers must have an objective basis supporting belief that bystander was armed to justify pat-down search).

- *United States v. Crews*, 445 U.S. 463 (1980) (if defendant was unconstitutionally arrested, the Fourth Amendment does not require the defendants' body to be suppressed; defendant thus can be compelled to attend a trial, although any evidentiary fruits of the illegal arrest, including a confession, typically are subject to suppression).

- *Payton v. New York*, 445 U.S. 573 (1980) (absent exigent circumstances, police officers may not enter a suspect's residence to arrest them without an arrest or search warrant, even if officers possess probable cause that the defendant committed a felony offense).

- *Rawlings v. Kentucky*, 448 U.S. 98 (1980) (to make a Fourth Amendment challenge to a police officer's search for evidence or contraband in the possession of a third party, a defendant must assert a legitimate privacy interest in the area searched; "arcane concepts of property law," such as the law of bailment, do not necessarily define whether the defendant possessed such a privacy interest regarding the search of the third party).

- *Steagald v. United States*, 451 U.S. 204 (1981) (although police officers may enter a suspect's residence without a separate search warrant if the officers obtained a valid arrest warrant naming the suspect, the officers may not enter a third party's residence to execute an arrest warrant on the defendant without a separate search warrant; an arrest warrant naming the suspect, but not the third party will not authorize an entry into the third party's residence).

- *Michigan v. Summers*, 452 U.S. 692 (1981) (officers may temporarily detain the occupants of a residence without an arrest warrant during the time that officers execute a search warrant for the residence).

- *New York v. Belton*, 453 U.S. 454 (1981) (if police officers possess probable cause to arrest an occupant of an automobile, the officers may engage in a warrantless search of the entire passenger compartment of the car, including closed containers therein, but may not search the closed trunk without probable cause to believe evidence or contraband is in the trunk).

- *Texas v. Brown*, 460 U.S. 730 (1983) (contraband or incriminating evidence in plain view of a police officer who views the item from a lawful vantage point may be seized without a warrant where the incriminating or evidentiary nature of the item is immediately apparent).

- *Illinois v. Gates*, 462 U.S. 213 (1983) (if the totality of the circumstances demonstrate that a police informant is reliable, probable cause may be based on the information provided by the informant if sufficiently detailed).

- *United States v. Place*, 462 U.S. 696 (1983) (police canine sniff of airspace around the outside of luggage placed in a public place, such as a luggage conveyor at an airport, is not a search under the Fourth Amendment; if there is reasonable suspicion that such luggage contains contraband, it may be detained temporarily under *Terry* without a warrant to allow for such a dog sniff; luggage that otherwise would be retrieved by its owner may not be detained for any substantial length of time in order to await the arrival of a canine without a search warrant).

- *Michigan v. Long*, 463 U.S. 1032 (1983) (holding that if a police officer has a legal basis to stop an automobile under *Terry*, the officer may engage in a warrantless "protective sweep" of the passenger compartment of the car to look for weapons if the officer has reasonable suspicion that weapons are present; such a protective sweep, however, is not as extensive as a *Belton* search when probable cause exists).

- *United States v. Jacobsen*, 466 U.S. 109 (1984) (Fourth Amendment's protections do not apply to "private" searches by citizens who are not working with law enforcement at the time of the search).

- *Oliver v. United States*, 466 U.S. 170 (1984) (discussing difference between "curtilage" of a home and "open fields" for purposes of the Fourth Amendment).

- *Welsh v. Wisconsin*, 466 U.S. 740 (1984) (discussing the fleeing felon/hot pursuit exception to the warrant requirement; specifically holding that when officers are not in hot pursuit of a fleeing suspect and no other exigent circumstances exist, officers may not enter into the suspect's residence without an arrest warrant; even if exigent circumstances exist, Court suggests in dicta that only "serious" offenses would permit a warrantless entry into the suspect's residence).

- *United States v. Leon*, 468 U.S. 897 (1984) (setting forth good-faith exception to search warrant requirement).

- *United States v. Sharpe*, 470 U.S. 675 (1985) (leading modern decision discussing warrantless *Terry* stops; holding that a *Terry* stop's duration may extend as long as is reasonably necessary to dispel or confirm an investigating officer's suspicion, but no longer; rejecting bright-line rules and, in so doing, upholding a twenty-minute *Terry* stop where such a length of time was reasonably necessary under the circumstances).

- *California v. Carney*, 471 U.S. 386 (1985) (leading modern decision discussing automobile exception to the Fourth Amendment's warrant requirement; specifically holding that readily movable mobile homes are subject to the automobile exception).

- *Colorado v. Bertine*, 479 U.S. 367 (1987) (leading modern decision discussing the inventory search exception to the Fourth Amendment's warrant requirement).

- *Maryland v. Garrison*, 480 U.S. 79 (1987) (leading modern decision discussing the Fourth Amendment's particularity requirement).

- *Arizona v. Hicks*, 480 U.S. 321 (1987) (police officer's warrantless movement of a record player a few inches to see the serial number on it constituted a search under the Fourth Amendment; plain view exception not applicable because, despite officer's lawful presence in defendant's residence, officer did not have probable cause to believe that record player was stolen before he moved it).

- *Murray v. United States*, 487 U.S. 533 (1988) (discussing independent source exception to Fourth Amendment exclusionary rule).

- *James v. Illinois*, 493 U.S. 307 (1990) (impeachment of third-party witness with illegally seized evidence not permitted, although impeachment of defendant with such evidence is permitted if defendant testifies).

- *Maryland v. Buie*, 494 U.S. 325 (1990) (permitting brief, warrantless protective sweep of any area of a defendant's residence in connection with an in-home arrest when officers have reasonable suspicion to believe that another person poses a danger to the officers and is present in such an area of the residence; extension of *Chimel v. California*, 395 U.S. 752 (1969), which held that officers could search only the area within the immediate control of a defendant who was arrested in their residence).

- *Minnesota v. Olson*, 495 U.S. 91 (1990) (overnight guest at a residence has a reasonable expectation of privacy in the residence and, thus, may object to an unlawful entry into the residence by officers that resulted in a warrantless search or seizure of the guest or their property).

- *Alabama v. White*, 496 U.S. 325 (1990) (anonymous tip that correctly predicted specific actions of defendant in connection with an alleged drug deal provided reasonable suspicion once the predictive information was proved to be correct; at that point, reliability of tipster was sufficiently established and a *Terry* stop was upheld).

- *Illinois v. Rodriguez*, 497 U.S. 177 (1990) (if police officers have a good-faith, reasonable factual basis for believing that a third party possesses common authority over a place along with a defendant and, thus, may give valid third-party consent under *Matlock*, then the warrantless search pursuant to such consent is constitutional even if it later turns out that the person did not in fact have the authority to give third-party consent).

- *California v. Hodari D.*, 499 U.S. 621 (1991) (holding that a suspect fleeing from a police officer is not "seized" until the suspect either stops and submits to the police officer's authority or until the officer applies physical force to the suspect, however slight; also holding that if a defendant voluntarily abandons property prior to being seized in the foregoing manner, the defendant loses any right to challenge officer's warrantless search or seizure of the abandoned property).

- *Florida v. Jimeno*, 500 U.S. 248 (1991) (unless a defendant specifically limits the scope of a warrantless search upon giving consent, the scope of a consensual search is what a reasonable person would have believed the officer's request encompassed under the circumstances; specifically holding that when a police officer requests consent to search a car for illegal drugs and the driver gives general consent, the scope of the search reasonably encompasses closed containers inside the car that could contain drugs).

- *California v. Acevedo*, 500 U.S. 565 (1991) (under the automobile exception, closed containers inside a car may be searched without a search warrant if there is probable cause to believe they contain contraband or evidence).

- *Florida v. Bostick*, 501 U.S. 429 (1991) (a person is seized under the Fourth Amendment when based on a law enforcement officer's words or actions, the person does not "feel free to disregard the officer and go about their own business"; mere fact that a police officer approaches a person and asks him incriminating questions is not by itself sufficient to turn such a police-citizen encounter into a seizure).

- *Soldal v. Cook County*, 506 U.S. 56 (1992) (a seizure of property occurs under the Fourth Amendment when a law enforcement officer engages in "meaningful interference with an individual's possessory interests" even if the individual's privacy interests are not violated; "the Amendment protects property as well as privacy").

- *Minnesota v. Dickerson*, 508 U.S. 366 (1993) (recognizing the plain feel exception to the Fourth Amendment's warrant requirement; officers who are legally engaging in a *Terry* frisk of a suspect may not extend the intrusiveness of such a limited pat down unless the superficial frisk results in probable cause justifying a more in-depth search).

- *Whren v. United States*, 517 U.S. 806 (1996) (whether police had probable cause to engage in a warrantless arrest is measured by an objective test: as long as, from an objective standpoint, arresting officer knew information that amounted to probable cause, the warrantless arrest is valid, even if officer would not have arrested the defendant but for a pretextual reason not amounting to probable cause).

- *Pennsylvania Board of Probation & Parole v. Scott*, 524 U.S. 357 (1998) (Fourth Amendment exclusionary rule not applicable to parole or probation revocation hearings).

- *Minnesota v. Carter*, 525 U.S. 83 (1998) (persons who are solely commercial visitors are not tantamount to overnight guests and, thus, do not have a basis to object to an unconstitutional search of a residence in which they were visiting; specifically holding that a person in another's home engaging in an illegal drug transaction cannot object to police officers' unconstitutional search of the home).

- *Knowles v. Iowa*, 525 U.S. 113 (1998) (if police officers stop a car for a traffic offense and issue a citation, but do not engage in a formal arrest on the traffic charges, then a *Belton* search is not permitted; rather, to search the inside of the defendant's car, the officer must have at least reasonable suspicion that weapons are inside the car).

- *Illinois v. Wardlow*, 528 U.S. 119 (2000) (holding that a defendant's "head-long flight" from a police officer gives the officer reasonable suspicion to engage in a *Terry* stop, at least when such flight occurs in a high-crime area).

- *Florida v. J.L.*, 529 U.S. 266 (2000) (an anonymous tip alleging that a defendant is engaging in criminal activity, without sufficient predictive information about the defendant's future conduct, does not give a police officer reasonable suspicion; distinguishing *Alabama v. White*, 496 U.S. 325, and also holding that there is no exception for anonymous tips about firearms offenses).

- *Bond v. United States*, 529 U.S. 334 (2000) (law enforcement officer's physical manipulation of a person's luggage placed on public transportation, beyond the type of third-party handling that a traveler would reasonably expect to occur, constitutes a search under the Fourth Amendment).

- *City of Indianapolis v. Edmond*, 531 U.S. 32 (2000) (police roadblock employing narcotics canine was unconstitutional where there was no individualized suspicion justifying search of individual cars; DUI and license-check roadblocks distinguished on the ground that the latter are not unconstitutional because they were primarily concerned with roadway safety as opposed to crime detection).

- *Atwater v. City of Lago Vista*, 532 U.S. 318 (2001) (Fourth Amendment does not require a "breach of the peace" for there to be a warrantless arrest for misdemeanor offense; footnote 11 leaves open question of whether a warrantless arrest for a misdemeanor is prohibited unless the misdemeanor offense occurs in the presence of the arresting officer).

- *Kyllo v. United States*, 533 U.S. 27 (2001) (any device that enhances police officers' naked senses that is directed inside a person's residence and that could detect innocent as well as criminal activity is a search that ordinarily requires a search warrant; specifically holding that a thermal imagining device used without a search warrant to detect the heat from marijuana plants inside a person's home was an unconstitutional search because it also could have detected innocent activity).

- *United States v. Arvizu*, 534 U.S. 266 (2002) (leading modern decision discussing what constitutes reasonable suspicion justifying a *Terry* stop).

- *United States v. Drayton*, 536 U.S. 194 (2002) (holding that "[l]aw enforcement officers do not violate the Fourth Amendment[] . . . merely by approaching individuals . . . in public places and putting questions to them if they are willing to listen"; specifically holding that police officers need not inform public bus passengers that they have a right to refuse consent for consent to search passengers' luggage to be valid).

- *United States v. Banks*, 540 U.S. 31 (2003) (police officers' fifteen- to twenty-second wait after knocking and announcing before forcibly entering a home of a suspected drug dealer to execute a warrant was reasonable under the Fourth Amendment's knock and announce rule).

- *Maryland v. Pringle*, 540 U.S. 366 (2003) (although mere proximity of a person to criminal activity or contraband does not give probable cause to arrest, other factors in addition to mere presence may give probable cause; specifically holding that the presence of the defendant and three others in a car at a late-night hour where illegal drugs were in plain view gave probable cause to arrest all four persons when none admitted to ownership of drugs).

- *Illinois v. Lidster*, 540 U.S. 419 (2004) (police roadblock to question motorists concerning whether they had witnessed a specific crime that recently had occurred in the area was reasonable under the Fourth Amendment; *Enmond* distinguished because it held that roadblocks aimed primarily at crime detection involving the motorists, as opposed to others, was unconstitutional).

- *Groh v. Ramirez*, 540 U.S. 551 (2004) (a warrant that fails to meet the Fourth Amendment's particularity requirement will not pass muster merely because the police officer's affidavit submitted in support of the warrant was sufficiently detailed, unless the warrant incorporates the affidavit).

- *United States v. Flores-Montano*, 541 U.S. 149 (2004) (dismantling of car's gas tank by law enforcement officers that did not cause irreparable damage at an international border was a "routine border search" that did not require reasonable suspicion or probable cause).

- *Thornton v. United States*, 541 U.S. 615 (2004) (permitting *Belton* search of a defendant's car even if, at the time police first encountered the defendant, they already had gotten out of their car and closed the car's door; *Belton* searches permitted if defendant is a recent occupant of car).

- *Illinois v. Caballes*, 543 U.S. 405 (2005) (police canine sniff of outside of automobile detained for a lawful traffic stop is not unconstitutional as long as it does not prolong the traffic stop beyond the time it ordinarily would have ended; if probable cause is developed during such a permissible canine sniff, then the automobile may be searched without a warrant under the automobile exception).

- *United States v. Grubbs*, 547 U.S. 90 (2006) (upholding anticipatory search warrant where probable cause of condition precedent for valid search existed at time warrant was issued).

- *Georgia v. Randolph*, 547 U.S. 103 (2006) (invalidating third-party consent to search defendant's residence by defendant's co-occupant where defendant, who possessed an equal or greater interest in the property, objected to consensual search).

- *Brigham City, Utah v. Stuart*, 547 U.S. 398 (2006) (police officers may enter a private residence without a warrant if, objectively, they have a reasonable basis to believe that someone inside is seriously injured or is facing imminent, serious injury or death).

- *Hudson v. Michigan*, 547 U.S. 586 (2006) (Fourth Amendment exclusionary rule does not apply to violations of the Fourth Amendment knock and announce rule applicable to execution of warrants).

- *Samson v. California*, 547 U.S. 843 (2006) (upholding warrantless, suspicionless searches of parolees).

- *Brendlin v. California*, 551 U.S. 249 (2007) (passenger of automobile has standing to challenge unconstitutional seizure of automobile and subsequent search of it).

- *Herring v. United States*, 555 U.S. 136 (2009) (police officer's negligently mistaken, but good faith belief that an arrest warrant existed based on computer error precluded application of Fourth Amendment exclusionary rule to fruits of arrest).

- *Arizona v. Johnson*, 555 U.S. 323 (2009) ([1] police may frisk passenger of car detained during lawful traffic stop based solely on reasonable suspicion of danger posed by passenger; [2] during lawful traffic stop, police may ask questions about alleged criminal activity other than traffic violation as long as the questions do not measurably extend the duration of the traffic stop).

- *Arizona v. Gant*, 556 U.S. 332 (2009) (limiting the *Belton* rule by prohibiting warrantless searches of inside an arrestee's car incident to arrest unless the driver or any passengers are not secured and within reach of the passenger compartment or unless a reasonable basis exists to believe that evidence related to the offense of arrest is inside the car).

- *Kentucky v. King*, 563 U.S. 452 (2011) (police officers did not unjustifiably create exigent circumstances by knocking on drug suspect's door and announcing their presence, even if that action foreseeably caused suspects to try to destroy drugs, thus authorizing the officers to enter the residence without a warrant).

- *Davis v. United States*, 564 U.S. 229 (2011) (applying good-faith exception to warrantless search that was authorized by binding appellate precedent at time of search, even though a subsequent Supreme Court decision overruled that precedent and declared that the search had been unconstitutional).

- *United States v. Jones*, 565 U.S. 400 (2012) (warrantless placement of GPS tracking device on defendant's car was an unconstitutional search when used to track defendant's movements because the placement of the device would have been deemed a trespass of chattels at time of Fourth Amendment's adoption in 1791).

- *Florida v. Jardines*, 569 U.S. 1 (2013) (warrantless entry of police dog into curtilage of defendant's home to detect drug particles coming from within the defendant's home was an unconstitutional search because the entry was a trespass).

- *Riley v. California*, 573 U.S. 373 (2014) (police officers may not search digital data on an arrested person's cellular phone as a search incident to arrest).

- *Heien v. North Carolina*, 574 U.S. 54 (2014) (a police officer's stop of defendant's car based on a reasonably mistaken belief that the defendant's car violated the state's traffic laws did not violate the Fourth Amendment; at time of stop, traffic law in question was ambiguous).

- *Rodriguez v. United States*, 575 U.S. 348 (2015) (any incriminating evidence obtained after a police officer has "measurably extended" a traffic stop without valid consent or exigent circumstances is tainted fruit of the unconstitutional detention and must be suppressed).

- *Byrd v. United States*, 138 S. Ct. 1518 (2018) (a person driving a rental car with the permission of the authorized driver—who was the only one on the rental contract—possesses standing to object to an unconstitutional seizure and search of the car even when that person was driving it alone).

- *Collins v. Virginia*, 138 S. Ct. 1663 (2018) (the automobile exception generally does not apply to vehicles parked within the curtilage of a home).

- *Carpenter v. United States*, 138 S. Ct. 2206 (2018) (the Fourth Amendment is violated by police officers' warrantless tracking of a suspect's movements by use of GPS monitoring or by accessing phone company records of the cell towers to which the defendant's cell phone sent signals when such monitoring was at least seven days in duration).

- *Kansas v. Glover*, 140 S. Ct. 1183 (2020) (an officer possesses reasonable suspicion that an unknown driver of an automobile is the registered owner—thus permitting a stop of the car when a police computer check of the car's license plate showed that the registered owner had their license suspended).

CHAPTER SIX

MOTIONS TO SUPPRESS CONFESSIONS

There are four main types of motions to suppress a defendant's confession:

1) a motion to suppress the confession as tainted fruit of an illegal search or seizure in violation of the Fourth Amendment;

2) a motion to suppress the confession based on a *Miranda* violation;[1]

3) a motion to suppress the confession as involuntary under the Due Process Clause; and

4) a motion to suppress a confession or other incriminating statement as having been obtained in violation of the Sixth Amendment right to counsel.

6.1 Motions to Suppress a Confession as Tainted Fruit of an Unconstitutional Search or Seizure

In Chapter Five, it was noted that a defendant's confession can be the type of derivative evidence that may be subject to suppression based on a Fourth Amendment violation. When applying the tainted fruit doctrine to Fourth Amendment violations, it is important to distinguish between unconstitutional arrests and unconstitutional searches and seizures of property. In *Brown v. Illinois*,[2] the Court held that when a defendant is unconstitutionally arrested and then confesses, the confession must be suppressed unless the prosecution can establish that the taint of the illegal arrest was dissipated by the time of the defendant's confession. The Court set forth a four-part test regarding whether the taint was dissipated at the time of the confession: 1) the temporal proximity between the illegal arrest and the defendant's confession; 2) whether *Miranda* warnings were read to the defendant before they confessed; 3) whether any intervening circumstances occurred (such as the defendant's consultation with an attorney or meeting with family members); and 4) the degree of flagrancy of the Fourth Amendment violation involved in the illegal arrest.[3] A court must balance the four factors when determining whether the

---

1. Miranda v. Arizona, 384 U.S. 436 (1966).
2. Brown v. Illinois, 422 U.S. 590 (1975).
3. *Id.* at 603–04.

taint was sufficiently attenuated; the mere fact that the defendant's confession was obtained in accordance with *Miranda* and was otherwise voluntary is not by itself dispositive.[4] In subsequent cases, the Court has strictly applied *Brown's* test to suppress confessions, even ones given after repeated *Miranda* waivers.[5]

It is important here to distinguish between a confession following an unconstitutional arrest and a confession following the defendant's being confronted with evidence or information obtained as a result of an unconstitutional search or seizure (where defendant has standing to assert the Fourth Amendment claim). If a defendant confesses after an unconstitutional search or seizure of evidence—and does so only after learning of the results of the search or seizure—then there is no four-part *Brown* taint attenuation analysis. Rather, a defendant need only establish that the antecedent search or seizure induced their confession or consent.[6]

6.2 *Miranda v. Arizona*

The most common type of motion to suppress a defendant's confession is based on an alleged violation of the Supreme Court's famous decision in *Miranda*, which is rooted in the Self-Incrimination Clause of the Fifth Amendment.[7] *Miranda* holds that before a defendant's custodial statement may be introduced at a trial, a police officer must have warned a suspect that 1) they have a right to remain silent; 2) anything they say can and will be used against them in a court proceeding; 3) they have a right to consult with a lawyer both before and during any interrogation; and 4) a lawyer will be appointed if the suspect cannot afford one.[8] The Supreme Court has held that although no specific wording is required to be a part of a *Miranda* warning, the warnings actually given must "reasonably convey to a suspect [all of] his rights as required by *Miranda*."[9] Put another way, the warnings actually given must be in substantial compliance with *Miranda*.[10] When a particular warning is omitted by an interrogating officer and the essence of that component is not

---

4. *Id.; see also* Lanier v. South Carolina, 474 U.S. 25 (1985) (per curiam).

5. *See* Kaupp v. Texas, 538 U.S. 626 (2003) (per curiam); Taylor v. Alabama, 457 U.S. 687 (1982); Dunaway v. New York, 442 U.S. 200 (1979); *but cf.* Rawlings v. Kentucky, 448 U.S. 98, 106–11 (1980).

6. Fahy v. Connecticut, 375 U.S. 85, 90–91 (1963) (remanding so that the defendant could have "a chance to show that his admissions were induced by being confronted with the illegally seized evidence"); *see also* State v. Hodges, 851 P.2d 352, 363 (Kan. 1993); State v. Abdouch, 434 N.W.2d 317, 328 (Neb. 1989); State v. Pinder, 489 A.2d 653, 657 (N.H. 1985); People v. Robbins, 369 N.E.2d 577 (Ill. 1977).

7. *Miranda*, 384 U.S. 436.

8. *Id.* at 467–74, 479.

9. Duckworth v. Eagan, 492 U.S. 195, 203 (1989) (citation, internal quotation marks, and brackets omitted); *see also* Florida v. Powell, 559 U.S. 50 (2010); California v. Prysock, 453 U.S. 355 (1981) (per curiam).

10. State v. Bopp, 519 P.2d 1277, 1280 (Or. Ct. App. 1974).

conveyed to the defendant who proceeds to confess, the confession is obtained in violation of *Miranda*.[11]

Miranda's requirements are "prophylactic" in nature, although the Court has held that they nonetheless are mandated by the Fifth Amendment's privilege against self-incrimination.[12] Remember that the "Fifth Amendment right to counsel" under *Miranda* is distinct from the Sixth Amendment right to counsel.[13] The right to counsel discussed in *Miranda* has been deemed a "necessary corollary" to the Fifth Amendment right to silence.[14] The Fifth Amendment right to counsel applies even in cases where the Sixth Amendment right to counsel never "attaches" (such as misdemeanor cases in which ultimately only a fine was imposed as the sentence).[15] And even in cases where a defendant's Sixth Amendment right to counsel later attaches, typically the Sixth Amendment right to counsel has not yet attached at the time that an officer's custodial interrogation causes the "*Miranda* right to counsel" to attach. Litigation about the *Miranda* right to counsel typically concerns police officers' failure to advise a defendant about their right to counsel or failure to honor a defendant's invocation of that right.

Confessions given in violation of *Miranda* should be distinguished from involuntary confessions. An involuntary confession is one where the defendant's self-incrimination was the product of law enforcement "techniques and methods offensive to due process" that interfered with the defendant's free will in giving an incriminating statement, while an officer's lack of compliance with *Miranda* does not necessarily (and usually does not) render the defendant's confession involuntary.[16] Nevertheless, if a confession is obtained in violation of *Miranda*'s prophylactic requirements, the confession is inadmissible even if in fact the defendant gave the confession freely and voluntarily.[17] The sole remedy for a *Miranda* violation is the suppression of a tainted confession.[18] Contrary to popular belief, a police officer's failure to administer *Miranda* warnings to an arrestee is not by itself a violation of

---

11. *See, e.g.*, Lujan v. Garcia, 734 F.3d 917, 932–33 (9th Cir. 2013) (holding that *Miranda* warnings read to defendant were constitutionally insufficient because they failed to reasonably convey that the defendant had a right to counsel to be present before and during the interrogation).

12. Dickerson v. United States, 530 U.S. 428, 437–38 (2000). The Court in *Dickerson* was asked to overrule *Miranda* in view of a post-*Miranda* congressional statute, 18 U.S.C. § 3501, that provided that only involuntary confessions were inadmissible. The Court, relying primarily on stare decisis, characterized *Miranda*'s rule as constitutional in nature and, thus, not subject to being overruled by the legislature. *Id.* at 437–38.

13. The Sixth Amendment right to counsel is discussed in Chapter Three.

14. State v. Salmon, 537 S.E.2d 829, 831 (N.C. Ct. App. 2000).

15. *See* Berkemer v. McCarty, 468 U.S. 420, 430–34 (1984); *see also* State v. Buchholz, 462 N.E.2d 1222 (Ohio 1984).

16. Oregon v. Elstad, 470 U.S. 298, 304 (1985).

17. *Id.* at 307.

18. Bennett v. Passic, 545 F.2d 1260, 1263 (10th Cir. 1976).

the arrestee's rights; a violation of the defendant's rights occurs only when an "un-Mirandized" confession thereafter is introduced at a criminal trial.[19]

6.2.1 *"Custodial" Interrogation*

A suspect must be in custody before *Miranda*'s prophylactic rule applies. Being in "custody" for *Miranda* purposes means that the suspect either has been arrested (within the meaning of the Fourth Amendment) "or otherwise deprived of [their] freedom of action in any significant way."[20] The critical inquiry is an objective one: whether, under the totality of the circumstances, a reasonable person in the defendant's circumstances would have felt free to stop the officer's questioning and leave.[21] This condition is typically met when a defendant is handcuffed or similarly restrained by a law enforcement officer at the time of the interrogation.[22] Similarly, when officers interrogate the defendant at gunpoint, the person is in custody under *Miranda*,[23] although some courts have held that the subsequent reholstering of the guns by the officers may deactivate *Miranda*'s requirements.[24] The Supreme Court has made it clear that the mere questioning of a suspect by a police officer—even if that officer requests that the suspect come down to the police station—does not by itself activate *Miranda*'s requirements.[25]

Custody under *Miranda* is ordinarily determined by an objective standard that does not consider the defendant's subjective characteristics, but an exception exists for juveniles who are interrogated.[26] When police officers knew or had reason to believe that a suspect in custody was a juvenile, a court must decide whether a

---

19. Chavez v. Martinez, 538 U.S. 760 (2003).
20. *Miranda*, 384 U.S. at 444 (1966); *see also* Stansbury v. California, 511 U.S. 318, 322 (1994) (per curiam).
21. *See* Thompson v. Keohane, 516 U.S. 99, 111–13 (1995); *see also Stansbury*, 511 U.S. at 323; United States v. Kim, 292 F.3d 969, 973–74 (9th Cir. 2002); United States v. Salvo, 133 F.3d 943, 949 (6th Cir. 1998).
22. *See* United States v. Smith, 3 F.3d 1088, 1097–98 (7th Cir. 1993) (finding "custody" under *Miranda* in case in which defendant was handcuffed and guarded by officers); *see also* State v. Miranda, 672 N.W.2d 753, 760 (Iowa 2003) ("Critically, the fact [the defendant] was handcuffed strongly indicates he was not free to leave . . . '[A] court . . . is likely to find custody if there was physical restraint such as handcuffing . . . .'") (citation and internal quotation marks omitted). In Colorado v. Connelly, 479 U.S. 157 (1986), the Supreme Court accepted the prosecution's concession that the act of handcuffing a suspect is a sufficient restraint to constitute custody under *Miranda. See id.* at 169 n.3 ("Petitioner conceded at oral argument that when Officer Anderson handcuffed respondent, the custody requirement of *Miranda* was satisfied. For purposes of our decision, we accept that concession . . . ."). And in New York v. Quarles, 467 U.S. 649 (1984), the Court found a defendant was in custody under *Miranda* where he was in handcuffs and surrounded by four police officers. *Id.* at 655.
23. *See, e.g.*, United States v. Perdue, 8 F.3d 1455, 1464 (10th Cir. 1993).
24. *See, e.g.*, Cruz v. Miller, 255 F.3d 77, 85–86 (2d Cir. 2001).
25. *See* California v. Beheler, 463 U.S. 1121 (1983) (per curiam); Oregon v. Mathiason, 429 U.S. 492, 495 (1977) (per curiam); Beckwith v. United States, 425 U.S. 341 (1976).
26. J.D.B. v. North Carolina, 564 U.S. 261 (2011).

reasonable juvenile in the defendant's position would have believed that they were in custody.[27]

Although the issue of whether a defendant is "in custody" under *Miranda* is superficially similar to the Fourth Amendment issue of whether a defendant has been "seized," the two questions are distinct.[28] In certain situations, a suspect will be seized in a limited manner under the Fourth Amendment—i.e., the suspect does not feel free to leave from an objective point of view—but will not be in custody under *Miranda*. For instance, if a police officer engages in a brief *Terry* stop, but does not significantly restrain the suspect (e.g., the officer does not display a weapon and does not use handcuffs), ordinarily the defendant is not in custody for purposes of *Miranda* during that brief period.[29] However, a more restraining *Terry* stop (even one that under the circumstances does not rise to the level of a full-fledged arrest under the Fourth Amendment) would require *Miranda* warnings.[30]

Similarly, the mere fact that a person has been temporarily detained during the execution of a search warrant at their residence pursuant to *Michigan v. Summers*[31] does not by itself constitute custody under *Miranda*.[32] However, when an officer temporarily detaining a person under *Summers* either engages in a type of physical restraint that exceeds the ordinary scope of *Summers* (e.g., handcuffs the person or keeps them at gunpoint) or proceeds to interrogate the suspect in a manner beyond limited questions (such as the person's identity and whether they live at the residence being searched), the *Miranda* warnings are required.[33]

A person is not ordinarily in custody for *Miranda* purposes when asked questions—even incriminating ones—by their probation or parole officer, and thus the probation or parole officer ordinarily need not administer *Miranda* warnings.[34] Likewise, a person who is incarcerated in a prison is not automatically in *Miranda* custody if law enforcement officers come to the prison to interrogate the person

---

27. *Id.* at 272–81.
28. *See Salvo*, 133 F.3d at 949.
29. Berkemer v. McCarty, 468 U.S. 420 (1984); *see also* Pennsylvania v. Bruder, 488 U.S. 9 (1988) (per curiam).
30. *See, e.g.*, United States v. Newton, 369 F.3d 659, 675–76 (2d Cir. 2004).
31. Michigan v. Summers, 452 U.S. 692 (1981).
32. *See Kim*, 292 F.3d at 976; *see also* United States v. Newton, 181 F. Supp. 2d 157, 172–73 (E.D.N.Y. 2002).
33. *See, e.g., Kim,* 292 F.3d at 976 (noting that a limited detention under *Summers* ordinarily does not require *Miranda* warnings when questions such as a person's identity are asked by officers; however, when officers ask more probing, incriminating questions during such a detention, *Miranda* warnings are required); *see also* United States v. Ritchie, 35 F.3d 1477, 1486 (10th Cir. 1994) ("[O]ur opinion today should not be interpreted as an exhaustive pronouncement that the procedural protections required by *Miranda* are never implicated when a person is detained pursuant to *Summers*.") (citation and internal quotation marks omitted).
34. Minnesota v. Murphy, 465 U.S. 420 (1984); Brown v. Butler, 811 F.2d 938, 940–41 (5th Cir. 1987); Baumann v. United States, 692 F.2d 565, 576 (9th Cir. 1982).

about a crime unrelated to the one for which the person is incarcerated (and one that allegedly occurred outside the prison).[35]

6.2.2 *"Interrogation"*

For *Miranda*'s exclusionary rule to apply to a custodial statement given by a defendant, there must have been an interrogation by law enforcement officials—that is, incriminating questioning or its functional equivalent.[36] The "functional equivalent" of questioning would include statements made by an officer to the defendant that the officer "should have known" were "reasonably likely" to elicit an incriminating response from the defendant.[37]

In *Rhode Island v. Innis*, a defendant had been arrested for allegedly killing a cab driver with a shotgun; when he was arrested, he did not possess the shotgun, which he had hidden. After his arrest, the defendant invoked his *Miranda* rights. Subsequently, while two police officers were driving him to the police station, one officer made the comment to the second officer—in the presence of the defendant, who was sitting in the back seat—that he hoped that no "handicapped children" who attended a neighborhood school for handicapped youth would find the shotgun and hurt themselves. In response to this remark, the defendant stated that he would show the officers where he had hidden the murder weapon. The Supreme Court held that the officer's remark was not "interrogation" under *Miranda*.[38]

If police officers intentionally use a third party (such as a suspect's spouse) as an agent of the police to ask incriminating questions to a defendant in custody, then *Miranda* applies to such third-party questioning.[39] However, where police merely monitor conversation between a defendant in custody and a third party without such an agency relationship—even if officers expect the defendant to make incriminating statements to the third party—there is no custodial interrogation under *Miranda*.[40]

---

35. Howes v. Fields, 565 U.S. 499 (2012) (holding that the prisoner was not in custody within the meaning of *Miranda* because the officers told him that he was free to return to his cell at any time and also was not physically restrained during the interrogation).

36. Rhode Island v. Innis, 446 U.S. 291 (1980).

37. *Id.* at 301. *Innis*'s standard for what constitutes "custodial interrogation" under *Miranda* and the Fifth Amendment should be contrasted with the Court's distinct standard for what constitutes impermissible questioning of a defendant whose Sixth Amendment right to counsel has attached. *Id.* at 300 n.4 (discussing Brewer v. Williams, 430 U.S. 387 (1977)) (applying the "deliberate elicitation" test). The Sixth Amendment issue is discussed in section 6.4.

38. *Innis*, 446 U.S. at 293–304.

39. Gilchrist v. State, 585 So. 2d 165, 175 (Ala. Crim. App. 1991).

40. Arizona v. Mauro, 481 U.S. 520 (1987); *see also* Illinois v. Perkins, 496 U.S. 292 (1990) (undercover officer who pretended to be then-unindicted defendant's cellmate did not need to give *Miranda* warnings before engaging in conversation with the defendant and, in the process, eliciting incriminating statements; there was no "interrogation" in such a situation because the defendant assumed he was talking to another inmate rather than a police officer).

6.2.3 Invocation of Miranda *Rights*

A common issue in the *Miranda* context is whether a defendant sufficiently invoked their rights. The Supreme Court has held that for a defendant to trigger *Miranda*'s protections after being given the warnings, the defendant's words seeking to invoke their right to silence or right to counsel must be unambiguous; an ambiguous or equivocal invocation does not prevent officers from continuing their questioning.[41] For example, a defendant's statement to police officers that "[m]aybe I should talk to a lawyer" was deemed insufficient to invoke their *Miranda* rights,[42] at least when the defendant had previously waived their *Miranda* rights.[43] A defendant's invocation of their *Miranda* right to counsel also must be in response to custodial interrogation; it cannot be done anticipatorily[44]—that is, at a point before it becomes apparent that police officers want to question the defendant. The same appears true of the Fifth Amendment right to silence, although the Supreme Court has never expressly held that the right to silence cannot be anticipatorily invoked prior to custodial interrogation.[45]

In *Berghuis v. Thompkins*, the Supreme Court held that a defendant's mere silence in response to a *Miranda* warning—even an extended period of silence (in *Berghuis*, it was approximately three hours)—is not necessarily an invocation of *Miranda* rights.[46] Thus, after *Thompkins*, a suspect must make some type of unambiguous assertion (words or a clear head shake) indicating that they do not wish to be interrogated. Merely remaining silent is not sufficient to invoke *Miranda* rights.

---

41. Davis v. United States, 512 U.S. 452, 459–60 (1994); *see also* Smith v. Illinois, 469 U.S. 91 (1984) (per curiam). A defendant does not invoke their *Miranda* rights by stating that they are unwilling to sign anything, but will give an oral statement. *See* Connecticut v. Barrett, 479 U.S. 523, 528–29 (1987) (defendant's unwillingness to put his confession in writing without his attorney being present did not invoke his *Miranda* rights when he was willing to give an oral confession without the presence of counsel).

42. *Davis*, 512 U.S. at 462.

43. In Davis, the defendant's ambiguous invocation of his Miranda right to counsel occurred after he had initially waived his Miranda rights unambiguously. After Davis, a majority of lower courts held that Davis does not apply to an ambiguous invocation by a defendant who has not yet validly waived their Miranda rights. See, e.g., United States v. Rodriguez, 518 F.3d 1072, 1078–79 & n.6 (9th Cir. 2008). However, in Berghuis v. Thompkins, 560 U.S. 370 (2010), the Supreme Court applied Davis to an initial ambiguous invocation of Miranda rights. See id. at 382–88.

44. McNeil v. Wisconsin, 501 U.S. 171, 178–79 (1991).

45. McNeil only addressed the right-to-counsel component of Miranda. See id. However, the vast majority of lower courts have held that the right to silence cannot be invoked anticipatorily (so as to prevent future interrogation under Michigan v. Mosley, 423 U.S. 96 (1975)); instead, it only may be invoked when a person is subject to custodial interrogation. See, e.g., United States v. Bautista, 145 F.3d 1140, 1149 (10th Cir. 1998) (refusing to permit anticipatory invocation of the right to silence before custodial interrogation); United States v. Grimes, 142 F.3d 1342, 1348 (11th Cir. 1998) (same); cf. Salinas v. Texas, 570 U.S. 178 (2013) (prosecution did not violate Fifth Amendment by offering evidence of defendant's pre-custody, pre-*Miranda* silence in response to questioning by police officers as proof of his guilt).

46. Berghuis v. Thompkins, 560 U.S. 370 (2010).

If a person does sufficiently invoke their *Miranda* rights during a custodial interrogation, then *Miranda* instructs that police officers immediately must cease interrogating the defendant.[47] In subsequent cases, the Supreme Court has drawn a line with respect to situations when police officers thereafter may reinitiate custodial interrogation between a suspect's invocation of the *Miranda* right to counsel and a suspect's invocation of the Fifth Amendment right to silence. If a defendant invokes their right to counsel, then police must cease questioning the defendant about any criminal matter; any incriminating statements thereafter obtained during custodial interrogation will be suppressed[48]—unless the defendant initiated the subsequent communication with the police and a valid *Miranda* waiver is then obtained.[49] The Court has held that the *Edwards* rule does not apply to situations where a defendant has had a "break in custody" for two weeks or more; in such a situation, officers may approach the defendant and interrogate them (assuming the defendant at that juncture chooses to waive their *Miranda* rights).[50]

In contrast to an invocation of the *Miranda* right to counsel, if the defendant invokes only their Fifth Amendment right to silence, then police officers under some circumstances may reinitiate communication with the defendant at a later time even without a break in custody.[51] In *Michigan v. Mosley*, a police officer read Mosley his *Miranda* rights, and Mosley then invoked his right to silence (but not his right to counsel) in response to questioning about alleged robberies. The police officer ceased questioning about the robberies and placed the defendant in a jail cell. After an interval of more than two hours, a different police officer went to Mosley's cell, read him *Miranda* warnings, and began to question him about a murder that was unrelated to the robberies. Mosley proceeded to confess to the murder. The Supreme Court held that based on this sequence of events, the police had

---

47. *Miranda*, 384 U.S. at 479.
48. Edwards v. Arizona, 451 U.S. 477 (1981); Arizona v. Roberson, 486 U.S. 675 (1988) (*Edwards*'s rule applies to offenses other than one that the officers initially questioned the defendant about); Minnick v. Mississippi, 498 U.S. 146 (1990) (*Edwards* rule applies even after a defendant has consulted with counsel); *see also Smith*, 469 U.S. at 91–100 (*Edwards*'s "bright-line rule" applies to new officers who question defendant after invocation of right to counsel whether "deliberate[ly] or unintentional[ly]").
49. Oregon v. Bradshaw, 462 U.S. 1039 (1983) (finding that the defendant's statement to police after initially invoking the right to counsel—"Well, what is going to happen to me now?"—was an initiation of the conversation by the defendant that permitted the police officers to seek a waiver of the defendant's *Miranda* rights and continue interrogation).
50. Maryland v. Shatzer, 559 U.S. 98 (2010). Note that *Shatzer*'s fourteen-day break-in-custody component of the *Edwards* rule would not apply if police officers approached the defendant and interrogated him within fourteen days of his release when at the time of that interrogation he was not in "custody." *Cf.* People v. Storm, 52 P.3d 52, 63–64 (Cal. 2002) (*Edwards* rule does not apply if police officers interrogate the defendant after he had been released from custody and was not taken back into custody at the time of the second interrogation, at which time he confessed).
51. Michigan v. Mosley, 423 U.S. 96 (1975). A defendant may "selectively" invoke their right to silence about certain offenses and proceed with the interrogation concerning different offenses. *See* United States v. Soliz, 129 F.3d 499, 504 (9th Cir. 1997).

"scrupulously honored" Mosley's invocation of his right to silence because: 1) the police waited a "significant period" of time (i.e., over two hours) between Mosley's invocation of his right to silence in connection with the robberies and the subsequent interrogation about the unrelated homicide; 2) Mosley was given a "fresh set" of *Miranda* warnings before he confessed to the murder; and 3) the subject matter of the second interrogation (a homicide) was entirely unrelated to the subject of the first interrogation (the robberies).[52] Since *Mosley*, the lower courts have been lenient in allowing police officers to reinitiate custodial interrogation after a defendant has invoked their right to silence, but did not invoke their right to counsel.[53]

6.2.4   *Waiver of* Miranda *Rights*

According to dicta in *Miranda*, there is a "heavy burden" placed on the prosecution to show that a defendant knowingly and intelligently waived their *Miranda* rights.[54] However, subsequent cases have only required the prosecution to demonstrate a valid waiver by a preponderance of the evidence.[55] When judging the validity of a defendant's waiver of *Miranda* rights, a court must consider the "totality of the circumstances."[56] Waiver may be express or implied.[57] However, proof that a defendant was read their *Miranda* warnings and then confessed is not by itself sufficient to prove a valid waiver.[58] Rather, in a case where the defendant did not state that they understood their rights before confessing, the prosecution must offer evidence that shows that the defendant was intellectually capable of understanding and waiving those rights.[59] For a waiver to be valid, the suspect need not be informed—in advance of giving a waiver—of the alleged crimes about which the police wish to question them.[60] Nor must a suspect know that their family or friends have already retained a lawyer for them for their waiver of the *Miranda* right to counsel to be valid.[61]

---

52. *See Mosley*, 423 U.S. at 97–107. The last factor was the most important in the Court's analysis. *See id.* at 105 (the police officer's "questioning of Mosley about an unrelated homicide was quite consistent with a reasonable interpretation of Mosley's earlier refusal to answer any questions about the robberies"). The lower courts are divided over whether questioning about the same offense violates *Miranda* and *Mosley. See, e.g.*, Jackson v. Wyrick, 730 F.2d 1177, 1180 (8th Cir. 1984) (finding no *Miranda* violation even though questioning involved the same offense); People v. Quezada, 731 P.2d 730, 733 (Colo. 1987) ("Some courts have interpreted *Mosley* to mean that in the absence of different crimes . . it is [always] unlawful for the police to attempt to question a suspect who has previously asserted the right to remain silent") (citing cases).
53. *See, e.g.*, Vujosevic v. Rafferty, 844 F.2d 1023, 1029 (3d Cir. 1988) (discussing cases).
54. *Miranda*, 384 U.S. at 475.
55. *See, e.g.*, Colorado v. Connelly, 479 U.S. 157, 168 (1986).
56. Fare v. Michael C., 442 U.S. 707 (1979).
57. North Carolina v. Butler, 441 U.S. 369 (1979); *see also* Berghuis v. Thompkins, 560 U.S. 370, 386–88 (2010).
58. Tague v. Louisiana, 444 U.S. 469 (1980) (per curiam).
59. *See id.* at 471.
60. Colorado v. Spring, 479 U.S. 564 (1987).
61. Moran v. Burbine, 475 U.S. 412 (1986).

6.2.5 What Is "Testimonial" for Purposes of **Miranda?**

The Supreme Court has held that certain types of oral statements or actions by a defendant in custody do not amount to "testimonial" statements or nonverbal communication for purposes of *Miranda* and the Fifth Amendment right against self-incrimination.[62] For example, a defendant's refusal to give a breath or blood test to a police officer who suspects that the defendant was driving under the influence of alcohol is not a testimonial statement; it may be admitted into evidence at a trial, regardless of whether *Miranda* warnings were given.[63] However, a DUI suspect's custodial statement to a police officer that they could not remember their birth date (or similar responses to questions that seek to determine the suspect's state of mental impairment) do qualify as testimonial statements that cannot be introduced at a trial without *Miranda* rights first having been waived.[64] Similarly, certain nonverbal, yet testimonial acts of a defendant in custody are inadmissible without a defendant's prior waiver of *Miranda* rights.[65] For instance, a defendant's act of showing a stolen item in direct response to a question from a law enforcement officer was a testimonial act that under *Miranda* had to be suppressed where no prior *Miranda* warnings were given.[66]

6.2.6 Limits and Exceptions to **Miranda's Exclusionary Rule**

The exclusionary rule applicable to *Miranda* violations has significant limitations. Much like evidence obtained in violation of the Fourth Amendment, an incriminating statement obtained in violation of *Miranda* is inadmissible during the prosecution's case-in-chief at trial. However, a defendant's un-Mirandized statement can be used for impeachment if the defendant testifies in a contrary manner at trial[67] and also may be admitted at noncapital sentencing hearings or hearings at which a defendant's probation or parole is revoked.[68]

Unlike a Fourth Amendment violation,[69] a suspect's confession obtained in violation of *Miranda* generally will not taint subsequent confessions or other evidence

---

62. *See* United States v. Dionisio, 410 U.S. 1 (1973).
63. South Dakota v. Neville, 459 U.S. 553 (1983).
64. Pennsylvania v. Muniz, 496 U.S. 582 (1990).
65. *See* United States v. Barte, 868 F.2d 773, *on rehearing,* 878 F.2d 829 (5th Cir. 1989).
66. *Id.*
67. Harris v. New York, 401 U.S. 222 (1971); but cf. Mincey v. Arizona, 437 U.S. 385 (1978) (involuntary confessions—as opposed to those merely obtained in violation of Miranda—cannot be used to impeach a defendant who testifies).
68. United States v. MacKenzie, 601 F.2d 221, 222 (5th Cir. 1979); see also Del Vecchio v. Ill. D.O.C., 31 F.3d 1363, 1388 (7th Cir. 1994) (en banc) (citing numerous noncapital decisions); but cf. Estelle v. Smith, 451 U.S. 454 (1981) (Miranda applicable to defendant's statements given during a custodial interrogation that the prosecution later sought to introduce during a capital sentencing hearing).
69. The difference between Fourth Amendment violations and Miranda violations—in terms of the "tainted fruit" doctrine—is discussed in United States v. Guerra, 237 F. Supp. 2d 795, 801 (E.D. Mich. 2003).

obtained as a result of information contained in the inadmissible confession.[70] A limited exception to this general rule exists when police officers *deliberately* violate *Miranda*; in that situation, a subsequent Mirandized confession generally will be inadmissible.[71]

In addition to the foregoing limits to *Miranda* and its exclusionary rule, there are two commonly applied exceptions to *Miranda*. First, under the public safety exception announced in *New York v. Quarles*,[72] police officers need not read *Miranda* warnings to a suspect before asking incriminating questions about the location of a firearm (or other dangerous instrumentality) that, from an objectively reasonable point of view, poses an imminent threat to the public (including police officers). Since *Quarles*, lower courts have grappled with the issue of under what circumstances police officers who are interrogating a suspect may ask about firearms and other weapons. The consensus appears to be that officers may ask about weapons on the defendant's person without first giving *Miranda* warnings if the officers have arrested the defendant (which would give them the right to search the defendant's person as an incident to arrest).[73] If officers are interrogating the defendant in or near their residence or automobile, officers also may ask about the presence of weapons inside the house or vehicle only if they have an objectively reasonable basis for believing that weapons could be present in the residence or automobile and could be used to hurt the officers.[74]

A second well-established exception to *Miranda* is referred to as the booking exception.[75] Under that exception, police officers may ask a defendant questions about their identity, age, and similar questions commonly asked when police officers book an arrested person into the jail without first giving *Miranda* warnings.[76] However, such questions must be true "booking" questions and cannot be designed to elicit

---

70. Michigan v. Tucker, 417 U.S. 433 (1974) (witness located as a result of information contained in defendant's confession given in violation of *Miranda* is not suppressible as a tainted fruit of the *Miranda* violation); Oregon v. Elstad, 470 U.S. 298 (1985) (defendant's second confession given after police officers' compliance with *Miranda* will not be suppressed even if defendant's first confession obtained in violation of *Miranda* as long as the initial confession was not obtained as a result of a deliberate *Miranda* violation); United States v. Patane, 542 U.S. 630 (2004) (physical evidence obtained as a result of a confession given in violation of *Miranda* should not be suppressed as long as confession was voluntary).
71. Missouri v. Seibert, 542 U.S. 600 (2004) (plurality) (police officer's deliberate violation of *Miranda* requires suppression of subsequent confession obtained in compliance with *Miranda*); *id.* at 2614–15 (Kennedy, J., concurring in judgment).
72. New York v. Quarles, 467 U.S. 649 (1984).
73. *See, e.g.*, United States v. Lackey, 334 F.3d 1224 (10th Cir. 2003).
74. *See, e.g.*, United States v. Newton, 369 F.3d 659, 677–78 (2d Cir. 2004); United States v. Mobley, 40 F.3d 688, 693 (4th Cir. 1994); United States v. Brady, 819 F.2d 884, 888 (9th Cir. 1987); State v. Stephenson, 796 A.2d 274 (N.J. Super. Ct. App. Div. 2002).
75. *See* Pennsylvania v. Muniz, 496 U.S. 582 (1990) (plurality).
76. *See, e.g.,* State v. Rheaume, 853 A.2d 1259 (Vt. 2004).

incriminating information, even if such questions occurred during the booking process and are related to legitimate booking questions.[77]

6.3   Involuntary Confessions

Prior to *Miranda*, the primary basis for suppressing a defendant's confession was a court's conclusion that the confession was involuntary under the Due Process Clause, which also was deemed an equivalent violation of the Fifth Amendment's Self-Incrimination Clause.[78] In a long series of cases in the twentieth century, the Supreme Court held that defendants' confessions were involuntary based on a variety of factual scenarios (typically involving extended incommunicado interrogations of uneducated or otherwise unsophisticated suspects without adequate provisions of nutrition or sleep).[79] An involuntary confession always is inadmissible because it is irrebuttably presumed to be unreliable (even if it is shown in fact to be true).[80] After *Miranda*, which was intended to prevent such involuntary confessions, the frequency of such cases diminished.

Nevertheless, just because police officers complied with *Miranda* and a defendant voluntarily waived their *Miranda* rights does not mean that a subsequent confession given by the defendant was per se voluntary.[81] Likewise, the fact that a defendant was not in custody (for *Miranda* purposes) does not foreclose a challenge to a confession as being involuntary.[82] Rather, a court must consider the totality of the circumstances, focusing both on the nature of the accused and the techniques used by the police officers.[83] As the Court stated in *Miller v. Fenton*:[84]

> [T]he admissibility of a confession turns as much on whether the techniques for extracting the statements, as applied to [a particular] suspect, are compatible with a system that presumes innocence and assures that a conviction will not be secured by inquisitorial means as on whether the defendant's will was in fact overborne [i.e., whether their confession was a product of their free will].[85]

---

77. *Muniz*, 496 U.S. at 601–02 & n.14; *see also* Rosa v. McCray, 396 F.3d 210 (2d Cir. 2005).
78. *See, e.g.*, Brown v. Mississippi, 297 U.S. 278 (1936); Bram v. United States, 168 U.S. 532 (1897).
79. *See, e.g.*, Culombe v. Connecticut, 367 U.S. 568 (1961); Haynes v. Washington, 373 U.S. 503 (1963); Davis v. North Carolina, 384 U.S. 737 (1966); Arizona v. Fulminante, 499 U.S. 279 (1991).
80. Rogers v. Richmond, 365 U.S. 534 (1961).
81. Henderson v. DeTella, 97 F.3d 942, 945–47 (7th Cir. 1996); *but cf.* Berkemer v. McCarty, 468 U.S. 420, 433 n.20 (1984) ("[C]ases in which a defendant can make a colorable argument that a self-incriminating statement was 'compelled' despite the fact that the law enforcement authorities adhered to the dictates of *Miranda* are rare.").
82. *See, e.g.*, United States v. Swint, 15 F.3d 286, 289 (3d Cir. 1994).
83. Dickerson v. United States, 530 U.S. 428, 433–34 (2000); *Fulminante*, 499 U.S. at 285; Clewis v. Texas, 386 U.S. 707, 708 & n.3 (1967).
84. Miller v. Fenton, 474 U.S. 104 (1985).
85. *Id.* at 116.

The constitutional standard thus appears to have both objective and subjective components.[86] The standard applies equally "whether a confession is the product of physical intimidation or psychological pressure."[87]

With respect to challenged interrogation techniques, "[t]he [initial] question [for a court in assessing the voluntariness of a confession] is whether the technique used here risks overcoming the will of the run-of-the-mill suspect, even if it did not overcome the will of this particular suspect."[88] The next line of inquiry is whether the "police conduct [was] causally related to the confession"—a question that focuses on the suspect's subjective mental state.[89] The Court repeatedly has suggested, however, that the second factor applies according to a sort of sliding scale—the more egregious the interrogation technique, the less focus on the second issue of whether the particular defendant's will was overborne by the police misconduct.[90]

Only one type of interrogation technique—the use or threat of significant physical force in connection with the interrogation[91]—is per se unconstitutional and thus will always render a confession involuntary (even if it did not in fact impair the free will of the defendant).[92] Other techniques offensive to due process are assessed on a case-by-case basis and consider things such as the defendant's age, education, mental condition, and prior experience in the criminal justice system.[93] Such subjective factors concerning a defendant's characteristics are relevant only if the police officers who interrogate the defendant somehow exploit the factors in a way that overcomes the defendant's free will. Thus, for example, if a seriously mentally ill person approaches the police and confesses to a crime, their confession will not be suppressed unless the police somehow knowingly exploited the defendant's mental condition to elicit a confession.[94]

---

86. *See, e.g.*, United States v. Miggins, 302 F.3d 384, 397 (6th Cir. 2002) (looking both at whether the interrogation techniques were "objectively coercive" and also at whether the techniques were the "crucial motivating factor" that led the defendant to confess).

87. Townsend v. Sain, 372 U.S. 293, 307 (1963).

88. Collazo v. Estelle, 940 F.2d 411, 426 (9th Cir. 1991) (en banc) (Kozinski, J., concurring).

89. Colorado v. Connelly, 479 U.S. 157, 164 (1986).

90. See, e.g., Miller, 474 U.S. at 115–16; Culombe, 367 U.S. at 603–05 (opinion of Frankfurter, J., announcing the judgment of the Court); Blackburn v. Alabama, 361 U.S. 199, 207–08 (1960); see also DeTella, 97 F.3d at 946–47 (discussing the Supreme Court's jurisprudence on involuntary confessions).

91. A confession will not be deemed per se involuntary (and instead will be subject to the totality of the circumstances test) if a defendant was arrested through the use of physical force (which is common), but later confessed when no physical force was used or threatened. *See, e.g.*, United States v. Carroll, 207 F.3d 465, 472 (8th Cir. 2000).

92. See State v. Fields, 827 A.2d 690, 698 (Conn. 2003) (discussing Stein v. New York, 346 U.S. 156, 182–84 (1953)).

93. *See, e.g.*, Hardaway v. Young, 302 F.3d 757, 762 (7th Cir. 2002); Knight v. State, 850 A.2d 1179, 1188 (Md. 2004).

94. *Connelly*, 479 U.S. at 164.

Perhaps the most common interrogation technique that is challenged in the post-*Miranda* era is a police officer's promise concerning the potential benefit to a defendant for confessing.[95] The vast majority of courts have held that an officer's general statement that there were "advantages" to cooperating and that a defendant's cooperation would be made known to the prosecutor or court was not improper and rarely—if ever—would render a confession involuntary.[96] Specific promises of a particular sentence, conversely, are more likely to be deemed a constitutionally offensive technique, at least when the officer has misrepresented the actual benefit of confessing.[97]

Another commonly challenged interrogation technique is deception or trickery by law enforcement officials. The Supreme Court has held that a law enforcement officer's outright lie to a suspect that the officers have strong incriminating evidence against the defendant—such as an eyewitness or fingerprint evidence—will not by itself render a subsequent confession involuntary.[98] However, "[w]hile law enforcement agents may employ some degree of trickery in obtaining a confession, a deceptive practice that distorts the suspect's rational choice might, in the totality of circumstances, render the confession involuntary."[99] Thus, if an officer falsely informed a suspect that the officer possessed powerfully incriminating evidence and also informed the suspect that their punishment would be significantly less if they confessed, most courts would find that a confession resulting from such an interrogation technique was involuntary.[100]

The exclusionary rule applies with its greatest force to involuntary confessions. Unlike a confession that is obtained in violation of *Miranda*, but otherwise deemed

---

95. In *Hutto v. Ross*, 429 U.S. 28 (1976) (per curiam) and *Bram v. United States*, 168 U.S. 532, 542–43 (1897), the Supreme Court equated promises and physical threats as being equally repugnant interrogation techniques. "The test [governing voluntariness] is whether the confession was . . . 'obtained by any direct or indirect promises, however slight, [or] by the exertion of any improper influence.'" *Ross*, 429 U.S. at 30 (quoting *Bram*). In a more recent case, however, the Court disavowed *Bram*'s per se holding regarding "promises, however slight," and held that promises to the defendant by law enforcement officers must be assessed under the totality-of-the-circumstances standard. *See* Arizona v. Fulminante, 499 U.S. 279, 285 (1991) ("[I]t is clear that this passage from *Bram* . . . under current precedent does not state the [proper] standard for determining the voluntariness of a confession.").
96. *See, e.g.,* United States v. Ornelas-Rodriguez, 12 F.3d 1339, 1347–48 (5th Cir. 1994).
97. *See* United States v. Long, 852 F.2d 975, 978 (7th Cir. 1988) ("[L]eading the defendant to believe that he or she will receive lenient treatment when this is quite unlikely is improper, whereas, making a promise to bring the defendant's cooperation to the attention of the prosecutor or to seek leniency [from the court], without more, typically is not."); *see also* Sprosty v. Buchler, 79 F.3d 635, 646 (7th Cir. 1996) (an "empty prosecutorial promise" about the benefit of a defendant's confession impairs defendant's "rational choice . . . by distorting the alternatives among which [the defendant] is being asked to choose" during an interrogation).
98. Frazier v. Cupp, 394 U.S. 731, 739 (1969).
99. United States v. Drake, 934 F. Supp. 953, 963 (N.D. Ill. 1996); *see also* Lincoln v. State, 882 A.2d 944, 951–52 (Md. App. 2005).
100. *See, e.g.,* Commonwealth v. Scroggins, 789 N.E.2d 1080, 1084 (Mass. 2003).

voluntary, an involuntary confession cannot be used to impeach a defendant who testifies at trial.[101] Furthermore, a defendant's trial testimony regarding a confession later found to be involuntary cannot be introduced at a subsequent trial.[102] The tainted fruit of an involuntary confession—including physical evidence—ordinarily is inadmissible.[103]

6.4 Motions to Suppress Confessions or Incriminating Statements Obtained in Violation of the Sixth Amendment Right to Counsel

Sixth Amendment right-to-counsel issues arise in two main contexts. The first, which is discussed in Chapter Three, involves a defendant who challenges their conviction or sentence based on alleged deprivation of the assistance of counsel during one or more critical stages of the prosecution.[104] The second, which is discussed in this chapter, involves motions to suppress pretrial confessions or other incriminating statements made after a defendant's right to counsel had attached under the Sixth Amendment.

As discussed in Chapter Three, the Supreme Court has held that a defendant's right to counsel under the Sixth Amendment "attaches" with the "initiation of adversary judicial criminal proceedings—whether by way of formal charge, preliminary hearing, indictment, information, or arraignment."[105] Until that time, the law affords no protection of a suspect's Sixth Amendment right to counsel, although *Miranda* and its progeny afford some protection of the Fifth Amendment right to counsel if the defendant has been subjected to custodial interrogation.[106]

Once the Sixth Amendment right to counsel attaches, law enforcement officers cannot interrogate a defendant—whether or not they are "in custody" for *Miranda* purposes—unless the defendant first validly waives their Sixth Amendment right to counsel. If law enforcement officers deliberately elicit an incriminating statement from a defendant after their Sixth Amendment right to counsel attaches, then the confession must be suppressed unless a defendant had validly waived their right to counsel.[107] Officers "deliberately elicit" a confession when they directly question the defendant about a charged offense or otherwise make statements designed to

---

101. Mincey v. Arizona, 437 U.S. 385 (1978).
102. Harrison v. United States, 392 U.S. 219 (1968).
103. *See* Oregon v. Elstad, 470 U.S. 298, 305–10 (1985) (contrasting involuntary confessions with otherwise voluntary confessions resulting from Miranda violations); see also Commonwealth v. McAndrews, 430 A.2d 1165, 1166–67 (Pa. 1981) (murder weapon suppressed as tainted fruit because its location was learned from defendant's involuntary confession).
104. *See, e.g.*, Iowa v. Tovar, 541 U.S. 77 (2004); Alabama v. Shelton, 535 U.S. 654 (2002).
105. Texas v. Cobb, 532 U.S. 162, 167–68 (2001) (citation and internal quotation marks omitted).
106. *See* section 6.2.
107. Fellers v. United States, 540 U.S. 519 (2004); Brewer v. Williams, 430 U.S. 387 (1977).

prompt the defendant to incriminate themself.[108] Similarly, certain other evidence obtained during a "critical stage" of the prosecution and after a defendant's Sixth Amendment right to counsel has attached—such as evidence that eyewitnesses picked a defendant out of post-indictment lineup without counsel being present—should be suppressed unless the defendant validly waived their right to counsel.[109]

Ordinarily, a valid out-of-court waiver of the Sixth Amendment right to counsel occurs when a defendant (who has not yet been appointed counsel by a court or retained private counsel) waives their Fifth Amendment *Miranda* rights.[110] In-court waivers of the Sixth Amendment right to counsel (e.g., at a defendant's initial appearance in court following an indictment) usually require something more than a simple *Miranda* waiver.[111]

In *Michigan v. Jackson*,[112] the Supreme Court announced a "prophylactic rule" that if a defendant requested the assistance of counsel after their Sixth Amendment right had attached (by accepting the appointment of court-appointed counsel at a court appearance, for example), then law enforcement officers were prohibited from initiating communication with the defendant about the charged offense, even if a defendant thereafter purported to waive their right to counsel. In *Montejo v. Louisiana,* however, the Supreme Court overruled *Jackson*.[113] Therefore, if a police officer initiates communication with a defendant who previously invoked their Sixth Amendment right to counsel and the defendant validly waives the right (by agreeing to talk after being given *Miranda* warnings), their statement generally will be admissible. *Montejo's* allowance for police interrogation, however, does not permit continued interrogation if a defendant, once in custody, has invoked the Fifth Amendment (*Miranda*) right to counsel, as *Edwards v. Arizona*[114] remains good law after *Montejo*.

Montejo also did not overrule the Supreme Court's earlier Sixth Amendment decisions holding that police officers (or their agents, such as a jailhouse informant) may not deliberately elicit an incriminating statement from a defendant whose Sixth Amendment right to counsel had attached and who did not validly waive the

---

108. *See id.* at 399–400. There is a difference between "deliberately eliciting" a confession (for Sixth Amendment purposes) and "interrogating" a suspect (for Miranda purposes). See also Rhode Island v. Innis, 446 U.S. 291, 300 n.4 (1980). It generally is easier for a defendant to prove that officers deliberately elicited a confession in violation of the Sixth Amendment than it is for a defendant to prove interrogation under Miranda.
109. United States v. Wade, 388 U.S. 218 (1967); Gilbert v. California, 388 U.S. 263 (1967); Moore v. Illinois, 434 U.S. 220 (1977); *but cf.* United States v. Ash, 413 U.S. 300 (1973) (post-indictment photographic lineup is not a "critical stage" under the Sixth Amendment).
110. Patterson v. Illinois, 487 U.S. 285 (1988)
111. In-court waivers of the Sixth Amendment right to counsel are discussed in section 3.2.
112. Michigan v. Jackson, 475 U.S. 625 (1986).
113. Montejo v. Louisiana, 556 U.S. 778 (2009).
114. Edwards v. Arizona, 451 U.S. 477 (1981).

National Institute for Trial Advocacy

right to counsel.[115] Just as with confessions given to police officers, though, such incriminating statements made to agents of law enforcement will not be suppressed under the Sixth Amendment if the defendant made the statements without being prompted in any manner.[116]

Unlike a defendant's invocation of the *Miranda* right to counsel—which, under *Edwards v. Arizona*,[117] requires officers to cease questioning the defendant about any offense[118]—the Sixth Amendment right to counsel is "offense specific."[119] This means that police officers or their agents are prohibited from deliberately eliciting incriminating statements only about the charged crime(s) or any other crime(s) that would be considered the "same offense" for double jeopardy purposes.[120] If the officers elicit a confession about a crime that is not the "same offense" as the one charged, then the Sixth Amendment is not violated.[121]

The Supreme Court has not definitively addressed the operation of the exclusionary rule with respect to Sixth Amendment violations. Unlike *Miranda* (Fifth Amendment) violations, the Court has held that physical evidence that is tainted by a direct Sixth Amendment violation—that is, an incriminating statement deliberately elicited without a valid waiver of the Sixth Amendment right to counsel—must be suppressed unless the prosecution can show that the evidence would have been obtained by wholly independent means.[122] If a defendant testifies at trial in a manner inconsistent with such an otherwise inadmissible confession, the prosecution may use the confession for the limited purpose of impeaching the defendant.[123] The Court has left open the question of whether a defendant's otherwise

---

115. Massiah v. United States, 377 U.S. 201 (1964); United States v. Henry, 447 U.S. 264 (1980); Maine v. Moulton, 474 U.S. 159 (1985). Contrast the situation when an undercover officer poses as a fellow inmate and elicits incriminating statements from an incarcerated defendant before the Sixth Amendment right to counsel has attached; in that situation, the defendant's incriminating statements are admissible as long as they were voluntary. See Illinois v. Perkins, 496 U.S. 292, 300 n.* (1990) (Brennan, J., concurring in judgment).
116. Kuhlmann v. Wilson, 477 U.S. 436, 459 (1986) (the undercover officer must do something "beyond mere listening" to elicit the incriminating statement from a defendant for there to be a Sixth Amendment violation).
117. *Edwards*, 451 U.S. 477.
118. Arizona v. Roberson, 486 U.S. 675 (1988).
119. McNeil v. Wisconsin, 501 U.S. 171 (1991).
120. Cobb, 532 U.S. at 172–74 (2001) (adopting the Blockburger test, see Blockburger v. United States, 284 U.S. 299 (1932), to determine the meaning of "same offense" for Sixth Amendment purposes). The Blockburger test is discussed in Chapter Four. An open question is whether the "dual sovereignty" doctrine applicable to the Double Jeopardy Clause applies in the Sixth Amendment context. Compare United States v. Avants, 278 F.3d 510 (5th Cir. 2002), with United States v. Mills, 412 F.3d 325 (2d Cir. 2005).
121. Cobb, 532 U.S. at 173–74.
122. Wade, 388 U.S. at 239–42 (1967); see also Nix, 467 U.S. at 441–50 (1984); United States v. Terzado-Madruga, 897 F.2d 1099, 1113–14 (11th Cir. 1990).
123. Kansas v. Ventris, 556 U.S. 586 (2009).

valid confession should be suppressed if it was tainted by a prior incriminating statement deliberately elicited in direct violation of the Sixth Amendment.[124]

6.5 Leading Supreme Court Decisions Concerning Constitutional Issues Raised in Pretrial Motions to Suppress Confessions

- *Fahy v. Connecticut*, 375 U.S. 85 (1963) (holding that a defendant's confession must be suppressed under the Fourth Amendment if it was induced by a police officer who confronted the defendant with unconstitutionally obtained evidence).

- *Massiah v. United States*, 377 U.S. 201 (1964) (holding that after defendant's Sixth Amendment right to counsel had attached, his incriminating statement "deliberately elicited" by a confidential informant working for law enforcement had to be suppressed).

- *Miranda v. Arizona*, 384 U.S. 436 (1966) (setting forth the warnings that a police officer must give to a suspect before a confession given during a custodial interrogation will be admissible at a trial, including a warning that anything the suspect says can be used against the suspect in a court proceeding, and also that the suspect has a right to counsel, including appointed counsel if they cannot afford to retain an attorney; the sole remedy for violation of this constitutional prophylactic rule is suppression of the confession).

- *Frazier v. Cupp*, 394 U.S. 731 (1969) (a police officer's lie to a suspect during interrogation ordinarily will not render a subsequent confession involuntary unless the lie distorted the suspect's free will in some manner).

- *Harris v. New York*, 401 U.S. 222 (1971) (although a confession given in violation of *Miranda* may not be offered during the prosecution's case-in-chief at trial, a defendant who testifies at trial may be impeached with their confession given in violation of *Miranda*; however, a defendant may not be impeached with an involuntary confession).

- *Brown v. Illinois*, 422 U.S. 590 (1975) (setting forth four-part standard governing when a defendant's confession following an illegal arrest must be suppressed).

- *Michigan v. Mosley*, 423 U.S. 96 (1975) (holding that a defendant's invocation of the right to remain silent must be "scrupulously honored" and

---

124. *See Fellers*, 540 U.S. at 525.

that failure to do so will result in the suppression of a confession given after such an invocation; however, in contrast to a defendant's invocation of the right to counsel, which flatly prohibits further interrogation, police officers may initiate further questioning under some circumstances following a defendant's invocation of the right to silence).

- *Brewer v. Williams*, 430 U.S. 387 (1977) (holding that a law enforcement officer violates the Sixth Amendment by "deliberately eliciting" an incriminating statement from a suspect after the Sixth Amendment right to counsel has attached without first securing a valid waiver of that right, regardless of whether the person is in custody for *Miranda* purposes).

- *North Carolina v. Butler*, 441 U.S. 369 (1979) (holding that a defendant may implicitly waive their *Miranda* rights by choosing to speak after being read *Miranda* warnings).

- *Tague v. Louisiana*, 444 U.S. 469 (1980) (per curiam) (although *Butler* held that a defendant may implicitly waive their *Miranda* rights, the prosecution has the burden to establish that the defendant possessed the intellectual capacity to do so; if no such evidence is offered at the suppression hearing, a trial court may not find that such an implicit waiver occurred).

- *Rhode Island v. Innis*, 446 U.S. 291 (1980) (discussing what amounts to "interrogation" for purposes of *Miranda*, which is a related, but distinct concept from "deliberately eliciting" an incriminating statement in violation of the Sixth Amendment right to counsel).

- *Edwards v. Arizona*, 451 U.S. 477 (1981) (once a defendant invokes their *Miranda* right to counsel, any subsequent custodial confession must be suppressed unless defendant reinitiated the conversation with police officers and also validly waived their *Miranda* rights).

- *Oregon v. Bradshaw*, 462 U.S. 1039 (1983) (even after defendant initially had invoked his *Miranda* rights, his subsequent initiation of communications about a criminal offense with police officers permitted police to re-initiate interrogation after securing valid *Miranda* waiver; no violation of *Edwards* under these circumstances).

- *California v. Beheler*, 463 U.S. 1121 (1983) (per curiam) (police officer's mere questioning of a suspect about an alleged crime, without more, does not require *Miranda* warnings because mere questioning does not constitute custody).

- *Nix v. Williams*, 467 U.S. 431 (1984) (discussing the inevitable discovery exception to constitutional exclusionary rules ordinarily applicable to unconstitutionally obtained confessions and evidence).

- *New York v. Quarles*, 467 U.S. 649 (1984) (discussing the public safety exception to *Miranda*).

- *Berkemer v. McCarty*, 468 U.S. 420 (1984) (holding that an ordinary traffic stop of a defendant's car does not amount to custody requiring *Miranda* warnings unless the defendant is formally arrested during the course of the traffic stop; further holding that *Miranda* warnings are required regardless of the severity of the offense leading to the arrest and includes arrests for petty misdemeanors).

- *Oregon v. Elstad*, 470 U.S. 298 (1985) (a subsequent, Mirandized confession given after an initial un-Mirandized statement is admissible and is not tainted fruit of the initial, inadmissible statement).

- *Miller v. Fenton*, 474 U.S. 104 (1985) ("the admissibility of a confession turns as much on whether the techniques for extracting the statements, as applied to [a particular] suspect, are compatible with a system that presumes innocence and assures that a conviction will not be secured by inquisitorial means as on whether the defendant's will was in fact overborne.").

- *Kuhlmann v. Wilson*, 477 U.S. 436 (1986) (an undercover officer or confidential informant must do something "beyond mere listening" to "deliberately elicit" an incriminating statement from a defendant in violation of the Sixth Amendment violation under *Massiah*).

- *Colorado v. Connelly*, 479 U.S. 157 (1986) (for a confession to be rendered involuntary, law enforcement officials must engage in some type of improper conduct; specifically holding that the spontaneous confession of a seriously mentally ill man to a police officer was voluntary because the officer did nothing to cause him to confess or exploit his mental illness).

- *Arizona v. Roberson*, 486 U.S. 675 (1988) (once a defendant has invoked the *Miranda* right to counsel with respect to one crime, *Edwards*'s prophylactic rule applies to police-initiated interrogation about a different offense; *Miranda* right to counsel, unlike Sixth Amendment right to counsel, is not "offense-specific" and, once invoked, applies to all criminal offenses).

- *Patterson v. Illinois*, 487 U.S. 285 (1988) (in situations where a defendant's Sixth Amendment right to counsel has attached, but the defendant has not yet invoked the right to counsel or been appointed counsel, a valid out-of-court waiver of the Sixth Amendment right to counsel ordinarily occurs when the defendant validly waives their *Miranda* rights; distinguishing in-court from out-of-court waivers of the Sixth Amendment right to counsel).

- *Duckworth v. Eagan*, 492 U.S. 195 (1989) (requiring substantial compliance, but not perfection with respect to the content of *Miranda* warnings).

- *Illinois v. Perkins*, 496 U.S. 292 (1990) (undercover officer who pretended to be then-unindicted defendant's cellmate did not need to give *Miranda* warnings before engaging in conversation with the defendant and, in the process, deliberately eliciting incriminating statements; there was no interrogation in such a situation because the defendant assumed he was talking to another inmate rather than a police officer; no Sixth Amendment violation because defendant's Sixth Amendment right to counsel had not yet attached).

- *Pennsylvania v. Muniz*, 496 U.S. 582 (1990) (discussing booking exception to *Miranda*).

- *Arizona v. Fulminante*, 499 U.S. 279 (1991) (holding that whether a confession is involuntary is judged by the totality of the circumstances in a particular case; a mere promise by law enforcement official to a suspect will not automatically render a subsequent confession involuntary; disavowing contrary language in *Bram v. United States*, 168 U.S. 532 (1897)).

- *McNeil v. Wisconsin*, 501 U.S. 171 (1991) (a defendant cannot anticipatorily invoke *Miranda* rights before actually being subjected to custodial interrogation).

- *Stansbury v. California*, 511 U.S. 318 (1994) (per curiam) (holding that "custody" for *Miranda* purposes occurs when a suspect is formally under arrest or is subjected to restraints traditionally associated with arrest; whether a defendant was in custody is an objective standard, with neither the defendant's nor an interrogating officer's subjective views being dispositive).

- *Davis v. United States*, 512 U.S. 452 (1994) (a defendant must unambiguously invoke their *Miranda* rights before an interrogating officer must cease questioning, at least when defendant previously waived their *Miranda* rights in an unambiguous manner).

- *Dickerson v. United States*, 530 U.S. 428 (2000) (reaffirming *Miranda* and describing its holding as constitutional in nature, although characterizing it as a prophylactic rule).

- *Texas v. Cobb*, 532 U.S. 162 (2001) (Sixth Amendment right to counsel is "offense-specific," meaning that a defendant's invocation of the Sixth Amendment right to counsel concerning one charged offense will not prevent officers from interrogating the defendant regarding a separate, uncharged offense; test for whether officers violated the Sixth Amendment right to counsel by questioning a suspect about a particular offense when the right had attached concerning another offense is whether the two crimes were the "same offense" within the meaning of *Blockburger v. United States*, 284 U.S. 299 (1932)).

- *Missouri v. Seibert*, 542 U.S. 600 (2004) (police officer's deliberate violation of *Miranda* in obtaining initial confession ordinarily requires suppression of subsequent confession obtained in compliance with *Miranda*; *Elstad* distinguished on the ground that the initial confession was not obtained in deliberate violation of *Miranda* in that case).

- *United States v. Patane*, 542 U.S. 630 (2004) (physical evidence obtained as a result of a confession given in violation of *Miranda* should not be suppressed as long as confession was voluntary, at least where *Miranda* violation was not deliberate).

- *Montejo v. Louisiana*, 556 U.S. 778 (2009) (overruling the Court's earlier decision in *Michigan v. Jackson*, 475 U.S. 625 (1986), which had created a Sixth Amendment prophylactic rule prohibiting police officers from interrogating a defendant after they invoked the Sixth Amendment right to counsel in a noncustodial situation where *Miranda* did not apply).

- *Kansas v. Ventris*, 556 U.S. 586 (2009) (defendant may be impeached with confession given in violation of the Sixth Amendment right to counsel).

- *Berghuis v. Thompkins*, 560 U.S. 370 (2010) (holding that [1] a defendant's mere silence in response to *Miranda* warnings, even for an extended period of time, does not by itself constitute invocation of *Miranda* rights; and [2] defendant's decision to speak to officers after such silence constitutes implied waiver of the rights as long as the defendant understood them and decided to confess voluntarily).

- *J.D.B. v. North Carolina*, 564 U.S. 261 (2011) (when determining whether a defendant was in custody for purposes of *Miranda*, a court must consider the defendant's status as a juvenile if the interrogating officer knew or should have known that the defendant was a juvenile).

- *Howes v. Fields*, 565 U.S. 499 (2012) (mere fact that defendant imprisoned for one crime does not automatically constitute custody for purposes of *Miranda* regarding unrelated crimes allegedly occurring outside of the prison).

CHAPTER SEVEN

THE RIGHT TO A JURY TRIAL AND THE JURY SELECTION PROCESS

7.1 The Right to an Impartial Jury

7.1.1 Introduction

The Sixth Amendment provides that a criminal defendant—other than a juvenile not tried as an adult[1] or a member of the military charged in court martial proceedings[2]—has a right to a "trial[] by an impartial [petit] jury" in all felony cases and also in "non-petty" misdemeanor cases.[3] According to the Supreme Court, "[t]he purpose of a jury is to guard against . . . the overzealous or mistaken prosecutor" and the "overconditioned or biased . . . judge."[4] The Court has deemed the right to a jury trial one of a criminal defendant's most "fundamental"[5] rights.

The constitutional right to a jury trial does not apply to defendants in "petty" misdemeanor cases, meaning cases in which the authorized (potential) jail sentence that a defendant faces is six months or less.[6] This is true even if a defendant faces multiple petty misdemeanor charges that, if "stacked" by the sentencing judge, would result in a cumulative jail sentence in excess of six months.[7] The right to a jury trial in misdemeanor cases should be contrasted with the Sixth Amendment right to counsel in misdemeanor cases: the latter turns not on authorized punishment, but instead on the punishment actually imposed (with the right attaching

---

1. McKeiver v. Pennsylvania, 403 U.S. 528 (1971).
2. *See* Solorio v. United States, 483 U.S. 435 (1987).
3. Duncan v. Louisiana, 391 U.S. 145 (1968). As discussed in section 1.3, the right to a grand jury—as opposed to the right to a petit jury—has not been applied to the states.
4. Taylor v. Louisiana, 419 U.S. 522, 530 (1975).
5. Schriro v. Summerlin, 542 U.S. 348, 358 (2004).
6. Blanton v. City of North Las Vegas, 489 U.S. 538 (1989); Bloom v. Illinois, 391 U.S. 194 (1968). Some states nonetheless provide a right to a jury trial in petty misdemeanor cases under state law. *See, e.g.*, People v. Antkoviak, 619 N.W.2d 18 (Mich. Ct. App. 2000).
7. Lewis v. United States, 518 U.S. 322 (1996).

only if a sentence of one day or more in jail ultimately is imposed, even if it is suspended).[8]

Although a defendant may waive the right to a jury trial and proceed with a bench trial (at which a judge rather than a jury renders the verdict), ordinarily a defendant has no right to waive a jury and proceed with bench trial without the consent of the court and prosecution.[9] A defendant may, of course, always plead guilty to the court, which necessarily waives their right to a jury trial.[10] A valid waiver of the right to a jury trial will "not be presumed" on appeal if the record is silent concerning the circumstances of the waiver.[11] A waiver is not constitutionally valid unless it is both knowing and voluntary.[12] Thus, for example, if a defendant erroneously is informed that they have the right to the assistance of counsel or the right to testify on their own behalf only if they waive the right to a jury trial and that defendant proceeds with a bench trial based on that erroneous assumption, then that waiver of the right to a jury trial is involuntary.[13] Unlike virtually all other rights afforded to criminal defendants in the Bill of Rights, the right to a jury trial is a "personal" one—meaning that presumably it must be personally waived by the defendant and cannot be waived by defense counsel (on the defendant's behalf) without the defendant's consent.[14]

The Sixth Amendment right to a jury trial does not apply to the decision of what sentence to impose in a criminal case, at least in non-capital cases.[15] However, the Supreme Court has held that any fact (other than a prior conviction) that increases the statutory mandatory minimum or maximum punishment that a defendant may receive is constitutionally equivalent to an element of the charged offense and that a defendant has a constitutional right to have that alleged fact found by a jury (rather than a judge)—even if such a fact is deemed a "sentencing factor" by the legislature.[16] Furthermore, each factual element of a charged offense must be found by a

---

8. The right to counsel in misdemeanor cases is discussed in section 3.1.

9. Singer v. United States, 380 U.S. 24 (1965).

10. Adams v. United States ex rel. McCann, 317 U.S. 269, 275 (1942); *see also* Parke v. Raley, 506 U.S. 20, 29 (1993) (valid guilty plea waives the right to a jury trial).

11. United States ex rel. Wandick v. Chrans, 869 F.2d 1084, 1087 (7th Cir. 1989).

12. *Adams*, 317 U.S. at 275.

13. *See, e.g.*, Abrams v. State, 777 So. 2d 1205 (Fla. Dist. Ct. App. 2001); Commonwealth v. Miller, 366 A.2d 299 (Pa. Super. Ct. 1976).

14. *See, e.g.*, United States v. Diaz, 540 F.3d 1316, 1321–22 (11th Cir. 2008). Justice Scalia contended in a concurring opinion that defense counsel may unilaterally waive a defendant's right to a jury trial. *See* Gonzalez v. United States, 553 U.S. 242, 1773 (2008) (Scalia, J., concurring in judgment).

15. The Supreme Court initially held that there was no Sixth Amendment right to a jury at capital or non-capital sentencing, *see* Spaziano v. Florida, 468 U.S. 447 (1984*); but cf.* Hurst v. Florida, 136 S. Ct. 616 (2016) (Sixth Amendment right to a jury trial requires jury to find "eligibility" aggravating factor in a death penalty case). *Hurst* is discussed in section 12.1.6.

16. Alleyne v. United States, 570 U.S. 99 (2013); United States v. Booker, 534 U.S. 220 (2005); Blakely v. Washington, 542 U.S. 296 (2004); Ring v. Arizona, 536 U.S. 584 (2002); Apprendi v.

jury, whether or not the element involves a pure fact (such as an allegation that the defendant lied to a law enforcement officer) or instead involves a mixed question of fact and law (such as an allegation that a defendant's lie was "material").[17] "The jury's function is not merely to determine the existence vel non of the factual components underlying the essential elements, but to apply the law to those facts and draw the ultimate conclusion of guilt or innocence."[18]

Although provided in the vast majority of jurisdictions, a twelve-person jury is not required by the Sixth Amendment,[19] at least in state cases.[20] The Supreme Court has approved six-person juries—but no fewer than six.[21] Overruling its prior precedent permitting non-unanimous juries, the Supreme Court, in 2020 in *Ramos v. Louisiana*,[22] held that the Sixth Amendment requires unanimous guilty verdicts, regardless of the size of the jury.

7.1.2 Constitutional Challenges to How the "Venire" Is Selected

Before a petit jury is empaneled in a case, a defendant may lodge a constitutional objection to the manner in which the "venire" (also called the "array" or "panel")—the pool from which petit jurors are selected—is chosen. In the vast majority of jurisdictions, such an objection usually is made in the form of a motion to quash the venire and must be filed before the voir dire process begins.[23]

There are two primary constitutional challenges to the manner in which the venire is selected: 1) a claim that the venire was chosen in a manner that does not represent a "fair cross-section of the community" within the meaning of the Sixth Amendment's right to an impartial jury;[24] and 2) a related, but distinct claim that the venire was selected in a manner that discriminated against a "cognizable" class of persons protected by the Equal Protection Clause of the

---

New Jersey, 530 U.S. 466 (2000). The *Apprendi* line of cases is discussed further in Chapter Twelve.

17. United States v. Gaudin, 515 U.S. 506 (1995).

18. United States v. Terry, 257 F.3d 366, 371 (4th Cir. 2001) (King, J., concurring in judgment) (citation and internal quotation marks omitted).

19. Williams v. Florida, 399 U.S. 78 (1970).

20. It is apparently an open question whether the twelve-person jury requirement exists in federal criminal cases as a constitutional element. *See* United States v. Curbelo, 343 F.3d 273, 279 n.5 (4th Cir. 2003).

21. Burch v. Louisiana, 441 U.S. 130 (1979); Ballew v. Georgia, 435 U.S. 223 (1978).

22. Ramos v. Louisiana, 140 S. Ct. 1390 (2020) (overruling Apodaca v. Oregon, 406 U.S. 404 (1972) (approving ten-to-two guilty verdict) and Johnson v. Louisiana, 406 U.S. 356 (1972) (approving nine-to-three guilty verdict)).

23. *See, e.g.*, United States v. Grismore, 546 F.2d 844, 848 (10th Cir. 1976); United States v. Greene, 971 F. Supp. 1117, 1137–38 (E.D. Mich. 1997); Miller v. State, 452 A.2d 180, 185 (Md. App. 1982). In contrast, a similar objection to the manner in which a grand jury is selected is typically made in a pretrial motion to dismiss the indictment. *See* Chapter Four.

24. *See, e.g.*, Taylor v. Louisiana, 419 U.S. 522 (1975); *see also* Berghuis v. Smith, 559 U.S. 314 (2010).

Fourteenth Amendment (or the equivalent equal protection provided by the Due Process Clause of the Fifth Amendment in federal prosecutions).[25] Both such constitutional challenges are similar in nature to the type raised in a pretrial motion to dismiss the indictment based on improper discrimination during the process of selecting grand jurors (discussed in Chapter Four).[26] As is true with challenges to the grand jury selection process, a defendant has third-party "standing" to challenge the petit jury selection process irrespective of race or gender or membership in any protected class (for example, a white male defendant may move to quash the venire based on the underrepresentation or exclusion of African-Americans or women).[27]

7.1.2.1   Fair Cross-Section Claim

A Sixth Amendment fair cross-section claim[28] contends that the manner in which the petit jury venire is selected in a particular jurisdiction fails to ensure an impartial jury by excluding all or significant portions of a distinctive group in that particular community from the pool of prospective jurors.[29] In *Duren v. Missouri*,[30] the Supreme Court has set forth the elements of a prima facie fair cross-section violation:

> To establish a prima facie violation of the fair-cross-section requirement, the defendant must show (1) that the group alleged to be excluded is a "distinctive" group in the [relevant] community; (2) that the representation of this group in venires from which juries are selected is not fair and reasonable in relation to the number of such

---

25. *See* Castaneda v. Partida, 430 U.S. 482 (1977); United States v. Biaggi, 909 F.2d 662, 677 (2d Cir. 1990).

26. Although a federal grand jury can be challenged on the ground that it does not reflect a fair cross-section of the community under the Sixth Amendment, it is an open question, which has divided the lower courts, whether state grand juries (as well as petit juries) are subject to the Sixth Amendment's implied "fair-cross-section" requirement. *Compare* Ford v. Seabold, 841 F.2d 677, 687–88 (6th Cir. 1988) (fair cross-section requirement only applies to state petit juries), *with* State v. Jenison, 405 A.2d 3, 6–8 (R.I. 1979) (fair cross-section requirement applies to both state grand and petit juries); *see also* Ford v. Kentucky, 469 U.S. 984 (1984) (Marshall, J., dissenting from denial of certiorari) (contending that the question is still an open one in the Supreme Court's jurisprudence).

27. *Taylor*, 419 U.S. at 526.

28. Although a defendant may lodge a "fair cross-section" objection concerning the petit jury venire at the time that the particular venire in their case is seated, realistically speaking such an objection should be preceded by pretrial investigation into the manner in which venires are chosen and the development of statistical evidence about the composition of prior venires in that particular jurisdiction. *See* McGinnis v. Johnson, 181 F.3d 686, 690–91 (5th Cir. 1999) (noting that a one-time example of substantial under-representation of a particular group on a particular venire does not make out a prima facie case in violation of the fair cross-section requirement of the Sixth Amendment; additional evidence of underrepresentation on prior venires is required).

29. *Taylor*, 419 U.S. at 526–31.

30. Duren v. Missouri, 439 U.S. 357 (1979).

persons in the community; and (3) that this underrepresentation is due to systematic exclusion of the group in the jury-selection process.[31]

The Court repeatedly has stated that this does not mean that a defendant is entitled to a particular petit jury that contains representatives from each "distinctive" group in the relevant community; it only means that the venire selection process cannot improperly exclude such groups.[32]

The first prong of *Duren*—a "distinctive group" under the Sixth Amendment—is a related, but distinct concept from a "cognizable group" under the Equal Protection Clause.[33] Such a distinctive group for Sixth Amendment purposes must be a significantly sized "identifiable segment[] playing [a] major role[] in the community,"[34] which has "basic similarit[ies] in attitudes or ideas or experience."[35] Although the Supreme Court's decisions have been limited to such obvious groups as women and racial minorities[36]—who also are cognizable groups under the Equal Protection Clause—a handful of lower courts have gone beyond cognizable classes and treated as distinctive groups such classes of persons as city dwellers (in areas with large rural communities),[37] specific religious groups,[38] young people,[39] and poor persons living in a housing project.[40] It is doubtful that the current Supreme Court would deem poor persons, rural or urban persons, or young persons as distinctive groups. It is a much closer question concerning specific religious groups.[41]

Even if the meanings of distinctive group (for fair cross-section purposes) and cognizable group (for equal protection purposes) are essentially the same,[42] there

---

31. *Id.* at 364.
32. *Taylor*, 419 U.S. at 538.
33. *See* State v. McDougal, 699 A.2d 872, 880–81 (Conn. 1997).
34. *Taylor*, 419 U.S. at 530.
35. State v. Tillman, 600 A.2d 738, 743 (Conn. 1991) (citations and internal quotation marks omitted).
36. *See, e.g., Taylor*, 419 U.S. 522; *Duren*, 439 U.S. 357.
37. *Tillman*, 600 A.2d at 743.
38. United States v. Gelb, 881 F.2d 1155, 1161 (2d Cir. 1989) (Jews); State v. Fulton, 566 N.E.2d 1195 (Ohio 1991) (Amish).
39. *See generally* Thomas M. Fleming, *Age Group Underrepresentation in Grand Jury or Petit Jury Venire*, 62 A.L.R. 4th 859 (1988) (citing conflicting decisions of lower courts).
40. State v. Cage, 337 So. 2d 1123 (La. 1976); *but cf.* Mitchell S. Zuklie, *Rethinking the Fair Cross-Section Requirement*, 84 CALIF. L. REV. 101, 116–18 & nn.127–48 (1996) (citing a large amount of case law holding that poor persons are not a distinctive group within the meaning of the fair cross-section requirement of the Sixth Amendment).
41. The Court has not yet addressed the related issue of whether religious groups are cognizable groups under the Equal Protection Clause for purposes of Batson v. Kentucky, 476 U.S. 79 (1986). *See* Davis v. Minnesota, 511 U.S. 1115 (1994) (Thomas, J., joined by Scalia, J., dissenting from denial of certiorari).
42. *See* Andrew D. Leipold, *Constitutionalizing Jury Selection in Criminal Cases: A Critical Evaluation*, 86 GEO. L. J. 945, 968–69 & nn.110–29 (Feb. 1998) ("[W]ith isolated exceptions, courts routinely limit the application of the [fair] cross-section requirement to groups that already receive heightened protection under the Equal Protection Clause.") (citing numerous lower court cases).

still is an important difference between a Sixth Amendment claim and an equal protection claim. The latter requires proof of intentional discrimination, whereas the former only requires proof of systematic exclusion—that as a result of state action (whether intentional or not), a distinctive group is entirely absent or significantly underrepresented on petit jury venires.[43]

The second prong of the *Duren* test—proof of a significant underrepresentation of a distinctive group—must be proven through the use of statistical data concerning prior venires.[44] To meet the second prong's requirements, such data must show that the actual number of persons within the distinctive group who were members of past petit jury venires constitute a statistically significant underrepresentation in relation to the number of such persons in the relevant community.[45] There are no hard and fast rules here; what is statistically significant in a given case will depend on the "absolute" and "comparative" degree of statistical underrepresentation.[46]

Assuming such statistical underrepresentation is shown, the third prong of *Duren* requires the defendant to demonstrate that some type of state action is responsible for it—as opposed to being the result of "voluntary behavior patterns, unencouraged by state action."[47] For instance, in a jurisdiction that randomly selects members of petit jury venires from nondiscriminatory voter registration rolls, a defendant attacking the selection process will lose their challenge if an underrepresented distinctive group simply failed to register to vote in the same percentages as other groups.[48] In such a case, there is no state action responsible for the distinctive group's underrepresentation on the venires; rather, it is the group's voluntary behavior that explains their underrepresentation. Only in a case where a defendant could prove that state action resulted in the underrepresentation could the defendant prevail.

If a prima facie fair cross-section violation is shown, the prosecution still has the opportunity to show that a "significant state interest" clearly outweighs the systemic exclusion or significant underrepresentation of a particular distinctive group.[49] Such an opportunity would appear to pose a high hurdle, although not an impossible one,[50] to overcome in most cases where a prima

---

43. *Duren*, 439 U.S. at 368 n.26; *see also* United States v. Rioux, 97 F.3d 648, 658 (2d Cir. 1996); People v. Taylor, 743 N.Y.S.2d 253, 264 (N.Y. Super. Ct. 2002).
44. *Duren*, 439 U.S. at 364–65.
45. *See* United States v. Weaver, 267 F.3d 231, 240–43 (3d Cir. 2001).
46. *Id.* The statistical analysis employed here is identical to the type employed in analyzing an equal protection challenge to the racial composition of grand juries. *See* Chapter Four.
47. *Taylor*, 743 N.Y.S.2d at 264 n.18.
48. *See, e.g.*, United States v. Cecil, 836 F.2d 1431, 1444–55 (4th Cir. 1988) (en banc).
49. *Duren*, 439 U.S. at 367–68.
50. *See, e.g.*, United States v. Benmuhar, 658 F.2d 14 (1st Cir. 1981) (holding that the fact that Puerto Ricans were statistically underrepresented on petit jury venires was explained by the fact that many of them did not show proficiency in English and that the government had a "significant interest" in limiting jury service to proficient English speakers).

facie violation has been established. However, in the overwhelming majority of modern cases—cases since *Duren*—lower courts have rejected criminal defendants' fair cross-sections claims on the ground that no prima facie case had been shown, thus obviating the need to address whether a "significant state interest" was presented.[51] There have only been a handful of successful fair-cross-section claims in the modern era.[52]

7.1.2.2 Equal Protection Claim

With three exceptions, an equal protection challenge to the systematic exclusion of certain classes of persons from petit jury venires[53] is equivalent to a fair cross-section challenge, at least when a defendant relies on circumstantial evidence (i.e., statistical evidence).[54] The three differences are: 1) an equal protection claim is limited to "cognizable" classes under the Equal Protection Clause (i.e., racial/ ethnic groups and genders) as opposed to theoretically broader "distinctive groups;"[55] 2) an equal protection claim requires the showing of intentional discrimination, which a fair cross-section does not require;[56] and 3) a prima facie case in the equal protection context does not require the defendant to offer statistical evidence of underrepresentation of relevant groups in past venires—instead, the defendant may rely on underrepresentation in the specific venire in their own case as long as

---

51. *See, e.g.*, Melissa K. Gee, *A Jury Drawn from a Fair Cross-Section of the Community—A Fading Memory?*: People v. Sanders, 26 U.S.F. L. REV. 785 (1992).
52. See, e.g., Garcia-Dorantes v. Warren, 801 F.3d 584 (6th Cir. 2015) (granting habeas corpus relief based on the defendant's fair-cross-section claim); State v. Lilly, 930 N.W.2d 293 (Iowa 2019) (remanding for an evidentiary hearing on the defendant's fair-cross-section claim).
53. Analysis of an equal protection challenge to a petit jury array is identical to an equal protection challenge to a grand jury. Alexander v. Louisiana, 405 U.S. 625, 626 n.3 (1972). The latter is discussed in Chapter Four.
54. In the rare case where direct evidence of invidious discrimination exists, a defendant need not rely on statistical evidence. See, e.g., State v. Lozano, 616 So. 2d 73, 76 (Fla. Dist. Ct. App. 1993) ("We agree . . that the trial court [in selecting a venue site] deliberately acted so as to increase the number of [potential] Black jurors. In doing this, the trial court virtually guaranteed the absence of Hispanic jurors. [P]urposeful racial discrimination in selection of the venire violates a defendant's right to equal protection because it denies him the protection that a trial by jury is intended to secure.") (citation and internal quotation marks omitted).
The same is true regarding direct evidence of a fair cross-section claim. *See, e.g., Cage*, 337 So. 2d at 1125 (finding a fair cross-section violation where undisputed evidence showed that the jury selection process intentionally excluded a large housing project that contained large numbers of poor minority persons).
55. *See* Lindsey v. Smith, 820 F.2d 1137, 1145–46 (11th Cir. 1987) (citing cases). As discussed above, for all practical purposes a cognizable group is equivalent to a distinctive group.
56. *Duren*, 439 U.S. at 368 n.26.

the defendant shows that the venire selection process provided an "opportunity for discrimination."[57]

If a defendant presents an adequate prima facie equal protection violation, the burden shifts to the prosecution to rebut a presumption of intentional discrimination by offering a race-neutral reason for the underrepresentation.[58]

A race-neutral reason need not qualify as a "significant state interest" (for fair cross-section purposes), and thus it appears that in theory at least, it is easier to rebut a prima facie case in the equal protection context.[59] However, because a mere affirmation of good faith on the part of jury selection officials (such as denials of discriminatory intent) will not suffice to rebut a prima facie case,[60] in most cases the prosecution will try to offer evidence explaining the statistical disparities that serves the same purpose as proving a significant state interest.

7.2 Legal Issues Related to the Process of Removing Objectionable or Undesirable Members of the Venire

The jury selection process is commonly called "voir dire," which roughly translates, "to speak the truth" in French.[61] During voir dire, the trial judge and attorneys explain the applicable rules of law to the members of the venire and seek to expose and remove those members who are unable or unwilling to fairly apply those rules during the trial.

Jury "selection" is a misnomer. The parties do not in fact select jurors. Rather, they remove objectionable or undesirable members of the venire through the use of peremptory "strikes" and challenges "for cause." Depending on the jurisdiction, each side is given a set number of peremptory strikes to use during voir dire.[62] There is no limit to the number of "for cause" challenges that can be made.

7.2.1 Constitutional Requirements Concerning the Manner of Questioning Prospective Jurors

The Supreme Court has held that trial judges have a great deal of discretion in conducting voir dire and that the Due Process Clause requires specific questions

---

57. Smith v. State, 658 N.E.2d 910, 916 (Ind. Ct. App. 1995); *see also* Cunningham v. Zant, 928 F.2d 1006, 1014 n.9 (11th Cir. 1991) (citing Batson v. Kentucky, 476 U.S. 79, 95 (1986)).
58. Davis v. Zant, 721 F.2d 1478, 1482 n.6 (11th Cir. 1983); Ramirez v. State, 575 S.E.2d 462, 466–67 (Ga. 2003); *see also* Castaneda v. Partida, 430 U.S. 482, 494 (1977).
59. *Gee, supra* n.51, at 793.
60. Whitus v. Georgia, 385 U.S. 545, 551 (1967); *Davis*, 721 F.2d at 1485.
61. BLACK'S LAW DICTIONARY 1605 (8th ed. 2004).
62. *See, e.g.*, FED. R. CRIM. P. 24(b)(1)–(3) (specifying the number of peremptory challenges given to the prosecution and defense in capital cases, noncapital felony cases, and misdemeanor cases).

to be posed to prospective jurors only in certain circumstances.[63] The two types of questions that are constitutionally required in noncapital cases,[64] at least in some situations, concern race and pretrial publicity. If an alleged noncapital crime involves special circumstances concerning race or racial issues that are inextricably bound up with the alleged offense, then the due process requires the trial judge, in at least a brief manner, to question prospective jurors about their views on race and determine whether any members of the venire possess racial prejudices that would interfere with their ability to be fair and impartial jurors in that case.[65] However, if the alleged noncapital offense merely involved a confrontation between persons of two different races without any other racial dimension, such questioning is not constitutionally required.[66]

With respect to questions about pretrial publicity, the Supreme Court has held that a trial judge need only ask general questions of prospective jurors about whether they could set aside any preexisting knowledge about the case (learned from the media) and render a fair and impartial verdict based solely on the evidence admitted during the trial.[67] A trial judge is not constitutionally required as a general rule to ask individual members of the venire about specific information they had learned from the pretrial publicity,[68] although in cases with extensive pretrial publicity, failure to do so could result in a reversal of a defendant's conviction on appeal.[69]

7.2.2 Constitutional Challenges "For Cause"[70]

Under the Sixth Amendment to the Constitution, each and every member of a jury must be "impartial."[71] There are countless potential bases for challenging a prospective juror for cause on the ground that the person is not impartial—most relate to the person's preexisting opinions or knowledge about the alleged offense

---

63. *See generally* Mu'Min v. Virginia, 500 U.S. 415, 422–24 (1991).
64. As discussed in Chapter Twelve, additional questions are constitutionally required in death penalty cases.
65. *See* Ristaino v. Ross, 424 U.S. 589, 596–97 (1976) (discussing Ham v. South Carolina, 409 U.S. 524 (1973)).
66. *Id.*; *see also* Rosales-Lopez v. United States, 451 U.S. 182 (1981) (for questions about race to be required during voir dire, there must be a "reasonable possibility" based on specific circumstances in a particular case that racial prejudice could impair the jury's impartiality).
67. *Mu'Min*, 500 U.S. at 431.
68. *Id.*
69. Irvin v. Dowd, 366 U.S. 717 (1961).
70. In theory at least, a defendant can move to challenge an entire venire for cause based on extensive pretrial publicity (in the form of a motion for a change of venue). *See, e.g.*, Rideau v. Louisiana, 373 U.S. 723 (1963). As discussed in Chapter Four, the modern Supreme Court would be extremely unlikely to uphold such a challenge to an entire venire. *See, e.g.*, Skilling v. United States, 561 U.S. 358 (2010).
71. Dyer v. Calderon, 151 F.3d 970, 973 (9th Cir. 1998) (en banc).

or the defendant.[72] A prospective juror may be either biased "in fact" or, instead, "conclusively presumed" to be biased "as a matter of law."[73] The former is referred to as "actual bias"; the latter is referred to as "implied bias."[74]

A prospective juror with actual bias is one who is found to be actually biased against a party in a litigation to the extent that the bias affects the prospective juror's ability to be fair and impartial. Such bias ordinarily may be determined to exist—or not to exist—as a factual matter during voir dire, when the parties and judge are permitted to question the prospective juror and the trial court is permitted to hear the answers and observe the prospective juror's demeanor.[75] Conversely, in certain extreme cases of prospective jurors with "implied bias," such bias is established where there are "specific facts" showing "a close connection to the circumstances" of the defendant's case.[76] In the latter situation, irrespective of whether the prospective juror claims to have been unbiased and irrespective of whether the trial court finds that the juror is actually unbiased, the extreme circumstances of the case require the court to imply bias as a matter of law.[77]

An example of implied bias was found in *Leonard v. United States*,[78] in which the Supreme Court held that a prospective juror who had heard the trial court announce the defendant's guilty verdict in a prior trial of "a similar case" should be presumed biased and unfit to serve as a juror in the subsequent case.[79] Conversely, the Court refused to find implied bias in *Smith v. Phillips*,[80] a case in which a juror

---

72. Sometimes, a prospective juror reveals their bias during voir dire; other times, the bias of a juror is not detected until after a defendant has been convicted following a jury trial. In the former situation, the trial court is required to rule on the question of whether a prospective juror is biased during voir dire; in the latter situation, the trial court in ruling on a motion for a new trial or other postconviction challenges to a defendant's conviction is required to determine whether a juror (who actually sat in judgment of the defendant) was biased. For a discussion of such a postconviction claim of juror misconduct, see Chapter Thirteen.

73. Smith v. Phillips, 455 U.S. 209, 221–24 (1982) (O'Connor, J., concurring); *see also* Miller v. Webb, 385 F.3d 666, 673–74 (6th Cir. 2004).

74. *Smith*, 455 U.S. at 221 (O'Connor, J., concurring); *see also* J.E.B. v. Alabama ex rel. T.B., 511 U.S. 127, 143 (1994) (recognizing both "actual" and "implied" juror bias); United States v. Wood, 299 U.S. 123, 134 (1936) (same).

75. *Smith*, 455 U.S. at 222 (O'Connor, J., concurring).

76. United States v. Scott, 854 F.2d 697, 699 (5th Cir. 1988); Gonzalez v. Thomas, 99 F.3d 978, 987 (10th Cir. 1996); *see also* Willie v. Maggio, 737 F.2d 1372, 1379 (5th Cir. 1984) ("A juror is presumed to be biased when he or she is apprised of such inherently prejudicial facts about the defendant that the court deems it highly unlikely that the juror can exercise independent judgment, even if the juror declares to the court that he or she will decide [or did decide] the case solely on the evidence presented.").

77. Brooks v. Dretke, 444 F.3d 328 (5th Cir. 2006).

78. Leonard v. United States, 378 U.S. 544 (1964) (per curiam).

79. *Id.* at 545.

80. Smith v. Phillips, 455 U.S. 209 (1982).

(shortly before being called for jury duty) had submitted an employment application to work as a criminal investigator at the prosecutor's office.[81]

7.2.3 *Peremptory Strikes and* Batson v. Kentucky

Peremptory strikes, unlike challenges for cause, do not require a litigant to state a reason for removing a prospective juror. One of the most common legal issues that arises during the parties' exercise of their peremptories is a *"Batson* claim"—an argument by one side that the opposing side used one or more of its peremptory strikes in an impermissibly discriminatory manner.[82] The Supreme Court has held that peremptory strikes cannot be used on the basis of a prospective juror's race,[83] ethnicity, or gender.[84] The Court has not yet addressed whether *Batson* applies when a prospective juror is removed based on their religious views or affiliation.[85]

The Court has held that defense counsel as well as prosecutors cannot use peremptory strikes in a discriminatory manner; likewise, the Court has extended *Batson* to lawyers in civil cases.[86] Any party—regardless of race or gender—has standing to challenge the opposing side's improper use of a peremptory strike in violation of the Equal Protection Clause.[87] The rule in *Batson* was an extension of prior cases in which the Supreme Court held that discrimination in the selection of

---

81. *Id.* at 216–17.
82. Batson v. Kentucky, 476 U.S. 79 (1986); *see also* Miller-El v. Dretke, 545 U.S. 231 (2005). The Court has extended *Batson* to "for cause" challenges based on impermissibly discriminatory reasons. *See* Hernandez v. New York, 500 U.S. 352, 362 (1991) ("If we deemed the prosecutor's reason for striking these jurors a racial classification on its face, it would follow that a trial judge could not excuse for cause a juror [for the same reasons]. If the explanation is not race-neutral for the prosecutor, it is no more so for the trial judge.").
83. Although the Supreme Court has never specifically addressed the issue of whether *Batson* applies to peremptory strikes of Caucasian members of the venire based on their race, the apparent consensus among lower courts is that *Batson* applies to members of racial majorities as well as racial minorities. *See, e.g.*, Caudill v. Commonwealth, 120 S.W.3d 635, 657 (Ky. 2003).
84. *See J.E.B.*, 511 U.S. 127 (gender); *Batson*, 476 U.S. 79 (race and ethnicity).
85. *See* Davis v. Minnesota, 511 U.S. 1115 (1994) (Thomas, J., joined by Scalia, J., dissenting from denial of certiorari). The lower courts are divided on whether *Batson* applies to strikes based solely on a prospective juror's religious affiliation (as opposed to specific religious beliefs held by the person, e.g., a Jehovah's Witness's belief that she cannot sit in judgment of another person). *Compare* United States v. Brown, 352 F.3d 654, 668–69 (2d Cir. 2003) (*Batson* applies to peremptory strikes based on religious affiliation, but not to strikes based on specific religious beliefs), *with* Casarez v. State, 913 S.W.2d 468 (Tex. Crim. App. 1994) (*Batson* inapplicable to religious affiliation). No lower court appears to have applied *Batson* to a peremptory strike based on specific religious beliefs possessed by a prospective juror.
86. *See* Georgia v. McCollum, 505 U.S. 42 (1992); Edmonson v. Leesville Concrete Co., 500 U.S. 614 (1991). In Rivera v. Illinois, 556 U.S. 148 (2009), the Supreme Court held that a trial court's erroneous, but good-faith, ruling that defense counsel violated *Batson* by using a peremptory strike does not amount to reversible error on appeal (based on the wrongful denial of the peremptory strike) unless the defendant can show the jury actually seated was biased.
87. *See* Campbell v. Louisiana, 523 U.S. 392 (1998).

petit jury venires violated equal protection.[88] *Batson* goes one step further by prohibiting discrimination against individual members of a specific venire.[89]

A *Batson* claim involves a three-step process. As the Supreme Court has stated:

> Under our *Batson* jurisprudence, once the opponent of a peremptory challenge has made out a prima facie case of racial discrimination (step one), the burden of production shifts to the proponent of the strike to come forward with a race-neutral [or gender-neutral] explanation (step two). If a . . . neutral explanation is tendered, the trial court must then decide (step three) whether the opponent of the strike has proved purposeful . . . discrimination.[90]

Step one—the prima facie case—requires a showing that the opposing counsel's peremptory strikes were used in a manner that raises an inference of improper discrimination against a "cognizable" class under the Equal Protection Clause.[91] A prima facie case usually has two components: 1) establishing the use of peremptory strikes against a significant number of the cognizable class (looking both at the absolute number of such persons in the venire and the number of strikes used against such persons);[92] and 2) a showing "that there exist facts and other relevant circumstances sufficient to raise an inference" that the opposing side "used its peremptory challenges to exclude" members of the venire based on their membership in the cognizable class.[93] Such facts and circumstances may include, for instance,

---

88. *See, e.g.*, Whitus v. Georgia, 385 U.S. 545 (1967).

89. *Batson*, 476 U.S. at 88–90. *Batson* overruled a prior case, Swain v. Alabama, 380 U.S. 202 (1965). In *Swain*, the Court had held that the Equal Protection Clause did not require a prosecutor in a particular case to give a "race-neutral" explanation for his use of peremptory strikes against racial minorities in the venire in that case and that a defendant was required to show a pattern of peremptory strikes against minority members of venires in prior cases to make out a prima facie case (thus shifting the burden to the prosecutor to explain his strikes). *Id.* at 221–33. *Batson* eliminated *Swain*'s requirement that a defendant offer evidence of a pattern of exclusion of members of a cognizable group in past cases to make out a prima facie case and permitted a defendant to establish a prima facie case based on a prosecutor's use of peremptories in the case at bar. *See Batson*, 476 U.S. at 87–91.

90. Purkett v. Elem, 514 U.S. 765, 767 (1995) (per curiam).

91. *Batson*, 476 U.S. at 96–97.

92. Note, however, that a party's allowing one or more members of the cognizable class to sit on the jury is not necessarily sufficient to foreclose a prima facie case, as long as there is sufficient proof to raise an inference that the party exercised peremptory challenges against other members of the class with a discriminatory motive. People v. Childress, 614 N.E.2d 709, 711 (NY 1993); *see also* Miller-El v. Dretke, 545 U.S. 231 (2005) (while noting that one African American was not struck by the prosecution, finding nevertheless a prima facie case under *Batson* based on prosecution strikes used against ten other African Americans).

93. *Childress*, 614 N.E.2d at 711. In Johnson v. California, 545 U.S. 162 (2005), the Supreme Court held that a party making a *Batson* motion need not make out a prima facie case by a preponderance of the evidence; instead, the evidence need only support a rational inference of discrimination. A related question that has divided the lower courts and not yet been addressed by the Supreme Court is whether a trial court's threshold ruling that no prima facie case was shown—the first step of the

"a showing that members of the cognizable group were excluded while others with the same relevant characteristics were not" or a showing that the opposing side "has stricken [certain] members of [the cognizable] group who, because of their background and experience, might otherwise be expected to be favorably disposed to" that side.[94]

The Supreme Court has said of step two in the *Batson* process:

> The second step of this process does not demand an explanation that is persuasive, or even plausible. At this [second] step of the inquiry, the issue is the facial validity of the prosecutor's explanation. Unless a discriminatory intent is inherent in the prosecutor's explanation, the reason offered will be deemed race neutral [or gender neutral].[95]

A recurring issue that has divided the lower courts and has not yet been addressed by the Supreme Court[96] is whether the requirement of the second step is satisfied by a "mixed motive" explanation for a peremptory strike. For example, is a criminal defense lawyer's admission that a peremptory strike against a female member of the venire was in part on her gender, but also based in part on her conservative political views, a "neutral" explanation that shifts the burden back to the prosecutor? Some lower courts have held that *Batson* does not apply to a mixed motive strike and, instead, only applies if the strike was solely based on an impermissible factor.[97] Other courts (an apparent majority) have held that a mixed motive strike is invalid under *Batson* unless the party who exercised the strike can establish that the prospective juror would have been struck even without consideration of the impermissible factor.[98] A third group of courts has held that a mixed motive peremptory is always invalid.[99]

Step three under *Batson*—shifting the burden to the party opposing the peremptory strike to overcome the other side's "neutral" explanation—requires the trial court to make a factual finding concerning discriminatory intent.[100] In making such a factual finding, the trial court should consider the totality of the facts and circumstances, including the demeanor of the attorney whose strikes have been

---

Batson inquiry—is a mixed question of fact and law subject to de novo review on appeal or, instead, is a factual finding subject to deferential appellate review. *See* Saiz v. Ortiz, 392 F.3d 1166, 1175 n.5 (10th Cir. 2004) (citing conflicting lower court cases). In Hernandez v. New York, 500 U.S. 352 (1991), the Court held that the third step of a *Batson* analysis is a factual finding subject to deferential appellate review.

94. *Childress*, 614 N.E.2d at 711.

95. *Purkett*, 514 U.S. at 767–68 (internal quotes and citations omitted).

96. *See* Wilkerson v. Texas, 493 U.S. 924 (1989) (Marshall, J., joined by Brennan, J., dissenting from the denial of certiorari).

97. *See, e.g.*, Davidson v. Gengler, 852 F. Supp. 782, 789 (W.D. Wis. 1994).

98. *See, e.g.*, Howard v. Senkowski, 986 F.2d 24 (2d Cir. 1993).

99. *See, e.g.*, Payton v. Kearse, 495 S.E.2d 205 (S.C. 1998).

100. *Hernandez*, 500 U.S. at 364.

questioned and the plausibility or implausibility of the attorney's reasons, when determining whether the asserted neutral explanation is credible or, instead, whether the explanation was merely pretextual (i.e., masking an impermissibly discriminatory motive).[101] The Supreme Court has required judges reviewing the plausibility of an attorney's motive in striking particular members of the venire to engage in a comparative analysis—that is, by looking at comparable members (of a different race or gender) who were *not* struck by the attorney.[102]

7.3 Leading Supreme Court Decisions on the Right to a Jury Trial and the Jury Selection Process

- *Adams v. United States ex rel. McCann*, 317 U.S. 269 (1942) (defendant's waiver of right to a jury trial must be knowing, voluntary, and intelligent; presumably, defendant must personally waive the right).

- *Duncan v. Louisiana*, 391 U.S. 145 (1968) (guaranteeing state and federal criminal defendants the right to a jury trial in all felony cases).

- *Williams v. Florida*, 399 U.S. 78 (1970) (twelve-person juries not constitutionally required under the Sixth Amendment in state cases; juries as small as six persons are constitutional as long as their verdicts are unanimous).

- *Taylor v. Louisiana*, 419 U.S. 522 (1975) (holding that the Sixth Amendment right to a jury trial includes a "fair cross-section" requirement and that the exclusion of "distinctive groups" of the community during the selection of the venire violates the Sixth Amendment).

- *Castaneda v. Partida*, 430 U.S. 482 (1977) (holding that intentional discrimination against any "cognizable" class of persons under the Equal Protection Clause during the selection of the venire is unconstitutional).

- *Duren v. Missouri*, 439 U.S. 357 (1979) (setting forth a three-part test for determining whether a defendant has made out a prima facie case that a "distinctive group" was excluded from the venire in violation of the Sixth Amendment right to a jury trial; the prosecution may rebut such a prima facie case only by showing that a "significant state interest" justifies such exclusion).

- *Smith v. Phillips*, 455 U.S. 209 (1982) (leading decision on what constitutes a biased juror who must be removed for cause under the Sixth Amendment right to an impartial jury; *see also id.* at 221–24 (O'Connor,

---

101. Miller-El v. Cockrell, 537 U.S. 322, 338–48 (2003).
102. *See* Snyder v. Louisiana, 552 U.S. 472 (2008); *see also* Foster v. Chatman, 136 S. Ct. 1737 (2016); Flowers v. Mississippi, 139 S. Ct. 2228 (2019).

J., concurring, noting that in exceptional cases a juror must be irrebuttably presumed to be biased as a matter of law even if the trial court finds that the juror is not "actually" biased).

- *Batson v. Kentucky*, 476 U.S. 79 (1986) (a prosecutor's use of a peremptory strike based on a prospective juror's race or ethnicity violates equal protection).

- *Spaziano v. Florida*, 468 U.S. 447 (1984) (no right to a jury sentencing in capital or noncapital cases).

- *Blanton v. City of North Las Vegas*, 489 U.S. 538 (1989) (right to a jury trial in a misdemeanor case exists only for non-"petty" misdemeanors, i.e., those in which the authorized punishment exceeds six months in jail, irrespective of the actual sentence imposed on a defendant in a particular case; contrasting right to counsel in misdemeanor cases, which depends on the actual punishment imposed rather than that authorized by law).

- *Mu'Min v. Virginia*, 500 U.S. 415 (1991) (trial court has wide latitude in conducting voir dire; as a general matter, the Sixth Amendment only requires limited questioning of prospective jurors about pretrial publicity).

- *Georgia v. McCollum*, 505 U.S. 42 (1992) (extending *Batson* to defense counsel's use of peremptory strikes in a discriminatory manner).

- *J.E.B. v. Alabama ex rel. T.B.*, 511 U.S. 127 (1994) (extending *Batson* to peremptory strikes based on a prospective juror's gender).

- *United States v. Gaudin*, 515 U.S. 506 (1995) (under the Sixth Amendment right to a jury trial, any element of the offense, whether legal or factual in nature, must be submitted to a jury and cannot be found by a judge absent a valid waiver of the right to a jury trial by the defendant).

- *Campbell v. Louisiana*, 523 U.S. 392 (1998) (a criminal defendant, regardless of race or gender, has third-party standing to a raise a claim that a prospective juror or jurors are being excluded from the grand jury, petit jury venire, or petit jury in violation of the Sixth Amendment or Equal Protection Clause).

- *Apprendi v. New Jersey*, 530 U.S. 466 (2000) (any fact that, if proven, raises the statutory maximum prison sentence otherwise available is an element of the offense that must be submitted to a jury and cannot be found by a judge absent a valid waiver of the right to a jury trial by the defendant).

- *Ring v. Arizona*, 536 U.S. 584 (2002) (any aggravating factor that if found, renders a defendant eligible for capital punishment must be submitted to a jury and cannot be found by a judge absent a valid waiver of the right to a jury trial by the defendant).

- *Blakely v. Washington*, 542 U.S. 296 (2004) (any fact that if found, raises the maximum prison sentence available under mandatory sentencing guidelines is an element of the offense that must be submitted to a jury and cannot be found by a judge absent a valid waiver of the right to a jury trial by the defendant).

- *Snyder v. Louisiana*, 552 U.S. 472 (2008) (when determining whether an attorney's purportedly neutral reason for exercising a peremptory strike was in fact neutral, court faced with a *Batson* challenge must engage in comparative analysis of similarly situated members of the venire, who are of a different race or gender and who were not struck by the attorney).

- *Ramos v. Louisiana*, 140 S. Ct. 1390 (2020) (Sixth Amendment requires unanimous jury guilty verdicts in state and federal court; overruling *Apodaca v. Oregon*, 406 U.S. 404 (1972) (approving ten-to-two guilty verdict) and *Johnson v. Louisiana*, 406 U.S. 356 (1972) (approving nine-to-three guilty verdict)).

CHAPTER EIGHT

CONSTITUTIONAL ISSUES THAT ARISE DURING TRIAL

After all pretrial motions have been ruled on and the jury has been selected, the trial on the merits commences when a criminal defendant has persisted in a plea of not guilty.[1] Beginning with the opening statements of the lawyers, continuing through the presentation of testimony and evidence, and finally during closing arguments, there are numerous disputed legal issues that can arise during a criminal trial. These issues are typically raised in the form of an oral objection by defense counsel or the prosecutor—usually the former. The most common types of constitutional issues arising during a trial will be discussed below.

Legal objections must be made in a specific and timely manner. Failure to make a timely objection that clearly and specifically states the legal point at issue generally will "procedurally default" or "waive" a claim of error on appeal.[2] Merely stating "objection" is insufficient. The specific ground for the objection must be articulated to a reasonable degree.[3] Furthermore, counsel must ensure that a trial court rules on an objection, even if counsel fully expects the trial court to deny it. Failure to obtain an adverse ruling on an otherwise meritorious objection likewise may prevent reversal on appeal.[4]

8.1 Impermissible Comments on a Defendant's Invocation of the Fifth Amendment Privilege Against Self-Incrimination

One of the most common constitutional issues that arises during a trial is a direct or indirect comment on a defendant's invocation of the Fifth Amendment right to silence by a prosecutor or prosecution witness. Such comments are typically made for the purpose of suggesting that a silent defendant must be guilty. There are two main types of such impermissible comments. The first is a comment on

---

1. Depending on the particular jurisdiction, only a small fraction of criminal defendants charged with felonies actually go to trial. The vast majority of criminal defendants ultimately plead guilty rather than proceed to trial. *See* Missouri v. Frye, 566 U.S. 134, 143 (2012) (noting that 97 percent of federal convictions and 94 percent of state convictions resulted from guilty pleas). Constitutional issues related to guilty pleas will be discussed in Chapter Eleven.
2. The procedural default doctrine is further discussed in Chapter Fourteen.
3. Osborne v. Ohio, 495 U.S. 103, 124–25 (1990).
4. *See, e.g.*, McKinney v. Estelle, 657 F.2d 740 (5th Cir. 1981).

the defendant's pretrial silence. The second is a comment on the defendant's silence during the trial itself.

8.1.1 Comment on a Defendant's Invocation of the Miranda *Right to Silence or* Miranda *Right to Counsel*

The Supreme Court has forbidden the prosecution—either in its case-in-chief or on cross-examination of the defendant—from referring to a defendant's invocation of the right to silence after being arrested and read *Miranda* warnings.[5] Although this issue most commonly arises when prosecutors make such remarks during their opening statements or closing arguments, it also can occur when prosecution witnesses comment on a defendant's silence during their testimony (at least when not intentionally elicited by defense counsel).[6] Furthermore, this rule prohibits comments on a defendant's pretrial invocation of the Fifth Amendment (*Miranda*) right to counsel because such an invocation is an implicit invocation of the right to silence (in other words, a defendant's request to be permitted to remain silent until afforded an opportunity to consult with an attorney).[7] The Supreme Court has not yet addressed whether the prosecution may introduce evidence of a defendant's pre-arrest, post-*Miranda* silence as substantive evidence of guilt, and the lower courts are divided on this issue.[8]

The prosecution may offer evidence of the defendant's pre-custody, pre-*Miranda* silence as substantive evidence of the defendant's guilt in a case where the defendant did not affirmatively invoke the right to silence.[9] Evidence of a defendant's pretrial silence before being read *Miranda* warnings—even after the defendant was arrested—is admissible to impeach a defendant who chooses to testify at trial or raises an affirmative defense that is inconsistent with their pretrial silence.[10]

---

5. Doyle v. Ohio, 426 U.S. 610 (1976) (prohibiting prosecutor from impeaching a defendant with his post-*Miranda* silence); Wainwright v. Greenfield, 474 U.S. 284 (1986) (prohibiting substantive use of post-*Miranda* silence).

6. *See, e.g.*, Pezzella v. State, 405 So. 2d 1032 (Fla. Ct. App. 1981). The Supreme Court has not addressed the issue of whether this rule applies to comments on a defendant's silence by a codefendant's attorney. *See* United States v. Anderson, 879 F.2d 369, 379 n.4 (8th Cir. 1989) (noting the division among the lower courts on this issue).

7. *Greenfield*, 474 U.S. at 295 n.13; State v. Hull, 556 A.2d 154, 159–60 (Conn. 1989).

8. *Compare* Fencl v. Abrahamson, 841 F.2d 760 (7th Cir. 1988) (applying *Doyle* to post-*Miranda*, pre-arrest silence), *with* State v. Robinson, 496 A.2d 1067, 1072 (Me. 1985) (refusing to apply *Doyle* to post-*Miranda*, pre-arrest silence).

9. Salinas v. Texas, 570 U.S. 178 (2013).

10. Jenkins v. Anderson, 447 U.S. 231 (1980) (no constitutional violation if prosecutor cross-examines defendant concerning their pre-*Miranda*, pre-arrest silence); Fletcher v. Weir, 455 U.S. 603 (1982) (per curiam) (no constitutional violation if prosecutor cross-examines defendant concerning their pre-*Miranda*, post-arrest silence); *see also* United States v. Fambro, 526 F.3d 836, 841 & n.19 (5th Cir. 2008) (*Doyle* applies to situations where a defendant's post-*Miranda* silence is used to rebut the theory of the defense at trial even if the defendant does not testify).

8.1.2 Comment on Defendant's Silence During Trial

Because the Fifth Amendment prohibits the prosecution from forcing criminal defendants to take the stand and testify at their trials, the Supreme Court has held that a prosecutor ordinarily may not comment on the defendant's silence at trial when the defendant has chosen not to testify.[11] If a defendant chooses to testify, however, the prosecutor may cross-examine him about any subject relevant to proper cross-examination and the defendant may not selectively invoke the right to silence to avoid answering such relevant questions.[12]

What constitutes an improper indirect comment on a defendant's invocation of the right to silence during trial is often a close question. For instance, in a case where the defendant did not testify, a prosecutor's comment that the prosecution's case was "unrefuted" or "uncontradicted" may violate the defendant's Fifth Amendment right to silence depending on the circumstances.[13] If the defense never communicated to the jurors that it intended to offer its own evidence and the only or most likely potential defense witness who could have contradicted the prosecution's evidence was the defendant, most courts have held that such a comment by the prosecutor is a violation of the defendant's right to silence.[14] However, if defense counsel in opening statements promised jurors that the defendant would take the stand (but ultimately did not do so) or if the prosecution's comment referred to other potential defense witnesses besides the defendant, courts have not found a violation of the defendant's right to silence.[15]

Although the general rule is that a prosecutor may not comment on a defendant's decision not to testify at trial, not all such statements—even direct ones—are unconstitutional. For instance, where defense counsel makes comments that invite a fair response from the prosecutor that focus on the defendant's decision not to testify, there is no error.[16] If a defendant invokes the right to silence at their first trial, but takes the stand at a retrial, the prosecution may impeach the defendant with their silence at the initial trial.[17]

---

11. Griffin v. California, 380 U.S. 609 (1965).

12. *See* Brown v. United States, 356 U.S. 148, 154–55 (1958).

13. As discussed below, depending on the circumstances, such an argument by the prosecutor also may impermissibly shift the burden of proof to the defense.

14. *See, e.g.,* United States v. Triplett, 195 F.3d 990, 995 (8th Cir. 1999); Williams v. Lane, 826 F.2d 654, 664–66 (7th Cir. 1987); Raper v. Mintzes, 706 F.2d 161, 166 (6th Cir. 1983); *but see* People v. Jones, 786 N.E.2d 243, 249 (Ill. App. Ct. 2003) (permitting such argument as long as the prosecutor does not explicitly refer to the defendant as being the potential witness who could rebut the prosecution's case).

15. *See, e.g.,* Lockett v. Ohio, 438 U.S. 586, 595 (1978); United States v. Mulder, 273 F.3d 91, 109 (2d Cir. 2001); Boyd v. United States, 473 A.2d 828, 833 (D.C. 1984).

16. *See* United States v. Robinson, 485 U.S. 25 (1988) (holding that defense counsel invited the prosecutor's comment on the defendant's silence by stating in closing arguments that the defendant never had an opportunity to tell their side of the story).

17. Raffel v. United States, 271 U.S. 494 (1926).

8.2 Defendant's Right to Testify in Their Own Behalf and Right to "Present a Defense"

A criminal defendant has a constitutional right to testify in their own behalf at trial—a right nowhere explicitly found in the Constitution, but one that emanates from various provisions of the Bill of Rights.[18] That right is not absolute and may be outweighed by a countervailing governmental interest. For instance, with a sufficient showing that a defendant's post-hypnosis memory is unreliable, the prosecution can limit a defendant to testimony about their pre-hypnosis memory of the relevant events.[19] However, a state may not adopt a per se rule that prohibits all testimony by a defendant about post-hypnosis memory and, instead, must limit its prohibition to unreliable memory.[20]

The right to testify is a "personal" right, which cannot be waived by defense counsel without the defendant's consent.[21] The lower courts are divided over whether a defendant must expressly waive the right on the record to validly waive the right to testify or whether, instead, a defendant's silent acquiescence in their attorney's statement that "the defense rests" (without having called the defendant to testify) is generally sufficient to waive the right (as long as the attorney had informed the defendant that it was the defendant's choice whether to testify and the defendant had informed defense counsel that they did not wish to testify).[22]

Regardless of whether the defendant testifies in their own behalf, a criminal defendant has a similar constitutional right to present a defense through other evidence and witnesses.[23] However, like a defendant's right to testify in their own behalf, the right to present a defense is "subject to reasonable restrictions" if there is a sufficient countervailing governmental interest.[24] Thus, for example, in *United States v. Scheffer*, the Supreme Court held that excluding the favorable results of a

---

18. Rock v. Arkansas, 483 U.S. 44 (1987).

19. *Id.* at 60–62.

20. *Id.* at 62.

21. Ward v. Sternes, 334 F.3d 696, 704–05 (7th Cir. 2003).

22. Brown v. Artuz, 124 F.3d 73, 78–79 (2d Cir. 1997) (discussing the conflicting lower court decisions).

23. United States v. Scheffer, 523 U.S. 303, 308 (1998); Chambers v. Mississippi, 410 U.S. 284 (1973).

24. *Scheffer*, 523 U.S. at 308. A related issue is whether a state may categorically prohibit a defendant from offering a particular type of evidence that is not unreliable, but is, in the legislature's judgment, inadmissible based on public policy grounds—such as voluntary intoxication—to defeat an essential element of the prosecution's case. In *Montana v. Egelhoff*, 518 U.S. 37 (1996), the justices split four to four on whether such a categorical restriction violated a defendant's constitutional right to present a defense. *Compare id.* at 39–56 (plurality op. of Scalia, J.), *with id.* at 61 (O'Connor, J., dissenting, joined by Stevens, Souter, & Breyer, JJ.). Justice Ginsburg concurred in the judgment on the ground that Montana's prohibition on a defendant's ability to offer evidence of voluntary intoxication to defeat a mens rea element was constitutionally permissible because it merely defined an essential mens rea element in a manner that made voluntary intoxication irrelevant under state law. *Id.* at 57 (Ginsburg, J., concurring in the judgment).

defendant's polygraph examination concerning the alleged offense did not violate the defendant's right to present a defense because polygraph tests have not yet been shown to be sufficiently reliable.[25] Conversely, in *Chambers v. Mississippi*,[26] and later in *Holmes v. South Carolina*,[27] the Supreme Court held that application of a state's evidentiary rules that unreasonably excludes reliable exculpatory evidence would violate a defendant's right to present a defense. The lower courts have grappled with applying this constitutional rule to a variety of state evidentiary rules.[28]

With respect to use of a defendant's mental illness as a defense—either to raise a reasonable doubt about the mens rea element or as an affirmative insanity defense—the Supreme Court has held that a state does not violate due process either by: 1) excluding psychiatric evidence concerning a defendant's mental state at the time of a crime if it is offered in the attempt to raise a reasonable doubt concerning the mens rea element so long as some version of the insanity defense may be raised; or 2) prohibiting the insanity defense so long as the state allows the defense to offer evidence of the defendant's mental state in the attempt to negate the mens rea element.[29]

8.3   Confrontation Clause Issues During Trial

The Confrontation Clause of the Sixth Amendment, which applies equally in federal and state prosecutions,[30] states: "In all criminal prosecutions, the accused shall enjoy the right to . . . be confronted with the witnesses against him."[31] There are three main lines of Supreme Court decisions that have interpreted the Confrontation Clause: 1) cases addressing the issue of when the prior in-court testimony of a subsequently unavailable witness or a declarant's out-of-court hearsay statement may be admitted into evidence by the prosecution; 2) cases discussing what limits a trial court may place on a criminal defendant's right to "face-to-face" confrontation with a witness in the presence of the jury; and 3) cases addressing a defendant's right to impeach a prosecution witness.

---

25. *Scheffer*, 523 U.S. at 309–17.
26. *Chambers*, 410 U.S. at 302–03.
27. Holmes v. South Carolina, 547 U.S. 319 (2006).
28. *See, e.g.*, Rice v. McCann, 339 F.3d 546 (7th Cir. 2003) (holding that the state evidentiary rule at issue in that case did not violate *Chambers*); *id.* at 550–53 (Posner, J., dissenting) (contending that the state evidentiary rule violated *Chambers*).
29. *See* Kahler v. Kansas, 140 S. Ct. 1021, 1037 (2020); Clark v. Arizona, 548 U.S. 735, 756–79 (2006).
30. Pointer v. State of Texas, 380 U.S. 400 (1965).
31. U.S. CONST. Amend. VI.

8.3.1 Hearsay/Prior Testimony Cases

8.3.1.1 Prior Sworn Testimony

If a prosecution witness testified under oath at a prior adversarial hearing and the defendant was both represented by counsel at that prior hearing and had a meaningful opportunity to cross-examine the witness, then as a general rule, it does not violate the Confrontation Clause to introduce that prior testimony as substantive evidence if the witness has become unavailable by the time of trial.[32] Whether a witness is unavailable for Confrontation Clause purposes is generally the same as whether a witness is unavailable under the applicable rules of evidence.[33]

8.3.1.2 *Crawford, Roberts*, and "Testimonial" Hearsay

Before the Supreme Court's landmark decision in *Crawford v. Washington*,[34] the constitutional test for determining whether the admission of hearsay violated the Confrontation Clause was governed by *Ohio v. Roberts*[35] and its progeny.[36] *Roberts* set forth a two-pronged test for judging the admissibility of all types of hearsay under the Confrontation Clause: 1) in cases involving prior in-court testimony of a subsequently unavailable witness (discussed above), the prosecution had a burden to show that the witness had become unavailable and that the defendant had a meaningful opportunity to cross-examine the witness in the prior adversarial proceeding; 2) in all other situations involving hearsay statements, the prosecution only needed to show that the hearsay statement was sufficiently reliable.[37] Under *Roberts*'s second prong, reliability could be shown in one of two different ways: 1) that the hearsay fell within a "firmly rooted" hearsay exception (such as business records);[38] or 2) even if the hearsay did not fall within such a firmly rooted exception to the hearsay rule, the hearsay statement in question had "particularized

---

32. Ohio v. Roberts, 448 U.S. 56 (1980), *overruled on other grounds by* Crawford v. Washington, 541 U.S. 36 (2004); California v. Green, 399 U.S. 149 (1970).

33. *See, e.g.*, FED. R. EVID. 804(a)(1)–(5) (listing the grounds for deeming a witness to be "unavailable," including a witness's invocation of a recognized privilege; a witness's refusal to testify despite a court order; a witness's lack of memory; a witness's death or "then existing physical or mental illness or infirmity" that prevents the witness from testifying; and the witness's absence from court combined with the lack of the ability to compel the witness's attendance through a subpoena or other reasonable means). A witness will not be deemed unavailable if the proponent of the prior testimony was responsible for the witness's unavailability "for the purpose of preventing the witness from attending or testifying." *Id.*

34. Crawford v. Washington, 541 U.S. 36 (2004)

35. Ohio v. Roberts, 448 U.S. 56 (1980).

36. *See, e.g.*, Idaho v. Wright, 497 U.S. 805 (1990).

37. *Id.* at 820–24. In addition, hearsay would not be admissible under either the rules of evidence or under the Confrontation Clause unless there is an adequate showing that the out-of-court declarant "actually made the [hearsay] statement in question." United States v. Seavoy, 995 F.2d 1414, 1420 (7th Cir. 1993).

38. *Wright*, 497 U.S. at 817.

guarantees of trustworthiness" and "indicia of reliability" when the "totality of circumstances" were considered.[39]

In *Crawford*, after engaging in an "original intent" analysis of the Confrontation Clause, Justice Scalia, writing for the Court, overruled *Roberts*'s holding concerning hearsay statements other than prior in-court testimony of a subsequently unavailable witness. The Court held that any such hearsay[40] that is "testimonial" in nature is per se inadmissible under the Confrontation Clause unless: 1) the declarant is unavailable at the time of the trial; and 2) the defendant had a prior opportunity to cross-examine the declarant under oath at an adversarial hearing.[41] To qualify as "testimonial," the hearsay need not be in-court statements (such as testimony at a grand jury proceeding). Rather, without giving an exhaustive definition of testimonial, the Court suggested that testimonial hearsay would include sworn or unsworn "statements that declarants would reasonably expect to be used prosecutorially" or "statements that were made under circumstances which would lead an objective witness reasonably to believe that the statement would be available for use at a later trial."[42]

The Court in *Crawford* applied this definition and held that a tape-recorded out-of-court unsworn statement of the defendant's wife that implicated the defendant in an attempted homicide was testimonial and thus inadmissible because the declarant had never been subject to cross-examination by the defendant.[43] *Crawford* confirms that *Bruton v. United States*[44] remains good law, and thus motions to sever codefendants' trials when there is a confession of one codefendant implicating another codefendant—and the confessing codefendant does not intend to testify—are still viable in both state and federal prosecutions.[45]

In the wake of *Crawford*, the lower courts grappled with the issue of what is testimonial and what is nontestimonial hearsay for Confrontation Clause purposes.[46] Further clarification from the Supreme Court came in several subsequent cases. In the companion cases of *Davis v. Washington* and *Hammon v. Indiana*,[47] the Court applied the *Crawford* standard to incriminating hearsay in

39. *Id.* at 818–22.
40. If out-of-court statements are offered not "to prove the truth of the matter asserted" and thus are not "testimonial"—but, instead, are offered for other purposes—then the Confrontation Clause (and, thus, *Crawford*) would not be implicated. *See* United States v. Trala, 386 F.3d 536, 543–44 (3d Cir. 2004); *see also* Tennessee v. Street, 471 U.S. 409, 414 (1985).
41. *Crawford*, 541 U.S. at 49–52.
42. *Id.* at 51–52.
43. *Id.* at 68.
44. Bruton v. United States, 391 U.S. 123 (1968).
45. *Bruton* motions are discussed in Chapter Four.
46. *See, e.g.*, People v. Geno, 683 N.W.2d 687, 692 (Mich. App. 2004) (holding that victim's out-of-court statement made to a social worker at the Child Assessment Center that implicated the defendant was not testimonial); Snowden v. State, 846 A.2d 36 (Md. App. 2004) (holding that victim's statement to social worker at Child Assessment Center was testimonial).
47. Davis v. Washington, 547 U.S. 813 (2006).

a 911 call (in which the caller excitedly reported an ongoing emergency) and a hearsay statement to a police officer who arrived on the scene shortly after the crime was completed and the suspect was gone. The Court held that the 911 call was nontestimonial, but that the statement to the police officer was testimonial.[48] In reaching these conclusions, the Court asked whether the "primary purpose" of the official questioning of the witnesses was to "enable police assistance to meet an ongoing emergency."[49]

Thereafter, in a series of cases, the Court addressed whether forensic lab reports—such as those containing the results of a drug test or DNA test—qualify as testimonial hearsay. Initially, in *Melendez-Diaz v. Massachusetts*, the Court held that a defendant's right to confrontation was violated when the trial court permitted the prosecutor to offer a testimonial lab report of a state crime laboratory analyst (concluding that the substance possessed by the defendant was an illegal controlled substance) without affording the defendant the right to cross-examine the analyst.[50] In *Bullcoming v. New Mexico*,[51] the Court held that the defendant's right to confrontation was violated by admission of a testimonial lab report of a forensic analyst who had performed a chemical test to determine the defendant's blood-alcohol level. However, in *Williams v. Illinois*,[52] a splintered Court held that it did not violate the Confrontation Clause to allow an expert witness to testify in court about the out-of-court DNA test conducted by an analyist who was not called to testify.[53] There likely will be additional cases in the future concerning the admissibility of the results of forensic tests conducted by an analyst who did not testify.

In *Michigan v. Bryant*, the Court held that an out-of-court statement made by a dying gunshot victim to police officers at the scene of the shooting (in which the victim identified the defendant as the shooter) was not "testimonial" and thus could be admitted at trial because the "primary purpose" of such a statement (from an "objective" standpoint) was not for law enforcement purposes; instead, the statement was elicited by the officers in their capacity as "first responders" to an emergency.[54] And in *Ohio v. Clark*,[55] the Court held that an incriminating statement

---

48. *Id.* at 826–34.
49. *Id.* at 822.
50. Melendez-Diaz v. Massachusetts, 557 U.S. 305 (2009).
51. Bullcoming v. New Mexico, 564 U.S. 647 (2011).
52. Williams v. Illinois, 567 U.S. 50 (2012).
53. In *Williams*, four justices held that *Melendez-Diaz* and *Bullcoming* were distinguishable primarily because they did not involve an in-court expert who merely relied in part on the out-of-court analyst's test results in rendering an expert conclusion, *see id.* at 68–73, while a fifth justice (Justice Thomas) reasoned that the out-of-court testing "lacked the requisite formality and solemnity to be considered testimonial for purposes of the Confrontation Clause." *Id.* at 103 (citation and internal quotation marks omitted).
54. Michigan v. Bryant, 562 U.S. 344 (2011).
55. Ohio v. Clark, 576 U.S. 237 (2015).

given by a small child (aged three) to his preschool teachers about sexual abuse committed by the defendant was not testimonial. The Court stated that "[s]tatements by very young children will rarely, if ever, implicate the Confrontation Clause" because such children will necessarily not have the "primary purpose" of implicating another person in a criminal prosecution.[56]

The Supreme Court in *Crawford* did not explicitly overrule *Roberts*'s reliability test as applied to nontestimonial hearsay. The Court intimated, however, that the question of *Roberts*'s continued viability regarding that type of hearsay is an open one in the Court's Confrontation Clause jurisprudence.[57] Subsequently, in *Whorton v. Bockting*,[58] the Court stated in dicta that *Roberts*'s reliability test has been entirely abandoned—for all types of hearsay, testimonial and nontestimonial alike. Thus, the only constitutional limitation on hearsay evidence offered as substantive evidence appears to be the rule in *Crawford*, which applies solely to testimonial hearsay.

8.3.2 Face-to-Face Confrontation

For the time being at least, a majority of the Supreme Court believes that the hoary requirement that a criminal defendant be permitted to see every witness against them—while, at the same time, the witnesses be permitted to see the defendant, with the jurors permitted to see both the defendant and witnesses—is not an absolute requirement. Rather, if a trial court finds special circumstances that outweigh the need for a "face-to-face" confrontation (e.g., a frightened child complainant in a rape case), then the Confrontation Clause is not violated by using a device such as a closed-circuit video monitor or a screen between the defendant and the sensitive witness.[59] A per se rule against face-to-face confrontation in certain types of cases that does not require a case-by-case approach, however, violates the Confrontation Clause.[60] Arguably, the case-by-case test is subject to being reconsidered in light of Justice Scalia's majority opinion in *Crawford*, which eschewed the Court's former, less rigorous application of the Confrontation Clause (as evidenced by *Roberts*) in favor of a more categorical approach to interpreting the Clause based on the original intent of the framers of the Constitution and Bill of Rights.[61]

---

56. *Id.* at 2182.
57. *Crawford*, 541 U.S. at 68.
58. Whorton v. Bockting, 549 U.S. 406, 420 (2007).
59. Maryland v. Craig, 497 U.S. 836 (1990).
60. Coy v. Iowa, 487 U.S. 1012 (1988); *id.* at 1022–23 (O'Connor, J., joined by White, J., concurring).
61. *See* Danner v. Kentucky, 525 U.S. 1010 (1998) (Scalia, J., joined by Thomas, J., dissenting from the denial of certiorari) (contending that *Craig* was wrongly decided).

8.3.3   Cross-Examination/Impeachment

A defendant's right to cross-examine with the opportunity to impeach an adverse witness—a prosecution witness as well as a hostile defense witness[62]—"is the main and essential purpose" of the Confrontation Clause.[63] While the right to unlimited cross-examination concerning any topic is not constitutionally guaranteed, a criminal defendant does have a right within reasonable limits to cross-examine an adverse witness concerning matters that could reveal biases for the prosecution or against the defendant or a motivation to lie (for example, a witness's expectation that in exchange for their testimony, the prosecution will dismiss pending charges against them) or matters that call into question the credibility of the witness (such as prior inconsistent statements that the witness has given).[64]

Sometimes Confrontation Clause challenges are aimed at statutes that categorically limit the scope of cross-examination in some manner (a "rape shield" statute, for example). In such cases, courts must balance the state's legitimate interest in enacting such laws against a defendant's right to confront a particular witness with relevant matters concerning the witness's credibility.[65] Depending on the circumstances of a particular case, courts have held that the application of such a law may violate the Confrontation Clause.[66]

The right to cross-examine a witness does not guarantee that a witness will remember or otherwise be mentally capable of addressing the topic of the questions.[67] Thus, for instance, the Confrontation Clause is not violated by a prosecution witness who previously picked the defendant out of a lineup shortly after the alleged offense, but who, by the time of the trial, could not remember having done so because of a mental defect. Although the defense contended that it was unable to meaningfully cross-examine the witness because of this total memory loss, the Supreme Court held that the witness's presence on the witness stand under oath was sufficient to satisfy the Confrontation Clause.[68] The special situation that arises when a prosecution witness invokes the Fifth Amendment right against self-incrimination on cross-examination by the defense—after having testified on direct-examination for the prosecution—is discussed below.

---

62. *See, e.g.*, United States v. Stephenson, 887 F.2d 57, 60 (5th Cir. 1989).

63. Delaware v. Van Arsdall, 475 U.S. 673, 678 (1986).

64. *Id.* at 678–79; *see also* Olden v. Kentucky, 488 U.S. 227 (1988); Davis v. Alaska, 415 U.S. 308 (1974); Vasquez v. Jones, 496 F.3d 564, 570–74 (6th Cir. 2007).

65. *See* Michigan v. Lucas, 500 U.S. 145, 149–51 (1991); *see also* Clifford S. Fishman, *Consent, Credibility, and the Constitution: Evidence Relating to a Sex Offense Complainant's Past Sexual Behavior*, 44 CATH. U. L. REV. 709 (Spring 1995) (discussing constitutional challenges to rape shield laws).

66. *Compare, e.g.*, Davis v. State, 749 N.E.2d 552 (Ind. Ct. App. 2001) (finding a constitutional violation); State v. Atkinson, 80 P.3d 1143 (Kan. 2003) (same), *with* Quinn v. Haynes, 234 F.3d 837 (4th.Cir. 2000) (finding no violation).

67. Delaware v. Fensterer, 474 U.S. 15 (1985).

68. United States v. Owens, 484 U.S. 554 (1988).

8.4 Compulsory Process Clause Issues During Trial

The Compulsory Process Clause applies equally to federal and state prosecutions.[69] It is most often associated with the subpoena power, which is discussed in Chapter Four in the context of a pretrial motion for issuance of a subpoena. However, Compulsory Process issues can arise during a trial as well.

The Supreme Court has stated that the Compulsory Process Clause affords a criminal defendant two protections: 1) the right to compel favorable witnesses at trial (the subpoena power); and 2) the right to actually "have the witness's testimony heard by the trier of fact"; in other words, to "put before a jury evidence that might influence the determination of guilt."[70] The latter is not absolute and is not violated during a trial if a trial court justifiably refuses to allow a defense witness to testify on the ground that the defense willfully violated a discovery rule or procedural rule.[71] In *Taylor v. Illinois*, the Court concluded that Compulsory Process Clause was not violated when a trial court refused to allow the defense to call a subpoenaed witness after finding that defense counsel intentionally violated a state discovery rule by withholding the witness's name until the middle of the trial.[72] The Court has held, however, that not every violation of a state discovery or procedural rule will forfeit a defendant's right to call a subpoenaed witness; if a trial court's refusal to permit a favorable defense witness is "disproportionate" to the seriousness of the rule violation, then the Compulsory Process Clause will be violated.[73]

A trial judge or prosecutor can violate the Compulsory Process Clause by unjustifiably intimidating a favorable defense witness to prevent them from testifying.[74] In *Webb v. Texas*, the trial court first advised a defense witness of his right against self-incrimination and then, without any basis to believe that the witness was about to commit perjury, warned the defense witness that if he lied, the judge would personally refer his case to the grand jury. In response, the witness invoked his right to silence and refused to testify for the defense. The Supreme Court held that the "threatening" remarks of the trial judge violated the Compulsory Process Clause.[75] Since *Webb*, lower courts have held that trial judges and prosecutors are not strictly prohibited from advising potential defense witnesses about their right to silence nor about the possibility that they could be prosecuted for perjury if they were to lie under oath. Rather, if a judge or prosecutor has a "particular basis" to believe that

---

69. Washington v. Texas, 388 U.S. 14 (1967).
70. Taylor v. Illinois, 484 U.S. 400, 408–09 (1988) (citation and internal quotation marks omitted).
71. *Id.*
72. *Id.* at 410–18.
73. *Lucas*, 500 U.S. at 151.
74. Webb v. Texas, 409 U.S. 95 (1972) (per curiam).
75. *Id.* at 97–98.

the witness is about to lie, then such an admonition is permitted[76] as long as it does not unduly interfere with the witness's free will.[77]

A related Compulsory Process issue that occasionally arises during a trial is whether the trial court or prosecution must grant a favorable defense witness some type of immunity if the witness invokes the right to silence under the Fifth Amendment, thereby refusing to testify for the defense. The Supreme Court has never addressed this issue,[78] but the majority of lower courts have held that no such forced immunity is constitutionally required where there is no prosecutorial misconduct related to the witness's decision to invoke their right to silence.[79] Some courts have left open the possibility, however, that in an exceptional situation—when, for instance, the prosecution immunizes key prosecution witnesses and a potential defense witness has strong exculpatory testimony to offer that contradicts the prosecution witnesses, but will not testify without immunity—the Constitution would require immunity for the defense witness.[80]

As discussed in Chapter Four, the Supreme Court has not yet addressed the type of materiality a defendant needs to show to prove a violation of the Compulsory Process Clause in the trial setting. Although the Supreme Court has stated that a defendant must show that a witness or evidence will be "material" as well as "favorable" for the Compulsory Process Clause to require a subpoena to issue,[81] the Court has not specifically addressed the issue of whether the *Brady* doctrine's somewhat demanding materiality standard[82] applies in the trial context—as it does in the special pretrial situation involving the deportation of potential defense witnesses before the defense had a chance to interview them or subpoena them.[83] The lower courts are divided on the type of "materiality" required in the trial context.[84]

---

76. *See, e.g.*, United States v. Smith, 997 F.2d 674, 679–80 (10th Cir. 1993) (permitting such an admonition where the court had a "particular basis" to do so).

77. *See, e.g.*, United States v. Arthur, 949 F.2d 211, 215–16 (6th Cir. 1991) (holding that *Webb* was violated where the trial judge not only advised a witness of their right to silence, but also stated that it would be "against [the witness's] interest" to testify).

78. *See* Autry v. McKaskle, 465 U.S. 1085, 1087–88 & n.3 (1984) (Marshall, J., joined by Brennan, J., dissenting from the denial of certiorari).

79. *See, e.g.*, Curtis v. Duval, 124 F.3d 1, 9 (1st Cir. 1997); United States v. Whittington, 783 F.2d 1210, 1220 (5th Cir. 1986); State v. Axley, 646 P.2d 268, 273–74 (Ariz. 1982); *but see* United States v. Straub, 538 F.3d 1147 (9th Cir. 2008) (denial of immunity for defense witness is constitutional error where it has the "effect" of "distorting the fact-finding process"); Gov't of the Virgin Islands v. Smith, 615 F.2d 964, 974 (3d Cir. 1980) (requiring forced immunity where a defense witness is clearly exculpatory and essential to the defense).

80. *See, e.g.*, United States v. Praetorius, 622 F.2d 1054, 1064 (2d Cir. 1979).

81. Washington v, Texas, 388 U.S. 14, 16–18 (1967).

82. *See* Brady v. Maryland, 373 U.S. 83 (1963) (due process violated by prosecution's suppression of material evidence). The *Brady* doctrine is discussed in Chapter Thirteen.

83. *See* United States v. Valenzuela-Bernal, 458 U.S. 858, 873 & n.9 (1982).

84. *Compare, e.g.*, Richmond v. Embry, 122 F.3d 866, 873 & n.5 (10th Cir. 1997) (applying the *Brady*-type materiality standard), *with id.* at 876–77 (Henry, J., concurring) (applying a more traditional relevancy standard of materiality); State v. Carlos, 17 P.3d 118, 123 (Ariz. 2001) (same).

8.5 Invocation of the Fifth Amendment Privilege Against Self-Incrimination by a Defendant or Witness During Trial

The Fifth Amendment privilege against self-incrimination extends to any person (whether or not already charged with a crime) in any type of proceeding who is called on to answer a question or make "any disclosures that the [person] reasonably believes could be used in a [present or future] criminal prosecution or could lead to other evidence that might be used"—including in any criminal, civil, bankruptcy, tax, or administrative proceedings in the state or federal systems.[85] Criminal defendants, of course, possess a Fifth Amendment privilege against self-incrimination; indeed, they may make a "blanket" invocation of their right to silence and refuse to take the witness stand at their own criminal trial.[86] If a defendant takes the witness stand in their own defense, however, they cannot invoke privilege against self-incrimination regarding any matter properly brought out on cross-examination (such as whether the defendant committed other, uncharged crimes similar to the one charged in the indictment).[87]

A third-party witness typically may not make a blanket invocation of the right to silence, whether called as a witness by the prosecution or the defense.[88] Rather, outside the presence of the jurors, the trial court initially should require counsel to state the specific questions that they wish to ask the witness and then require a "question-by-question" invocation of the right to silence by the witness.[89] The standard governing whether a particular question exposes the witness to self-incrimination is quite generous to the witness—only requiring them to state a good-faith basis that their answer could directly or indirectly incriminate them even in the slightest respect.[90] A witness may properly invoke the right to silence when reasonably fearing their answer could "furnish a link in the chain of evidence needed to prosecute" them, even if that link is not directly incriminating (such as an admission that the witness was at or near the crime scene around the time of the crime).[91] A trial court cannot order the witness to answer a particular question unless it is "perfectly clear"

---

85. *See* Kastigar v. United States, 406 U.S. 441, 444–45 (1972).

86. Littlejohn v. United States, 705 A.2d 1077, 1081 (D.C. 1997).

87. Brown v. United States, 356 U.S. 148, 154–56 (1958) (scope of defendant's waiver of right to silence is "coextensive with the scope of relevant cross-examination").

88. A possible exception exists for a case of a codefendant/witness who is being tried separately from the defendant, but charged with the same crime. *See, e.g.,* State v. Edwards, 419 So. 2d 881, 892 (La. 1982).

89. *Littlejohn*, 705 A.2d. at 1086; *see also* United States v. Argomaniz, 925 F.2d 1349, 1355 (11th Cir. 1991); State v. Cecarelli, 631 A.2d 862, 866 (Conn. 1993).

90. *See* Hoffman v. United States, 341 U.S. 479, 486–87 (1951); *see also* Emspak v. United States, 349 U.S. 190, 199 & n.18 (1955); United States v. Coffey, 198 F.2d 438 (3d Cir. 1952).

91. *Hoffman*, 341 U.S. at 486; *see also* In re Proceedings Before a Grand Jury, 768 N.E.2d 1102 (Mass. App. 2002) (witness's mere presence at crime scene shortly before crime was committed was a sufficient basis on which to invoke right to silence).

that an answer to the question posed "cannot possibly" incriminate the witness directly or indirectly in any state or federal (although not a foreign) prosecution.[92]

Even a witness who asserts their innocence may invoke the right to silence as long as the witness has a good-faith belief that their answers could be used, along with other evidence, to incriminate them.[93] The Supreme Court has said that the Fifth Amendment protects the guilty and the innocent alike from self-incrimination; indeed, it protects the innocent "who otherwise might be ensnared by ambiguous circumstances."[94]

The trial court ultimately must decide whether each question in response to which the witness "invokes the Fifth" is proper.[95] The trial court cannot force the witness (or the witness's attorney) to provide their answer in ruling on whether the question is permissible; the court generally is limited to considering the question and the context in which it is asked when determining whether an answer would potentially incriminate the witness.[96] One limited exception is that a trial court may require the witness (along with their attorney, if they wish) to appear in an in camera, ex parte hearing at which the court may require additional—yet extremely limited—statements concerning why the witness believes that a particular answer will incriminate him.[97]

If the trial court permits one or more questions to be asked and the answers given are potentially relevant, then the witness should be called to testify before the jury and answer the questions allowed by the court; a witness who refuses to answer the nonincriminating questions is subject to being held in contempt of court.[98] Although the Supreme Court has never definitively addressed the issue,[99] the majority

---

92. Malloy v. Hogan, 378 U.S. 1, 11–12 (1964); *Hoffman*, 341 U.S. at 488.

93. Ohio v. Reiner, 532 U.S. 17, 21–22 (2001) (per curiam).

94. *Id.* at 21 (citation and internal quotation marks omitted).

95. *Hoffman*, 341 U.S. at 486–87.

96. United States v. Balsys, 524 U.S. 666, 672 (1998); *Malloy*, 378 U.S. at 11–12 (quoting *Hoffman*, 341 U.S. at 488).

97. *See, e.g.*, United States v. Goodwin, 625 F.2d 693, 702 (5th Cir. 1980); Commonwealth v. Martin, 668 N.E.2d 825, 831–32 (Mass. 1996).

98. *See, e.g.*, Commonwealth v. Long, 625 A.2d 630 (Pa. 1993). If a contempt order is entered, the ordinary course of action is for the convicted contemnor to seek a stay of the contempt order and then seek an expedited appeal of the order. The appeals court then decides whether the trial court erred in ordering the witness to answer the question and, if the appeals court so concludes, it will reverse the contempt order. *See, e.g.*, United States v. Costello, 198 F.2d 200, 202 (2d Cir. 1952); In re Kefalidis, 714 N.E.2d 243 (Ind. Ct. App. 1999). If the court or prosecution provides sufficient immunity to the witness, then ordinarily the witness has no basis to refuse to testify and the contempt order will be upheld on appeal. *See* United States v. Wilson, 421 U.S. 309 (1975). Unless the witness is afforded sufficient immunity, an attorney representing the witness cannot be held in contempt for advising the witness to refuse to answer the question and risk being held in contempt as long as the attorney's advice is in good faith (i.e., is based on a good-faith belief that the witness's answer will in fact incriminate him). Maness v. Meyers, 419 U.S. 449, 460–68 (1975).

99. Lindsey v. United States, 484 U.S. 934, 934 (1987) (White, J., joined by Brennan, J., dissenting from the denial of certiorari).

of lower courts have held that neither the prosecution nor the defense has a right to call a witness to testify before the jury when it is known in advance that the witness will legitimately invoke the Fifth Amendment right to silence in response to all questions that are posed.[100]

Occasionally, the prosecution or defense will call a witness who testifies without limitation on direct examination, but who proceeds to invoke the privilege against self-incrimination (or some other privilege that prevents questioning) on cross-examination by the opposing party.[101] The apparent consensus among the lower courts is that if the witness invoked the right to silence about a significant matter—as opposed to a "collateral" matter—that potentially impacted the jury's ability to assess the witness's credibility concerning a subject discussed during the direct examination, the trial court ordinarily should strike the relevant portion of the direct examination.[102]

8.6   Prosecutorial Arguments that Shift the Burden of Persuasion to the Defense or Diminish the Meaning of "Reasonable Doubt"

Under the Due Process Clause, the "burden of proof" or "burden of persuasion"[103] in a criminal case rests on the prosecution to prove each and every element of the charged offense beyond a reasonable doubt; that burden never shifts to the defense at any point during the trial.[104] Certain prosecutorial arguments have been

---

100. *See, e.g.,* United States v. Deutsch, 987 F.2d 878, 883–84 (2d Cir. 1993); United States v. Johnson, 488 F.2d 1206, 1211 (1st Cir. 1973); Littlejohn, 705 A.2d at 1086; Cecarelli, 631 A.2d at 866; People v. Dyer, 390 N.W.2d 645 (Mich. 1986); *but see* United States v. Vandetti, 623 F.2d 1144, 1147 (6th Cir. 1980) (permitting the prosecutor to call a witness in front of the jury who will invoke their right to silence to all questions posed). In dicta, the Supreme Court suggested that the prosecution's intentionally calling a witness whom it knows will invoke their right to silence could amount to reversible error if the prosecution relied on the improper inference that the witness's silence was tantamount to an incriminating answer. *See* Namet v. United States, 373 U.S. 179, 185–88 (1963).

101. *See* Combs v. Commonwealth, 74 S.W.3d 738, 742–43 (Ky. 2002).

102. *See, e.g.,* United States v. Wilmore, 381 F.3d 868 (9th Cir. 2004); United States v. Gary, 74 F.3d 304, 309–12 (1st Cir. 1996); United States v. Cardillo, 316 F.2d 606, 612 (2d Cir. 1963).

103. The "burden of persuasion" and "burden of proof" are essentially synonymous terms in a criminal case. *See* State v. Rolle, 560 So. 2d 1154, 1160 n.8 (Fla. 1990) (Barkett, J., concurring, joined by Kogan, J.). Those terms should be distinguished from the "quantum of proof" that governs the prosecution's burden of proof or persuasion; the quantum of proof required of each element "beyond a reasonable doubt." *See* United States v. Hartsock, 347 F.3d 1, 7–8 (1st Cir. 2003). Further, the concept of the "burden of production" is a distinct one from the concept of the burden of proof or persuasion. The burden of production is the burden of coming forward with enough evidence to shift the ultimate burden of proof to the other party. *Id.* With the exception of affirmative defenses and burden shifting presumptions (both discussed in Chapter Ten), the concept of the burden of production rarely appears in criminal cases, as opposed to civil cases.

104. *See* Sandstrom v. Montana, 442 U.S. 510 (1979) (discussing the prosecution's burden of proof and prohibiting that burden from being shifted to the defense); Mullaney v. Wilbur, 421 U.S. 684

held to violate this constitutional requirement by improperly shifting the burden to the defense.[105] For instance, if a prosecutor contends that a defendant (who invoked the right to silence during trial and did not offer any other evidence) must "come forward" with an explanation of their "side of the story," the burden has been effectively shifted to the defense (in addition to violating the defendant's right to silence).[106] However, if a prosecutor simply responds in rebuttal to a defensive theory (whether supported by the defendant's own testimony or other evidence) and contends that there is insufficient evidence supporting such a theory, the prosecutor does not improperly shift the burden to the defense.[107] Courts also have condemned prosecutorial arguments that once a certain amount of evidence has been presented by the prosecution during the trial, the defendant's presumption of innocence disappears.[108]

Certain prosecutorial arguments also may violate the Due Process Clause by diminishing the constitutional reasonable-doubt standard.[109] For instance, some courts have held that definitions of "reasonable doubt" based on percentages (for example, "a reasonable doubt means that you are not at least 90 percent certain of guilt") or by analogy to the "scales of justice"—that is, definitions that define reasonable doubt quantitatively rather than qualitatively—are improper.[110] Courts also have condemned certain arguments that refer to the degree of doubt that a person has when making everyday decisions (even important ones)[111] or that have defined the quantum of proof necessary for a conviction as a "gut feeling" by jurors.[112] Such arguments, however, typically will not constitute reversible error on appeal if the trial court sustained a defendant's objection to the prosecutor's argument and correctly instructed the jurors on the definition of reasonable doubt.[113] Some appeals

---

(1975) (holding that every element of a charged offense must be proved beyond a reasonable doubt); In re Winship, 397 U.S. 358 (1970) (same); *see also* Taylor v. Kentucky, 436 U.S. 478 (1978) (discussing the defendant's presumption of innocence); *but cf.* Patterson v. New York, 432 U.S. 197 (1977) (due process not violated by placing the burden on the defense to prove an affirmative defense, which is distinct from the elements of the charged offense).

105. The issue of "burden-shifting" in the context of jury instructions is discussed in Chapter Ten.

106. People v. Kent, 509 N.Y.S.2d 841, 842 (N.Y. App. Div. 1986).

107. *See, e.g.*, People v. Fields, 538 N.W.2d 356, 366–68 (Mich. 1995).

108. *See, e.g.*, State v. Trimble, 371 N.W.2d 921, 926–27 (Minn. Ct. App. 1985).

109. *See generally* Cage v. Louisiana, 498 U.S. 39 (1990) (per curiam) (discussing the constitutional reasonable doubt standard). This issue also arises in the context of jury instructions on the meaning of reasonable doubt. *See* Chapter Ten.

110. *See, e.g.*, Commonwealth v. Sullivan, 482 N.E.2d 1198, 1200–01 (Mass. App. Ct. 1985); McCullough v. State, 657 P.2d 1157, 1158–59 (Nev. 1983).

111. *See, e.g.*, People v. Nguyen, 46 Cal. Rptr. 2d 840, 844–45 (Cal. Ct. App. 1995) (criticizing a prosecutor's argument that ordinary people rely on the equivalent of "reasonable doubt" in everyday situations, such as making the decision to change lanes on the highway).

112. Randolph v. State, 36 P.3d 424, 430–31 (Nev. 2001).

113. *See, e.g., id.* at 431–32.

courts have prohibited trial courts or lawyers from attempting to define reasonable doubt for jurors.[114]

8.7 Improper Extraneous Influences on the Jury in the Courtroom During Trial

A defendant's Sixth Amendment right to an impartial jury—along with a defendant's constitutional presumption of innocence—require that there be no extraneous, prejudicial influences on the jurors during the trial.[115] Such prejudicial, extraneous influences typically occur in two scenarios: 1) the presence of certain types of persons in the courtroom during trial; and 2) the defendant's appearance in jail clothes or shackles in the presence of jurors.[116]

The Supreme Court has held that the presence of an unnecessarily large number of uniformed law enforcement officers situated near a defendant during trial (for security purposes) may be unconstitutional if the presence of such officers would tend to cause jurors to believe that the defendant is dangerous or must be guilty.[117] In *Holbrook v. Flynn*, the Court concluded that the presence of only four uniformed officers near the defendant acting as security personnel did not violate the Constitution because it was not "inherently prejudicial."[118] The Supreme Court has not yet addressed[119]—and the lower courts are divided over—the issue of whether the presence of a large number of uniformed officers as spectators in the courtroom gallery is inherently prejudicial and, thus, unconstitutional.[120] Likewise, the lower courts are divided on whether the presence of a large number of civilian spectators wearing prejudicial buttons during trial results in inherent prejudice.[121] The Supreme

---

114. *See, e.g.*, United States v. Glass, 846 F.2d 386, 387 (7th Cir. 1988). Such courts have held that if defense counsel offers a definition of reasonable doubt, prosecutors are free to respond with their own definition as long as such a definition does not diminish the quantum of proof required for a conviction. *See, e.g.*, United States v. Dominguez, 835 F.2d 694, 701 (7th Cir. 1987).

115. Holbrook v. Flynn, 475 U.S. 560 (1986); Estelle v. Williams, 425 U.S. 501 (1976). Extraneous influences on members of the jury that occur outside of the courtroom or during jury deliberations will be discussed in Chapter Thirteen.

116. *See* Deck v. Missouri, 544 U.S. 622 (2005).

117. *Holbrook*, 475 U.S. at 569–71.

118. *Id.* The Court recognized that some types of extraneous influences on a jury may be "inherently" prejudicial—thus relieving the defendant's burden of establishing "actual" prejudice.

119. *See* Palumbo v. Ortiz, 89 F. App'x 3 (9th Cir. 2004).

120. *Compare* Woods v. Dugger, 923 F.2d 1454, 1458–60 (11th Cir. 1991) (finding that the large number of uniformed prison guards present as spectators during the trial of a defendant charged with murdering a prison guard violated Constitution), *with* Howard v. State, 941 S.W.2d 102, 117–18 & n.15 (Tex. Crim. App. 1996) (refusing to reverse the defendant's conviction based on presence of large number of uniformed police officers during the trial of a defendant charged with murdering a police officer; distinguishing *Woods*).

121. *Compare* Norris v. Risley, 918 F.2d 828 (9th Cir. 1990) (presence of large number of women wearing "Women Against Rape" buttons during defendant's rape trial violated Constitution); State v. Franklin, 327 S.E.2d 449, 454–55 (W. Va. 1985) (presence of large number of spectators wearing

Court specifically left open this issue in *Carey v . Musladin*,[122] noting that the lack of "state action" may distinguish such a situation from one involving "government-sponsored practices."[123]

The Supreme Court and lower courts also have held that unless there is a valid governmental interest justifying it (such as a dangerous defendant or one who is an escape risk), a criminal defendant's constitutional rights are violated by forcing him to wear shackles or other restraints visible to jurors in the courtroom.[124] Similarly, the Supreme Court has held that forcing a defendant to wear identifiable jail clothes in the presence of jurors during trial violates the Constitution, at least when the defense has objected to the defendant being forced to do so.[125] However, if jurors inadvertently only caught a brief glimpse of a defendant in shackles or jail clothes, it is highly unlikely that a court will find a constitutional violation warranting a new trial.[126]

8.8 Defendant's Right to Be Present During "Critical Stages" of Trial

Under the Due Process Clause, a criminal defendant has a "right to personal presence at all critical stages" of a prosecution.[127] The right to be present is related to, but distinct from the Sixth Amendment right to confront witnesses.[128] The latter specifically concerns the right of a defendant to face a prosecution witness and (usually through counsel) cross-examine the witness under oath; the former is a broader right and does not necessarily depend on the prosecution's presentation of witnesses or evidence.[129] The Supreme Court has held that a criminal defendant has a right to be present "whenever his presence has a relation, reasonably substantial, to

---

MADD buttons during defendant's DUI/manslaughter trial violated Constitution), *with* State v. McNaught, 713 P.2d 457, 467–68 (Kan. 1986) (refusing to find inherent prejudice caused by presence of spectators wearing MADD buttons during defendant's DUI/manslaughter trial).

122. Carey v. Musladin, 549 U.S. 70 (2006).

123. *Id.* at 75.

124. *See Deck*, 544 U.S. at 629; *see also* Bagwell v. Dretke, 372 F.3d 748, 754 (5th Cir. 2004) (placing defendant in shackles was not a constitutional violation because trial court found that defendant was violent and had made specific threats of violence before trial); Rhoden v. Rowland, 172 F.3d 633, 637–38 (9th Cir. 1999) (placing defendant in visible shackles during their trial violated their constitutional rights when trial court did not articulate a valid reason for doing so); Commonwealth v. Conley, 959 S.W.2d 77 (Ky. 1997) (placing defendant in visible shackles not a constitutional violation because trial court found that defendant posed a serious escape risk).

125. *Estelle*, 425 U.S. at 512–13.

126. *See, e.g.*, *Rhoden*, 172 F.3d at 636.

127. Rushen v. Spain, 464 U.S. 114, 117–18 (1983) (per curiam). The related issue of what constitutes a critical stage of the proceedings for right-to-counsel purposes is discussed in Chapter Three.

128. Kentucky v. Stincer, 482 U.S. 730, 745 (1987).

129. *Id.*

the fullness of his opportunity to defend against the charge."[130] Thus, for example, a defendant's right to be present was violated when they were excluded from voir dire,[131] the reading of jury instructions, or closing arguments,[132] and arguably even when they were excluded from the jury's return of a guilty verdict in open court.[133] Conversely, a defendant's right to presence was not violated by their absence from a pretrial hearing at which no substantive factual or legal issues were discussed by counsel and the judge[134] nor by their absence from a bench conference at which the judge and attorneys briefly discussed a juror's concern over the fact that the defendant appeared to be sketching the jury on a note pad during the trial.[135] The Supreme Court has held that a defendant's constitutional right to be present during trial was not infringed by a prosecutor's closing argument that the defendant had the opportunity to tailor their own trial testimony based on what they heard other witnesses say prior to the defendant taking the stand.[136]

The right to be present is not absolute and can be waived by a defendant in a variety of ways. Waiver can occur explicitly (by a refusal to appear in court) or constructively (by repeated misconduct in the courtroom or by a defendant's becoming a fugitive after attendance at the beginning of trial).[137] Because the right to presence is a personal, fundamental constitutional right, defense counsel may not waive the defendant's right to presence without first obtaining the consent or acquiescence of the defendant.[138]

In *Illinois v. Allen*, the Court held that although "courts must indulge every reasonable presumption against the loss [of the defendant's constitutional right to be present during trial], . . . a defendant can lose his right to be present at trial if, after he has been warned by the judge that he will be removed if he continues his disruptive behavior, he nevertheless [continues to be] . . . disruptive."[139] "Once lost, the right to be present can, of course, be reclaimed as soon as the defendant is willing to conduct himself consistently with the decorum and respect inherent in the

---

130. *Id.* (citation and internal quotation marks omitted).
131. *See, e.g.*, United States v. Hernandez, 873 F.2d 516 (2d Cir. 1989).
132. *See, e.g.*, Larson v. Tansy, 911 F.2d 392, 396 (10th Cir. 1990) (closing argument, jury instructions); United States v. Fontanez, 878 F.2d 33 (2d Cir. 1989) (jury instructions).
133. *See Larson*, 911 F.2d at 396. In *Rice v. Wood*, 77 F.3d 1138, 1140 n.2 (9th Cir. 1996) (en banc), the court noted that the Supreme Court has never addressed the issue of whether the jury's return of a guilty verdict is a critical stage.
134. *See, e.g.*, United States v. Oles, 994 F.2d 1519 (10th Cir. 1993).
135. United States v. Gagnon, 470 U.S. 522, 526 (1985) (per curiam).
136. Portuondo v. Agard, 529 U.S. 61 (2000).
137. Taylor v. United States, 414 U.S. 17 (1973) (per curiam) (to be tried in abstensia after jumping bail or escaping from pretrial detention, defendant must have been present when trial began); Illinois v. Allen, 397 U.S. 337 (1970) (defendant's right to presence constructively waived by "disruptive" behavior).
138. *See, e.g.*, Lee v. State, 509 P.2d 1088, 1091–92 (Alaska 1973).
139. *Allen*, 397 U.S. at 343.

concept of courts and judicial proceedings."[140] Justice Brennan, who concurred in the majority opinion in *Allen*, added that a defendant should not be removed from the courtroom "except after he has been fully and fairly informed that his conduct is wrong and intolerable, and warned of the possible consequences of continued misbehavior."[141]

8.9 Inflammatory Closing Arguments by Prosecutors

As discussed above, a variety of prosecutorial arguments can violate specific constitutional rights of a criminal defendant, such as comments on a defendant's right to silence and arguments that shift to the defense or diminish the "reasonable doubt" quantum of proof. In addition to such arguments that violate a "specific trial right" of a defendant,[142] other prosecutorial arguments that are "inflammatory" also can violate due process if they are sufficiently prejudicial and not "invited" by prior arguments of the defense.[143] To result in a reversal of a defendant's conviction or sentence on appeal, such arguments must have "so infected the trial with unfairness as to make the resulting conviction [or sentence] a denial of due process."[144] Appellate decisions finding that such unconstitutional unfairness resulted are relatively rare, and in the cases where reversals have occurred, the prosecutors' inflammatory arguments usually involved repeated improper arguments[145] or improper appeals to jurors' racial prejudices[146] or religious views.[147]

8.10 Leading Supreme Court Decisions Concerning Constitutional Violations During Trial

- *Hoffman v. United States*, 341 U.S. 479 (1951) (third-party witness may invoke Fifth Amendment right against self-incrimination and avoid testifying at trial, absent being immunized, if the question(s) posed would directly or indirectly incriminate the witness if answered; trial court cannot order the witness to answer, absent immunity, unless it is "perfectly clear" that the answer would not incriminate the witness).

---

140. *Id.*

141. *Id.* at 350 (Brennan, J., concurring); *see also* State v. Aceto, 100 P.3d 629, 635–36 (Mont. 2004) (reversing conviction where trial court did not give defendant a proper warning before removing him from the courtroom during the trial).

142. United States v. Mietus, 237 F.3d 866, 870 (7th Cir. 2001).

143. Darden v. Wainwright, 477 U.S. 168 (1986); Donnelly v. DeChristoforo, 416 U.S. 637 (1974).

144. *Donnelly*, 416 U.S. at 643.

145. *See, e.g.*, Bates v. Bell, 402 F.3d 635 (6th 2005).

146. *See, e.g.*, Bennett v. Stirling, 842 F.3d 319 (4th Cir. 2016); Moore v. Morton, 255 F.3d 95, 113–20 & n.15 (3d Cir. 2001).

147. *See, e.g.*, Sandoval v. Calderon, 241 F.3d 765, 776–77 (9th Cir. 2001); Romine v. Head, 253 F.3d 1349, 1368–69 (11th Cir. 2001).

- *Griffin v. California*, 380 U.S. 609 (1965) (holding that a prosecutor violates a defendant's Fifth Amendment privilege against self-incrimination by commenting on a nontestifying defendant's silence during the trial).

- *Bruton v. United States*, 391 U.S. 123 (1968) (defendant's constitutional right to confront nontestifying codefendant is violated by admission of codefendant's confession during a joint trial if it implicates the defendant in the alleged crime, even if trial court were to give a limiting instruction).

- *Illinois v. Allen*, 397 U.S. 337 (1970) (although a criminal defendant has a constitutional right to be present during all "critical stages" of the prosecution, the defendant can constructively waive that right by engaging in "disruptive" behavior after being fairly warned that such behavior will lead to the removal of the defendant from the courtroom).

- *Webb v. Texas*, 409 U.S. 95 (1972) (per curiam) (neither trial judge nor prosecutor may unjustifiably threaten a defense witness with perjury charges—and in so doing dissuade the witness from testifying—without running afoul of the Compulsory Process Clause).

- *Chambers v. Mississippi*, 410 U.S. 284 (1973) (leading case on defendant's constitutional right to "present a defense"; specifically holding that a state's rules of evidence cannot be applied mechanistically to exclude reliable evidence of a defendant's innocence).

- *Doyle v. Ohio*, 426 U.S. 610 (1976) (prosecutor may not impeach a defendant who testifies at trial with their post-*Miranda* silence).

- *Estelle v. Williams*, 425 U.S. 501 (1976) (a trial judge who forces a defendant to go to trial in jail clothes over the defendant's objection violates due process).

- *Ohio v. Roberts*, 448 U.S. 56 (1980) (a prosecution witness's testimony under oath in a prior adversary proceeding, such as a preliminary hearing, may be introduced in a subsequent trial as long as the witness since has become unavailable and the defendant had a meaningful opportunity to cross-examine the witness in the prior proceeding through counsel, *overruled on other grounds by Crawford v. Washington*, 541 U.S. 36 (2004)).

- *Fletcher v. Weir*, 455 U.S. 603 (1982) (per curiam) (no violation of the Fifth Amendment to impeach a defendant who testifies in their own behalf with their pre-*Miranda* silence).

- *Wainwright v. Greenfield*, 474 U.S. 284 (1986) (prohibiting prosecution from using defendant's post-*Miranda* silence as substantive evidence at trial).

- *Holbrook v. Flynn*, 475 U.S. 560 (1986) (holding that the presence of a limited number of uniformed security personnel during a criminal trial does not violate due process; however, suggesting that the presence of an excessive number of security personnel could under some circumstances violate due process by suggesting to jurors that a defendant is dangerous or guilty).

- *Delaware v. Van Arsdall*, 475 U.S. 673 (1986) (as a general rule, a defendant has a right under the Confrontation Clause to impeach a hostile witness with anything that would reveal bias or a motive to lie—e.g., the witness's prior criminal record or pending charges—although the trial court may impose reasonable limits on such cross-examination).

- *Darden v. Wainwright*, 477 U.S. 168 (1986) (leading decision on constitutional limits to prosecutors' inflammatory closing arguments to juries).

- *Rock v. Arkansas*, 483 U.S. 44 (1987) (defendants have a constitutional right to testify in their own behalf at trial; trial court may limit that right only based on sufficient reasons, such as a finding that a defendant's testimony about their post-hypnotic memories is unreliable).

- *Taylor v. Illinois*, 484 U.S. 400 (1988) (leading decision on Compulsory Process Clause, which as a general matter gives the defendant the right to subpoena favorable and material defense witnesses, yet permits the trial court to impose reasonable restrictions on calling such witnesses to testify if the defense engaged in willful misconduct).

- *Maryland v. Craig*, 497 U.S. 836 (1990) (rejecting a categorical "face-to-face" requirement under the Confrontation Clause; as long as trial court finds that there is a sufficient reason to do so based on the specific circumstances of a particular case, the court may block a sensitive witness from seeing defendant during witness's testimony, e.g., in a child-rape case).

- *Crawford v. Washington*, 541 U.S. 36 (2004) (admission of "testimonial" hearsay at trial violates the Confrontation Clause unless the defendant had a meaningful opportunity to cross-examine the declarant under oath in a prior proceeding and the declarant is unavailable to testify at trial; reliability of such "testimonial" hearsay irrelevant (overruling *Ohio v. Roberts*)).

- *Deck v. Missouri*, 544 U.S. 622 (2005) (unconstitutional to require a defendant to wear shackles during trial unless sufficient showing is made that the defendant is dangerous or a flight risk).

- *Clark v. Arizona*, 548 U.S. 735 (2006) (due process not violated by excluding psychiatric evidence concerning a defendant's mental state at the time of a crime if it is offered in the attempt to raise a reasonable doubt concerning the mens rea element so long as some version of the insanity defense may be raised).

- *Melendez-Diaz v. Massachusetts*, 557 U.S. 305 (2009) (state crime laboratory report concluding that the substance that the defendant possessed was a controlled substance was "testimonial," and its admission violated the Confrontation Clause when the analyst was not available to be cross-examined about it).

- *Michigan v. Bryant*, 562 U.S. 344 (2011) (an out-of-court statement made by a dying gunshot victim to police officers at the scene of the shooting, in which the victim identified the defendant as the shooter, was not "testimonial" and thus could be admitted at trial because the "primary purpose" of such a statement, from an "objective" standpoint, was not law enforcement; instead, the statement was elicited by the officers in their capacity as first responders to an emergency).

- *Bullcoming v. United States*, 564 U.S. 647 (2011) (state crime laboratory report about defendant's blood-alcohol level was testimonial, and its admission violated the Confrontation Clause when the analyst was not available to be cross-examined about it).

- *Williams v. Illinois*, 567 U.S. 50 (2012) (splintered Court, in a 4-1-4 vote, ruled that prosecution's expert witness' reliance on results of DNA test conducted by out-of-court analyst did not violate the Confrontation Clause).

- *Ohio v. Clark*, 576 U.S. 237 (2015) (testimony about three-year-old victim's out-of-court statement to his preschool teacher did not violate Confrontation Clause because the hearsay was not "testimonial" insofar its "primary purpose" was not to further criminal prosecution of the defendant).

- *Kahler v. Kansas*, 140 S. Ct. 1021 (2020) (due process not violated by prohibiting the insanity defense so long as the state allows the defense to offer evidence of the defendant's mental state in the attempt to negate the mens rea element).

CHAPTER NINE

MOTIONS FOR JUDGMENT OF ACQUITTAL

After the prosecution has rested its case, defense counsel typically moves for a "judgment of acquittal." Closely analogous to a motion for a "directed verdict" in civil cases, a motion for a judgment of acquittal in a criminal case is a procedural device whereby defense counsel requests—usually in an oral motion—that the trial court "take the case away from the jury" and render a "not guilty" verdict based on legally insufficient evidence.[1] Conversely, the prosecution in a criminal case may not move the trial court to take the case away from the jury and enter a judgment of conviction; to do so would violate the defendant's Sixth Amendment right to a jury trial.[2]

9.1 The *Jackson v. Virginia* Standard

The constitutional standard governing the trial court in ruling on a motion for judgment of acquittal is the same standard governing an appellate court asked to reverse a conviction based on insufficient evidence—namely, whether a "rational jury," viewing the evidence in a light most favorable to the prosecution, could conclude that the prosecution proved each and every element of the charged offense beyond a reasonable doubt.[3] After viewing the evidence in such a light, a trial court, if it concludes that no rational jury could find each and every element of the charged offense(s) beyond a reasonable doubt, will take the case away from the jury and enter a judgment of acquittal.[4]

This "*Jackson v. Virginia* standard" erects a high hurdle for defendants. Motions for judgment of acquittal are thus granted on an infrequent basis. Nevertheless, they should be made by defense counsel in every case, even if only in a perfunctory manner. The prosecution occasionally makes a critical mistake—overlooked by the

---

1. *See, e.g.*, FED. R. CRIM. P. 29(a).
2. United States v. Martin Linen Supply Co., 430 U.S. 564, 572–73 (1977).
3. *See* Jackson v. Virginia, 443 U.S. 307 (1979); Glasser v. United States, 315 U.S. 60, 80 (1942); *see also* Fiore v. White, 531 U.S. 225, 228–29 (2001).
4. Sometimes trial courts grant motions for judgment of acquittal on some counts of the indictment, but not on others. In such cases of partial acquittals, the remaining counts of the indictment are submitted to the jury for deliberation.

parties and the trial judge—by failing to offer some piece of evidence that constitutes a fatal gap in the prosecution's case.[5]

If a trial court grants a motion for judgment of acquittal, it usually does so before the jury has deliberated and returned a verdict. Occasionally, however, a trial judge inclined to grant a motion will allow a jury the opportunity to return a not guilty verdict first; if the jury ultimately does not acquit, then the judge can enter a judgment of acquittal after the jury's guilty verdict[6] or after a mistrial following a hung jury. The critical difference between a trial court's judgment of acquittal granted before a jury returns a verdict and one granted after a guilty verdict from the jury is the significance for double jeopardy purposes. A pre-verdict judgment of acquittal by the trial court prevents a retrial under the Double Jeopardy Clause and also prevents an appeal of the court's ruling by the prosecution; a post-verdict judgment of acquittal does not prevent an appeal by the prosecution, which, if successful, will result in the reinstatement of the jury's guilty verdict.[7]

In some jurisdictions, a trial court also has the option of granting a new trial after concluding that a jury's guilty verdict is unjust because it is "against the great weight and preponderance of the evidence" even if there was legally sufficient evidence to support the verdict under the *Jackson v. Virginia* standard.[8] Because it is not tantamount to a jury's not guilty verdict, a finding of "factual insufficiency" does not bar a retrial under the Double Jeopardy Clause.[9]

In many jurisdictions, to preserve a sufficiency issue for appeal, a defendant not only must make a motion for judgment of acquittal immediately after the prosecution has rested its case-in-chief, but also must renew the motion after both sides have rested following the close of all the evidence in the case (assuming that the defense does not rest its case without putting on any evidence).[10] If defense counsel fails to renew its motion at the close of all the evidence, then an appellate court will either refuse to address a claim of insufficient evidence or engage in some type of restricted review, less than de novo.[11]

---

5. *See, e.g.*, United States v. Schultz, 17 F.3d 723 (5th Cir. 1994) (federal bank fraud conviction reversed based on insufficient evidence as a result of the prosecution's failure to offer readily available proof that bank was FDIC-insured on date of fraud).

6. Such a post-verdict judgment of acquittal is analogous to what was formerly known as a "judgment notwithstanding the verdict" (or a "JNOV") in a civil case. *Cf.* FED. R. CIV. P. 50(b)(3).

7. *See* United States v. Scott, 437 U.S. 82, 91 n.7 (1978).

8. *See, e.g.*, United States v. Ashworth, 836 F.2d 260, 266 (6th Cir. 1988) (discussing FED. R. CRIM. P. 33).

9. Tibbs v. Florida, 457 U.S. 31 (1982). The Double Jeopardy Clause is further discussed in Chapter Four.

10. *See, e.g.*, United States v. Burton, 324 F.3d 768, 770 (5th Cir. 2003). Note that, in some jurisdictions, a motion for a judgment of acquittal is not required to preserve the sufficiency issue for appeal when the defendant was convicted at a bench trial rather than a jury trial. *See, e.g.*, United States v. Rosas-Fuentes, 970 F.2d 1379, 1381 (5th Cir. 1992).

11. *See, e.g.*, United States v. Carpenter, 95 F.3d 773, 775 (9th Cir. 1996).

If the trial court erroneously added an "element" to the charged offense in the jury instructions, an appellate court performing a sufficiency analysis under *Jackson* must assess the evidence in light of the statutory elements only and not consider the extra-statutory element erroneously added by the trial court in the jury instructions.[12]

9.2   Direct Versus Circumstantial Evidence

In theory at least, most courts ruling on motions for judgment of acquittal treat "direct evidence" cases and "circumstantial evidence" cases[13] in the same manner.[14] Traditionally, however, some courts have applied what has been referred to as the "reasonable hypothesis of innocence analytical construct," whereby circumstantial evidence that permits any reasonable hypothesis of innocence (as well as a hypothesis of guilt) is necessarily deemed insufficient as a matter of law, even if the greater weight of circumstantial evidence supports the hypothesis of guilt.[15] The vast majority of courts have abandoned this standard in circumstantial evidence cases.[16]

Nonetheless, many courts still conclude that where the prosecution's circumstantial evidence shows "equal or nearly equal circumstantial support to a theory of guilt and a theory of innocence," the evidence is necessarily insufficient under the *Jackson v. Virginia* standard.[17] Similarly, in criminal cases that involve charges that a defendant illegally possessed contraband (e.g., a controlled substance or an illegal firearm), courts faced with circumstantial evidence that the defendant was present in a place jointly occupied by other persons and that the contraband was hidden from plain view will find insufficient evidence as a matter of law if there is no proof specifically linking the defendant to the hidden contraband.[18] Likewise, a

---

12. Musacchio v. United States, 136 S. Ct. 709 (2016).

13. "'Direct evidence' is the testimony of one who asserts actual knowledge of a fact, such as an eyewitness. 'Circumstantial evidence' is proof of a chain of events and circumstances indicating that something is or is not a fact." COMMITTEE ON PATTERN JURY INSTRUCTIONS, FIFTH CIRCUIT PATTERN JURY INSTRUCTIONS (CRIMINAL CASES), § 1.07, at 16 (2012).

14. *See, e.g.*, Geesa v. State, 820 S.W.2d 154 (Tex. Crim. App. 1991), *overruled on other grounds by* Paulson v. State, 28 S.W.3d 570 (Tex. Crim. App. 2000).

15. *Geesa*, 820 S.W.2d at 157; *see also* State v. Derouchie, 440 A.2d 146, 148–49 (Vt. 1981); State v. Bell, 560 P.2d 925 (N.M. 1977).

16. *See* Holland v. United States, 348 U.S. 121, 139–40 (1954); United States v. Jackson, 863 F.2d 1168, 1173 (4th Cir. 1989); United States v. Bell, 678 F.2d 547 (5th Cir. 1982); *Geesa*, 820 S.W.2d at 160–61; State v. Grim, 854 S.W.2d 403 (Mo. 1993).

17. *See, e.g.*, United States v. Brown, 186 F.3d 661, 664 (5th Cir. 1999); United States v. Morillo, 158 F.3d 18, 22–23 (1st Cir. 1998); United States v. Wright, 835 F.2d 1245, 1249 n.1 (8th Cir. 1987); McRee v. State, 732 So. 2d 246, 250 (Miss. 1999).

18. *See, e.g.*, United States v. Mergerson, 4 F.3d 337, 349 (5th Cir. 1993) ("[W]here . . . a residence is jointly occupied, the mere fact that contraband is discovered at the residence will not, without more, provide evidence sufficient to support a conviction based upon constructive possession against any of the occupants . . . [S]omething else (e.g., some circumstantial indicium of possession) is required besides mere joint occupancy before constructive possession is established."); Guiton v. State, 742 S.W.2d 5 (Tex. Crim. App. 1987).

defendant's mere association with, or proximity to, other persons engaging in criminal activity does not, by itself, prove beyond a reasonable doubt that the defendant also was engaging in that criminal conduct.[19]

Conversely, in cases in which there was "direct" evidence introduced concerning each element of the charged offense—such as testimony from an eyewitness or accomplice—it is highly unlikely that a trial court will take the case away from the jury and enter a judgment of acquittal under the *Jackson v. Virginia* standard. This is because "[a]ssessing the credibility of witnesses and weighing the evidence is the exclusive province of the jury."[20] Even substantial inconsistencies between the testimony of two witnesses or internal inconsistencies in a witness's testimony will not ordinarily render the evidence insufficient concerning one or more elements of the charged offense. Only if the testimony of a witness is incredible "on its face" (e.g., it defies the laws of nature) will a reviewing court discredit the testimony as a matter of law.[21] Therefore, unless "direct" evidence offered by the prosecution simply fails to address one or more essential elements of a charged offense, a trial court ordinarily must assume that rational jurors could believe direct evidence in reaching a guilty verdict and permit the case to go to the jury.

9.3 Venue as an Element

Occasionally, defendants raise sufficiency challenges to venue. In the federal system, in light of the venue provision in Article III, § 2 of the Constitution and the "vicinage" requirement of the Sixth Amendment, venue is a quasi "element" of all criminal offenses but—unlike essential elements—only must be proved by a preponderance of the evidence (rather than beyond a reasonable doubt).[22] Furthermore, if a federal court enters a judgment of acquittal based on lack of sufficient proof of venue after jeopardy has attached at trial, the Double Jeopardy Clause does not bar a retrial.[23] The state courts vary in their approaches to venue; some treat venue as the equivalent of an essential element—barring retrial under the Double Jeopardy Clause if insufficient proof of venue was offered at the first trial—while others follow the federal courts' approach.[24]

---

19. *See, e.g.*, United States v. Starks, 309 F.3d 1017, 1025–26 (7th Cir. 2002); United States v. Perry, 624 F.2d 29, 31 (5th Cir. 1980).

20. United States v. Greenwood, 974 F.2d 1449, 1457–58 (5th Cir. 1992); *see also* United States v. Necoechea, 986 F.2d 1273, 1282 (9th Cir. 1993).

21. *Necoechea*, 986 F.2d at 1282; *see also* State v. Hornsby, 858 S.W. 2d 892 (Tenn. 1993).

22. *See, e.g.*, United States v. Strain, 407 F.3d 379, 379–80 (5th Cir. 2005); United States v. Perez, 280 F.3d 318, 330 (3d Cir. 2002); *but see* United States v. Rommy, 506 F.3d 108, 119 (2d Cir. 2007) (holding that venue is not an "element").

23. *See, e.g.*, United States v. Kayto, 868 F.2d 1020, 1021 (9th Cir. 1988); Wilkett v. United States, 655 F.2d 1007, 1011–12 (10th Cir. 1981).

24. *Compare, e.g.*, Williams v. State, 634 N.E.2d 849, 853 & n.3 (Ind. Ct. App. 1994) (although characterizing venue as a quasi-element, nonetheless holding that insufficient evidence of venue requires an entry of a judgment of acquittal and bars a retrial under the Double Jeopardy Clause),

9.4 Leading Supreme Court Decisions Concerning Judgments of Acquittal

- *United States v. Martin Linen Supply Co.*, 430 U.S. 564 (1977) (under Double Jeopardy Clause, the prosecution may neither retry a defendant nor appeal following a trial court's entry of a judgment of acquittal entered before a jury returns a guilty verdict or after the jury is dismissed following a "deadlock" in deliberations, although prosecution may appeal a trial court's judgment of acquittal entered after the jury has returned a guilty verdict).

- *Jackson v. Virginia*, 443 U.S. 307 (1979) (defendant entitled to judgment of acquittal at trial if a "rational jury" could not find each element of the charged offense beyond a reasonable doubt based on the evidence presented at the trial).

- *Tibbs v. Florida*, 457 U.S. 31 (1982) (Double Jeopardy Clause does not bar either a retrial or a prosecution appeal following a trial court's post-trial ruling that the "weight" of the evidence was contrary to the jury's guilty verdict—as opposed to a finding that a "rational jury" could not convict under the *Jackson v. Virginia* standard).

- *Musacchio v. United States*, 136 S. Ct. 709 (2016) (if the trial court erroneously added an element to the charged offense in the jury instructions, an appellate court must assess the sufficiency of the evidence in light of the statutory elements only and not consider the extra-statutory element).

---

with Grier v. State, 569 S.E.2d 837, 839 (Ga. 2002) (finding that venue is not an element of a criminal offense under state law and that insufficient proof of venue did not bar a retrial under the Double Jeopardy Clause); State v. Roybal, 132 P.3d 598, 604–05 (N.M. Ct. App. 2006) (same).

CHAPTER TEN

CONSTITUTIONAL ISSUES IN INSTRUCTING THE JURY AND DURING JURY DELIBERATIONS

10.1 Jury Instructions

After both sides have rested following the close of evidence, but prior to the jury's deliberations, a trial court will instruct the jury—usually in a multipage written set of instructions that also is read aloud to jurors—on the legal rules applicable to criminal cases generally and also on the law relating to the specific charges at issue in the case.[1] These are called "jury instructions" or the "jury charge." Most parts of the jury instructions are taken from boilerplate, standardized "pattern" jury instructions. Some pattern jury instructions have received the official imprimatur of a court, while others have been drafted by a legal scholar and were not prepared under the official auspices of a court.[2] What follows is a discussion of the most common constitutional issues that arise in the context of a trial court's instructing the jury on the relevant legal principles.

10.1.1 Lesser Included Offense Instructions

One of the most common disputes about jury instructions concerns what are referred to as "lesser included offenses." According to the majority position—adopted in the federal system and most states—a lesser included offense is a less serious crime (usually not charged) whose elements are a subset of a more serious ("greater"), charged offense.[3] In the vast majority of jurisdictions, either the defense

---

1. In most jurisdictions, the jury instructions are read aloud to the jury prior to closing arguments by the attorneys. In some jurisdictions, the lawyers must give closing arguments prior to the reading of the jury instructions.

2. *Compare, e.g.*, COMMITTEE ON PATTERN JURY INSTRUCTIONS, FIFTH CIRCUIT PATTERN JURY INSTRUCTIONS (CRIMINAL CASES) (2019), *with* Elizabeth Berry & George Gallagher, TEXAS CRIMINAL JURY CHARGES (2020).

3. *See* Schmuck v. United States, 489 U.S. 705, 715–22 (1989); *see also* John F. Yetter, *Truth in Jury Instructions: Reforming the Law of Lesser Included Offenses*, 9 ST. THOMAS L. REV. 603, 610 n.41 (Spring 1997) (collecting cases). The majority rule is referred to as the "statutory elements" test, which is analytically equivalent to the test in *Blockburger v. United States*, 284 U.S. 299 (1932), to determine whether a conviction or acquittal of a lesser offense bars a subsequent prosecution for the

or the prosecution may request a lesser included offense instruction (or the trial court may submit such an instruction sua sponte) when the evidence would permit a "rational jury" to find the defendant not guilty of the greater offense, but guilty of a lesser offense.[4] Usually, it is the defense that requests such an instruction over the objection of the prosecutor, although occasionally the prosecutor requests a lesser included offense instruction over the objection of the defense (who believes that it stands a good chance of an acquittal on the greater offense, but a conviction on a lesser offense).[5]

The Supreme Court has held that in death penalty cases, due process requires a trial court to grant a defendant's request for the submission of a jury instruction on at least one lesser included offense if both the evidence and the jurisdiction's law support it.[6] In *Beck v. Alabama*, the Court specifically declined to address whether due process required a lesser included offense instruction in a noncapital case.[7] In a prior noncapital case, the Court observed that failure to submit a defendant's requested lesser included offense instruction (where the evidence and law supported it) "would raise difficult constitutional questions,"[8] and the lower courts are divided on that question.[9] The debate is largely academic, however, since as a matter of nonconstitutional law there is "nearly universal acceptance of the rule" in some fashion or the other in capital and noncapital cases alike.[10]

The primary issue that is debated in the context of lesser included offenses is what quantum of evidence must exist to justify the submission of a lesser-included offense instruction requested by the defense. The various states and lower federal courts "vary in their descriptions of the quantum of proof necessary" for the submission of such an instruction.[11] The two main approaches are best described as the

---

greater offense or vice-versa. *See* Catherine L. Carpenter, *The All-or-Nothing Doctrine in Criminal Cases: Independent Trial Strategy or Gamesmanship Gone Awry*, 26 AM. J. CRIM. L. 257, 265–66 & nn.20–25 (Spring 1999) (collecting cases). A minority of courts opt for the "cognate pleading/ evidence" approach, which eschews a strict statutory-element analysis and instead looks at the allegations and the actual evidence offered at the trial to determine whether a jury could acquit on the greater offense and convict of the lesser offense. *Id.* at 267–68; *see also* Hopkins v. Reeves, 524 U.S. 88, 96 n.6 (1998) (discussing the different approaches of the state and federal courts).

4. *See* Beck v. Alabama, 447 U.S. 625, 634–37 & n.12 (1980) (citing cases from numerous jurisdictions).

5. *See, e.g.,* Hampton v. State, 109 S.W.3d 437 (Tex. Crim. App. 2003).

6. *Beck*, 447 U.S. at 637–38; *see also Hopkins*, 524 U.S. at 96–98.

7. *Beck*, 447 U.S. at 638 & n.14.

8. Keeble v. United States, 412 U.S. 205, 213 (1973).

9. *Compare, e.g.,* Vujosevic v. Rafferty, 844 F.2d 1023, 1027 (3d Cir. 1988) (applying *Beck* to noncapital cases); Moore v. United States, 599 A.2d 1381, 1386 (D.C. 1991) (same), *with* Valles v. Lynaugh, 835 F.2d 126, 127 (5th Cir. 1988) (failure to submit a lesser included offense charge in a noncapital case does not violate Constitution); Tata v. Carver, 917 F.2d 670, 671 (1st Cir. 1990) (failure to submit a lesser included offense instruction would violate due process only where it resulted in a fundamental miscarriage of justice).

10. *Beck*, 447 U.S. at 637.

11. *Id.* at 636–37 n.12 (citing cases).

　　　　　　　　　　　　　　　　　　　National Institute for Trial Advocacy

liberal "any evidence" standard and the more demanding "substantial evidence" standard. Under the "any evidence" standard, a trial court should submit a requested lesser included offense instruction if there is any evidence, "however weak," that would permit jurors to conclude the defendant was innocent of the greater offense and guilty only of the lesser.[12] The more demanding standard, conversely, focuses on whether there is "substantial" enough evidence to permit a rational jury to convict of the lesser included offense and acquit of the greater.[13]

A related question is under what circumstances a trial court is permitted to submit a lesser included offense instruction—either on the court's own motion or at the request of the prosecution—when the defense objects to it. The consensus among the lower courts appears to be that submission of a lesser offense instruction would be proper if there is "substantial" evidence for a "rational jury" to convict the defendant of the lesser offense[14] and, furthermore, only if the lesser offense is one that is fairly encompassed within the greater, charged offense (so as to comport with the Sixth Amendment's fair notice requirement and, in federal cases, the Fifth Amendment's Grand Jury Clause).[15]

10.1.2 Instructions on Affirmative Defenses

Another instruction commonly requested by criminal defendants concerns "affirmative defenses." An affirmative defense contends that the defendant should be acquitted not because the prosecution has failed to prove one or more essential "elements" of a charge, but instead because of some other factor that exculpates the defendant. Affirmative defenses include insanity, entrapment, self-defense, necessity,

---

12. *See, e.g.,* United States v. Humphrey, 208 F.3d 1190, 1207 (10th Cir. 2000); United States v. Thornton, 746 F.2d 39, 47 (D.C. Cir. 1984); Ex parte Hannah, 527 So. 2d 675, 677–78 (Ala. 1988). The Supreme Court has applied a similar liberal standard in an old case addressing the related issue of the quantum of evidence required for the submission of an affirmative defense instruction, *see* Stevenson v. United States, 162 U.S. 313, 314–15 (1896), but it has not addressed the issue in the context of lesser included offenses.

13. *See, e.g.,* United States v. Wright, 131 F.3d 1111, 1113 (4th Cir. 1997); People v. Breverman, 960 P.2d 1094, 1105 (Cal. 1998). Courts applying the substantial evidence standard have likened it to the "rational jury" standard governing judicial review of the sufficiency of the evidence supporting a jury's guilty verdict as set forth in Jackson v. Virginia, 443 U.S. 307 (1979). *See, e.g.,* United States v. Monger, 185 F.3d 574, 577 (6th Cir. 1999). It is questionable whether a *Jackson*-type standard is appropriate to apply to a defendant's request—as opposed to the prosecutor's request—for a lesser included offense instruction. *See* United States v. White, 972 F.2d 590, 605 n.4 (5th Cir. 1992) (King, J., concurring in part and dissenting in part) (explaining that, while superficially similar, the *Jackson* standard, which focuses on the amount of evidence necessary for a rational jury to convict, sets a higher evidentiary standard than the lesser included offense standard, which concerns the amount of evidence necessary for a rational jury to acquit). "A rational jury obviously need not find a fact beyond a reasonable doubt to rationally acquit." *Id.* at 605 n.4 (King, J., dissenting).

14. *See, e.g.,* People v. Barton, 906 P.2d 531, 535–36 (Cal. 1995); State v. Cox, 851 A.2d 1269 (Del. 2003); Hagans v. State, 559 A.2d 792 (Md. 1989).

15. *See Schmuck,* 489 U.S. at 717–18; People v. Cooke, 525 P.2d 426 (Colo. 1974).

duress, and justification.[16] Just as with lesser included offense instructions, there also is disagreement among judges on the lower courts regarding the quantum of evidence required for submission of an affirmative defense instruction.[17]

The Supreme Court has held that it does not unconstitutionally shift the prosecution's burden of persuasion to require a defendant to prove an affirmative defense, even if the defendant has the burden to do so beyond a reasonable doubt.[18] The Court has drawn a line between placing the burden on the defendant to disprove an element of the charged offense (usually by way of a mandatory presumption, which is discussed below) and placing the burden of proving an affirmative defense on the defendant. The former is unconstitutional burden shifting; the latter is not.[19] How the legislature defines a particular issue—as an "element" or an "affirmative defense"—is what matters.[20] Courts must examine both the statutory language and legislative intent to determine whether a particular fact in a case is an element under the relevant penal statute or, instead, is an affirmative defense.[21]

In some state jurisdictions, absent an explicit legislative directive to the contrary, a defendant has only the initial "burden of production" to come forward with enough evidence to make out a prima facie case of an affirmative defense—which entitles the defendant to a jury instruction on the affirmative defense—at which point the ultimate burden of persuasion shifts to the prosecution to disprove the affirmative defense beyond a reasonable doubt.[22] Yet the Supreme Court has held that

---

16. *See, e.g.*, United States v. Bailey, 444 U.S. 394 (1980) (discussing the affirmative defenses of necessity and duress); Mathews v. United States, 485 U.S. 58 (1988) (discussing the affirmative defense of entrapment).

17. *Compare, e.g.*, United States v. Branch, 91 F.3d 699, 712 (5th Cir. 1996) (requiring substantial enough evidence for a "reasonable juror" to find the affirmative defense), *with id.* at 745–46 & n.1 (Schwarzer, J., dissenting) (contending that "any evidence" of the lesser offense, "regardless how weak, inconsistent, or dubious," requires submission of an affirmative defense instruction) (citation and internal quotation marks omitted); United States v. Burt, 410 F.3d 1100, 1103–04 (9th Cir. 2005); Cassels v. People, 92 P.3d 951, 955 (Colo. 2004) (same). There is a dispute among lower court judges in the federal system whether the "any evidence" standard set forth in *Stevenson*, 162 U.S. at 323, was overruled by *Mathews*, 485 U.S. at 63–64 (1988) (which cited *Stevenson*, but stated that an affirmative defense instruction was proper if a "reasonable jury" could find the affirmative defense). *Compare* United States v. Perez, 86 F.3d 735, 736 (7th Cir. 1996), *with Branch*, 91 F.3d at 746 n.2 (Schwarzer, J., dissenting). Some lower courts have held that failure to submit a jury instruction on an affirmative defense, when supported by the evidence, violates due process. *See, e.g.*, Jackson v. Edwards, 404 F.3d 612 (2d Cir. 2005).

18. Patterson v. New York, 432 U.S. 197 (1977); Leland v. Oregon, 343 U.S. 790 (1952).

19. *Compare Patterson*, 432 U.S. 197, *with* Mullaney v. Wilbur, 421 U.S. 684 (1975); *see also* Martin v. Ohio, 480 U.S. 228 (1987) (state court's placement of burden of defendant to prove affirmative defense by a preponderance of the evidence does not violate due process).

20. *Patterson*, 432 U.S. at 210.

21. *See, e.g.*, People v. Reed, 932 P.2d 842 (Colo. App. 1996).

22. *See, e.g.*, People v. Janes, 962 P.2d 315, 318 (Colo. App. 1998).

the due process clause does not require the prosecution to disprove common-law affirmative defenses (such as duress) beyond a reasonable doubt.[23]

10.1.3   Burden-Shifting Presumptions

Traditionally, criminal law has permitted the trial court to instruct the jury that certain facts, if found by jurors as a threshold matter, give rise to a "presumption" of another fact. One of the oldest of such presumptions is that if jurors find that a defendant possessed stolen property that was recently stolen and the defendant did not satisfactorily explain how they legally came into possession of such property, jurors may infer that the defendant knew the property had been stolen.[24] Prior to *In re Winship*,[25] which held that the prosecution must prove each element of a charged offense beyond a reasonable doubt, most constitutional challenges to such presumptions were based on a claim that there was no "rational connection between the facts proved and the ultimate fact presumed."[26]

The Supreme Court applied that constitutional test to invalidate presumptions as "irrational" where it could not be "said with substantial assurance that the presumed fact is more likely than not to flow from the proved fact on which it is made to depend."[27] For instance, in *Leary v. United States*, the Court invalidated a presumption that a defendant who possessed marijuana also must have known that it had been illegally imported into the United States (a violation of former 21 U.S.C. § 176a).[28]

After *Winship*, the Supreme Court invalidated certain presumptions on a separate ground:[29] that a presumption, even a rebuttable one, in some situations unconstitutionally shifted the burden of persuasion from the prosecution to the defense concerning one or more elements of the offense.[30] In the leading case, *Sandstrom*,

---

23. Dixon v. United States, 548 U.S. 1 (2006).
24. Barnes v. United States, 412 U.S. 837 (1973).
25. In re Winship, 397 U.S. 358 (1970).
26. Tot v. United States, 319 U.S. 463, 467 (1943).
27. Leary v. United States, 395 U.S. 6, 36 (1969).
28. *Id.* at 46–54.
29. The original constitutional challenge is viable after *Winship*. *See, e.g.*, County Court of Ulster County v. Allen, 442 U.S. 140, 160–67 (1979). The two challenges, although both rooted in the Due Process Clause, are distinct.
30. *See* Sandstrom v. Montana, 442 U.S. 510 (1979); Connecticut v. Johnson, 460 U.S. 73 (1983); Francis v. Franklin, 471 U.S. 307 (1985); Rose v. Clark, 478 U.S. 570 (1986); Yates v. Aiken, 484 U.S. 211 (1988); Carella v. California, 491 U.S. 263 (1989) (per curiam); Yates v. Evatt, 500 U.S. 391 (1991); *cf.* Mullaney v. Wilbur, 421 U.S. 684 (1975). In *Morissette v. United States*, 342 U.S. 246 (1952), the Court rejected a "mandatory" presumption on the ground that it would remove the essential fact-finding function from the jury and violate a criminal defendant's presumption of innocence. *See id.* at 274–75. However, the Court made these statements in an era before the Court had "constitutionalized" the reasonable doubt standard and had applied the constitutional rule to state and federal criminal cases alike.

a homicide case in which the defendant claimed the killing was not deliberate, the Court held that a jury instruction that told jurors that the "law presumes that a person intends the ordinary consequences of [their] voluntary acts" unconstitutionally shifted the burden to the defense.[31]

Sandstrom drew a line between a "mandatory" presumption and a "permissive" presumption (or "inference"): the former unconstitutionally shifts the prosecution's burden whereas the latter generally does not.[32] A mandatory presumption requires jurors to find a fact if another fact is proved by the prosecution; a permissive presumption or inference permits—but does not require—jurors to find certain facts.[33] A mandatory presumption is unconstitutional even if it is rebuttable by the defendant because it shifts the burden to the defendant.[34] A permissive presumption is not unconstitutional unless it is irrational (as discussed above).[35]

10.1.4   Definitions of "Reasonable Doubt"

As discussed in Chapter Eight (concerning prosecutorial arguments), defining "reasonable doubt" for jurors implicates the Due Process Clause, and erroneous definitions that diminish the constitutionally required quantum of proof will cause a conviction to be reversed on appeal.[36] Although the Supreme Court has stated in dicta that "the Constitution does not require that any particular form of words be used in advising the jury of the [prosecution's] burden of proof,"[37] the Court has held that if the term "reasonable doubt" is defined, the definition must not unconstitutionally diminish the quantum of proof.[38]

In *Cage v. Louisiana*, the Supreme Court held that a jury instruction that defined "reasonable doubt" as "such doubt as would give rise to a grave uncertainty"

---

31. *Sandstrom*, 442 U.S. at 514–25.

32. *Id.* at 518–24.

33. *Yates*, 500 U.S. at 402–03; *Francis*, 471 U.S. at 314–15; *Allen*, 442 U.S. at 157.

34. *Francis*, 471 U.S. at 314–15. A mandatory presumption that is not rebuttable is referred to as a "conclusive" mandatory presumption. *Id.*

35. *Allen*, 442 U.S. at 157.

36. Cage v. Louisiana, 498 U.S. 39 (1990) (per curiam) (reversing conviction based on erroneous definition of "reasonable doubt" standard); *see also* Sullivan v. Louisiana, 508 U.S. 275 (1993) (finding this type of constitutional violation is "structural error" that is not amenable to harmless-error analysis); *but cf.* Victor v. Nebraska & Sandoval v. California, 511 U.S. 1 (1994) (finding that two different definitions of "reasonable doubt" were constitutional; distinguishing definitional instruction in case); *see generally* Robert C. Power, *Reasonable and Other Doubts: The Problem of Jury Instructions*, 67 TENN. L. REV. 45 (Fall 1999).

37. *Victor*, 511 U.S. at 5; *but see id.* at 26 (Ginsburg, J., concurring in part and concurring in the judgment) ("[W]e need not decide whether the Constitution required [a definition of 'reasonable doubt.'] . . [H]owever, the argument for defining the concept is strong."). Numerous courts refuse to require definitions of "reasonable doubt." *See* United States v. Walton, 207 F.3d 694, 697–98 & nn.3–5 (4th Cir. 2000) (opinion of Ervin, J., for half of an equally divided en banc court) (noting the many jurisdictions not requiring a definition).

38. *Id.* at 5–6, 22–23.

and stated that such doubt must be "an actual substantial doubt" was unconstitutional.[39] Conversely, in *Sandoval v. California*,[40] the Court upheld a definitional instruction that stated that "reasonable doubt . . . is not a mere possible doubt," but instead is the kind of doubt that causes reasonable persons to be unable to "say they feel an abiding conviction, to a moral certainty, of the truth of the charge."[41]

In *Victor v. Nebraska*, the Court upheld an instruction that defined the "reasonable doubt" standard in a way that permitted jurors to convict based on "the strong probabilities of the case, provided such probabilities are strong enough to exclude any doubt . . . that is reasonable"; the instruction also stated that "reasonable doubt" is "an actual and substantial doubt . . . as distinguished from a doubt arising from mere possibility, from bare imagination, or from fanciful conjecture."[42] Although the Court in *Victor* found this instruction "somewhat problematic" in that it referred to "actual substantial doubt"—just as the unconstitutional instruction in *Cage* had done—the Court ultimately concluded that the instruction in *Victor* was distinguishable from the one in *Cage* because the former (unlike the latter) contained the additional language that contrasted "substantial" doubt with a "mere possibility" or "conjecture."[43]

In *Victor*, the Court also affirmed the constitutionality of the widely used definition of "reasonable doubt" that draws an analogy to "the most important affairs" that a person has in their own life and defines reasonable doubt as being the type of doubt that would cause a reasonable person to "hesitate to act" in such affairs.[44] In a concurring opinion, Justice Ginsburg noted that critics of this definition contend that many people in the real world make critically important decisions without hesitation, even when they have objectively reasonable doubts.[45] Lower courts have invalidated definitions of "reasonable doubt" that draw analogies to the type of certainty required in important personal affairs, but that do not include the "hesitate to act" formulation.[46]

---

39. *Cage*, 498 U.S. at 41.
40. Sandoval v. California, 511 U.S. 1 (1994). *Sandoval* was a companion case to the lead case, Victor v. Nebraska, 511 U.S. 1 (1994), and is addressed separately in that opinion.
41. *Sandoval*, 511 U.S. at 7–17.
42. *Victor*, 511 U.S. at 17–23.
43. *Id.* at 5–6, 22–23.
44. *Id.* at 20.
45. *Id.* at 24–25 (Ginsburg, J., concurring in part and concurring in judgment).
46. *See, e.g.*, Commonwealth v. Bonds, 677 N.E.2d 1131 (Mass. 1997) (invalidating instruction that told jurors that reasonable doubt was "moral certainty," like the type of certainty that people have when they decide to marry, buy a house, or leave a long-held job).

10.1.5   *Omission of an Essential Element of the Offense*

As a general rule, omission of an essential element of the charged offense from jury instructions is constitutional error.[47] A related issue is whether the Due Process Clause requires a jury instruction on a mens rea element when a penal statute appears to leave out a mens rea element (or only requires a minimal mens rea such as mere negligence). In a series of cases interpreting federal criminal statutes, the Supreme Court has been able to avoid addressing the question of whether such a statute would violate due process by reading into the statutes an implicit mens rea requirement of knowledge or intent.[48] The Court has stated that a penal statute "completely bereft" of a mens rea element—other than one criminalizing a minor "public welfare" or "regulatory" offense"[49]—would "raise serious constitutional doubts."[50] Nevertheless, the Court has never squarely held that such a statute, state or federal, would violate the Constitution.[51]

10.1.6   *Instructions on the Defendant's Right to Silence During Trial*

On request, a trial court must instruct the jurors that they may not draw adverse inferences against a criminal defendant based on their invocation of the Fifth Amendment right to silence at trial.[52] A trial court may properly submit such an instruction over the defendant's objection that it would cause jurors to focus on the defendant's silence.[53]

10.1.7   *Instructions on the Defendant's Presumption of Innocence*

Unlike an instruction that the jury not draw adverse inferences from a defendant's decision to remain silent at trial, which must be submitted on request of the

---

47. United States v. Gaudin, 515 U.S. 506 (1995); *but cf.* Neder v. United States, 527 U.S. 1 (1999) (omission of an essential element, although constitutional error, is subject to harmless-error analysis on appeal).

48. *See, e.g.*, United States v. X-Citement Video, Inc., 513 U.S. 64 (1994) (reading a knowledge mens rea into a federal statute criminalizing the possession of child pornography); Staples v. United States, 511 U.S. 600 (1994) (reading a knowledge mens rea into a federal statute criminalizing the possession of a machine gun).

49. What qualifies as a minor criminal offense has caused much judicial debate. *See, e.g.*, Hanousek v. United States, 528 U.S. 1102, 1102–03 (2000) (Thomas, J., joined by O'Connor, J., dissenting from the denial of certiorari) (noting that the lower federal courts are divided over whether the criminal provision of the Clean Water Act is a "regulatory" or "public welfare" offense).

50. *X-Citement Video, Inc.*, 513 U.S. at 78. The Court also has stated that a criminal statute that entirely omits a mens rea requirement could be subject to a constitutional vagueness challenge. *See* Colautti v. Franklin, 439 U.S. 379, 395 (1979). The void-for-vagueness doctrine is discussed in Chapter Four.

51. The lower courts therefore consider this to be an open question. *See, e.g.*, Lady J. Lingerie v. City of Jacksonville, 176 F.3d 1358, 1367–68 (11th Cir. 1999).

52. Carter v. Kentucky, 450 U.S. 288 (1981).

53. Lakeside v. Oregon, 435 U.S. 333 (1978); *see also* Hunter v. Clark, 934 F.2d 856, 858–59 (7th Cir. 1991) (en banc).

National Institute for Trial Advocacy

defendant, the Constitution does not compel a trial court in every case to submit a requested instruction that a defendant is presumed innocent.[54] However, depending on the circumstances of a particular case, such an instruction may be constitutionally required—for instance, if the prosecutor has made arguments that suggest otherwise.[55]

10.1.8 Constructive Amendments to Indictments

A federal trial court violates the Grand Jury Clause by submitting jury instructions to a petit jury that permit jurors to convict the defendant of an offense that differs from the offense charged in the grand jury's indictment, even if it differs by only one additional or different element.[56] Thus, for example, if a federal grand jury returned an indictment that charged a defendant with distributing a controlled substance, it would constitute an impermissible "constructive amendment" if the jury instructions at trial instructed jurors on the distinct crime of possession with the intent to distribute because the two offenses contain distinct elements.[57] An unresolved question in the Supreme Court's grand jury jurisprudence is whether a constructive amendment to the indictment in a federal prosecution rises to the level of "structural error,"[58] requiring automatic reversal of a conviction on appeal.[59]

Note that the Fifth Amendment's Grand Jury Clause does not apply to state criminal prosecutions; there cannot, therefore, be a "constructive amendment"

---

54. Kentucky v. Whorton, 441 U.S. 786 (1979) (per curiam).
55. Taylor v. Kentucky, 436 U.S. 478 (1978).
56. Stirone v. United States, 361 U.S. 212 (1960).
57. United States v. Randall, 171 F.3d 195 (4th Cir. 1999). It does not constitute a constructive amendment to charge the petit jury on an uncharged, lesser included offense of the greater offense charged in the indictment. *See* United States v. Miller, 471 U.S. 130 (1985). Likewise, a "variance" between the factual allegations in the indictment and proof at a jury trial that does not alter the elements of the offense charged ordinarily does not constitute a constructive amendment to the indictment. *See generally* United States v. Adams, 778 F.2d 1117, 1122–24 (5th Cir. 1985) (discussing the difference between a constructive amendment and a variance). Only variances that "affect the substantial rights" of a defendant will result in a reversal of the conviction on appeal. *See* Berger v. United States, 295 U.S. 78, 82 (1935); *see also* United States v. Tsinnhnahijinnie, 112 F.3d 988 (9th Cir. 1997); Gollihar v. State, 46 S.W.3d 243 (Tex. Crim. App. 2001).
58. "Structural errors" are discussed in Chapter Thirteen.
59. *See* United States v. Resendiz-Ponce, 549 U.S. 102, 103 (2007) (after granting certiorari to resolve question, Court avoided addressing it by reversing on a different issue); *see also id.* at 116-17 (Scalia, J., dissenting) (addressing the issue and contending that a constructive amendment violates the Constitution and constitutes a "structural error"). In *Stirone*, decided in 1960, the Supreme Court held that a reversal of a federal defendant's conviction was automatic when the trial court "constructively amended" the indictment by submitting jury instructions that broadened the elements contained in the indictment. *Stirone*, 361 U.S. at 217. However, four decades later, in *United States v. Cotton*, 535 U.S. 625 (2002), the Court held that at least where a defendant failed to object to such a "constructive amendment" at the jury trial, a petit jury's guilty verdict demonstrated that any error did not prejudice the defendant. After *Cotton*, some lower federal courts have held that *Cotton* effectively overruled *Stirone*. *See, e.g.*, United States v. Robinson, 367 F.3d 278 (5th Cir. 2004).

to a state indictment in violation of the federal Grand Jury Clause.[60] However, the Sixth Amendment explicitly provides that a defendant is entitled to be informed of the "nature and cause of the accusation" before trial,[61] and the Due Process Clause has been interpreted to require similar pretrial notice in state prosecutions, which can be a basis for challenging a state trial court's jury instructions that "constructively amend" the state's charging instrument (whether or not it was returned by a state grand jury).[62] However, a state defendant must establish actual prejudice (for example, that they did not actually have pretrial notice of the constructively amended charge and was prejudiced thereby at the trial), which is difficult to do in most cases.[63] If the defense can establish that they learned of the prosecution's amendment of the charges for the first time after the trial proceedings were underway and were prejudiced thereby, a due process violation would be established.[64]

10.1.9 Jury Instructions on Alternate Means of Commission of the Charged Offense and "Patchwork" Guilty Verdicts[65]

The Supreme Court has held that in all federal cases a jury "cannot convict unless it unanimously finds that the [prosecution] has proved each element."[66] As discussed in Chapter Seven, in state cases the Court has held that the Constitution requires at least nine of twelve jurors to agree that the prosecution has proved each element.[67]

An issue that often arises is how the court must instruct jurors when there is more than one way for a defendant to have committed an element of a charged offense (for example, at a trial at which the charge is aggravated assault with a deadly weapon, there was conflicting evidence about whether the defendant used a knife or gun to commit the assault). The Supreme Court has held that as long as the jury unanimously agrees (in a federal case) or a sufficient majority agrees (in a state case) that there is proof beyond a reasonable doubt of a particular element, jurors need not be of one mind about how the element was proved (in the above example, a guilty verdict would be constitutional even if six jurors believed the

---

60. *See* Lanfranco v. Murray, 313 F.3d 112, 118 & n.1 (2d Cir. 2002); Hartman v. Lee, 283 F.3d 190, 195 n.4 (4th Cir. 2002).

61. *See* Hunter v. New Mexico, 916 F.2d 595, 598 & n.5 (10th Cir. 1990).

62. Cole v. Arkansas, 333 U.S. 196, 201 (1948); Watson v. Jago, 558 F.2d 330, 337–38 (6th Cir. 1977).

63. *See, e.g.,* Hain v. Gibson, 287 F.3d 1224 (10th Cir. 2002).

64. *Cf.* In re Ruffalo, 390 U.S. 544, 551 (1968) ("The charge must be known before the proceedings commence. They become a trap when, after they are underway, the charges are amended on the basis of testimony of the accused.") (disbarment proceedings).

65. This jury instruction issue is conceptually related to a motion to dismiss a charge in an indictment as being duplicitous, which is discussed in Chapter Four.

66. Richardson v. United States, 526 U.S. 813, 817 (1999).

67. *See* Chapter Seven.

defendant used a gun, but the other six jurors believed that the defendant used a knife).[68] Put another way, if there was proof of alternate means of committing a particular element, jurors need not agree on a single means as long as jurors do agree that the defendant engaged in one of the alternate means of committing the element.[69]

As a general rule, such "patchwork" guilty verdicts[70] are constitutionally permissible when the jury's patchwork verdict consists of "stitching" together multiple alternate means as opposed to "stitching" together alternate elements. Sometimes it is not clear, however, whether multiple alternate means are in fact multiple alternate elements.[71] If multiple elements are at issue—rather than multiple means of committing a single element—the court must instruct jurors that they must be of one mind concerning each element in order to return a guilty verdict.[72] To decide whether "several sets of underlying facts" are separate elements rather than separate means to commit a single element under the relevant statute, a court must engage in traditional statutory interpretation analysis and determine what the legislature intended in enacting the statute.[73]

The Supreme Court has recognized that in rare situations a jury instruction would violate the Constitution by labeling facts as separate means of committing a single element—as opposed to labeling such facts as separate elements—"where that definition risks serious unfairness and lacks support in history or tradition."[74] For example, at a trial in which the defendant was charged with a single count of possessing illegal drugs and the prosecution's proof at the trial concerned two distinct and unrelated possessions—one in the defendant's workplace and the other in their home, each on separate dates—the trial court would violate the Constitution by permitting jurors to convict the defendant without an instruction to jurors that to convict, they must agree that the defendant possessed the drugs in at least one of the two locations.[75]

---

68. *Richardson*, 526 U.S. at 817; Schad v. Arizona, 501 U.S. 624, 631–32 (1991) (plurality). The plurality in *Schad* suggested that a constitutional violation in this context would be a due process violation rather than a violation of the Sixth Amendment right to a jury trial; thus, the rule would apply equally in federal and state cases. *Schad*, 501 U.S. at 634 n.5.
69. *Richardson*, 526 U.S. at 817.
70. United States v. Navarro, 145 F.3d 580, 586 (3d Cir. 1998).
71. *Schad*, 501 U.S. at 634–36.
72. *Id.*
73. *See Richardson*, 526 U.S. at 819–20; *see also* United States v. Pleasant, 125 F. Supp. 2d 173, 176 & n.2 (E.D. Va. 2000).
74. *Richardson*, 526 U.S. at 820.
75. *See, e.g.,* State v. Stempf, 627 N.W.2d 352 (Minn. App. 2001).

10.2   Jury Deliberations and the Verdict[76]

10.2.1   Allen *Charges*

The Supreme Court has held that if jurors indicate to the trial court that they are deadlocked or otherwise unable to reach a verdict after a period of deliberating, the court may instruct jurors that they should continue deliberating and attempt to reach a verdict of some type.[77] However, in *Allen v. United States*, the Court cautioned that a trial court's charge should not "coerce" jurors into reaching a guilty verdict; doing so would render the guilty verdict unconstitutional.[78] To determine whether a particular *Allen* charge is coercive, the charge must be considered "in its context and under all the circumstances."[79] Giving deadlocked jurors a single "simple" *Allen* charge almost never will be deemed coercive. Such a charge not only instructs jurors that they should attempt to reach a verdict after further deliberations, but also tells jurors that they should "not hesitate to reexamine [their] own views and to change [their] opinion if [jurors] are convinced [they] are wrong but do not [change their position] . . . for the mere purpose of returning a verdict."[80]

An *Allen* charge that goes beyond this type of basic admonition risks coercing jurors into an unconstitutional guilty verdict. For instance, a charge that explicitly or implicitly singles out jurors in the minority and suggests that the majority of jurors are correct in their position likely will be deemed coercive, particularly when the jury knows that the trial court is aware of its numerical breakdown.[81] Similarly, a charge that explicitly or implicitly instructs jurors that they must reach a verdict— and that they have no "right to fail to agree"—will be found coercive.[82] Courts are more likely to find an *Allen* charge to be coercive when jurors return a guilty verdict shortly after receiving the charge.[83] Multiple *Allen* charges are more likely to be deemed coercive than a single charge.[84]

10.2.2   *Inconsistent Verdicts*

With one possible narrow exception, the Constitution is not violated by inconsistent jury verdicts (e.g., a split verdict of guilty on one count and not guilty on

---

76. The issue of jury misconduct, including during the jury's deliberations, is discussed in Chapter Thirteen.

77. Allen v. United States, 164 U.S. 492 (1896).

78. Lowenfield v. Phelps, 484 U.S. 231, 237–38 (1988); *see also* Early v. Packer, 537 U.S. 3 (2002) (per curiam).

79. *Lowenfield*, 484 U.S. at 237 (citation and internal quotation marks omitted).

80. *Id.* at 235.

81. Tucker v. Catoe, 221 F.3d 600, 610–11 (4th Cir. 2000); Smalls v. Batista, 191 F.3d 272, 282–83 (2d Cir. 1999); United States v. Burgos, 55 F.3d 933, 937–40 (4th Cir. 1995).

82. *See, e.g.,* United States v. Paniagua-Ramos, 135 F.3d 193 (1st Cir. 1998).

83. *See, e.g.,* Weaver v. Thompson, 197 F.3d 359, 366 (9th Cir. 1999).

84. *See, e.g.,* United States v. Seawell, 550 F.2d 1159 (9th Cir. 1977).

another count where logically the judge or jury returning the verdict should have returned a uniform verdict on all counts).[85] This is true regarding inconsistent verdicts among codefendants at a joint trial and inconsistent verdicts at a single defendant's trial (involving multiple counts against that defendant).[86] The one possible exception exists when a trial judge finds legally insufficient evidence of a conspiracy with respect to all coconspirators except one (where all coconspirators were tried in a joint trial); some courts have held that because a conspiracy necessarily involves at least two coconspirators, a finding of insufficient evidence of guilt with respect to all but one member of the conspiracy necessarily means insufficient evidence of guilt with respect to the remaining coconspirator.[87]

10.3　Leading Supreme Court Decisions Regarding Jury Instruction Issues

- *Cole v. Arkansas*, 333 U.S. 196 (1948) (defendant's constitutional right to be informed of the "nature and cause of the accusation" against him forbids a trial court from submitting a jury instruction on an offense when the defendant did not receive adequate pretrial notice of that specific offense or a greater variation of it).

- *Stirone v. United States*, 361 U.S. 212 (1960) (in federal cases, the Grand Jury Clause of the Fifth Amendment prohibits a federal district court from instructing a jury on a felony offense not charged in the indictment unless that offense is a lesser version of the charged offense).

- *Leary v. United States*, 395 U.S. 6 (1969) (a "presumption" in a trial court's jury instructions, whether mandatory or permissive in nature, violates due process if there is no "rational connection between the facts proved [at trial] and the fact presumed" in the jury instructions).

- *Keeble v. United States*, 412 U.S. 205 (1973) (trial court's refusal to submit a lesser included offense instruction requested by defendant in a noncapital case would raise "difficult constitutional questions" if the evidence at trial permitted a rational jury to acquit on the greater offense and convict on the lesser offense).

---

85. Harris v. Rivera, 454 U.S. 339 (1981); United States v. Powell, 469 U.S. 57 (1984); *see also* Bravo-Fernandez v. United States, 137 S. Ct. 352, 356–57 (2016).
86. *See Harris*, 454 U.S. 399 (inconsistent verdicts among codefendants); *Powell*, 469 U.S. 57 (inconsistent verdicts in single defendant trial).
87. *See, e.g.*, United States v. Velasquez, 885 F.2d 1076 (3d Cir. 1989); *but cf.* United States v. Nichols, 374 F.3d 959, 970 & n.9 (10th Cir. 2004) (noting that the vast majority of courts have held that a jury's acquittal of all but one conspirator at a joint trial does not equate to legally insufficient evidence with respect to the remaining coconspirator).

- *Mullaney v. Wilbur*, 421 U.S. 684 (1975) (if the applicable penal law defines a certain factual issue as an "element" of the charged offense rather than as an "affirmative defense," then due process requires the prosecution to prove or disprove the relevant fact—whichever the case may be— beyond a reasonable doubt, and the burden concerning that fact cannot be shifted to the defense).

- *Patterson v. New York*, 432 U.S. 197 (1977) (no due process violation to place burden on defendant to prove an "affirmative defense" at trial).

- *Kentucky v. Whorton*, 441 U.S. 786 (1979) (per curiam) (trial court need not in all cases submit a jury instruction explaining a defendant's "presumption of innocence," but must do so if the prosecution has made arguments denigrating the presumption of innocence).

- *Sandstrom v. Montana*, 442 U.S. 510 (1979) (a "mandatory" presumption, as opposed to a "permissive" presumption, violates due process by effectively shifting the burden of proof to the defense, even if the presumption is a rational one under *Leary*).

- *Carter v. Kentucky*, 450 U.S. 288 (1981) (upon request from the defendant, the trial court must charge the jury that it cannot consider a defendant's silence at trial in any way against the defendant or draw any "adverse inferences" therefrom).

- *United States v. Powell*, 469 U.S. 57 (1984) (as a general rule, "inconsistent" verdicts by a jury do not violate the Constitution as long as a guilty verdict is supported by sufficient evidence).

- *Lowenfield v. Phelps*, 484 U.S. 231 (1988) (leading modern decision discussing "*Allen* charges," *see Allen v. United States*, 164 U.S. 492 (1896)).

- *Cage v. Louisiana*, 498 U.S. 39 (1990) (per curiam) (trial court's jury instruction on "reasonable doubt" may not define that concept in a manner that undercuts the constitutionally required quantum of proof).

- *Victor v. Nebraska*, 511 U.S. 1 (1994) (in dicta, stating that there is no constitutional requirement that the concept of "reasonable doubt" be specifically defined for jurors beyond a bare statement that the prosecution must prove each element of the charged offense "beyond a reasonable doubt").

- *United States v. X-Citement Video, Inc.*, 513 U.S. 64 (1994) (a trial court's refusal to instruct a jury on a mens rea element concerning a "serious" offense, even when the penal statute mentions no mens rea element, would raise "serious constitutional doubts").

- *United States v. Gaudin*, 515 U.S. 506 (1995) (jury, rather than trial judge, must find each element of the charged offense beyond a reasonable doubt unless the defendant waives the right to a jury trial; trial court cannot "direct" the jury's verdict on any element in the trial court's jury instructions by informing jurors that the prosecution has met its burden regarding a particular element).

- *Richardson v. United States*, 526 U.S. 813 (1999) (jury instructions violate the Sixth Amendment right to a jury trial when they permit the jury to convict where jurors need not agree on one of alternate elements of the charged offense, although jurors generally need not be of one mind about alternate means of committing a single element).

CHAPTER ELEVEN

GUILTY PLEAS

Each year, the overwhelming majority of criminal defendants in both the state and federal court systems plead guilty or nolo contendere ("no contest")[1] rather than take their cases to trial (assuming that their cases were not dismissed as a result of a pretrial motion or for some other reason).[2] The hearing at which a defendant pleads guilty—which involves a colloquy between the defendant and the trial judge—is called an "arraignment," "rearraignment" or "guilty plea canvas," depending on the jurisdiction.[3] A defense lawyer may not enter a guilty plea—or its functional equivalent (i.e., waiving a jury trial and all of the rights associated with a trial and failing to contest the prosecution's evidence)—for their client without the client's consent to do so.[4] The entry of a guilty plea is an extremely significant event for a criminal defendant in that, with a few exceptions, it "waives all non-jurisdictional defects in the prosecution"[5]—meaning the vast majority of constitutional challenges to the conviction (e.g., Fourth Amendment search and seizure issues) are forever waived.[6]

---

1. A nolo contendere or "no contest" plea does not admit guilt and, instead, simply acknowledges that the prosecution has sufficient evidence to convict the defendant and that the defendant has chosen not to contest the charges. In the vast majority of jurisdictions, a no contest plea is equivalent to a guilty plea with a single exception—a no contest plea generally is inadmissible against the defendant in a subsequent civil case as an admission of the facts supporting the plea. *See, e.g.*, State v. Hebert, 846 So. 2d 60, 63 (La. Ct. App. 2003). The Supreme Court has held that it does not violate due process for a trial court to accept a guilty plea or no contest plea from a defendant who professes their innocence, but states that they nonetheless wish to plead guilty to avoid a more severe penalty or for some other rational purpose. North Carolina v. Alford, 400 U.S. 25 (1970). Henceforth, all references to "guilty pleas" refer as well to no-contest pleas.

2. *See, e.g.*, Missouri v. Frye, 566 U.S. 134, 143 (2012) (noting that 97 percent of federal convictions and 94 percent of state convictions resulted from guilty pleas).

3. *See, e.g.*, Bond v. Dretke, 384 F.3d 166, 167 (5th Cir. 2004); State v. Langarica, 822 P.2d 1110 (Nev. 1991).

4. Brookhart v. Janus, 384 U.S. 1 (1966); *but cf.* Florida v. Nixon, 543 U.S. 175 (2004) (holding that at least when a capital defendant does not object, a capital defense lawyer may concede a clearly guilty defendant's guilt during trial to increase the defendant's chance of avoiding the death penalty at the subsequent capital sentencing hearing).

5. Tollett v. Henderson, 411 U.S. 258, 261–67 (1973).

6. *Id.*

There are many constitutional issues, both substantive and procedural, that arise in the guilty plea context. Those issues, along with the few exceptions to the general rule that a guilty plea waives all nonjurisdictional challenges to the conviction, will be discussed below.

11.1 Substantive Constitutional Requirements for a Valid Guilty Plea: A "Knowing, Voluntary, and Intelligent" Plea

To satisfy due process, a defendant's guilty plea must be "knowing, voluntary, and intelligent."[7] This substantive constitutional requirement means not only that a defendant must be mentally competent at the time of the plea,[8] but also that the plea not be "induced by threats . . . , misrepresentation (including unfulfilled or unfulfillable promises), or . . . promises that are by their nature improper as having no proper relationship to the prosecutor's business (e.g., bribes)."[9] The Supreme Court has held that one particular type of "threat"—a threat by the prosecutor at the outset of the prosecution that greater charges will be filed (including charges making a defendant eligible for the death penalty) unless the defendant pleads guilty to lesser charges—is constitutionally permissible, at least where a prosecutor has probable cause supporting the more serious charges.[10]

A defendant's guilty plea is invalid if they pleaded guilty with an inadequate understanding of the constitutional rights that they were waiving by pleading guilty or an inadequate understanding of essential elements of the offense to which they pleaded.[11] For instance, in *Henderson v. Morgan*, the Supreme Court held that a defendant's guilty plea was invalid where the trial judge and lawyers in his case erroneously had led him to believe that a person could be convicted of second-degree murder under state law without possessing the requisite intent to cause

---

7. Brady v. United States, 397 U.S. 742 (1970); Bousley v. United States, 523 U.S. 614 (1998). The line between the terms "knowing," "voluntary," and "intelligent" is somewhat blurry. Indeed, the Supreme Court has treated "knowing" and "intelligent" as being synonymous in this context. *See* State v. Freese, 13 P.3d 442, 449 n.1 (Nev. 2000) (Agosti, J., dissenting, joined by Rose, C.J., & Leavitt, J.). "Voluntary" means an exercise of the defendant's free will in pleading guilty, while "knowing" or "intelligent" means a guilty plea with sufficient knowledge and understanding about all relevant matters (e.g., the elements of the charged offense and range of punishment the defendant is facing). Courts often collapse both concepts into the term "voluntary."
8. Godinez v. Moran, 509 U.S. 389 (1993) (standard for mental competency applies equally to a defendant who pleads guilty and a defendant who goes to trial). Mental competency is discussed in Chapter Four.
9. *Brady*, 397 U.S. at 755 (citation and internal quotation marks omitted).
10. Bordenkircher v. Hayes, 434 U.S. 357 (1978); *see also* Guam v. Fegurgur, 800 F.2d 1470, 1473 (9th Cir. 1986); *cf.* Corbitt v. New Jersey, 439 U.S. 212 (1978) (offering lenient treatment in return for guilty plea is a valid promise).
11. Henderson v. Morgan, 426 U.S. 637 (1976).

death at the time of the killing.[12] Likewise, if a defendant pleaded guilty based on "untenable sentencing information," that guilty plea is constitutionally invalid.[13] For example, when a trial court erroneously informed a defendant at the guilty plea hearing that the court had the authority to give the defendant a sentence below the statutory mandatory minimum prison sentence—when in fact the court had no such authority—the defendant's plea was involuntary.[14] When a defendant pleads guilty after being misinformed about the elements of the charged offense or the punishment range they are facing, the plea is constitutionally invalid even if the defendant would have pleaded "anyway," assuming that they had been given correct information.[15]

When a defense attorney gives significant misinformation to a defendant about the potential punishment a guilty plea will bring, the defendant's subsequent plea will be unintelligent if the defendant did not in fact know the actual range of punishment they were facing at the time they pleaded guilty.[16] A defense attorney's erroneous estimate of the potential sentence a defendant would receive, however, ordinarily will not render the guilty plea involuntary, provided that the estimate was objectively reasonable at the time it was given.[17] A defendant's erroneous belief about the punishment that they were facing will not render the plea involuntary as long as neither their attorney nor a "state actor" (e.g., a police officer, the prosecutor, or the judge) improperly influenced the defendant's erroneous belief.[18]

11.2 Procedural Constitutional Requirements for a Valid Guilty Plea: *Boykin v. Alabama*

In *Boykin v. Alabama*,[19] the Supreme Court held that due process requires an affirmative showing on the record that a defendant's guilty plea was voluntarily and

---

12. *Id.* at 644–46 & n.13.

13. *See, e.g.*, United States v. Amaya, 111 F.3d 386, 389 (5th Cir. 1997).

14. *Id.*

15. *See Henderson*, 426 U.S. at 644 & n.12; *see also Amaya*, 111 F.3d at 389.

16. Laycock v. New Mexico, 880 F.2d 1184, 1186 (10th Cir. 1989) (citing Blackledge v. Allison, 431 U.S. 63, 75 n.8 (1977)). A minority of courts have treated a defense lawyer's misinformation about the sentence that a defendant is facing exclusively as an allegation of ineffective assistance of counsel, which requires a defendant to make the further showing that there is a "reasonable probability" that they would not have pleaded guilty "but for" the erroneous advice. *See, e.g.*, United States ex rel. Bachman v. Hardy, 637 F. Supp. 1273, 1281 (N.D. Ill. 1986). In *Blackledge*, however, the Supreme Court appeared to view erroneous information from defense counsel to be equivalent to erroneous information from the trial court—thus only requiring a defendant to show that they pleaded guilty after being given the erroneous information. Whether a defendant would have pleaded guilty after having been given correct information is irrelevant. *Cf. Henderson*, 426 U.S. at 644 & n.12.

17. *Laycock*, 880 F.2d at 1186.

18. *Brady*, 397 U.S. at 757.

19. Boykin v. Alabama, 395 U.S. 238 (1969); *see also* Von Moltke v. Gillies, 332 U.S. 708 (1948) (plurality).

intelligently made.[20] The "on-the-record" prophylactic requirement can be satisfied by a court reporter's transcript of the guilty plea proceeding, a written waiver-of-rights form filled out by the defendant, or other memorialization that demonstrates the defendant's plea was knowing and voluntary.[21]

The Court's decision in *Boykin* referred in particular to making a contemporaneous record of the defendant's waiver of important constitutional rights, i.e., waiver of the right to silence, the right to a jury trial, and the right to confront the defendant's accusers.[22] In a portion of the text of the Court's opinion and a corresponding footnote (note 7), the *Boykin* Court also stated that the record must reflect that the defendant was aware of the nature of the charges (the elements of the charged offense and facts alleged by the prosecution)[23] and the consequence[s] of the plea, including the statutory range of punishment.[24] The dissenting justices in *Boykin*

---

20. *Boykin*, 395 U.S. at 242–44. Notably, *Boykin* was decided before the Supreme Court's 1970 decision in In re Winship, 397 U.S. 358 (1970), which held that the prosecution has the burden to prove each element of the charged offense beyond a reasonable doubt. That constitutional right is now deemed more important than the rights to silence, a jury trial, and confrontation. Indeed, the Supreme Court has refused to give retroactive application of its decisions applying the Fifth Amendment privilege against self-incrimination, right to a jury trial, and the right to confront witnesses. *See* Tehan v. United States ex rel. Shott, 382 U.S. 406 (1966) (refusing to apply Griffin v. California, 380 U.S. 609 (1965), retroactively); Schriro v. Summerlin, 542 U.S. 348, 356–57 (2004) ("Our decision in DeStefano v. Woods, 392 U.S. 631 (1968) (per curiam) . . . refused to give retroactive effect to Duncan v. Louisiana, 391 U.S. 145 (1968), which applied the Sixth Amendment's jury-trial guarantee to the States."); Whorton v. Bockting, 549 U.S. 406 (2007) (refusing to apply Crawford v. Washington, 541 U.S. 36 (2004), retroactively). Conversely, the Court has given *Winship* "complete retroactive effect." Ivan V. v. City of New York, 407 U.S. 203, 205 (1971) (per curiam) (retroactively applying "the constitutional standard of proof beyond a reasonable doubt announced in *Winship*"); *cf.* Sullivan v. Louisiana, 508 U.S. 275 (1993) (holding that a violation of the due-process requirement set forth in Cage v. Louisiana, (1990) (per curiam), concerning an erroneous definition of "reasonable doubt," was a "structural error" requiring automatic reversal on appeal). For that reason, some lower courts after *Boykin* have recognized that, "[a] plea of guilty also involves a waiver of other constitutional rights [including] the right to insist upon the prosecution's proof of guilt beyond a reasonable doubt at trial, In re Winship, 397 U.S. 358 (1970) . . ." *People v. Meyers*, 617 P.2d 808, 815 (Colo. 1980); *accord Commonwealth v. DelVerde*, 496 N.E.2d 1357, 1360 (Mass. 1986).
21. *See, e.g.,* Moore v. Anderson, 474 F.2d 1118 (10th Cir. 1973); Odom v. State, 962 S.W.2d 117 (Tex. Crim. App. 1997); McNalley v. State, 468 So. 2d 209 (Ala. Crim. App. 1985).
22. *Boykin*, 395 U.S. at 242–43.
23. The lower courts are divided on the question of whether *Boykin* requires a "factual basis" for a defendant's guilty plea to appear on the record in addition to a court's explanation of the abstract "nature of the charges." *Compare, e.g.*, Tillery v. State, 647 So. 2d 87, 89–90 (Ala. Crim. App. 1994) (*Boykin* does not mandate a factual basis), *with* State v. Moreno, 492 P.2d 440 (Ariz. App. 1972) (factual basis required under *Boykin*).
24. *Boykin*, 395 U.S. at 244 & n.7. The lower courts are divided on whether footnote 7 in *Boykin* was nonbinding dicta and thus, for instance, whether a trial court must inform a defendant of the statutory range of punishment. *Compare, e.g.*, Aguirre-Mata v. State, 125 S.W.3d 473, 476 (Tex. Crim. App. 2003) (footnote 7 was nonbinding dicta); Heptinstall v. State, 624 So. 2d 1111 (Ala. Crim. App. 1993) (same), *with* State v. Thornton, 533 A.2d 951, 955 (Md. App. 1987) (footnote 7 is a "constitutional mandate"). The Supreme Court's decision in Parke v. Raley, 506 U.S. 20 (1992)—discussing Boykin's procedural requirements—suggests that footnote 7 of *Boykin* was part

stated that the majority had created a rigid constitutional prophylactic requirement that the trial judge in each case in which a defendant is pleading guilty must engage in a detailed colloquy with the defendant similar to what Federal Rule of Criminal Procedure 11 requires in federal cases in which defendants plead guilty.[25]

After *Boykin*, lower courts have taken divergent approaches to its on-the-record prophylactic requirement, and the Supreme Court has not revisited the issue in terms of what specific procedures are constitutionally required at a guilty plea. Most lower courts have taken a less than rigid approach, merely requiring the record as a whole to indicate, directly or circumstantially, that a defendant understood the constitutional rights that they were waiving by pleading guilty, the factual and legal nature of the charges (including the elements of the charged offense), and the penalty range faced.[26] Only if a record is entirely silent concerning a defendant's waiver of an important constitutional right or their understanding of the consequences of pleading guilty will most appeals courts vacate a guilty plea under *Boykin*.[27]

Boykin's prophylactic rule applies with greatest force on direct review of a conviction resulting from a guilty plea as opposed to on habeas corpus or other collateral review. In the vast majority of jurisdictions, if on collateral review a defendant challenges their guilty plea based on the trial court's failure to have complied with *Boykin*, the defendant bears the initial burden of production of evidence that affirmatively shows that the trial court did not comply with *Boykin* (e.g., a court reporter's transcript of the guilty plea proceedings showing a lack of compliance with *Boykin*).[28] In other words, on collateral review, the mere absence of any record of the guilty plea proceedings will not result in reversal under *Boykin* (the way it would on direct appeal of the conviction).[29] Rather, a defendant must actually present affirmative proof that they were not given the necessary admonishments required by *Boykin*. Only if the defendant meets such an initial burden of production does the ultimate burden of persuasion shift to the prosecution to show that the defendant

---

of the Court's holding. *See id.* at 36–37; *see also* North Carolina v. Alford, 400 U.S. 25, 29 n.3 (1970) (stating that *Boykin*'s rule included the requirement that a defendant's knowledge of the consequences of their guilty plea must "affirmatively appear" on the record); Bradshaw v. Stumpf, 545 U.S. 175, 182–83 (2005) (assuming that *Boykin* requires a defendant to be informed of the elements of the charged offense).

25. *Boykin*, 395 U.S. at 244–45 (Harlan, J., dissenting, joined by Black, J.).

26. *See, e.g.*, McChesney v. Henderson, 482 F.2d 1101 (5th Cir. 1973); State v. Kirchoff, 452 N.W.2d 801, 804–05 (Iowa 1990); Davis v. State, 361 A.2d 113 (Md. 1976).

27. *See, e.g.*, State v. Lawson, 410 So. 2d 1101 (La. 1982) (because the record was totally devoid of any suggestion that the defendant was advised by anyone that a guilty plea waived his Fifth Amendment right to silence, appeals court vacated his guilty plea under *Boykin*).

28. *See, e.g.*, Parke v. Raley, 506 U.S. 20 (1992).

29. A minority of lower courts have held that the remedy for a *Boykin* violation on direct appeal is not an automatic reversal of the conviction, but, instead, a remand for an evidentiary hearing to determine whether the defendant was in fact aware of the omitted admonishments at the time of their guilty plea. *See, e.g.*, State v. Darling, 506 P.2d 1042, 1046 (Ariz. 1973).

did in fact understand the relevant rights they were waiving and the consequences of a guilty plea.[30]

11.3   Plea Agreements and Breaches

Defendants who plead guilty may do so with or without a plea agreement (also called a "plea bargain") with the prosecution.[31] In most plea bargains, prosecutors agree to dismiss one or more of the multiple charges in exchange for the defendant's guilty plea to a remaining charge or to dismiss a single charge in exchange for a defendant's guilty plea to a lesser charge, or agree that the prosecutor will recommend or not oppose a specific sentence (or simply stand mute at sentencing).[32] While plea agreements are analogous to civil contracts and thus the law of contracts provides a useful analogy when there are disputes about whether a party has breached a plea agreement, they are "constitutional contracts" that must be interpreted and enforced consistent with principles of due process.[33] Any ambiguity in a plea agreement's terms is construed in a manner favorable to a defendant.[34]

If the prosecutor or defendant alleges that the other side has breached the plea agreement, the trial court must determine whether an actionable breach in fact occurred.[35] If the trial court finds that one of the parties was in "material" breach of its contractual obligations,[36] then the remedy will depend on who breached it, the defendant or the prosecution. The Supreme Court has held that due process is violated by the prosecution's breach of a plea bargain after a guilty plea has been entered.[37] Until the defendant has actually pleaded guilty pursuant to the agreement, however, the prosecution may withdraw from the executory plea bargain without

---

30. *See* Fox v. Kelso, 911 F.2d 563, 569–70 (11th Cir. 1990) (citing cases from numerous jurisdictions).

31. Pleading guilty to the charges without a plea agreement is commonly referred to as pleading "straight up" to the charges. Wofford v. State, 819 So. 2d 891, 892 (Fla. Dist. Ct. App. 2002) (Miner, J., dissenting).

32. *See, e.g.,* FED. R. CRIM. P. 11(c)(1)(A)–(C).

33. Ricketts v. Adamson, 483 U.S. 1, 16 (1987) (Brennan, J., dissenting) (discussing a point not addressed by the majority).

34. *See, e.g.,* United States v. Cimino, 381 F.3d 124, 127 (2d Cir. 2004); Keller v. People, 29 P.3d 290, 297 (Colo. 2000).

35. *See, e.g.,* United States v. Simmons, 537 F.2d 1260, 1261–62 (4th Cir. 1976); Edwards v. State, 581 So. 2d 1260, 1261 (Ala. Crim. App. 1991).

36. A vast majority of courts apply the "substantial performance" standard or the equivalent "material breach" standard in determining whether an actionable breach occurred. *See, e.g.,* United States v. Castaneda, 162 F.3d 832, 837–38 (5th Cir. 1998); United States v. Hauptman, 111 F.3d 48, 51–52 (7th Cir. 1997); United States v. Crowell, 997 F.2d 146, 148 (6th Cir. 1993); United States v. Bulla, 58 M.J. 715, 720 (C.G.C.A. 2003); People v. McCormick, 859 P.2d 846, 856–57 (Colo. 1993).

37. Santobello v. New York, 404 U.S. 257 (1971).

violating the Constitution,[38] unless the defendant detrimentally relied on the prosecution's plea offer prior to the actual entry of the guilty plea.[39]

The remedy for a prosecution's material breach of a plea bargain is either specific performance of the agreement or permitting the defendant to withdraw their guilty plea. In *Santobello v. New York*, a majority of the seven justices of the Supreme Court who participated in that case held that ordinarily a trial court should give deference to a defendant's choice of the remedy.[40] However, the Court more recently has indicated that a trial court possesses discretion about what remedy to provide in the event of a breach.[41] If the prosecution's breach involved a recommendation concerning sentencing, then the specific performance remedy requires resentencing before a different judge.[42] If a defendant breaches a plea agreement, then the prosecution may move the trial court to vacate the defendant's conviction and sentence on the plea-bargained charges and reinstate any charges that were dismissed as part of the agreement.[43] The Supreme Court has held that when a defendant breaches a plea agreement that originally had resulted in the dismissal of charges, the reinstatement of those charges does not violate the Double Jeopardy Clause.[44]

11.4   Constitutional Challenges to Guilty Pleas

Although the Supreme Court has held that as a general matter a guilty plea waives the defendant's right to challenge nonjurisdictional defects in the prosecution, there are four main constitutional challenges to a guilty plea conviction that a defendant may make.[45] First, a defendant may challenge their guilty plea as not having been "knowing, voluntary, and intelligent" and thus in violation of

---

38. Mabry v. Johnson, 467 U.S. 504, 507–08 (1984). Arguably, a trial court may nonetheless enforce an executory plea agreement against the prosecution as a matter of "public policy" even if not compelled by the Constitution. *See* People v. Navarroli, 521 N.E.2d 891, 899 (Ill. 1988) (Clark, J., dissenting).

39. *See* Reed v. Becka, 511 S.E.2d 396, 402–03 (S.C. 1999); *cf.* People v. Starks, 478 N.E.2d 350, 355 (Ill. 1985) (defendant's waiver of their Fifth Amendment right to silence in exchange for prosecution's plea offer would entitle them to specific performance of the plea agreement even prior to their entry of the guilty plea).

40. *Santobello*, 404 U.S. at 267, 268 n.*; *see also* United States v. Kurkculer, 918 F.2d 295, 298–99 (1st Cir. 1990); State v. Miller, 756 P.2d 122, 126 (Wash. 1988); Miller v. State, 322 A.2d 527, 529–30 (Md. 1974).

41. Kernan v. Cuero, 138 S. Ct. 4, 8–9 (2017) (per curiam).

42. *Santobello*, 404 U.S. at 263.

43. *See, e.g.*, United States v. Wood, 780 F.2d 929 (11th Cir. 1986); People v. Collins, 53 Cal. Rptr. 2d 367 (Cal. App. 1996).

44. *Ricketts*, 483 U.S. 1; *see also* United States v. Bowe, 309 F.3d 234 (4th Cir. 2002).

45. A guilty plea by itself does not waive the defendant's right to challenge their sentence on appeal unless, as part of a plea bargain, the defendant waived their right to appeal the sentence. *See* State v. Morrison, 337 N.W.2d 825, 826 (S.D. 1983); *see also* United States v. Wiggins, 905 F.2d 51, 53 (4th Cir. 1990).

due process.[46] Second, a defendant may challenge their guilty plea conviction on the ground that it violated the Double Jeopardy Clause if the court can determine whether there was a double jeopardy violation from the "face of the record" before the court (no additional factual development is required and the record before the court contains all of the facts needed to show a double jeopardy violation).[47] Third, a defendant can challenge their guilty plea conviction on the ground that the penal statute under which they were charged is unconstitutional.[48] Finally, the defendant may challenge their guilty plea on the ground that the attorney who advised them to plead guilty afforded ineffective assistance of counsel by so advising the defendant.[49]

A claim of ineffective assistance of counsel made by a defendant who pleaded guilty requires a defendant to show not only that their attorney was "deficient" in advising a guilty plea, but also that there is a reasonable probability that the defendant would not have pleaded guilty but for the attorney's deficient performance.[50] An attorney can be constitutionally ineffective in this context by 1) failing to investigate evidence that if presented at a trial would have had a good chance of resulting in an acquittal,[51] or 2) failing to file a pretrial motion that had a reasonable probability of suppressing material prosecution evidence or dismissing the charges with prejudice.[52]

Occasionally, defendants plead guilty pro se after waiving their Sixth Amendment right to counsel at a guilty plea hearing. Just like a guilty plea itself, a defendant's waiver of the constitutional right to counsel at a guilty plea hearing must be

---

46. *See, e.g.,* Henderson v. Morgan, 426 U.S. 637 (1976).

47. United States v. Broce, 488 U.S. 563 (1989).

48. Class v. United States, 138 S. Ct. 798 (2018); Haynes v. United States, 390 U.S. 85, 87 n.2 (1968).

49. Hill v. Lockhart, 474 U.S. 52 (1985); *cf.* Missouri v. Frye, 566 U.S. 134 (2012) (criminal defense attorney has a constitutional obligation under the Sixth Amendment to convey prosecution's plea offer to the defendant); Lafler v. Cooper, 566 U.S. 156 (2012) (plea bargaining phase of a criminal case is a critical stage of the prosecution under the Sixth Amendment and, thus, defense counsel has an obligation to properly advise a defendant whether to accept a plea bargain offer made by the prosecution). A defendant's entry of a guilty plea to the trial judge is itself a "critical stage" of the proceeding at which a defendant possesses the right to the effective assistance of counsel under the Sixth Amendment. Boyd v. Dutton, 405 U.S. 1 (1972) (per curiam); *see also* Childress v. Johnson, 103 F.3d 1221 (5th Cir. 1997).

50. *Hill,* 474 U.S. 52. Ineffective assistance of counsel (IAC) claims are further discussed in Chapter Thirteen.

51. *See, e.g.,* United States v. Kauffman, 109 F.3d 186 (3d Cir. 1997).

52. *See* Kimmelman v. Morrison, 477 U.S. 365, 383–91 (1986). A defense lawyer's failure to have filed pretrial motions in a case in which the defendant ultimately pleaded guilty is not per se ineffective assistance of counsel. Ineffective assistance occurs only when a defense lawyer's failure to file a specific type of pretrial motion was both deficient performance and prejudicial to the defendant. *See* Premo v. Moore, 562 U.S. 115 (2011); *see also* Tollett v. Henderson, 411 U.S. 258, 264–67 (1973).

knowing, voluntary, and intelligent.[53] In most cases, however, a valid waiver of that right can occur during a simple colloquy with the trial judge in which the defendant is informed that they have the right to retained or appointed counsel (if financially eligible) and affirms that they are voluntarily waiving that right and wishes to plead guilty without the assistance of counsel.[54]

It is an open question in the Supreme Court's guilty-plea jurisprudence whether a defendant's guilty plea waives their right later to challenge the conviction on the ground that the prosecution failed to disclose material, exculpatory evidence in violation of *Brady v. Maryland*.[55] In *United States v. Ruiz*,[56] the Court held that a guilty plea waived a defendant's right to challenge their conviction based on the prosecution's failure to disclose mere "impeachment" evidence concerning one of its witnesses, but left open the question of whether a *Brady* claim based on material, exculpatory evidence is still viable after a defendant has pled guilty. The lower courts are divided on this question; however, a majority have held that a guilty plea does not waive a *Brady* claim based on the prosecution's nondisclosure of material, exculpatory evidence.[57]

11.5 Leading Supreme Court Decisions on Constitutional Issues Concerning Guilty Pleas

- *Boykin v. Alabama*, 395 U.S. 238 (1969) (defendant's statement of understanding the rights waived by their guilty plea and their understanding of the nature of the charges and consequences of the plea must appear "on the record" or an appellate court will reverse the conviction on direct appeal).

- *Brady v. United States*, 397 U.S. 742 (1970) (leading Supreme Court decision on what is required for a guilty plea to be "voluntary" in a constitutional sense).

- *Santobello v. New York*, 404 U.S. 257 (1971) (prosecutor violates due process by breaching plea agreement after defendant has entered a guilty plea pursuant to the agreement).

---

53. Iowa v. Tovar, 541 U.S. 77 (2004).
54. *Id.*; *but cf.* Faretta v. California, 422 U.S. 806, 835–36 (1975) (discussing procedures for waiving right to counsel at trial, which are more demanding on the trial court). A defendant's waiver of the right to counsel is discussed in Chapter Three.
55. Brady v. Maryland, 373 U.S. 83 (1963). The *Brady* doctrine is discussed further in Chapter Thirteen.
56. United States v. Ruiz, 536 U.S. 622 (2002).
57. *See* Matthew v. Johnson, 201 F.3d 353, 358 (5th Cir. 2000) (citing cases from various jurisdictions); *see also* McCann v. Mangialardi, 337 F.3d 782, 787–88 (7th Cir. 2003) (stating in dicta that the Supreme Court's decision in *Ruiz* implicitly supports the position that a guilty plea does not waive a *Brady* claim based on the prosecution's nondisclosure of material, exculpatory evidence).

- *Tollett v. Henderson*, 411 U.S. 258 (1973) (defendant's entry of knowing, voluntary, and intelligent guilty plea waives defendant's right to later challenge the vast majority of "nonjurisdictional defects" in prosecution).

- *Henderson v. Morgan*, 426 U.S. 637 (1976) (holding that defendant's guilty plea was rendered involuntary by erroneous information from trial judge about the essential elements of the offense to which he pleaded guilty; the fact that there was overwhelming evidence of his guilt of the charged offense and the fact that he would have pleaded guilty anyway if he had possessed correct information does not render the due process violation harmless).

- *Bordenkircher v. Hayes*, 434 U.S. 357 (1978) (prosecutor's good-faith threat to file more serious charge if defendant does not plead guilty to lesser charge does not render a defendant's plea to the lesser charge "involuntary").

- *Mabry v. Johnson*, 467 U.S. 504 (1984) (*Santobello*'s due process requirement not applicable to prosecutor's withdrawal from plea bargain prior to actual entry of defendant's guilty plea).

- *Hill v. Lockhart*, 474 U.S. 52 (1985) (a defendant claiming that their prior attorney provided ineffective assistance of counsel by advising them to plead guilty must show both that 1) the attorney was "deficient" in advising them to plead guilty and 2) there is a "reasonable probability" that but for the deficiency, the defendant would not have pleaded guilty).

- *Kimmelman v. Morrison*, 477 U.S. 365 (1986) (a defendant who pleaded guilty can show ineffective assistance under *Hill* by showing a reasonable probability that but for the attorney's failure to file a meritorious pretrial motion to suppress evidence, the defendant would not have pleaded guilty).

- *United States v. Broce*, 488 U.S. 563 (1989) (defendant's guilty plea does not waive a double jeopardy claim where, prior to the entry of the plea, the basis for the claim was apparent on the existing record).

- *Parke v. Raley*, 506 U.S. 20 (1992) (*Boykin* claim raised for the first time on collateral review requires a defendant to prove that they were actually unaware of the information that did not appear "on the record" at the time of their guilty plea, at least where no transcript of plea proceeding exists).

- *United States v. Ruiz*, 536 U.S. 622 (2002) (defendant who pleaded guilty thereby waived his right to later raise a claim under *Brady v. Maryland*, 373 U.S. 83 (1963), based on the prosecution's nondisclosure of "impeachment" evidence; Court leaves open the question of whether *Brady* claim based on material "exculpatory" evidence may be raised by a defendant who pleaded guilty).

- *Lafler v. Cooper*, 566 U.S. 156 (2012) (plea bargaining phase of a criminal case is a "critical stage" of the prosecution under the Sixth Amendment, and thus defense counsel has an obligation to properly advise a defendant whether to accept a plea bargain offer made by the prosecution).

- *Missouri v. Frye*, 566 U.S. 134 (2012) (criminal defense attorney has a constitutional obligation under the Sixth Amendment to convey prosecution's plea offer to the defendant).

- *Class v. United States*, 138 S. Ct. 798 (2018) (defendant's guilty plea does not waive the defendant's right to challenge the constitutionality of the penal statute in their case on appeal).

CHAPTER TWELVE

SENTENCING

After a defendant has been convicted of a criminal charge—at a trial or following a guilty plea—sentencing occurs. As discussed below, capital sentencing and noncapital sentencing involve dramatically different procedures as a result of the Supreme Court's repeated recognition that "death is different" under the Constitution as a type of punishment.[1]

In the vast majority of jurisdictions, sentencing in noncapital cases is done by the trial court (even if a jury convicted the defendant); in a small minority of jurisdictions, defendants have the option of jury sentencing in noncapital cases.[2] Conversely, jury sentencing is the norm in the vast majority of jurisdictions in death penalty cases.[3]

In many jurisdictions, noncapital sentencing usually is preordained by a plea bargain, and the trial court predictably sentences a defendant immediately after the guilty plea is taken in accordance with a plea bargain. In noncapital cases in other jurisdictions (including the federal system), sentencing is an entirely separate stage of the proceedings and often involves complex, contested legal issues (e.g., disputes over the application of "sentencing guidelines"). In all jurisdictions, capital sentencing is a "bifurcated" proceeding, separate and apart from the guilt-innocence phase of the trial.[4] As discussed below, the constitutional protections afforded to a convicted criminal defendant during a typical noncapital sentencing proceeding are significantly fewer in number than the myriad constitutional protections afforded to defendants during the preceding guilt-innocence phase[5] and those afforded to capital defendants in the sentencing phase of a death penalty case.

In many jurisdictions, a trial court in all noncapital cases and even some capital cases will order a presentence report (PSR) to be prepared after conviction, but before the sentencing hearing. A PSR, which usually is prepared by the probation office (an arm of the court in most jurisdictions), typically contains a great deal of

---

1. *See, e.g.*, Gardner v. Florida, 430 U.S. 349, 357 (1977) (plurality).
2. *See* Jenia Iontcheva, *Jury Sentencing as Democratic Practice*, 89 VA. L. REV. 311, 330 & n.101 (April 2003).
3. Harris v. Alabama, 513 U.S. 504, 516 (1995) (Stevens, J., dissenting).
4. *See, e.g.*, Gregg v. Georgia, 428 U.S. 153 (1976).
5. *See generally* Alan C. Michaels, *Trial Rights at Sentencing*, 81 N.C. L. REV. 1771 (June 2003).

social history about a defendant in addition to a thorough criminal history, often including adjudicated as well as unadjudicated prior offenses. At least in noncapital cases, the procedures governing both the probation officer's preparation of a PSR and a sentencing court's consideration of it are informal and involve virtually none of the constitutional protections applicable during the guilt-innocence phase of a criminal case.[6] A PSR can serve as a pivotal source of information at sentencing that can dramatically alter a court's sentencing decision.[7]

12.1 Constitutional Rules of Criminal Procedure Applicable to Noncapital Sentencing

12.1.1 *First Amendment Limitations at Sentencing*

Both the Free Exercise and Establishment Clauses of the First Amendment occasionally place limits on how a defendant may be sentenced. The Supreme Court has held that a defendant cannot be sentenced to a harsher punishment based solely on their constitutionally protected expression or associations (such as mere association with a white supremacist prison gang).[8] However, when the defendant's First Amendment expression or association goes beyond mere "abstract ideas" and implicates a legitimate state interest in criminal punishment, then it may be considered in assessing punishment (e.g., a defendant who commits an offense with racist motivations).[9]

Likewise, a defendant may not be sentenced more harshly solely because of their religious views or associations (or lack thereof),[10] although a defendant's religious views or associations may be considered in aggravation of punishment if they are related to the offense (e.g., a defendant committed a murder as part of a Satanic

---

6. *See, e.g.*, United States v. Johnson, 935 F.2d 47, 50 (4th Cir. 1991) (convicted defendant did not possess the right to the assistance of counsel under the Sixth Amendment during a probation officer's presentence interview of defendant); United States v. Sisk, 87 F. App'x 323, 331–32 (4th Cir. 2004) (no error for sentencing court to consider a PSR's damaging allegations that were based entirely on hearsay sources in increasing the defendant's sentence); Baumann v. United States, 692 F.2d 565, 576 (9th Cir. 1982) (*Miranda* warnings not required during presentence interview of defendant by probation officer).

7. *See Gardner*, 430 U.S. 349; Williams v. New York, 337 U.S. 241 (1949); *see also* Gary Maveal, *Federal Presentence Reports: Multitasking at Sentencing*, 26 SETON HALL L. REV. 544 (1996); Timothy Bakken, *The Continued Failure of Modern Law to Create Fairness and Efficiency: The Presentence Report and Its Effect on Justice*, 40 N.Y. L. SCH. L. REV. 363 (1996).

8. Dawson v. Delaware, 503 U.S. 159 (1992).

9. *Id.* at 166–67; *see also* Wisconsin v. Mitchell, 508 U.S. 476 (1993) (upholding sentencing enhancement based on defendant's racist motivation in committing the offense).

10. *See, e.g.*, Flanagan v. State, 846 P.2d 1053 (Nev. 1993) (citing *Dawson*, 503 U.S. 159).

National Institute for Trial Advocacy

ritual).[11] Furthermore, a sentencing judge or jury may not factor in the sentencer's own religious views into the assessment of punishment.[12]

12.1.2 Limited Applicability of the Exclusionary Rules of the Fourth, Fifth, and Sixth Amendments

Although the U.S. Supreme Court has not yet addressed the issue, the vast majority of lower courts that have done so have held that the Fourth Amendment's exclusionary rule has no application at sentencing—meaning that evidence that was unconstitutionally searched or seized is admissible at sentencing even if it was inadmissible during the trial.[13] According to some lower courts, the exclusionary rule may have limited application to exclude evidence intentionally seized in violation of the Fourth Amendment solely to increase a defendant's sentence (when independent, lawfully seized evidence gave the officers sufficient evidence to convict the defendant).[14]

Similarly, although the Supreme Court has not yet addressed the issue, the vast majority of lower courts to have done so have held that *Miranda*'s exclusionary rule is inapplicable to a defendant's "un-Mirandized" custodial statement introduced at sentencing.[15] Conversely, involuntary confessions (which are considered inherently unreliable)[16] and incriminating statements obtained in direct violation of the defendant's Fifth Amendment privilege against self-incrimination (e.g., immunized statements) are inadmissible at sentencing hearings.[17] It also appears that confessions obtained in direct violation of the Sixth Amendment right to counsel are inadmissible at sentencing (capital and noncapital alike).[18]

---

11. *See, e.g.*, People v. Shatner, 673 N.E.2d 258, 269 (Ill. 1996) (citing *Dawson*, 503 U.S. 159).
12. *See, e.g.*, United States v. Bakker, 925 F.2d 728 (4th Cir. 1991) (sentencing judge's consideration of his own religious opinions in assessing sentence was unconstitutional, although court relied on due process rationale rather than First Amendment); *see also* Oliver v. Quarterman, 541 F.3d 329, 336–39 (5th Cir. 2008) (capital sentencing jury's consideration of Bible during sentencing deliberations was unconstitutional); People v. Harlan, 109 P.3d 616 (Colo. 2005) (same).
13. *See, e.g.*, United States v. Acosta, 303 F.3d 78, 84–86 (1st Cir. 2002) (collecting federal cases); Smith v. State, 517 A.2d 1081 (Md. 1986).
14. *See, e.g.*, United States v. Kim, 25 F.3d 1426 (9th Cir. 1994).
15. *See, e.g.*, Del Vecchio v. Ill. D.O.C., 31 F.3d 1363, 1388 (7th Cir. 1994) (en banc); State v. Bryant, 776 So. 2d 532 (La. Ct. App. 2000).
16. *See, e.g.*, Jones v. Cardwell, 686 F.2d 754, 757 (9th Cir. 1982); State v. Conn, 669 P.2d 581 (Ariz. 1983).
17. *See, e.g.*, United States v. Abanatha, 999 F.2d 1246, 1249 (8th Cir. 1993); United States v. Chitty, 760 F.2d 425, 431–32 (2d Cir. 1985).
18. *See* Terry v. Commonwealth, 500 S.E.2d 843 (Va. Ct. App. 1998), *rev'd on other grounds*, 516 S.E.2d 233 (Va. Ct. App. 1999) (en banc); *see also* Estelle v. Smith, 451 U.S. 454 (1981); *cf.* Mitchell v. United States, 526 U.S. 314, 326, 330 (1999) (explaining that *Estelle*'s holding that a sentencing court could not draw an adverse inference from a defendant's invocation of their privilege against self-incrimination applied equally in capital and noncapital cases).

12.1.3 Defendant's Invocation of the Fifth Amendment Privilege Against Self-Incrimination in Connection with Sentencing

The Supreme Court has held that a sentencing court cannot consider as an "adverse inference" a defendant's invocation of the Fifth Amendment privilege against self-incrimination at or before sentencing as a basis for punishing the defendant more severely than the court otherwise would have done.[19] However, the Court has held that a sentencing court may impose a harsher sentence if a defendant simply refuses to cooperate (such as admitting their guilt and implicating any other persons involved in the crime), but never invokes their privilege against self-incrimination under the Fifth Amendment as a basis for not cooperating.[20] In *Mitchell v. United States*, the Court left open the issue of whether a sentencing court may refuse to impose a more lenient sentence based on a defendant's invocation of the right to silence after finding that a defendant thereby failed to show remorse or "accept responsibility" for their offense.[21] However, other decisions of the Court suggest—and many lower courts have held—that a sentencing court may refuse a more lenient sentence[22] based on a defendant's invocation of their constitutional right to silence concerning the offense or offenses of conviction at sentencing.[23] The lower courts are divided, however, on whether a sentencing court may deny a more lenient sentence based on a defendant's invocation of their Fifth Amendment privilege concerning uncharged conduct.[24]

12.1.4 Inapplicability of the Confrontation and Compulsory Process Clauses at Sentencing

In *Williams v. New York*,[25] the Supreme Court held that the Confrontation Clause does not apply at sentencing.[26] Therefore, hearsay is admissible at sentencing as long

---

19. *Mitchell*, 526 U.S. at 329–30.

20. Roberts v. United States, 445 U.S. 552, 559 (1980).

21. *Mitchell*, 526 U.S. at 330.

22. For instance, under some jurisdictions' sentencing guidelines, a defendant's sentencing range is less if he "accepts responsibility" for the offense of conviction. *See, e.g.*, USSG § 3E1.1.

23. *See, e.g.*, State v. Souder, 105 S.W.3d 602, 607–08 (Tenn. Crim. App. 2002); State v. Muscari, 807 A.2d 407, 415–17 (Vt. 2002); *cf.* McKune v. Lile, 536 U.S. 24 (2002) (prison early-release program that required inmates to admit criminal conduct did not violate privilege against self-incrimination); Ohio Adult Parole Authority v. Woodward, 523 U.S. 272, 286 (1998) (clemency procedure that required inmates to be interviewed by the parole board before being eligible for clemency did not violate privilege against self-incrimination); Corbitt v. New Jersey, 439 U.S. 212 (1978) (statute that rendered defendant ineligible for anything less than a life sentence if he were to go to trial, but rendered him eligible for a lesser sentence if he pleaded guilty did not violate the privilege against self-incrimination).

24. *See* Kinder v. United States, 504 U.S. 946 (1992) (White, J., dissenting from denial of certiorari) (collecting conflicting lower court cases).

25. Williams v. New York, 337 U.S. 241 (1949).

26. *Id.* at 250–52; *see also* United States v. Petty, 982 F.2d 1365, 1368 (9th Cir. 1993), *amended*, 992 F.2d 1015 (9th Cir. 1993). In recent years, the lower courts have divided over whether the

National Institute for Trial Advocacy

as it has a minimum degree of reliability.[27] In *Williams*, the Supreme Court concluded that a sentencing court was entitled to consider witnesses' out-of-court allegations that the defendant had committed other (uncharged) crimes—allegations made to a probation officer and included in a pre-sentence report submitted to the court.[28] Although some older decisions of lower courts held that *Williams* does not require a sentencing court to disclose such damaging allegations contained in the probation officer's presentence report to the defense,[29] the modern trend among the clear majority of lower courts is to hold that due process requires such disclosure prior to sentencing (although still permitting the sentencing court to consider hearsay).[30] Similarly, the vast majority of lower courts have held that it violates due process for a member of the prosecution team—as opposed to a probation officer or other court official—to engage in ex parte communication with the sentencing judge and convey damaging information about the defendant.[31]

Although the Supreme Court has not yet addressed the issue,[32] the consensus among lower courts is that the Compulsory Process Clause does not apply at sentencing, and thus, a defendant does not have a constitutional right to subpoena favorable witnesses solely for sentencing.[33] Although the lower courts agree that a defendant does not have a constitutional right to present the testimony of other witnesses at sentencing, the lower courts are divided over whether the defendant has a constitutional right to "allocute" (whether sworn or unsworn) before being sentenced.[34]

Confrontation Clause applies at capital sentencing hearings. *See* United States v. Fields, 483 F.3d 313, 363–64 & n.1 (5th Cir. 2007) (Benavides, C.J., dissenting) (citing conflicting cases).

27. *Petty*, 982 F.2d at 1368–69; *see also* United States v. Wise, 976 F.2d 393, 400–02 (8th Cir. 1992) (en banc).

28. *Williams*, 337 U.S. at 246–52.

29. *See, e.g.*, Fernandez v. Meier, 432 F.2d 426, 427 (9th Cir. 1970); United States v. Fischer, 381 F.2d 509, 511 (2d Cir. 1967).

30. *See, e.g.*, State v. Lipsky, 608 P.2d 1241, 1246–49 (Utah 1980) (citing cases). Such courts recognize that the many decisions of the Supreme Court in the 1960s and 1970s affording criminal defendants increased procedural protections at sentencing (including the right to counsel) "cast doubt on the constitutionality of the trial court's receipt of sentencing information adverse to the defendant without affording him an opportunity to respond [to it]." In re Calhoun, 549 P.2d 1235, 1240 (Cal. 1976).

31. *See, e.g.*, United States v. Wolfson, 634 F.2d 1217, 1221–22 (9th Cir. 1980); Haller v. Robbins, 409 F.2d 857 (1st Cir. 1969); *but cf.* Williams v. Oklahoma, 358 U.S. 576 (1959) (due process not violated when sentencing court relied on prosecutor's unsworn allegations about defendant's criminal record; such allegations were made in open court in the presence of the defendant and their attorney and were not contested by defense).

32. *See* McGautha v. California, 402 U.S. 183, 218 (1971).

33. *See, e.g.*, United States v. Jackson, 453 F.3d 302, 305–06 (5th Cir. 2006); Ruffin v. State, 683 So. 2d 565, 566 (Fla. Dist. Ct. App. 1996) (citing cases).

34. *Compare, e.g.*, State v. Greve, 681 N.W.2d 479, 488–89 (Wis. 2004) (holding that allocution is not a constitutional right), *with* Boardman v. Estelle, 957 F.2d 1523, 1525 (9th Cir. 1992) (holding that allocution is a constitutional right).

12.1.5 The Sixth Amendment Right to Counsel at Sentencing

Sentencing, capital or noncapital, is a critical stage of the proceedings at which the Sixth Amendment right to counsel applies unless validly waived.[35] In addition, the Sixth Amendment right to counsel includes the effective assistance of counsel at sentencing.[36] In *Glover v. United States*, the Supreme Court held that a defense lawyer deprived his client of the right to the effective assistance of counsel when there was a reasonable probability that the deficient performance of the lawyer resulted in any amount of additional punishment.[37]

Right-to-counsel issues at sentencing are often raised by way of a defendant's collateral challenge to a prior, uncounseled conviction being used to enhance the defendant's sentence in a subsequent case.[38] A defendant ordinarily cannot collaterally challenge a prior felony conviction being used at sentencing except on the ground that the prior conviction was obtained in violation of the Sixth Amendment right to the assistance of counsel; any other constitutional infirmity in the prior conviction must be raised in a separate proceeding directly challenging the conviction.[39] Claims of ineffective assistance of counsel are not cognizable in a collateral challenge to a prior conviction being used at sentencing—only claims of actual or constructive denial of the assistance of counsel are cognizable.[40]

It appears to be an open question in Supreme Court jurisprudence whether a defendant can collaterally attack a prior uncounseled misdemeanor conviction being used to enhance their punishment at sentencing in a subsequent case. In two cases, the Court has assumed such a collateral challenge is permitted.[41] However, some lower courts have held that only uncounseled misdemeanor sentences—as opposed to convictions—can be collaterally attacked.[42] Such courts have based their holding

---

35. Mempa v. Rhay, 389 U.S. 128, 134 (1967).
36. Glover v. United States, 531 U.S. 198 (2001). The right to the effective assistance of counsel is further discussed in Chapter Thirteen.
37. *Id.*
38. *See, e.g.*, United States v. Tucker, 404 U.S. 443 (1972); Burgett v. Texas, 389 U.S. 109 (1967). Such collateral challenges are discussed in Chapter Three.
39. *See* Custis v. United States, 511 U.S. 485 (1994); *see also* Parke v. Raley, 506 U.S. 20, 30 (1992) (noting that when defendants collaterally attack prior convictions in subsequent criminal prosecutions, as opposed to challenging them in separate postconviction proceedings, such challenges, if successful, merely "deprive [the prior convictions] of their normal force and effect in a proceeding that had an independent purpose other than to overturn the prior judgments").
40. *See Custis*, 511 U.S. at 493–97; *see also* Childress v. Johnson, 103 F.3d 1221 (5th Cir. 1997) (permitting a defendant to collaterally attack a prior conviction where, although counsel had been appointed, the counsel was a "potted plant" whose total lack of assistance "constructively" denied the defendant of his right to counsel in violation of *United States v. Cronic*, 466 U.S. 648 (1984)).
41. *See* Nichols v. United States, 511 U.S. 738, 748–49 (1994); *see also* Iowa v. Tovar, 541 U.S. 77, 88 n.10 (2004).
42. *See, e.g.*, United States v. Ortega, 94 F.3d 764, 769 (2d Cir. 1996); *but see* State v. Ferguson, 169 P.3d 423, 428–29 (Utah 2007).

on the fact that the Supreme Court in *Argersinger v. Hamlin*[43] held only that a misdemeanant could not be imprisoned if not afforded the assistance of counsel and did not appear to invalidate an uncounseled misdemeanor conviction on that ground. It also is an open question in the Supreme Court's jurisprudence whether a misdemeanor sentence of probation not tethered to a suspended jail sentence will activate the right to counsel in a misdemeanor case. The Supreme Court in *Alabama v. Shelton*[44] held that probation coupled with a suspended jail sentence activated the right to counsel in a misdemeanor case, but did not specifically address a sentence of "stand-alone" probation. The issue has divided judges on the lower courts.[45]

12.1.6 "Sentencing Factors" Versus "Elements": Applicable Quantum of Proof and the Right to a Jury Trial

Beginning with *Specht v. Patterson*[46] and continuing through to *United States v. Haymond*,[47] the Supreme Court has held that any fact (other than a defendant's prior criminal conviction)[48] that increases the maximum punishment that a defendant otherwise faces is "the functional equivalent of an element" of an offense that must be found by a jury beyond a reasonable doubt or admitted by a defendant at a guilty plea.[49] The most significant decision in this line of cases was *Apprendi v. New Jersey*; the cases are thus known as embodying the "*Apprendi* doctrine."[50] In

---

43. Argersinger v. Hamlin, 407 U.S. 25, 37–38 (1972).
44. Alabama v. Shelton, 535 U.S. 654 (2002).
45. *Compare* United States v. Pollard, 389 F.3d 101, 104–05 (4th Cir. 2004) (holding that sentence of probation without any suspended jail sentence does not trigger the right to counsel in a misdemeanor case), *with id.* at 106 (Titus, J., dissenting) (contending that a sentence of probation does trigger the right to counsel in a misdemeanor case).
46. Specht v. Patterson, 386 U.S. 605 (1967). *See also*:
   - Jones v. United States, 526 U.S. 227 (1999);
   - Apprendi v. New Jersey, 530 U.S. 466 (2000);
   - Ring v. Arizona, 536 U.S. 584 (2002);
   - Blakely v. Washington, 542 U.S. 296 (2004);
   - United States v. Booker, 543 U.S. 220 (2005);
   - Cunningham v. California, 549 U.S. 270 (2007);
   - Southern Union v. United States, 567 U.S. 343 (2012); and
   - Hurst v. Florida, 136 S. Ct. 616 (2016).
47. United States v. Haymond, 139 S. Ct. 2369 (2019); *see also id.* at 2385 (Breyer, J., concurring in judgment) (controlling opinion).
48. Almendarez-Torres v. United States, 523 U.S. 224 (1998) (holding that prior convictions used to enhance a defendant's sentence under a "recidivist" or "habitual offender" statute need not be found by a jury or found beyond a reasonable doubt); *but see* Shepard v. United States, 544 U.S. 13, 27–28 (2005) (Thomas, J., concurring in judgment) (contending that *Almendarez-Torres* should be overruled). The lower courts are divided on the issue of whether *Almendarez-Torres* applies to juvenile convictions (which are not subject to the same degree of constitutional protections applicable to adult convictions). *See* United States v. Wright, 594 F.3d 259, 264 (4th Cir. 2010) (citing conflicting lower court cases).
49. *Apprendi*, 530 U.S. at 494 n.19.
50. *Cunningham*, 549 U.S. at 295 (Kennedy, J., dissenting).

federal felony cases, such facts also must be pleaded in the indictment,[51] although in state cases there is no such constitutional requirement because the Grand Jury Clause does not apply to the states.[52] The legislature's classification of such facts as "sentencing factors"—as opposed to "elements" of a charged offense—is constitutionally irrelevant.[53]

While sentencing facts that increase the maximum penalty otherwise applicable must be found by a jury (unless a defendant admits them in their guilty plea), the Supreme Court has held that there is no constitutional right under the Sixth Amendment for the jury to impose punishment.[54] Until 2013, the Supreme Court held that facts that trigger a "mandatory minimum" sentence, but do not increase a defendant's maximum punishment from that otherwise authorized by law, did not have to be submitted to a jury or proven beyond a reasonable doubt. Instead, the Court held, a trial court may find the existence of such facts by a mere preponderance of the evidence.[55] In *Alleyne v. United States*, the Court changed its position and applied the *Apprendi* doctrine to any facts that trigger a mandatory minimum sentence as well as facts that raise the otherwise applicable statutory maximum sentence.[56] The Court refused to extend the *Apprendi* doctrine to facts on which a sentencing court relies when deciding to run a defendant's multiple sentences in a consecutive rather than concurrent manner.[57]

In *Blakely v. Washington* and *Booker v. United States*, the Supreme Court extended this constitutional principle to mandatory sentencing guidelines. Thus, any fact that increases a defendant's maximum guidelines sentence—even if such a sentence would fall below the larger, statutory maximum sentence—is functionally an element of the offense that must be submitted to a jury and proven beyond a reasonable doubt unless a defendant admits to that fact during a guilty plea.[58] The Court was careful to limit its holding regarding facts that increase maximum sentencing guideline punishment ranges to "determinate" sentencing systems, as opposed to "indeterminate" sentencing systems.[59] In a jurisdiction with an indeterminate

---

51. *See Jones*, 526 U.S. at 243 n.6.
52. *Apprendi*, 530 U.S. at 477 n.3.
53. *See Ring*, 536 U.S. at 610–13 (Scalia, J., joined by Thomas, J., concurring).
54. *See, e.g.*, Spaziano v. Florida, 468 U.S. 447 (1984).
55. Harris v. United States, 536 U.S. 545 (2002); McMillan v. Pennsylvania, 477 U.S. 79 (1986).
56. Alleyne v. United States, 570 U.S. 99 (2013) (overruling *Harris* and *McMillian*).
57. Oregon v. Ice, 555 U.S. 160 (2009). It is an open question whether *Apprendi* applies to a trial court's order of criminal restitution. *See Hester v. United States*, 139 S. Ct. 509, 509–11 (2019) (Gorsuch, J., joined by Sotomayor, J., dissenting from denial of certiorari).
58. *See Booker*, 543 U.S. at 242–44 (opinion of Stevens, J., for five members of the Court). In *Booker*, a different majority of the Supreme Court held that application of this constitutional principle to the U.S. Sentencing Guidelines would render them facially unconstitutional. Therefore, the Court held that the federal guidelines are now advisory only and thus do not bind judges, thus obviating the need to have juries find such facts beyond a reasonable doubt. *Id.* at 245–46 (opinion of Breyer, J., for five members of the Court).
59. *See Blakely*, 542 U.S. at 304–07.

scheme—in which sentencing decisions are constrained only by statutory ranges of punishment (e.g., from zero to twenty years in prison)—the Constitution does not require jury findings or impose any quantum of proof on the fact-finding process at sentencing as long as the sentence is within the statutory range of punishment; a judge may impose a sentence based on virtually any information as long as it is not unreliable or materially untrue.[60]

12.1.7 Limited Double Jeopardy Protections in the Noncapital Sentencing Context

Under the Double Jeopardy Clause, a defendant may only receive multiple convictions and sentences in the same prosecution when the crimes forming the basis of such convictions constitute the "same offense" under the *Blockburger* test[61] if the legislature intended for such multiple convictions and sentences.[62] If there is insufficient evidence of legislative intent for multiple convictions and sentences for the "same offense," multiple punishments, even if they run concurrently, would violate double jeopardy.[63] Thus, if the defendant in a single prosecution has been convicted of multiple offenses that constitute the "same offense" for double jeopardy purposes and there is no legislative intent for multiple punishments, the prosecution must "elect" which of the convictions it wishes to leave intact for sentencing purposes.[64]

It does not violate the Double Jeopardy Clause in a noncapital case for a defendant to be resentenced on remand from an appeal of the original sentence—whether the appeal was filed by the defendant or the prosecution—even if an appellate court concluded that there was insufficient evidence supporting the trial court's findings in support of the original sentence.[65]

Under the Supreme Court's current precedent, it does not violate the Double Jeopardy Clause for a sentencing court to consider a defendant's prior criminal conduct in aggravation of punishment even if, in the prior criminal prosecution, a defendant was acquitted of charges alleging such conduct.[66] In *United States v. Watts*, the Court reasoned that as long as such prior conduct need only be proved by a preponderance of the evidence at a subsequent sentencing (as opposed to beyond a reasonable doubt), it does not constitute double jeopardy or violate the collateral estoppel doctrine for a sentencing court to consider it in a subsequent case because

---

60. *See* Townsend v. Burke, 334 U.S. 736, 740–41 (1948).
61. Blockburger v. United States, 284 U.S. 299 (1932). The "multiple prosecution" component of the Double Jeopardy Clause, which also applies the *Blockburger* test, is discussed in Chapter Four.
62. Missouri v. Hunter, 459 U.S. 359 (1983).
63. *See, e.g.*, Ball v. United States, 470 U.S. 856, 864–65 (1985); United States v. Gibson, 820 F.2d 692 (5th Cir. 1987).
64. *Ball*, 470 U.S. at 864–65.
65. Monge v. California, 524 U.S. 721 (1998); *see also* Pennsylvania v. Goldhammer, 474 U.S. 28 (1985); United States v. DiFrancesco, 449 U.S. 117, 136–37 (1980).
66. United States v. Watts, 519 U.S. 148 (1997) (per curiam).

the prior acquittal was under the more demanding "reasonable doubt" standard.[67] A fortiori, it does not constitute double jeopardy for a court in a subsequent case to enhance a defendant's sentence based on a prior conviction.[68]

In *Witte v. United States*,[69] the Supreme Court addressed the flip side of *Watts*: a court had sentenced a defendant in a prior case based in part on uncharged conduct that was not part of the offense of conviction in the prior case. The *Witte* Court held that it did not constitute double jeopardy for the defendant to be prosecuted in a subsequent case for the same conduct previously used to enhance the sentence in the earlier prosecution because the prior court's consideration of the uncharged conduct did not place the defendant "in jeopardy" for that conduct for purposes of the Fifth Amendment.[70]

The Supreme Court's decision in *Blakely v. Washington*[71] might limit to some degree the holdings in *Watts* and *Witte*, however, because *Blakely* treats any factual finding that increases the otherwise applicable maximum sentence as an element that must be proved beyond a reasonable doubt.[72] The holdings of both *Watts* and *Witte* were premised on the rule that factual findings at noncapital sentencings were subject, at most, to the preponderance standard and were not elements of the charged offense. The Supreme Court may address the double jeopardy implications of *Blakely* in noncapital cases in the future.

12.1.8   No Sixth Amendment Right to "Speedy" Sentencing

In *Betterman v. Montana*, the Supreme Court held that the Speedy Trial Clause of the Sixth Amendment did not apply to the sentencing phase of a criminal case.[73] The Court left open the possibility of a due process challenge to a lengthy delay between conviction and sentencing.[74]

12.1.9   The Operation of the Ex Post Facto Clause at Sentencing

As discussed in Chapter Four (concerning a pretrial motion to dismiss a penal statute under the Ex Post Facto Clause),[75] the Ex Post Facto Clause also prevents the application of a statute or sentencing guideline increasing punishment that was

---

67. *Id.*

68. Gryger v. Burke, 334 U.S. 728, 732 (1948).

69. Witte v. United States, 515 U.S. 389 (1995).

70. *Id.* at 395–406.

71. Blakely v. Washington, 542 U.S. 296 (2004).

72. *See, e.g.*, United States v. Booker, 375 F.3d 508, 514–15 (7th Cir. 2004) (Posner, J.) (noting potential double jeopardy implications of Blakely), *aff'd on other grounds*, 543 U.S. 220 (2005).

73. Betterman v. Montana, 136 S. Ct. 1609 (2016).

74. *Id.* at 1618.

75. *See* section 4.4.2.6.

enacted after the date of the offense.[76] Not all retroactive applications of new sentencing provisions are impermissible ex post facto laws, however. Retroactive application of a sentencing statute or guideline that does not make the punishment "more onerous" or otherwise "disadvantage the offender affected by it" is constitutional.[77] The Supreme Court also has invalidated the ex post facto application of parole statutes that retroactively deny "early release" or "good time" credits earned by prison inmates whose convictions occurred prior to the enactment of such parole statutes.[78]

12.1.10 Due Process Protection Against Court's Reliance on "Unreliable" Information at Sentencing

The Supreme Court has long held that it violates due process for a court to sentence a defendant based on materially untrue information.[79] In *Townsend v. Burke*, the Court held that due process was violated when a trial court sentenced the defendant based on a mistaken belief that he had three prior felony convictions (when in fact those three cases had been dismissed or resulted in acquittals).[80] Lower courts have extended *Townsend*'s reliability principle to reverse sentencing decisions based on unreliable information or evidence in addition to outright untrue information.[81]

12.1.11 Judicial Vindictiveness Doctrine

Just as it prohibits a prosecutor from punishing a defendant for appealing (by adding more serious charges on remand),[82] the Due Process Clause prohibits a trial court from "vindictively" sentencing a defendant more harshly on remand from an appellate court's reversal of an original conviction or sentence.[83] Judicial

---

76. *See, e.g.*, Miller v. Florida, 482 U.S. 423 (1987); *see also* Peugh v. United States, 569 U.S. 530 (2013) (applying *Miller* to retroactive application of "advisory" federal sentencing guidelines that would yield a higher sentencing range).
77. Dobbert v. Florida, 432 U.S. 282 (1977) (upholding retroactive application of Florida's capital punishment statute enacted after the Supreme Court's *Furman* decision in 1972, which struck down capital punishment, because the new statute did not increase the available punishment, but instead simply made the capital sentencing procedures more fair to the defendant by complying with the Eighth Amendment).
78. *See, e.g.*, Lynce v. Mathis, 519 U.S. 433 (1997).
79. Townsend v. Burke, 334 U.S. 736, 739–41 (1948); *see also* United States v. Berry, 553 F.3d 273, 280 (3d Cir. 2009); United States v. Baylin, 696 F.2d 1030, 1039–40 (3d Cir. 1982); United States v. Tobias, 662 F.2d 381, 388 (5th Cir. 1981).
80. *Townsend*, 334 U.S. at 736–41.
81. *See, e.g.*, United States v. Weston, 448 F.2d 626, 633–34 (9th Cir. 1971) (reversing sentence in drug case where district court had relied on unsubstantiated claim from law enforcement officers that the defendant was a major drug supplier; defendant not required to prove that he was not a major drug supplier).
82. *See* Blackledge v. Perry, 417 U.S. 21 (1974), discussed in section 4.2.14.
83. North Carolina v. Pearce, 395 U.S. 711 (1969).

vindictiveness, like prosecutorial vindictiveness, can be "actual" or "presumed."[84] Because proving actual vindictiveness is almost always impossible, the Supreme Court in *North Carolina v. Pearce* created a rebuttable presumption: when a judge imposes a harsher sentence on remand from a defendant's successful appeal of their conviction after a trial (or a successful appeal of their sentence), the judge is presumed to have acted vindictively and in violation of due process. However, the sentencing judge may rebut the presumption by articulating on the record that there were objective intervening circumstances justifying the harsher sentence at the resentencing.[85] Such circumstances include the defendant's misconduct in prison during the pendency of the appeal or the fact that a defendant was convicted of other charges after the original sentencing.[86]

The Supreme Court has created many exceptions to the *Pearce* presumption. First, it does not apply to a different judge who resentences a defendant on remand from a successful appeal of their conviction or original sentence.[87] Second, it does not apply when a jury resentences a defendant on remand following the defendant's successful appeal of a prior jury's conviction and sentence.[88] Third, it does not apply to a judge who resentences after a jury's original sentence was reversed on appeal.[89] Fourth, it does not apply to the same judge's resentencing of a defendant who successfully appealed a conviction following a guilty plea and then proceeded to be convicted at a trial on remand.[90] Finally, although the Supreme Court has never addressed the issue, there is an apparent consensus among lower courts that the *Pearce* presumption does not apply when a trial court at resentencing increases the defendant's original sentence based on discovery of a legal error at the original sentencing hearing that resulted in a lesser sentence than should have been imposed under the applicable law.[91]

12.1.12 Limited Eighth Amendment Protections at Noncapital Sentencing

Unlike capital punishment (discussed in the following chapter), prison sentences imposed on adult offenders are subject to an extremely limited review under the

---

84. Wasman v. United States, 468 U.S. 559, 568–69 (1984).

85. *Pearce*, 395 U.S. at 721–23. Although *Pearce* concerned resentencing following a retrial on remand from an appellate court's reversal of the original conviction, *Pearce*'s logic has been applied to resentencing following an appellate court's reversal of a defendant's original sentence (while leaving the conviction intact). *See, e.g.*, United States v. Peyton, 353 F.3d 1080, 1085 (9th Cir. 2003).

86. *Wasman*, 468 U.S. at 570–72; *Pearce*, 395 U.S. at 722–23.

87. *See* Texas v. McCullough, 475 U.S. 134, 140 n.3 (1986).

88. Chaffin v. Stynchcombe, 412 U.S. 17 (1973).

89. *McCullough*, 475 U.S. at 140.

90. Alabama v. Smith, 490 U.S. 794 (1989). However, if a defendant were to again plead guilty on remand from the appellate court (rather than go to trial), the *Pearce* presumption would appear applicable. *Cf.* Turner v. Tennessee, 940 F.2d 1000, 1002 (6th Cir. 1991).

91. *See, e.g., Peyton*, 353 F.3d at 1086–87; State v. Lucas, 598 So. 2d 338 (La. 1992); Grobarchick v. State, 307 N.W.2d 170 (Wis. 1981).

Cruel and Unusual Punishments Clause of the Eighth Amendment,[92] and fines (including criminal forfeitures of money) are likewise subject to extremely limited review under the Excessive Fines Clause of the Eighth Amendment.[93] For a prison sentence or fine to be unconstitutional under the Eighth Amendment, it must be grossly disproportionate to the gravity of the offense of conviction and the defendant's criminal record.[94] Although there are a few instances of courts invalidating prison sentences or fines as constitutionally excessive in recent years,[95] it is exceedingly rare for a court to do so.[96]

The sole exception to the Supreme Court's otherwise limited noncapital Eighth Amendment jurisprudence concerns offenders who were juveniles at the time of the offense. The Court has held that the Eighth Amendment categorically prohibits imposition of a prison sentence of life without parole (LWOP) on a juvenile offender who was not convicted of a homicide offense.[97] In addition, the Court has held that a mandatory LWOP sentence violates the Eighth Amendment even if a juvenile offender was convicted of a homicide offense—a judge or jury must first consider any relevant mitigating evidence before deciding whether to impose a LWOP sentence.[98]

---

92. *See* Ewing v. California, 538 U.S. 11, 14–31 (2003) (plurality) (citing Harmelin v. Michigan, 501 U.S. 957, 996–97 (1991) (Kennedy, J., joined by O'Connor & Souter, JJ., concurring in part and concurring in judgment). Although a majority of the Court has never embraced Justice Kennedy's position, the lower courts have followed it because the plurality in *Ewing* and Justice Kennedy's concurring opinion in *Harmelin* represent the holding of the Court. *See, e.g.*, Hawkins v. Hargett, 200 F.3d 1279, 1282 (10th Cir. 1999); Close v. People, 48 P.3d 528, 535 (Colo. 2002). The Supreme Court also has held that, with respect to juvenile offenders, a sentence of life without the possibility of parole is cruel and unusual punishment in any case where the defendant was convicted solely of a "nonhomicide crime." Graham v. Florida, 560 U.S. 48 (2010).

93. *See* United States v. Bajakajian, 524 U.S. 321, 330–38 (1998). In *Timbs v. Indiana*, 139 S. Ct. 682 (2019), the Supreme Court held that the Eighth Amendment prohibition against "excessive fines" applied to the states as well as the federal government.

94. *Ewing*, 538 U.S. at 14–31; *Bajakajian*, 524 U.S. at 330–38.

95. *See, e.g.*, *Bajakajian*, 524 U.S. at 330–38 (five-to-four majority of Court concluded that the government's forfeiture of $357,144 in cash that a defendant failed to report to Customs as he was attempting to leave the United States was disproportionate because the money was legally obtained and intended to be used in a legal manner, and the defendant's failure to declare the money, although a crime, was a function of cultural differences); Ramirez v. Castro, 365 F.3d 755 (9th Cir. 2004) (two-to-one majority of court of appeals concluded that defendant's twenty-five-years-to-life "habitual" prison sentence for shoplifting a $199 VCR was grossly disproportionate where defendant's prior criminal record consisted of two minor unarmed robberies that involved minimal use of force); Humphrey v. Wilson, 652 S.E.2d 501 (Ga. 2007) (invalidating ten-year prison sentence as grossly disproportionate in case of seventeen-year-old convicted of consensual statutory rape of fifteen-year-old).

96. *Ramirez*, 365 F.3d at 763 (citations and internal quotation marks omitted).

97. Graham v. Florida, 560 U.S. 48 (2010).

98. Miller v. Alabama, 567 U.S. 460 (2012).

12.1.13 Due Process Protections Applicable to Revocations of Probation and Other Forms of Conditional Release

In all jurisdictions, courts are empowered to sentence certain offenders to probation, which may or may not be coupled with a suspended prison or jail sentence. If a probationer violates the conditions of probation (e.g., by committing a new offense or by failing to fulfill some condition such as community service), then the sentencing court is empowered to revoke the probation and sentence the probationer to serve prison or jail time.

In all jurisdictions, when inmates are released from prison many are conditionally released on what is commonly called parole (in most states) or supervised release (in the federal system). If a released inmate violates the terms of such conditional release, then they are subject to having the conditional release revoked and being sent back to prison. In jurisdictions with parole, the parole board conducts the revocation hearing; in the federal system, which has abolished parole and replaced it with supervised release, a trial court conducts a supervised release revocation hearing.

Under the Due Process Clause, defendants subject to such revocation hearings—whether concerning probation, parole, or any other type of conditional release—are entitled to certain minimum procedural protections.[99] The same essential procedural protections apply to all types of conditional release revocation hearings.[100]

The constitutional protections afforded to persons before their conditional release can be revoked include: 1) the right to a prompt preliminary hearing at which probable cause justifying the revocation is established; 2) written notice of the specific grounds for revocation; 3) the right to a revocation hearing at which a neutral and detached hearing officer presides (who need not be a judicial officer in the case of parole revocations); 4) the right to confront and cross-examine adverse witnesses unless good cause for denying that right can be shown; 5) the right to the disclosure of the adverse evidence or information being considered by the hearing officer or judge; 6) the right to testify, call favorable witnesses, and present favorable evidence; 7) the right to the assistance of counsel (including appointed counsel) when such assistance is necessary for a fair hearing;[101] and 8) the right to have a written statement of reasons from the hearing officer or judge who ordered that the probation or conditional release be revoked.[102] The two most commonly litigated issues

---

99. Morrissey v. Brewer, 408 U.S. 471 (1972); Gagnon v. Scarpelli, 411 U.S. 778 (1973).

100. *Gagnon*, 411 U.S. at 782; *see also* Young v. Harper, 520 U.S. 143 (1997).

101. A person facing revocation is constitutionally entitled to the assistance of counsel if they make a "colorable claim" that they have not committed the violation alleged or that their case raises "complex" issues concerning mitigation of punishment. *Gagnon*, 411 U.S. at 790; *see also* Wolff v. McDonnell, 418 U.S. 539, 559–60 (1974).

102. *Morrissey*, 408 U.S. at 489; *Gagnon*, 411 U.S. at 782–91.

National Institute for Trial Advocacy

concern the denial of the right to the assistance of counsel[103] and the denial of the right to confront adverse witnesses.[104]

The Supreme Court has stressed that revocation hearings are informal proceedings that are not tantamount to criminal trials and, thus, not all of the constitutional protections afforded to criminal defendants at trial are applicable at revocation hearings.[105] However, as the above litany of constitutional protections demonstrates, a defendant's constitutional rights at a revocation hearing are greater than they were at the original sentencing hearing.[106] Although the Supreme Court has not directly addressed the issue and instead has only implied that the quantum of proof applicable to revocation hearings is less than the reasonable doubt standard applicable at a criminal trial,[107] the vast majority of lower courts have held that the preponderance of the evidence standard satisfies due process.[108]

In addition to the foregoing procedural requirements, there also are certain substantive constitutional limitations at revocation hearings. Conditional release may not be revoked solely based on the defendant's nonwillful failure to pay a fine or restitution because of financial inability to pay where good-faith efforts have been made to do so.[109] Nor may conditional release be revoked solely based on a defendant's

---

103. *Compare, e.g.*, United States v. Dodson, 25 F.3d 385 (6th Cir. 1994) (concluding that lower court erred by denying the defendant's request for appointment of counsel at supervised release revocation hearing), *with* Byrd v. State, 717 So. 2d 874 (Ala. Crim. App. 1998) (concluding that lower court did not err in denying defendant's request for the appointment of counsel at probation revocation hearing).

104. *Compare, e.g.*, United States v. Martin, 382 F.3d 840 (8th Cir. 2004) (concluding that the defendant's right to confront adverse witnesses at supervised release revocation hearing was not violated because prosecution showed "good cause" for not producing the witness), *with* McBride v. Johnson, 118 F.3d 432 (5th Cir. 1997) (concluding that defendant's right to confront witnesses at parole revocation hearing was violated because prosecution had not shown "good cause"); *see also* United States v. Lloyd, 566 F.3d 341, 344 (3d Cir. 2009) (discussing the division in the lower courts concerning whether admission of "reliable" hearsay is admissible at a revocation hearing even if the prosecution cannot show "good cause" for a missing witness).

105. *See* Pennsylvania Board of Probation and Parole v. Scott, 524 U.S. 357, 365–66 (1998) (refusing to apply the Fourth Amendment exclusionary rule to unconstitutionally seized evidence offered during revocation hearing).

106. It should be noted that the procedural protections discussed above apply only to the court or hearing officer's determination of whether conditional release should be revoked; once revocation occurs, the defendant's rights at the sentencing that follows are essentially the same as those limited rights applicable at the original sentencing hearing. *See, e.g.,* United States v. Morin, 889 F.2d 328, 332 (1st Cir. 1989).

107. *Gagnon*, 411 U.S. at 789 n.12.

108. State v. Davis, 641 A.2d 370, 376–77 & nn.12–17 (Conn. 1994) (collecting cases); People v. Rodriguez, 795 P.2d 783, 786–90 & nn.4–7 (Cal. 1990) (collecting cases). A minority of courts applies what is referred to as the "reasonably satisfied" standard, which is even less than the preponderance standard. *See, e.g.,* United States v. Smith, 571 F.2d 370, 372 (7th Cir. 1978).

109. Bearden v. Georgia, 461 U.S. 660 (1983). Similarly, the Supreme Court has held that an indigent defendant may not be kept in prison longer than a non-indigent defendant based solely on the indigent's inability to pay a fine. *See* Tate v. Short, 401 U.S. 395 (1971); Williams v. Illinois, 399 U.S. 235 (1970).

---

invocation of their Fifth Amendment privilege against self-incrimination.[110] A defendant's probation cannot be revoked when their Sixth Amendment right to the assistance of counsel was violated at the original proceeding at which they were convicted and sentenced to probation.[111]

Finally, although courts and parole boards traditionally have been afforded "broad discretion" to impose conditions of supervision,[112] there are certain constitutional limitations on the conditions of probation or other conditional release. For instance, a condition that requires a probationer or parolee to attend religiously based substance abuse treatment classes runs afoul of the First Amendment's Establishment Clause.[113] Some courts have held that a probation condition permitting warrantless searches of the person's residence without a specification of any degree of objective suspicion (not even reasonable suspicion) would violate the Fourth Amendment.[114] Courts also have invalidated conditions that are unconstitutionally vague or overbroad, particularly regarding constitutionally protected activity or expression.[115]

12.2 Special Constitutional Rules of Criminal Procedure Applicable to Capital Sentencing[116]

After declaring the existing capital punishment laws to be in violation of the Eighth Amendment's ban on cruel and unusual punishments in 1972 in *Furman v.*

---

110. Minnesota v. Murphy, 465 U.S. 420, 438–39 (1984).

111. United States v. Reilley, 948 F.2d 648, 654 & n.11 (10th Cir. 1991); United States v. Foster, 904 F.2d 20, 21–22 (9th Cir. 1990); *cf.* Alabama v. Shelton, 535 U.S. 654 (2002).

112. *See, e.g.,* United States v. Bee, 162 F.3d 1232 (9th Cir. 1998).

113. *See, e.g.,* Warner v. Orange County Dep't of Probation, 173 F.3d 120 (2d Cir. 1999).

114. *See, e.g.,* State v. Moses, 618 A.2d 478 (Vt. 1992). The U.S. Supreme Court has not yet addressed that issue. *See* United States v. Knights, 534 U.S. 112, 118, 120 n.6 (2001).

115. *See, e.g.,* United States v. Loy, 237 F.3d 251, 267 (3d Cir. 2001) (concluding that a condition of supervised release that prohibited the defendant from possessing all types of pornography violated the First Amendment).

116. In addition to special constitutional rules of criminal procedure that apply only in capital cases, there also are substantive constitutional rules (rooted in the Eighth Amendment) that apply. *See* Kennedy v. Louisiana, 554 U.S. 407 (2008) (unconstitutional to execute defendants who rape but do not kill victim, whether child or adult); Panetti v. Quarterman, 551 U.S. 930 (2007) (unconstitutional to execute a death row inmate who is mentally incompetent at the time of the scheduled execution); Roper v. Simmons, 543 U.S. 551 (2005) (unconstitutional to execute defendants who were younger than eighteen at time of capital murder); Atkins v. Virginia, 536 U.S. 304 (2002) (unconstitutional to execute capital defendants who were mentally retarded at time of offense); Tison v. Arizona, 481 U.S. 137 (1987) (unconstitutional to execute a defendant who was not the "triggerman" in felony-murder case if he was not a "major" participant in the crime or did not at least have a "reckless indifference" whether the codefendant/triggerman would commit murder). The Supreme Court also has twice addressed equal protection issues related to racial discrimination in the application of capital punishment in the modern era and in both cases placed a heavy burden on capital defendants alleging racial discrimination to prevail on their claims. *See* United States v. Bass, 536 U.S. 862 (2002) (per curiam); McCleskey v. Kemp, 481 U.S. 279 (1987).

Georgia,[117] the Supreme Court in 1976 upheld the facial validity of most states' capital punishment laws that had been rewritten in the wake of *Furman*.[118] Currently, twenty-eight states and the federal government (including the military) authorize capital punishment as an optional penalty for certain types of aggravated murder (although three of them have long-term moratoria on the implementation of death sentences).[119] In scores of decisions since *Furman*, the Supreme Court has developed an extremely complex body of Eighth Amendment jurisprudence applicable only in death penalty cases that has evoked criticism from liberal and conservative jurists alike,[120] although a firm majority of the modern Court appears willing to maintain the status quo, with occasional "tweaking" of the Court's jurisprudential "machinery of death."[121]

Understanding the Court's post-*Furman* Eighth Amendment jurisprudence is aided by understanding the typical process in a capital prosecution, which significantly differs in certain respects from a typical noncapital felony prosecution. A typical capital prosecution involves a "bifurcated" jury trial, with separate proceedings on guilt-innocence and punishment, although with a single jury hearing both phases of the case.[122] A guilty verdict is virtually preordained in the vast majority of capital jury trials since prosecutors usually seek the death penalty only if the evidence of a defendant's guilt of capital murder is strong.[123] Outright acquittals occur in only a small percentage of capital trials; convictions on lesser included noncapital offenses (e.g., second-degree murder)—ones not carrying the death penalty as an available punishment[124]—are much more common than full acquittals.

---

117. Furman v. Georgia, 408 U.S. 238 (1972).

118. *See* Gregg v. Georgia, 428 U.S. 153 (1976); Proffitt v. Florida, 428 U.S. 242 (1976); Jurek v. Texas, 428 U.S. 262 (1976); *but see* Woodson v. North Carolina, 428 U.S. 280 (1976) (invaliding North Carolina's mandatory death penalty); Roberts v. Louisiana, 428 U.S. 325 (1976) (invalidating Louisiana's mandatory death penalty). Mandatory death penalty statutes are discussed below.

119. Death Penalty Information Center, *States with and without the Death Penalty*, www.deathpenaltyinfo.org/states-and-without-death-penalty (last visited February 13, 2021).

120. *See, e.g.*, Callins v. Collins, 510 U.S. 1141, 1142–59 (1994) (opinions of Scalia, J., concurring in denial of certiorari & Blackmun, J., dissenting from the denial of certiorari).

121. *Id.* at 1145 (Blackmun, J., dissenting); *see also* Glossip v. Gross, 135 S. Ct. 2726, 2756 (2015) (Breyer, J., dissenting, joined by Ginsburg, J.) (contending that "the death penalty, in and of itself, now likely constitutes a legally prohibited 'cruel and unusual punishment'").

122. On April 11, 2017, Alabama became the last death penalty jurisdiction to prohibit judges from making the ultimate decision about whether to impose a death sentence rather a life sentence. *See* Equal Justice Initiative, *Judge Override*, http://eji.org/death-penalty/judge-override (last visited April 13, 2017).

123. This is not to say that all convicted capital defendants are in fact guilty of capital murder. A significant number of persons have been released from death row after being exonerated in postconviction proceedings—well over 100 such persons since 1973, *see* Thompson v. McNeil, 556 U.S. 1114 (2009) (Stevens, J., respecting the denial of certiorari)—yet the actual percentage of such innocent death row inmates in relation to all death row inmates is relatively small.

124. *See* Beck v. Alabama, 447 U.S. 625 (1980) (discussing lesser included offenses in capital cases).

The "main event" in most capital prosecutions is the capital sentencing phase, where a jury (rather than the trial judge, who typically sentences in noncapital cases) must decide between imposing a life sentence or a death sentence. During the capital sentencing phase, jurors are asked to find "aggravating" and "mitigating" factors or circumstances and then impose a sentence.

The typical capital prosecution has the following stages:

- Events constituting the alleged crime;

- Arrest (which may occur before or after the filing of charges or issuance of an arrest warrant);

- Filing of criminal complaint/magistrate's ex parte determination of probable cause ("48-hour hearing")—if an arrest warrant is not issued prior to the arrest;

- Denial of bail in almost all capital cases;

- Preliminary hearing;

- Grand jury proceedings (virtually all jurisdictions use grand juries in capital cases);

- Arraignment;

- Filing of pretrial motions and pretrial "discovery" process;

- Pretrial hearing on motions;

- Jury trials in the vast majority of cases (very few capital defendants plead guilty or choose bench trials):

  lengthy individual voir dire, including on issues concerning capital punishment, and jury selection > opening statements > prosecution's case-in-chief > defendant's motion for judgment of acquittal > optional defense's case and optional prosecution's rebuttal case > defendant's renewed motion for judgment of acquittal > jury instructions > closing arguments > jury deliberations > verdict on guilt or innocence;

- Separate capital sentencing phase (involving sentencing juries in the vast majority of jurisdictions):

  opening statements > prosecution's case-in-chief > defense's case[125] > optional prosecution's rebuttal case > jury instructions > closing arguments > jury deliberations > jury's verdict on punishment;

---

125. Unlike the guilt-innocence phase of a typical criminal trial (capital or noncapital)—where

- Motion for new trial and hearing on motion;

- Mandatory direct appeal;

- Discretionary habeas corpus appeals in state and federal court systems;

- Clemency process;

- Execution after exhaustion of all appeals and clemency denied.

In the average American death penalty case leading to an execution, the process from arrest on capital murder charges to the execution of the death sentence takes over a decade because of the delays occasioned by direct and collateral appeals.[126]

The Supreme Court's Eighth Amendment jurisprudence has "distinguished between two different aspects of the capital sentencing process, the eligibility phase and the selection phase."[127] The "eligibility" phase is concerned with "narrowing" the potential class of capital murderers to a relatively small group who, because of the aggravated nature of their cases, are worthy of consideration for the death penalty.[128] The "selection" phase—which occurs after the eligibility phase—is concerned with allowing for a "broad inquiry into all relevant mitigating evidence" and permitting the sentencer to arrive at a sentence only after considering all aggravating and mitigating factors.[129]

As discussed below, the Supreme Court's cases concerning the "eligibility" phase have focused on constitutional issues concerning aggravating factors, while the Court's cases concerning the selection phase have focused primarily on mitigating factors.

12.2.1 Eighth Amendment Requirements Regarding Aggravating Factors

12.2.1.1 "Eligibility" Aggravating Factors as "Elements"

The Supreme Court in *Ring v. Arizona*[130] held that under the Sixth Amendment right to a jury trial, any aggravating factor or circumstance that must be found before a defendant is eligible for capital punishment under the applicable law is,

---

often the defense does not present a case—the defense typically offers mitigating evidence during the capital sentencing phase.

126. *McNeil*, 556 U.S. at 1114 (Stevens, J., dissenting from denial of certiorari) (noting that average time between imposition of death sentence and execution is thirteen years). Some post-*Furman* capital cases have taken well over two decades (in a few cases nearly three decades), which has led Justice Breyer (in dissenting opinions) to suggest that executions in cases of extraordinary delay constitute cruel and unusual punishment, at least where such delay was largely attributable to the state (i.e., by denying fair capital trials, resulting in multiple appeals and retrials). *See, e.g.*, Foster v. Florida, 537 U.S. 990, 991–93 (2002) (Breyer, J., dissenting from the denial of certiorari).

127. Buchanan v. Angelone, 522 U.S. 269, 275 (1998).

128. *Id.*

129. *Id.* at 275–76; *see also* Tuilaepa v. California, 512 U.S. 967, 971–72 (1994).

130. Ring v. Arizona, 536 U.S. 584 (2002).

functionally speaking, an element of the capital offense that must be found to exist by a jury beyond a reasonable doubt before a death sentence can be imposed.[131] Although *Ring* requires a capital sentencing jury to find such "eligibility" aggravating factors beyond a reasonable doubt, the Court's pre-*Ring* precedent (which was not overruled by *Ring*) permits the ultimate decision of whether to impose the death penalty—made during the subsequent selection phase—to be made by a judge rather than a jury, and the Court has refused to reconsider that pre-*Ring* precedent.[132] Common aggravating factors include the fact that a defendant committed the murder in the course of another felony (such as a rape, robbery, or burglary); the defendant knowingly or intentionally murdered a police officer; and a jury's belief that a defendant poses a future danger or continuing threat to society.[133]

A jurisdiction may allow for both statutory and nonstatutory aggravating factors to be used during the selection process as long as at least one statutory eligibility factor must be found as a threshold matter.[134] A nonstatutory selection-phase aggravating factor is one drafted by the prosecutor or trial court rather than by the legislature.[135]

12.2.1.2   Aggravating Factors Cannot Be Vague or Overbroad

Another constitutional requirement concerning aggravating factors—which, unlike the *Ring* requirement, is rooted in the Eighth Amendment—is that aggravating

---

131. *Id*. at 609–10.

132. *See* Spaziano v. Florida, 468 U.S. 447 (1984) (no right to jury sentencing in capital cases). In *Ring*, the Court expressly noted that it was not addressing the larger issue of whether, as a constitutional matter, a jury must make the ultimate decision about which sentence to impose in view of the totality of aggravating and mitigating circumstances. *Ring*, 536 U.S. at 597 n.4; *see also id*. at 612 (Scalia, J., concurring, joined by Thomas, J.) ("today's judgment has nothing to do with jury sentencing" in death penalty cases); *but see id*. at 613–19 (Breyer, J., concurring in the judgment) (contending that the Eighth Amendment requires the ultimate sentencing decision in a capital case to be made by a jury rather than a judge). In *Hurst v. Florida*, 136 S. Ct. 616 (2016), the Court ruled that Florida's former capital sentencing system—which did not require a jury to find that at least one aggravating circumstance existed for a judge to impose a death sentence—was unconstitutional because the jury was not required to find a fact (i.e., the existence of at least one aggravating factor) necessary for the defendant to be legally eligible for a death sentence. The Court did not directly address the additional question of whether a jury is constitutionally required to decide whether a death sentence should actually be imposed (i.e., whether the aggravating evidence outweighs the mitigating evidence). In a concurring opinion, Justice Breyer contended that the Constitution requires that the ultimate decision of whether to impose a death sentence instead of a life sentence must be made by a jury rather than a judge. *Hurst*, 136 S. Ct. at 624–25 (Breyer, J., concurring). However, in McKinney v. Arizona, 140 S. Ct. 702 (2020), the Court later held that "a jury (as opposed to a judge) is not constitutionally required to weigh the aggravating and mitigating circumstances or to make the ultimate sentencing decision within the relevant sentencing range." *Id*. at 707–08.

133. *See, e.g., Gregg*, 428 U.S. at 165 & n.9; *Jurek*, 428 U.S. at 269.

134. Barclay v. Florida, 463 U.S. 939, 957–58 (1983) (plurality); *id*. at 966–67 (Stevens, J., joined by Powell, J., concurring in judgment).

135. Jones v. United States, 527 U.S. 373, 402–03 (1999).

factors, whether included in the eligibility or selection process, cannot be vague[136] or overbroad.[137] A "vague" factor is one that "fails adequately to inform juries what they must find to impose the death penalty and as a result leaves them . . . with the kind of open-ended discretion which was held invalid in *Furman* . . ."[138] An "overbroad" factor is one defined in such a way that "[a] person of ordinary sensibility could fairly characterize almost every murder" as qualifying under that factor and, thus, is not a sufficient channel for "narrowing" the class of murderers eligible for capital punishment.[139]

The Supreme Court has stressed that in addressing whether an aggravating factor is vague or overbroad, a court's review of the factor is deferential, asking whether the words used in the factor have a common-sense core meaning that lay jurors will understand.[140] Even engaging in such deferential review, however, the Court has invalidated aggravating factors on a few occasions. For instance, the Court held that a jury instruction that permitted jurors to find an aggravating factor if they concluded that the murder was "especially heinous, atrocious, or cruel" was constitutionally invalid because such language was both vague and overbroad under the Eighth Amendment.[141] Such an aggravating factor without some type of judicial limiting instruction offered "no principled way to distinguish [a particular] case, in which the death penalty case is imposed, from the many cases in which it was not."[142] The Court has permitted state courts to cure such invalid statutory aggravating factors by limiting their reach with an adequate narrowing interpretation.[143] In *Brown v. Sanders*,[144] the Supreme Court further held that a vague or overbroad aggravating factor is not unconstitutional if "one of the other [valid aggravating] factors enables the sentencer to give aggravating weight to the same facts and circumstances [at issue with respect to the invalid factor]."[145]

---

136. Maynard v. Cartwright, 486 U.S. 356, 361–63 (1988); Godfrey v. Georgia, 446 U.S. 420 (1980); *see also Tuilaepa*, 512 U.S. at 971–80 (addressing vagueness challenge to aggravating factors in selection phase).
137. *Maynard*, 486 U.S. at 364; *see also Jones*, 527 U.S. at 401 (suggesting that even selection-aggravating factors could be unconstitutionally overbroad, but not defining how so). The Court's use of the terms "vague" and "overbroad" in this context differs from the use of the terms in the due process or First Amendment contexts, which is discussed in Chapter Four. *See Maynard*, 486 U.S. at 361–62.
138. *Maynard*, 486 U.S. at 361–62.
139. *Godfrey*, 446 U.S. at 428–29.
140. *Tuilaepa*, 512 U.S. at 973–74.
141. *Maynard*, 486 U.S. at 363–65.
142. *Id.* at 363.
143. *See, e.g.*, Arave v. Creech, 507 U.S. 463, 471–76 (1993) (holding that the statutory aggravating factor that the defendant had an "utter disregard for life" was sufficiently narrowed by the state supreme court's clarification that this meant the murder was "reflective of [a] cold-blooded, pitiless slayer").
144. Brown v. Sanders, 546 U.S. 212 (2006).
145. *Id.* at 220.

A state is free to make an aggravating factor part of the crime of capital murder to be decided during the guilt-innocence phase—for eligibility purposes—and need not include aggravating factors as part of the bifurcated sentencing process, although all states do so.[146] If a state chooses to make an aggravating factor an element of the crime of capital murder (as many states do), a state also may make the same aggravating factor part of the selection process without violating the Eighth Amendment.[147]

A state may permit jurors to consider "victim impact" evidence in aggravation of punishment—i.e., the effect of a murder on the victim's family as well as the positive attributes of the victim—without running afoul of the Eighth Amendment, even if the jury is not instructed that such evidence is a specific aggravating factor.[148] However, the Eighth Amendment does not permit the victim's family members to ask for a death sentence over a life sentence.[149] The prosecution also may introduce expert testimony from a mental health professional who opines that the defendant is a future danger to society as long as the witness is subject to cross-examination by the defense.[150]

There are some constitutional limits, however, on other types of aggravating evidence offered by the prosecution during the capital sentencing phase. "Constitutionally protected behavior" or other legal conduct that has no legitimate relationship to the crime or any sentencing factor—such as a defendant's unpopular religious or political views or unorthodox (yet legal) sexual practices—cannot be introduced during the sentencing phase.[151] Any such conduct that has a nexus to

---

146. Lowenfield v. Phelps, 484 U.S. 231, 244–45 (1988).

147. *Id.* at 245–46.

148. Payne v. Tennessee, 501 U.S. 808 (1991). The Court noted that the Due Process Clause might limit the admission of such evidence—or prosecutorial arguments based on such evidence—that renders the capital sentencing phase "fundamentally unfair" in a particular case. *Id.* at 825. In *Humphries v. Ozmint*, 366 F.3d 266, 272–76 (4th Cir. 2004), a panel of the Fourth Circuit held that a prosecutor's "comparative worth" argument (i.e., comparing the relative "moral worth" of the victim and defendant) was unconstitutional, yet the en banc Fourth Circuit ruled otherwise over a dissent. *See* Humpries v. Ozmint, 397 F.3d 206 (4th Cir. 2005) (en banc).

The Supreme Court has not yet addressed the converse scenario, i.e., whether a capital defendant has a constitutional right to offer as mitigation evidence the potential effect of execution on their family. The lower courts are divided concerning this issue. *Compare, e.g.*, State v. Stevens, 879 P.2d 162 (Or. 1994) (considering such evidence to be relevant mitigating evidence and reversing a death sentence when the trial court had excluded it), *with* Card v. State, 803 So. 2d 613, 628 & n.15 (Fla. 2001) (holding that such evidence is not "mitigating" and affirming a trial court's decision to exclude it during a capital sentencing hearing).

149. Bosse v. Oklahoma, 137 S. Ct. 1 (2016) (per curiam).

150. Barefoot v. Estelle, 463 U.S. 880 (1983).

151. Zant v. Stephens, 462 U.S. 862, 885 (19830; *see also* Dawson v. Delaware, 503 U.S. 159 (1992) (capital defendant's First Amendment association with a prison gang when no showing of actual violence or threats by the gang); Beam v. Paskett, 3 F.3d 1301, 1308–09 (9th Cir. 1993) (capital defendant's unorthodox sexual practices); Flanagan v. State, 846 P.2d 1053 (Nev. 1993) (capital defendant's Satanist beliefs and practices).

National Institute for Trial Advocacy

the capital offense, though, may be admitted.[152] An open question that has divided the lower courts is whether evidence of a capital defendant's alleged, unadjudicated crimes can be introduced during the capital sentencing phase (typically to prove future dangerousness); and, if so, whether jurors must be instructed that, to consider them in aggravation of punishment, jurors must find beyond a reasonable doubt that such unadjudicated crimes were committed by the capital defendant.[153]

Although the Supreme Court in *Dobbert v. Florida* held that a post-*Furman* capital sentencing statute may be applied to a pre-*Furman* murder without violating the Ex Post Facto Clause,[154] *Dobbert* does not foreclose all ex post facto claims in the capital sentencing context.[155] For instance, the prosecution cannot rely on an eligibility aggravating factor enacted after the date of a capital offense.[156] However, many courts have permitted reliance on post-offense selection aggravating factors (including nonstatutory aggravators),[157] although some courts have held that the prosecution cannot rely on such an aggravating factor that was not authorized at the time of the capital offense, even if there are other valid eligibility aggravators that exist, because the new factor may increase the chance of a death sentence.[158]

A defendant must be given pretrial notice that the prosecution will be seeking the death penalty,[159] but a majority of the Supreme Court has not yet addressed whether the Eighth Amendment requires advance notice of particular aggravating evidence that the prosecution intends to introduce during the capital sentencing phase.[160]

---

152. Barclay v. Florida, 463 U.S. 939, 948–50 (1983) (plurality) (capital defendant's racist motivations in committing murder).

153. *See* Williams v. Lynaugh, 484 U.S. 935 (1987) (Marshall, J., joined by Brennan, J., dissenting from the denial of certiorari); Hatch v. Oklahoma, 58 F.3d 1447, 1466–67 (10th Cir. 1995); *see also* Steven P. Smith, *Unreliable and Prejudicial: The Use of Extraneous Unadjudicated Offenses in the Penalty Phases of Capital Trials*, 93 COLUM. L. REV. 1249 (June 1993) (discussing the various approaches of the lower courts).

154. Dobbert v. Florida, 432 U.S. 282 (1977).

155. *Dobbert* was decided at a time when the Supreme Court's ex post facto analysis was based on a "substantive/procedural" dichotomy that since has been modified. *See* United States v. Church, 151 F. Supp. 2d 715, 719–20 (W.D. Va. 2001). Furthermore, *Ring's* treatment of "eligibility" aggravators as "elements" of a capital offense renders *Dobbert*—which was decided in pre-*Ring* era—inapposite to eligibility aggravators. *See* United States v. Higgs, 353 F.3d 281, 301 (4th Cir. 2003).

156. *Higgs*, 353 F.3d at 301; State v. Hootman, 709 So. 2d 1357, 1360–61 (Fla. 1998).

157. *See, e.g.*, United States v. McVeigh, 944 F. Supp. 1478, 1486 (D. Colo. 1996).

158. *See* Bowen v. State, 911 S.W.2d 555, 562–63 (Ark. 1995) (new "cruel and depraved" aggravating factor, enacted in 1993, impermissible ex post facto law when retroactively applied to 1991 capital murder).

159. Lankford v. Idaho, 500 U.S. 110 (1991).

160. Gray v. Netherland, 518 U.S. 152, 169–70 (1996) (holding that such a constitutional requirement would be a new rule that cannot be applied retroactively on federal habeas corpus review); *but see id.* at 180–86 (Ginsburg, J., joined by Stevens, Souter & Breyer, JJ., dissenting) (holding that such a rule was dictated by existing precedent).

12.2.2 *Eighth Amendment Requirements Regarding Mitigating Factors*

In a long line of post-*Furman* decisions, the Supreme Court has held that the Cruel and Unusual Punishments Clause of the Eighth Amendment requires that the capital sentencer—whether a judge or jury—must "be able to consider," must "not refuse to consider," and must be able to "give effect" to a capital defendant's mitigating evidence under the applicable law and the trial court's jury instructions.[161] The Court has broadly defined "mitigating evidence" as being any evidence "which tends logically to prove or disprove some fact or circumstance which a factfinder could reasonably deem to have mitigating value."[162] Such evidence includes anything that relates to a defendant's character, history, or the circumstances of the offense that would support a sentence less than death, including, for example, a defendant's history of child abuse or an underprivileged childhood; a defendant's relatively young age at the time of the crime (e.g., a nineteen-year-old capital defendant); a defendant's mental or emotional problems at the time of the crime; the fact that a defendant was intoxicated on drugs or alcohol at the time of the crime; and a defendant's good conduct in jail while awaiting trial.[163]

In applying this Eighth Amendment doctrine, the Court has reversed death sentences when there was a "reasonable likelihood" that jury instructions precluded even a single juror (among the twelve) from considering or "giving effect" to mitigating evidence that was introduced during the trial or sentencing phase.[164] Likewise, the Court has reversed death sentences when a trial court excluded mitigating evidence.[165] Because a capital sentencer must be able to consider and give mitigating effect to all mitigating evidence before deciding to impose the death penalty,

---

161. Hitchcock v. Dugger, 481 U.S. 393, 394 (1987); *see also* Lockett v. Ohio, 438 U.S. 586 (1978); Eddings v. Oklahoma, 455 U.S. 104 (1982); Skipper v. South Carolina, 476 U.S. 1 (1986); Mills v. Maryland, 486 U.S. 367 (1988); Penry v. Lynaugh, 492 U.S. 302 (1989); McKoy v. North Carolina, 494 U.S. 433 (1990); Penry v. Johnson, 532 U.S. 782 (2001); Abdul-Kabir v. Quarterman, 550 U.S. 233 (2007).

162. Smith v. Texas, 543 U.S. 37, 44 (2004).

163. *See, e.g., id.* at 44 (low IQ, even if it does not qualify as mental retardation); *Penry*, 532 U.S. at 788–89, 803–04 (child abuse); Johnson v. Texas, 509 U.S. 350, 367 (1993) (defendant's youth, i.e., nineteen years of age, at the time of the crime); Parker v. Dugger, 498 U.S. 308, 314 (1991) (defendant's "difficult childhood" and intoxication at the time of the crime); *Hitchcock*, 481 U.S. at 397–99 (underprivileged childhood and mental impairment resulting from childhood substance abuse); *Skipper*, 476 U.S. at 5 (defendant's good behavior in jail while awaiting trial); *Eddings*, 455 U.S. at 115 ("difficult family history," emotional disturbance at the time of the offense, and defendant's youth at the time of the offense).

164. *See, e.g., Penry*, 532 U.S. at 788–89, 803–04 (jury instructions precluded jury from giving mitigating effect to defendant's evidence of mental impairment and history of child abuse); *McKoy*, 494 U.S. at 442–44 (jury instructions impermissibly required jurors to be unanimous about existence of each mitigating factor before it could be considered); *Hitchcock*, 481 U.S. at 397–99 (jury instructions precluded jurors from considering defendant's mitigating evidence of a mental impairment and disadvantaged childhood).

165. *See, e.g., Skipper*, 476 U.S. at 7–9 (trial court improperly excluded mitigating evidence of defendant's good behavior in jail while awaiting trial).

National Institute for Trial Advocacy

the Court also has invalidated mandatory death sentences, including a mandatory sentence for the murder of a prison guard by an inmate already serving a life sentence.[166]

The Supreme Court has stressed that during the selection process of the capital sentencing phase, the trial court's instructions to the jury need not specify a "laundry list" of aggravating and mitigating factors and need not require any type of mathematical weighing of factors as long as jurors are not precluded from considering and giving meaningful effect to all mitigating evidence.[167] Indeed, the selection process can involve virtually "unbridled discretion" (subject only to a limitation on vague or overbroad aggravating factors).[168]

With respect to the constitutional requirement that jury instructions must permit jurors to "give effect" to all mitigating evidence offered by the defense during the selection process, the Court's decisions appear to conflict. In 1993, in *Johnson v. Texas*,[169] the Court held that a state has discretion to "structure" jurors' consideration of mitigating evidence. Five justices in *Johnson* held—over a vigorous dissenting opinion by Justice O'Connor—that jury instructions do not run afoul of the Eighth Amendment if they permit jurors to give some meaningful effect to particular types of mitigating evidence, even if they do not permit jurors to give "full" effect to the evidence.[170] However, in a series of recent decisions, a bare majority of the Court, citing Justice O'Connor's dissenting opinion in *Johnson*, has held that jury instructions must give a capital sentencing jury the ability to give "full effect" to mitigating evidence.[171]

Although the Supreme Court has held that a mandatory death penalty is unconstitutional insofar as it violates the Court's mitigation doctrine,[172] the Court has approved a state law that requires jurors to impose a death sentence if they find at least one aggravating factor and do not find any mitigating factors or if a jury concludes that one or more mitigating factors do not outweigh the aggravating factor(s).[173]

---

166. Sumner v. Shuman, 483 U.S. 66 (1987).
167. Buchanan v. Angelone, 522 U.S. 269 (1998) (upholding capital sentencing scheme in which the prosecution was required to prove an eligibility aggravating factor and the defense was permitted to offer mitigating evidence without limitation, but the trial court refused to instruct jurors concerning specific mitigating factors and refused to instruct jurors on the concept of mitigation); *accord* Weeks v. Angelone, 528 U.S. 225 (2000) (upholding such a capital sentencing scheme even when jurors asked about an instruction on mitigation).
168. Tuilaepa v. California, 512 U.S. 967, 979–80 (1994).
169. Johnson v. Texas, 509 U.S. 350 (1993).
170. *Johnson*, 509 U.S. at 369–73 (holding that as long as capital sentencing instructions give jurors the ability to give some meaningful effect to mitigating evidence, the instructions are constitutional; rejecting dissent's argument that instructions must allow "full" effect to be given to mitigating evidence, *see id*. at 379–80 (dissent)).
171. Smith v. Texas, 543 U.S. 37, 39 (2004) (per curiam); *Penry*, 532 U.S. at 797 (2002).
172. *Sumner*, 483 U.S. at 78–85.
173. Blystone v. Pennsylvania, 494 U.S. 299 (1989); *see also* Kansas v. Marsh, 548 U.S. 163 (2006).

12.2.3 "Death Is Different"/"Heightened Reliability" Jurisprudence

In addition to the foregoing constitutional requirements regarding aggravating and mitigating evidence, the Supreme Court has set forth a series of constitutional rules that recognize that "death is qualitatively different"[174] from noncapital criminal punishments and, thus, apply only in capital cases. Those special rules include: 1) a ban on a capital resentencing if a defendant originally received a life sentence from a judge or jury, but later successfully appealed the conviction and the case was then remanded for a retrial;[175] 2) the constitutional requirement that, when the evidence offered during the guilt-innocence phase of a capital trial would permit a rational jury to acquit the defendant of the capital offense and convict him for a lesser included noncapital offense under the applicable penal law, a lesser included offense instruction must be submitted if requested by the capital defendant;[176] 3) the rule that a capital sentencer cannot consider ex parte aggravating evidence that has not been disclosed to the defense at or before the sentencing hearing;[177] 4) the application of the *Miranda* exclusionary rule to a custodial statement given

---

174. Woodson v. North Carolina, 428 U.S. 280, 305 (1976) (plurality); *see also Eddings*, 455 U.S. at 117–18 (1982) (O'Connor, J., concurring) ("[T]his Court has gone to extraordinary measures to ensure that the prisoner sentenced to be executed is afforded a process that will guarantee, as much as humanly possible, that the sentence was not imposed out of whim, passion, prejudice, or mistake.").

175. Bullington v. Missouri, 451 U.S. 430 (1981); Arizona v. Rumsey, 467 U.S. 203 (1984); *but cf.* Sattazahn v. Pennsylvania, 537 U.S. 101 (2003) (no double jeopardy violation if death sentence imposed at a resentencing in a case in which a life sentence originally was imposed automatically under state law because of a deadlocked jury). For a discussion of the Double Jeopardy Clause and noncapital sentencing, see section 12.1.7.

The related collateral estoppel doctrine's application to aggravating factors has resulted in some confusion in the law. *Compare, e.g.*, Poland v. Arizona, 476 U.S. 147, 155–57 (1986) (although not explicitly invoking the collateral estoppel doctrine, holding that trial court's finding of insufficient evidence of one of two aggravating factors at first capital sentencing hearing where death sentence was imposed did not foreclose prosecution from relying on the same aggravating factors at the resentencing following the defendant's successful appeal of initial death sentence); Hill v. State, 962 S.W.2d 762, 766 (Ark. 1998) (holding same, yet explicitly addressing collateral estoppel doctrine), *with* Delap v. Dugger, 890 F.2d 285, 314 (11th Cir. 1989) (applying collateral estoppel doctrine to bar aggravating factor at capital sentencing phase based on insufficient evidence of same aggravating fact during guilt-innocence phase); Ex parte Mathes, 830 S.W.2d 596 (Tex. Crim. App. 1992) (plurality) (defendant given life sentence at first trial involving one of two murder victims after jury concluded he was not a future danger; appeals court applied collateral estoppel doctrine to prevent state from relying on "future dangerousness" aggravator at capital trial of defendant involving second murder victim).

176. *See* Beck v. Alabama, 447 U.S. 625 (1980); *but cf.* Hopkins v. Reeves, 524 U.S. 88 (1998) (lesser offense instruction not required when under applicable state law the "lesser" offense is not considered to be a "lesser included" offense of capital murder offense); Schad v. Arizona, 501 U.S. 624, 645–48 (1991) (lesser included offense instruction on one lesser offense not required when the trial court has submitted an instruction on a different lesser included offense). For a discussion of lesser included offense instructions in noncapital cases, see Chapter Ten.

177. Gardner v. Florida, 430 U.S. 349 (1977) (plurality). *Gardner* overruled this aspect of the pre-*Furman* decision of Williams v. New York, 337 U.S. 241 (1949), which is discussed *supra* in the context of noncapital sentencing.

by a defendant that is offered during the capital sentencing phase;[178] and 5) the defendant's right to have all prospective jurors questioned during voir dire concerning their views on race when the alleged capital murder was interracial (the defendant and victim were of different races).[179]

It should be noted, however, that the Supreme Court has not imported all of the constitutional rules of criminal procedure applicable to the guilt-innocence phase of a criminal trial to the capital sentencing phase.[180] Whether the Supreme Court's decision in *Ring v. Arizona*[181]—treating "eligibility" aggravating factors in the capital sentencing phase as "elements" of the capital offense for constitutional purposes—will result in the extension of additional guilt-innocence phase protections to the capital sentencing process is subject to an ongoing debate in the lower courts.[182]

In addition to creating a constitutional double standard for certain rules of criminal procedure in the capital sentencing context, the Supreme Court also has adopted certain constitutional rules uniquely applicable to the capital sentencing phase that, in the Court's view, result in "heightened reliability"[183] in the capital sentencing process. Such special rules include: 1) the submission of a jury instruction informing jurors that a "life" sentence means life without parole if a capital defendant's "future dangerousness" is an aggravating circumstance and also if under applicable law a "life" sentence actually means life without parole;[184] 2) a

178. Estelle v. Smith, 451 U.S. 454, 466–69 (1981); *see also* Powell v. Texas, 492 U.S. 680 (1989) (per curiam). The *Miranda* exclusionary rule does not apply in the noncapital sentencing context. *See* Chapter Six.
179. Turner v. Murray, 476 U.S. 28 (1986). As discussed in Chapter Seven, there is no such automatic right (as a constitutional matter) in a noncapital case involving an interracial offense.
180. *See Gardner*, 430 U.S. at 358 n.9 (plurality) (noting that "the entire panoply of criminal trial procedure rights" does not apply at the capital sentencing phase); *see also* Christopher K. Tahbaz, *Fairness to the End: The Right to Confront Adverse Witnesses in Capital Sentencing Proceedings*, 89 COLUM. L. REV. 1345, 1347 (Oct. 1989) (contending that the Sixth Amendment right to confront adverse witnesses should be extended to the capital sentencing phase, yet noting that the Supreme Court has not yet done so in the post-*Furman* era).
181. Ring v. Arizona, 536 U.S. 584 (2002); *see also* Hurst v. Florida, 136 S. Ct. 616 (2016) (applying *Ring* to invalidate Florida's capital sentencing statute, which did not require a jury to find at least one aggravating factor before a trial judge could impose a death sentence).
182. *See, e.g.*, United States v. Fell, 217 F. Supp. 2d 469 (D. Vt. 2002), *reversed*, 360 F.3d 135 (2d Cir. 2004) (Second Circuit reversed district court's decision that in view of *Ring*, the Confrontation Clause applies to evidence introduced in support of an eligibility aggravating factor).
183. Caldwell v. Mississippi, 472 U.S. 320, 329 n.2 (1985) (citation and internal quotation marks omitted).
184. Simmons v. South Carolina, 512 U.S. 154 (1994); Kelly v. South Carolina, 534 U.S. 246 (2002); Lynch v. Arizona, 136 S. Ct. 1818 (2016) (per curiam); *but cf.* California v. Ramos, 463 U.S. 992 (1983) (holding that it is not unconstitutional to accurately instruct a capital sentencing jury that a life sentence is not necessarily one without any possibility of release under the state's law). To date, the Court has not yet extended *Simmons* to situations when a life sentence means something less than "life without parole," although the Court has not foreclosed doing so in a future case on direct (as opposed to collateral) review. *See* Ramdass v. Angelone, 530 U.S. 156, 179–81 (2000)

prohibition on informing jurors that an appeals court will review the validity of a death sentence imposed by the jury in a manner that improperly "shifts" jurors' "sense of responsibility" for imposing the death penalty;[185] and 3) the rule that an aggravating factor based on a defendant's prior conviction in an earlier case is invalid if, after the death sentence is imposed, the defendant's conviction in the earlier case is reversed.[186]

12.2.4 Constitutional Requirements for Selecting a Capital Sentencing Jury

A corollary of the Supreme Court's capital sentencing jurisprudence is the Court's jurisprudence related to selection of a capital sentencing jury. In *Witherspoon v. Illinois*,[187] the Court held that under the Sixth Amendment's requirement that a jury reflect a "fair cross-section" of the community and thus embody the "conscience" of the community, a prospective juror with "scruples" concerning capital punishment may not automatically be removed "for cause" from service on a capital-sentencing jury. A trial court, however, may remove a prospective juror whose anti-death-penalty position is so strong that it would "prevent or substantially impair" the person's ability to follow their oath as a juror to apply the law fairly to both sides of the case.[188] A trial court's determination that a prospective juror's anti-death penalty views would "prevent or substantially impair" their ability to fairly apply the law is given great deference on appeal.[189] A trial court's improper removal of even a

---

(O'Connor, J., concurring in the judgment) (stating that extending *Simmons* to a situation where a defendant would not necessarily receive a sentence of life without parole if a death sentence were not imposed would create a new rule that cannot be announced on habeas corpus review); *see also* Brown v. Texas, 522 U.S. 940 (1997) (opinion of Stevens, J., joined by Souter, Ginsburg, & Breyer, JJ., respecting the denial of certiorari) (in a case on direct review, suggesting that *Simmons* is applicable to life sentences when, under a state's law, a convicted capital defendant would become eligible for parole only after a lengthy period of time in prison).

185. *Caldwell*, 472 U.S. at 328–29. In Romano v. Oklahoma, 512 U.S. 1 (1994), the Court held that a *Caldwell* violation only occurs when a prosecutor or trial judge shifts jurors' sense of responsibility by misdescribing the jury's role under relevant state law. *Id.* at 8–9.

186. Johnson v. Mississippi, 486 U.S. 578 (1988).

187. Witherspoon v. Illinois, 391 U.S. 510 (1968). A prosecutor may remove such a person with a peremptory strike without violating the *Witherspoon* rule. Gray v. Mississippi, 481 U.S. 648, 671–72 (1987) (Powell, J., concurring in part and concurring in the judgment). *Witherspoon* only applies to for-cause challenges to prospective jurors. *Id.* For a discussion of the difference between "peremptory" and "for cause" challenges during the jury selection process, see Chapter Seven.

188. *Gray*, 481 U.S. at 658; *see also* Uttecht v. Brown, 551 U.S. 1 (2007); Wainwright v. Witt, 469 U.S. 412 (1985); Adams v. Texas, 448 U.S. 38 (1980).

189. *See Witt*, 469 U.S. at 428–35 (treating trial court's ruling on *Witherspoon* issue as a "factual" finding concerning juror bias and, thus, requiring great deference to the trial court's ruling on federal habeas corpus review). Although such deference is required on federal habeas corpus review of a state court judgment, the Supreme Court has not yet addressed the issue of whether such deference is required on direct review of a state court's judgment. *See* Mead v. Texas, 465 U.S. 1041, 1043–49 (1984) (Rehnquist, J., joined by Burger, C.J., & O'Connor, J., dissenting from the denial of certiorari); *cf.* Hernandez v. New York, 500 U.S. 352, 364–69 (1991) (holding that a trial court's

single prospective juror for cause in violation of *Witherspoon* will result in automatic reversal of a death sentence on appeal (even if the prosecution could have removed the prospective juror with a peremptory strike).[190]

In *Morgan v. Illinois*,[191] the Supreme Court addressed the "reverse-*Witherspoon*" scenario, i.e., the situation when a prospective juror in a capital case has pro-death-penalty views. Consonant with its *Witherspoon* jurisprudence, the Court in *Morgan* held that such persons cannot sit on a capital-sentencing jury if their pro-death-penalty views would "prevent or substantially impair" their ability to follow their oath as a juror to follow the applicable law.[192] The Court's holding rested on a defendant's Sixth Amendment right to an impartial jury, but also implicated the Eighth Amendment insofar as a capital sentencer must be willing to consider mitigating evidence in deciding whether to impose a death sentence.[193] *Morgan* also held that during voir dire in a capital case, the trial court must sufficiently question prospective jurors about their pro-death-penalty views in a manner that permits the removal of persons with opinions that would prevent them from serving on a capital sentencing jury.[194]

Justice Scalia's dissenting opinion in *Morgan* suggested that the majority's holding logically would require prospective jurors in capital cases to be questioned about whether they could consider particular types of mitigating evidence and further would require the removal of prospective jurors unwilling to "consider" specific types of mitigating evidence.[195] Since *Morgan*, the Supreme Court has not addressed whether the Court's holding extends as far as the dissent suggested, and the lower courts are divided on the issue.[196]

---

finding that a peremptory strike was not racially motivated is a factual finding reviewed for "clear error" on direct appeal). In Greene v. Georgia, 519 U.S. 145 (1996) (per curiam), the Court held that state appellate courts are not constitutionally required to defer to a state trial court's ruling on a *Witherspoon* issue, but did not address whether the Supreme Court (or a federal court of appeals) would be required to afford such deference on a direct appeal. *Id.* at 146–17.

190. *Gray*, 481 U.S. at 664–68.

191. Morgan v. Illinois, 504 U.S. 719 (1992).

192. *Id.* at 729.

193. *Id.* at 729, 737–39.

194. *Id.* at 732–36.

195. *Id.* at 744 n.3 (Scalia, J., joined by Rehnquist, C.J., & Thomas, J., dissenting) ("Presumably, under today's decision a [prospective] juror who thinks a 'bad childhood' is never mitigating must also be excluded.").

196. *Compare, e.g.*, State v. Williams, 831 So. 2d 835, 845–48 (La. 2002) (agreeing with footnote 3 of Justice Scalia's dissenting opinion in *Morgan*), *with* Holland v. State, 705 So. 2d 307, 339 (Miss. 1997) (holding that the defense in a capital trial has no right to question prospective jurors concerning whether they would refuse to consider certain specific types of mitigating evidence).

12.2.5 Appellate Review and Clemency in Death Penalty Cases

Although the Supreme Court has held that there is no constitutional right to appeal in a noncapital criminal case,[197] the Court repeatedly has suggested that there is at least a limited right to appeal in death penalty cases.[198] The Court further has spoken of the need for "meaningful appellate review" of death sentences and that an appellate court, like a trial court or sentencing jury, may not refuse to consider any mitigating evidence offered in the trial court in performing appellate review of a death sentence.[199] However, the Supreme Court has held that in performing such appellate review, an appeals court is not required to engage in "comparative proportionality review" and compare the appropriateness of a death sentence in a particular case with all other capital prosecutions in the same jurisdiction in which a life or death sentence was imposed.[200]

Almost all of the Supreme Court's post-*Furman* decisions concerning appellate review have addressed harmless-error review[201] of Eighth Amendment violations related to aggravating factors. "An appellate court may choose to consider whether absent an invalid [aggravating] factor, the jury would have reached the same verdict or it may choose instead to consider whether the result would have been the same had the invalid aggravating factor [been submitted in a constitutional manner]."[202] Alternatively, state appellate courts also are permitted to reweigh the mitigating factors against the remaining, valid aggravating factors and decide whether a death

---

197. *See* Chapter Fourteen.

198. *See* Parker v. Dugger, 498 U.S. 308, 321 (1991); Pulley v. Harris, 465 U.S. 37, 45 (1984); *id.* at 54–57 (Stevens, J., concurring in part and concurring in judgment); *see also* State v. Creighton, 469 So. 2d 735, 740 n.8 (Fla. 1995). In dicta, four justices (in a plurality opinion) rejected the notion that there is a constitutional right to collateral review (as opposed to direct review) in a death penalty case. Murray v. Giarratano, 492 U.S. 1, 10 (1989) (plurality).

199. *See, e.g., Parker,* 498 U.S. at 321.

200. *Pulley,* 465 U.S. at 43–44.

201. *See, e.g.,* Jones v. United States, 527 U.S. 373, 402–03 (1999); Sochor v. Florida, 504 U.S. 527 (1992); Richmond v. Lewis; 506 U.S. 40 (1992); Clemons v. Mississippi, 494 U.S. 738 (1990); Zant v. Stephens, 462 U.S. 862 (1983); Barclay v. Florida, 463 U.S. 939 (1983).

   In cases in which a state appellate court does not opt to independently reweigh aggravating and mitigating factors when mitigating evidence was unconstitutionally excluded from consideration by a capital sentencing jury, the Supreme Court has assumed—but never expressly decided—that constitutional harmless-error analysis would be appropriate. *See, e.g.,* Hitchcock v. Dugger, 481 U.S. 393, 399 (1987). The lower courts have issued inconsistent decisions concerning this issue. *Compare* Nelson v. Quarterman, 472 F.3d 287, 314–15 (5th Cir. 2006) (en banc) (refusing to engage in harmless-error review of erroneous jury instructions that precluded consideration of mitigating evidence), *with* McKinney v. Ryan, 813 F.3d 798, 821–22 (9th Cir. 2015) (en banc) (engaging in harmless-error analysis of Eighth Amendment violation involving a state court's refusal to consider relevant mitigating evidence in a death penalty case).

202. *Jones,* 527 U.S. at 402–03. The Supreme Court formerly had a bifurcated harmless-error standard depending on whether a particular jurisdiction was a "weighing" or "non-weighing" capital sentencing statute. In *Brown v. Sanders,* 546 U.S. 212 (2006), the Court abolished the distinction. *See id.; see also* Karen Lamprey, Brown v. Sanders: *Invalid Factors and Appellate Review in Capital Sentencing,* 84 DENV. U. L. REV. 743 (2006).

sentence is appropriate.[203] Similarly, a state appellate court may reweigh aggravating and mitigating factors when a trial court wrongly refused to consider (or excluded a capital sentencing jury's consideration of) a specific mitigating factor.[204]

After a death row inmate has exhausted all direct and collateral appeals, they are entitled to some type of executive clemency review in all jurisdictions. Although a death row inmate has no constitutional right to such consideration for clemency, a plurality of the Supreme Court held that minimal procedural protections are required under the Due Process Clause, while four justices contended that no due process protections apply during the executive clemency process.[205]

12.3 Leading Supreme Court Decisions Concerning Sentencing

Noncapital Sentencing Cases

- *Townsend v. Burke*, 334 U.S. 736 (1948) (sentencing based on untrue or inherently unreliable information or evidence violates due process).

- *Williams v. New York*, 337 U.S. 241 (1949) (sentencing court need not disclose specific prejudicial information that the probation officer relied on in preparation of presentence report; Confrontation Clause inapplicable at sentencing phase), overruled in part by *Gardner v. Florida*, 430 U.S. 349 (1977) (in capital cases, sentencing court must disclose prejudicial information to defense at sentencing hearing).

- *Burgett v. Texas*, 389 U.S. 109 (1967) (prior, uncounseled convictions obtained in violation of Sixth Amendment right to counsel may not be used to enhance a defendant's sentence in a subsequent prosecution; defendant has a constitutional right to "collaterally" challenge such prior, uncounseled convictions during the sentencing phase of the subsequent prosecution).

- *North Carolina v. Pearce*, 395 U.S. 711 (1969) (discussing "judicial vindictiveness" doctrine applicable to higher sentences imposed by a trial judge at resentencing following a remand from a successful appeal).

- *Gagnon v. Scarpelli*, 411 U.S. 778 (1973) (setting forth constitutional procedural protections applicable to probation and parole revocations,

---

203. *Clemons*, 494 U.S. at 748–49.
204. McKinney v. Arizona, 140 S. Ct. 702 (2020).
205. *Compare* Ohio Adult Parole Authority v. Woodward, 523 U.S. 272, 284–85 (1998) (plurality op. of Rehnquist, C.J., joined by Scalia, Kennedy, & Thomas, JJ.) (no due process protections during capital clemency review), *with id.* at 288–89 (O'Connor, J., joined by Souter, Ginsburg, & Breyer, JJ., concurring in judgment) ("minimal" due process protections must be afforded).

including a limited right to counsel and somewhat limited right to confront witnesses).

- *Missouri v. Hunter*, 459 U.S. 359 (1983) (multiple sentences imposed in the same proceeding for two convictions constituting the "same offense" within the meaning of *Blockburger v. United States*, 284 U.S. 299 (1932), violate the Double Jeopardy Clause unless the legislature specifically intended for such multiple sentences).

- *Spaziano v. Florida*, 468 U.S. 447 (1984) (no right to jury sentencing in capital or noncapital cases).

- *Miller v. Florida*, 482 U.S. 423 (1987) (retroactive application of mandatory sentencing guideline or statute that increases a defendant's sentence for preenactment offense violates the Ex Post Facto Clause).

- *Alabama v. Smith*, 490 U.S. 794 (1989) (limiting *Pearce*'s "presumption of vindictiveness" to cases in which the same trial judge imposes a higher sentence on remand following successful appeal of a conviction at trial or appeal of the original sentence).

- *Dawson v. Delaware*, 503 U.S. 159 (1992) (defendant's sentence may not be increased based on their First Amendment expression or conduct when there is no "nexus" to the offense or otherwise no valid state interest in punishing the defendant for such First Amendment expression or conduct).

- *Custis v. United States*, 511 U.S. 485 (1994) (at sentencing, defendant possesses no constitutional right to collaterally challenge a prior conviction being used to enhance their sentence except on the ground that the prior conviction was obtained in violation of the right to the assistance of counsel).

- *Nichols v. United States*, 511 U.S. 738 (1994) (a defendant possesses no right to collaterally attack a prior, uncounseled misdemeanor conviction being used to enhance their sentence in a subsequent case if they possessed no right to counsel in the prior misdemeanor case).

- *Monge v. California*, 524 U.S. 721 (1998) (no double jeopardy protection against resentencing in a noncapital case).

- *United States v. Bajakajian*, 524 U.S. 321 (1998) (extremely limited review of whether a criminal fine is "excessive" under the Eighth Amendment).

- *Pennsylvania Board of Probation and Parole v. Scott*, 524 U.S. 357 (1998) (refusing to apply the Fourth Amendment exclusionary rule to unconstitutionally seized evidence offered during probation or parole revocation hearing; presumably, exclusionary rule likewise does not apply at original sentencing hearing).

- *Mitchell v. United States*, 526 U.S. 314 (1999) (sentencing court may not increase defendant's sentence based on their refusal to incriminate self at sentencing hearing, at least when a defendant specifically invokes their constitutional privilege against self-incrimination in response to the court's stated intention to increase the sentence based on the defendant's silence).

- *Apprendi v. New Jersey*, 530 U.S. 466 (2000) (except for a defendant's prior conviction, any fact that, if proved, would raise the available statutory maximum sentence is an "element" of the offense that must be submitted to a jury and proven beyond a reasonable doubt unless admitted by the defendant at a guilty plea proceeding).

- *Glover v. United States*, 531 U.S. 198 (2001) (noncapital as well as capital sentencing phase is a "critical stage" of the prosecution under the Sixth Amendment and, thus, a defendant has a right to the effective assistance of counsel; lawyer's deficient performance that results in any increase in defendant's sentence amounts to ineffective assistance of counsel).

- *Ewing v. California*, 538 U.S. 11 (2003) (providing for extremely limited Eighth Amendment "proportionality" review of a prison sentence).

- *Blakely v. Washington*, 542 U.S. 296 (2004) (applying *Apprendi* to mandatory sentencing guidelines and holding that, other than a prior conviction, any fact that, if proved, would raise the defendant's maximum guidelines sentence must be submitted to a jury and proven beyond a reasonable doubt, unless admitted by the defendant at a guilty plea hearing).

- *United States v. Booker*, 543 U.S. 220 (2005) (applying *Blakely* to U.S. Sentencing Guidelines and, as a remedy, holding that federal guidelines are merely "advisory" rather than "mandatory").

- *Cunningham v. California*, 549 U.S. 270 (2007) (applying *Blakely* to California's mandatory state sentencing guidelines).

- *Graham v. Florida*, 560 U.S. 48 (2010) (Eighth Amendment prohibits imposition of a life without parole prison sentence on a juvenile offender convicted of a nonhomicide offense).

- *Miller v. Alabama*, 567 U.S. 460 (2012) (Eighth Amendment prohibits imposition of a mandatory life without parole prison sentence on a juvenile offender convicted of a homicide offense).

- *Alleyne v. United States*, 570 U.S. 99 (2013) (applying *Apprendi* to hold that any fact that triggers a statutory mandatory minimum sentence is an "element" that must be submitted to a jury and proved beyond a reasonable doubt unless the defendant pleads guilty to such fact; overruling *Harris v. United States*, 536 U.S. 545 (2002)).

- *Betterman v. Montana*, 136 S. Ct. 1609 (2016) (Sixth Amendment right to a speedy trial does not apply to sentencing).

- *Timbs v. Indiana*, 139 S. Ct. 682 (2019) (holding that the Eighth Amendment prohibition against "excessive fines" applies to the states as well as the federal government).

Capital Sentencing Cases

- *Furman v. Georgia*, 408 U.S. 238 (1972) (invalidating capital punishment as applied in United States in 1972 as "cruel and unusual punishment" in violation of the Eighth Amendment).

- "1976 Cases": *Gregg v. Georgia*, 428 U.S. 153 (1976) (affirming facial validity of Georgia's post-*Furman*, "nonweighing" capital sentencing statute); *Proffitt v. Florida*, 428 U.S. 242 (1976) (affirming facial validity of Florida's post-*Furman*, "weighing" capital sentencing statute); *Jurek v. Texas*, 428 U.S. 262 (1976) (affirming facial validity of Texas's post-*Furman* capital sentencing statute that pivoted on a capital sentencing jury's finding that a capital defendant posed a "continuing threat" to society if not executed); *Woodson v. North Carolina*, 428 U.S. 280 (1976) (invaliding North Carolina's post-*Furman* mandatory death penalty); *Roberts v. Louisiana*, 428 U.S. 325 (1976) (invalidating Louisiana's post-*Furman* mandatory death penalty).

- *Godfrey v. Georgia*, 446 U.S. 420 (1980) (vague or overbroad aggravating factors in capital sentence phase violated the Eighth Amendment; however, state courts may interpret facially vague aggravating factors in a manner that renders them constitutional).

- *Beck v. Alabama*, 447 U.S. 625 (1980) (lesser included noncapital offense instruction must be submitted on request of defense in capital cases if a rational jury could acquit defendant of capital offense and convict on lesser offense, as long as supported by evidence and state law).

- *Bullington v. Missouri*, 451 U.S. 430 (1981) (when capital sentencer imposed a life sentence rather than the death penalty at the original capital sentencing hearing, Double Jeopardy Clause prevents prosecution from seeking the death penalty at a retrial following the reversal of original conviction).

- *Eddings v. Oklahoma*, 455 U.S. 104 (1982) (capital sentencer, whether judge or jury, may not "refuse to consider" mitigating evidence in deciding whether to impose capital punishment).

- *Skipper v. South Carolina*, 476 U.S. 1 (1986) (trial court may not refuse to admit mitigating evidence that capital sentencing jury could consider as a basis for a sentence of less than death penalty).

- *Gray v. Mississippi*, 481 U.S. 648 (1987) (prospective juror in a capital case with "scruples" concerning capital punishment may not be removed "for cause" unless trial court finds that the juror's views would "prevent or substantially impair" their ability to follow their oath as a juror to apply the law fairly to both sides of the case).

- *Sumner v. Shuman*, 483 U.S. 66 (1987) (mandatory death sentence unconstitutional, even for defendant who committed a capital murder while serving a sentence of life without parole, because it would exclude consideration of mitigating evidence in violation of the Eighth Amendment).

- *Mills v. Maryland*, 486 U.S. 367 (1988) (holding as unconstitutional jury instructions that foreclosed capital sentencing jurors' consideration of mitigating evidence unless jurors unanimously found a particular mitigating factor).

- *Blystone v. Pennsylvania*, 494 U.S. 299 (1989) (upholding a state capital sentencing statute that required a jury to impose death penalty if the jury found at least one aggravating factor but found no mitigating factors; distinguishing such a capital sentencing statute from a truly "mandatory" death penalty).

- *Parker v. Dugger*, 498 U.S. 308 (1991) ("meaningful appellate review" required in death penalty cases).

- *Morgan v. Illinois*, 504 U.S. 719 (1992) (prospective juror in a capital case with pro-death penalty views must be removed "for cause" if trial court finds that the juror's views would "prevent or substantially impair" their ability to follow their oath as a juror to apply the law fairly to both sides of the case, including the consideration of mitigating evidence; trial court must question members of the venire to determine if any members possess such pro-death-penalty views).

- *Simmons v. South Carolina*, 512 U.S. 154 (1994) (where applicable state law defines "life" sentence as life without parole, trial court must inform capital sentencing jury that a life sentence alternative to capital punishment means life without parole, at least where defendant's "future dangerousness" is an issue during the capital sentencing phase).

- *Tuilaepa v. California*, 512 U.S. 967 (1994) (discussing the differences between the "eligibility" and "selection" aspects of the capital sentencing phase for Eighth Amendment purposes).

- *Buchanan v. Angelone*, 522 U.S. 269 (1998) (during selection process of capital sentencing phase, Eighth Amendment does not require a capital sentencing jury to be instructed on specific mitigating factors as long as defense is not prohibited from introducing mitigating evidence and making arguments in mitigation).

- *Ring v. Arizona*, 536 U.S. 584 (2002) (applying *Apprendi* to eligibility aggravating factors in capital cases; such aggravating factors must be found by a jury beyond a reasonable doubt unless defendant admits them at guilty plea).

- *Brown v. Sanders*, 546 U.S. 212 (2006) (holding that a vague or overbroad aggravating factor does not constitute an Eighth Amendment violation if the same facts and circumstances at issue with respect to the invalid factor were given aggravating weight in another valid aggravating factor).

- *Abdul-Kabir v. Quarterman*, 550 U.S. 233 (2007) (instructions to capital sentencing jury must permit jurors to give full mitigating effect to all mitigating evidence introduced).

- *Bosse v. Oklahoma*, 137 S. Ct. 1 (2016) (per curiam) (although the Eighth Amendment permits victim impact evidence, it does not permit victims to request a death sentence rather than a life sentence).

- *Hurst v. Florida*, 136 S. Ct. 616 (2016) (applying *Ring* to invalidate Florida's former capital sentencing statute, which did not require a jury to find at least one aggravating factor before a trial judge could impose a death sentence).

- *McKinney v. Arizona*, 140 S. Ct. 702 (2020) (a capital sentencing jury, as opposed to a judge, is not constitutionally required to weigh the aggravating and mitigating factors or to make the ultimate sentencing of a life sentence or a death sentence).

CHAPTER THIRTEEN

COMMON EXTRA-RECORD POST-TRIAL CLAIMS

Every jurisdiction in the United States provides that within a certain amount of time after conviction,[1] a defendant may file a motion for new trial that seeks to set aside their conviction based on some error (usually constitutional error) having occurred during the prior proceedings. Often such claims are not discovered until long after trial (and well past the due date for a motion for a new trial) and thus are raised for the first time in a postconviction habeas corpus petition.[2] The main types of constitutional claims raised in a motion for new trial or habeas corpus petition are referred to as "extra-record" claims—meaning such claims rely at least in part on facts that are not apparent in the record of the prior proceedings.[3] Thus, such claims usually require factual development, typically at an evidentiary hearing conducted by the trial court or by submission of affidavits or by depositions.[4] Conversely, "record" claims—that is, claims based on facts apparent in the existing record—typically are raised on direct appeal.[5]

The three most common types of extra-record postconviction constitutional claims allege: 1) ineffective assistance of counsel by a defendant's prior attorney;[6] 2) prosecutorial or police misconduct that occurred before or during the trial; and 3) jury misconduct that occurred during the trial or during jury deliberations.

---

1. *See, e.g.*, FED. R. CRIM. P. 33(b)(1) & (2) (motion for new trial based on newly discovered evidence may be filed within three years of guilty verdict; all other motions for new trial must be filed within fourteen days of verdict); TEX. R. APP. P. 21.4 (motion for new trial must be filed within thirty days of sentence being imposed); *see also* Herrera v. Collins, 506 U.S. 390, 410–11 & nn.8–11 (1993) (collecting state statutes and procedural rules concerning time limits for motions for new trial).

2. Habeas corpus procedure is discussed in Chapter Fifteen.

3. *See, e.g.*, Morales v. Calderon, 85 F.3d 1387, 1388 (9th Cir. 1996); Commonwealth v. Grant, 813 A.2d 726, 736–37 (Pa. 2003).

4. *See, e.g.*, Massaro v. United States, 538 U.S. 500, 505–06 (2003).

5. Direct appeal procedure is discussed in Chapter Fourteen.

6. Under the rules of ethics, a defense lawyer cannot challenge their own conduct as ineffective. *See, e.g.*, Holmes v. Norris, 32 F.3d 1240, 1241 (8th Cir. 1994). Therefore, unless new counsel is appointed or retained by the due date for a motion for new trial, an ineffectiveness claim may not be raised until a habeas corpus petition has been filed by new counsel.

13.1 Claims of Ineffective Assistance of Counsel

As discussed in Chapter Three, the Sixth Amendment guarantees criminal defendants who are charged with all felonies and certain misdemeanors in state or federal court the right to the "assistance of coun[s]el"—including appointed counsel when a defendant cannot afford privately retained counsel.[7] The Supreme Court has interpreted this Sixth Amendment guarantee to include the "effective" assistance of counsel.[8]

There are three main types of ineffective assistance of counsel (IAC) claims: 1) a claim that defense counsel performed in an incompetent manner in some respect that actually prejudiced the defendant (a "*Strickland* claim"[9]); 2) a claim that there was a "constructive denial" of the assistance of counsel or that counsel's acts or omissions caused a "breakdown in the adversary system," thus requiring an irrebuttable presumption of prejudice to the defendant ("a *Cronic* claim"[10]); and 3) a claim that defense counsel labored under an impermissible conflict of interest without the defendant's valid waiver of the right to conflict-free counsel (a "conflict claim"). Each claim is analyzed under a different legal standard.

13.1.1 Strickland *Claims*

The first type of IAC claim—alleging defense counsel's incompetence—encompasses the vast majority of IAC scenarios and requires a defendant to establish two things to prevail: 1) that defense counsel performed "deficiently" in some respect—in other words, counsel's performance was incompetent when judged by an objective standard of competence generally applicable to criminal defense attorneys; and 2) that such deficient performance "prejudiced" the defendant.[11] Even if a defendant makes a strong showing concerning one of the two prongs, a court cannot grant relief unless both requirements are met.[12]

The first prong of the *Strickland* standard does not require "good lawyering." Rather, it measures the acts or omissions of the defense attorney in question against what courts would expect of an attorney of average competence[13] or, in the apt words of the Supreme Judicial Court of Massachusetts, "an ordinary fallible lawyer."[14]

---

7. Gideon v. Wainwright, 372 U.S. 335 (1963) (felonies); Alabama v. Shelton, 535 U.S. 654 (2002) (misdemeanors, when the sentence is a suspended jail sentence or any amount of time actually served in jail; no right to counsel if there is a fine-only sentence).
8. McMann v. Richardson, 397 U.S. 759 (1970).
9. Strickland v. Washington, 466 U.S. 668 (1984).
10. United States v. Cronic, 466 U.S. 648 (1984).
11. *Strickland*, 466 U.S. at 687–94; *see also* Wiggins v. Smith, 539 U.S. 510, 534–38 (2003) (discussing the *Strickland* standard); Rompilla v. Beard, 545 U.S. 374 (2005) (same).
12. *Strickland*, 466 U.S. at 687.
13. Riles v. McCotter, 799 F.2d 947, 954 (5th Cir. 1986) (Rubin, J., concurring, joined by Johnson, J.).
14. Commonwealth v. White, 565 N.E.2d 1185, 1189–90 (Mass. 1991).

National Institute for Trial Advocacy

The first prong is "highly deferential" to the challenged attorney and requires reviewing courts to afford a "strong presumption" that the lawyer was reasonably competent—thus erecting a relatively "high hurdle" for most defendants challenging their attorneys' competence under *Strickland*.[15]

Especially strong deference is given to legitimate "strategic" decisions made by defense counsel. If an attorney made an informed decision after a reasonable investigation to pursue one available option over another (for example, the attorney opted not to call a potential defense witness after interviewing them because it reasonably appeared that they would hurt the defense's case as much as or more than they would help it), the attorney's decision is "virtually unchallengeable" under the Sixth Amendment.[16] This strong deference to "strategic" or "tactical" decision-making recognizes that defense attorneys often are required to "make difficult choices among a number of legitimate options" and that reasonable legal minds can disagree about the best option to pursue.[17]

Merely because a challenged attorney describes their acts or omissions in a case as "strategic," however, does not insulate the acts or omissions of the attorney from scrutiny under *Strickland*; the attorney's conduct in fact must have been a reasonably informed choice after a reasonable investigation.[18] An attorney's decision not to investigate a particular matter will pass muster under *Strickland* only when the attorney's prior investigation or research made the decision to forego further investigation a reasonable conclusion at the time the decision was made.[19]

When deciding whether a defense attorney was "deficient," a reviewing court must judge the attorney's acts or omissions not based on current norms of what constitutes reasonable performance. Instead, a reviewing court must assess the attorney's acts or omissions based on the professional norms prevailing at the time of the alleged ineffectiveness.[20] This principle is important considering that many habeas corpus appeals in which defendants alleged their prior attorneys were ineffective occur decades after the alleged deficient performance.[21]

The second prong of the *Strickland* standard places the burden on the defendant to show a "reasonable probability" that "but for" the attorney's deficient

---

15. *Strickland*, 466 U.S. at 689–91; *see also* United States ex rel. McCall v. O'Grady, 908 F.2d 170, 173 (7th Cir. 1990) (*Strickland*'s first prong poses a "high hurdle").
16. *Strickland*, 466 U.S. at 690–91.
17. Lewis v. Lane, 832 F.2d 1446, 1461 (7th Cir. 1987).
18. Paine v. Massie, 339 F.3d 1194, 1200 (10th Cir. 2003); *accord* Hardwick v. Crosby, 320 F.3d 1127, 1182 (11th Cir. 2003); Silva v. Woodford, 279 F.3d 825, 846 (9th Cir. 2002); White v. McAninch, 235 F.3d 988, 995 (6th Cir. 2000); *see also Wiggins*, 539 U.S. at 521–38.
19. *See Wiggins*, 539 U.S. at 521–22; *Strickland*, 466 U.S. at 690–91.
20. *See* Maryland v. Kulbicki, 136 S. Ct. 2 (2015) (per curiam); Bobby v. Van Hook, 558 U.S. 4 (2009) (per curiam).
21. *See, e.g., Bobby, supra* (the challenged performance of the defense attorney occurred over two decades beforehand).

performance, the result of the proceeding would have been different.[22] This standard is essentially an "outcome-determinative" test[23] and makes it more difficult for a defendant to prevail than under the traditional "harmless-error" standard[24] applied to other types of constitutional violations.[25] Quantitatively speaking, *Strickland*'s reasonable probability standard requires a defendant to show that a different outcome would have occurred by a quantum of proof less than a preponderance of the evidence; qualitatively speaking, a reviewing court's "confidence in the verdict" must be "undermined."[26]

Strickland's two-prong standard applies to a defense attorney's alleged incompetence during all "critical stages" of a prosecution—including in pretrial motion practice;[27] an attorney's pretrial advice (or lack thereof) to a defendant concerning which plea to enter (including whether to accept a plea offer from the prosecutor);[28] an attorney's acts or omissions during the guilt-innocence phase of a trial;[29] and an attorney's representation of a defendant during a capital or noncapital sentencing proceeding.[30] (As discussed in Chapter Fourteen, it also applies to an attorney's representation of a defendant in connection with their first appeal.)

---

22. *Strickland*, 466 U.S. at 694–95.

23. *Id* at 697. The Court has held that *Strickland* prejudice is not solely an "outcome-determinative" test; a defendant must also show that an attorney's deficiency caused the result of the proceeding to be "unreliable" or "unfair." Lockhart v. Fretwell, 506 U.S. 364 (1993).

24. Chapman v. California, 386 U.S. 18 (1967). The harmless-error doctrine is discussed in Chapter Fourteen.

25. *See* United States v. Lott, 310 F.3d 1231, 1251–52 (10th Cir. 2002) (contrasting *Strickland* prejudice standard with *Chapman* harmless-error standard). *Strickland*'s prejudice prong differs from harmless-error analysis in another respect: without a showing of prejudice, a defendant has not established that the Sixth Amendment guarantee of the effective assistance of counsel was denied (even if their attorney performed deficiently). Harmless-error analysis applies only after a court determines that a constitutional error occurred.

26. *Strickland*, 466 U.S. at 694–95. Although the Court repeatedly has said that to establish *Strickland* prejudice, a defendant need not show by a preponderance of the evidence that the result of the proceeding would have been different, the Court also has suggested that *Strickland* prejudice and the preponderance standard are not significantly different. *See* Harrington v. Richter, 562 U.S. 86, 112 (2011).

27. Kimmelman v. Morrison, 477 U.S. 365 (1986) (defense counsel performs deficiently and prejudices the defendant under *Strickland* by failing to move to suppress material evidence in a pretrial motion when there was a reasonable probability under the facts and prevailing legal precedent that the motion would have been granted); *but cf.* Premo v. Moore, 562 U.S. 115 (2011) (counsel does not perform deficiently or prejudice the defendant by failing to move to suppress evidence in a pretrial motion when such a suppression motion would have been futile because the prosecution's other evidence that was not subject to suppression was formidable and the defendant faced a strong likelihood of conviction at trial based on that evidence).

28. Hill v. Lockhart, 474 U.S. 52 (1985); Lafler v. Cooper, 566 U.S. 156 (2012).

29. *Strickland*, 466 U.S. at 686–87; *see also* Hinton v. Alabama, 571 U.S. 263 (2014) (per curiam) (defense counsel performed deficiently in failing to challenge prosecution's expert witnesses during guilt-innocence phase of trial).

30. Glover v. United States, 531 U.S. 198 (2001); Buck v. Davis, 137 S. Ct. 759 (2017) (concluding that a defense attorney provided deficient, prejudicial performance under *Strickland* at the capital sentencing stage by calling as a defense expert a psychologist who opined that the capital defendant's African American race made him more likely to be violent in the future).

In *Hill v. Lockhart*, the Court applied *Strickland* to cases in which a defendant pleads guilty, but later alleges that their attorney was ineffective in advising them not to go to trial. The Court held that a defendant must show that there is a reasonable probability that but for a defense attorney's deficient performance, the defendant would not have pleaded guilty.[31] For all practical purposes, this requires a defendant who pleaded guilty to show a reasonable probability that they would have prevailed before or at trial (by winning a pretrial dismissal, for example, or acquittal at trial) or would have reduced their sentence by going to trial (by being convicted of a lesser-included offense at trial).[32] In *Padilla v. Kentucky*,[33] the Supreme Court held that a criminal defense counsel performs deficiently under *Strickland* by failing to advise a noncitizen defendant of the immigration consequences of a guilty plea; if the deportation consequences of a criminal conviction are clear, counsel must provide specific advice, and if the consequences are not clear, counsel need only provide a general warning.[34] The Court further held that a showing of deficiency under *Padilla* does not entitle alien defendants to relief unless they also can show "prejudice" under *Strickland*—meaning a defendant must show that there is a "reasonable probability" that but for defense counsel's failure to sufficiently warn the defendant about the immigration consequences of a guilty plea, the defendant would have insisted on going to trial.[35]

The Supreme Court addressed the converse of the situation in *Hill v. Lockhart* in two decisions in 2012.[36] The Court held that the plea bargaining phase of a criminal case is a critical stage of the prosecution under the Sixth Amendment, and thus, defense counsel has an obligation to properly advise a defendant whether to accept a plea bargain offer made by the prosecution; the fact that a defendant was convicted at a fair trial does not foreclose the ability to challenge counsel's effectiveness concerning plea bargaining.[37] In addition, a criminal defense attorney has a

---

31. *Hill*, 474 U.S. at 59–60.

32. *See* United States v. Del Rosario, 902 F.2d 55, 58 (D.C. Cir. 1990); Copas v. Comm'n of Corr., 662 A.2d 718, 729 n.18 (Conn. 1995). In other words, a defendant who wishes to withdraw their guilty plea based on alleged ineffective assistance of counsel must show not only that he had "nothing to lose" by going to trial, but also that he had "something to gain" by doing so. *Cf.* Lambert v. Blodgett, 248 F. Supp. 2d 988, 1001–04 (E.D. Wash. 2003).

33. Padilla v. Kentucky, 559 U.S. 356 (2010).

34. *Id.* at 368–71.

35. *Id.* at 374–75. In *Lee v. United States*, 137 S. Ct. 1958 (2017), the Court held that the Korean defendant had shown sufficient prejudice—namely, that if he had been advised that his guilty plea would result in mandatory deportation, he would have refused to accept the prosecution's plea offer and gone to trial (even though the evidence against him was overwhelming). The Court in *Lee* stressed that a defendant such as Lee need not show that he would have prevailed at trial—only that he would have insisted on going to trial rather than accept a guilty plea that preordained deportation. *Id.* at 1965–69.

36. Lafler v. Cooper, 566 U.S. 156 (2012); Missouri v. Frye, 566 U.S. 134 (2012).

37. *Frye*, 566 U.S. at 139–45; *Lafler*, 566 U.S. at 162–69.

constitutional obligation under the Sixth Amendment to convey prosecution's plea offer to the defendant.[38]

If a defense attorney performed deficiently under *Strickland* by failing to properly advise the defendant about whether to take a plea bargain offer (or in failing to convey the offer), then the defendant must show prejudice to have a guilty plea to a more serious offense vacated (or have the sentence reduced to what it would have been had the plea bargain occurred). "Prejudice" means a reasonable probability that the defendant would have agreed to the offer and also that the trial court would have accepted its terms.[39]

In *Buck v. Davis*,[40] the Supreme Court addressed a defense attorney's injection of racial bias against his African American client into the case. The Court found deficient performance and prejudice (notwithstanding the fact that the prosecution's case against the defendant was strong) because "[s]ome toxins can be deadly in small doses."[41]

13.1.2 Cronic *Claims*

The second type of IAC claim involves acts or omissions by defense counsel that, because of exceptionally bad lawyering or because of interference with the attorney-client relationship by the prosecution or the court, resulted in a "breakdown of the adversary system" or in a "constructive denial of the assistance of counsel."[42] Such cases are rarely established by defendants claiming ineffective assistance of counsel, but in those rare instances there is an irrebuttable presumption that the defendant was prejudiced and a new trial is required.[43] In other words, if an attorney's acts or omissions rose to the level of "*Cronic* IAC," then the defendant need not show actual prejudice under *Strickland*.[44]

The types of *Cronic* claims that courts have found meritorious involved: 1) defense counsel's sleeping or physical absence from the courtroom during an appreciable portion of the trial or other critical stage of the court proceeding;[45] 2) a trial

---

38. *Frye*, 566 U.S. at 144–47.
39. *Frye*, 566 U.S. at 146–50; *Lafler*, 566 U.S. at 169–74.
40. Buck v. Davis, 137 S. Ct. 759 (2017).
41. *Id.* at 777.
42. United States v. Cronic, 466 U.S. 648 (1984); *see also* Wright v. Van Patten, 552 U.S. 120, 124–26 (2008) (per curiam) (discussing *Cronic*); Bell v. Cone, 535 U.S. 685, 695–96 (2002) (same).
43. *See* Restrepo v. Kelly, 178 F.3d 634, 641 (2d Cir. 1999). For a thorough collection of lower cases applying (or refusing to apply) *Cronic's* irrebuttable presumption of prejudice in a wide variety of scenarios, *see* Keith Cunningham-Parmeter, *Dreaming of Effective Assistance: The Awakening of* Cronic*'s Call to Presume Prejudice from Representational Absence*, 76 TEMP. L. REV. 827 (Winter 2003).
44. *Cronic*, 466 U.S. at 659.
45. *See, e.g.*, French v. Jones, 332 F.3d 430 (6th Cir. 2003) (temporarily absent lawyer); Siverson v. O'Leary, 764 F.2d 1208 (7th Cir. 1985) (same); Burdine v. Johnson, 262 F.3d 336 (5th Cir. 2001)

court's refusal to allow defense counsel to communicate with the client during a significant period of time during the trial or a lengthy recess in the proceedings;[46] 3) defense counsel's racism or other bigotry toward the defendant that interfered with the attorney-client relationship;[47] 4) defense counsel's total failure to perform as an advocate during one or more critical stages of the proceeding;[48] and 5) an attorney whose law license had been permanently revoked at the time of their representation of a defendant or an "imposter attorney" (i.e., a person who had never passed a bar examination).[49]

Conversely, lower courts have refused to apply *Cronic*'s irrebuttable presumption of prejudice and instead have applied the *Strickland* actual prejudice standard to claims of: 1) a defense lawyer who was intoxicated on drugs or alcohol during a critical stage of the court proceedings (as long as the lawyer remained conscious);[50] 2) a defense lawyer who suffered from mental illness or other type of brain disorder during a critical stage of the proceedings;[51] 3) a defense lawyer who provided unusually "bad" or "maladroit" assistance of counsel, but who did not entirely fail to act as an advocate for the client;[52] and 4) an attorney whose law license had been temporarily suspended at the time of the representation, but who otherwise was

---

(en banc) (lawyer who dozed off repeatedly during trial); Tippins v. Walker, 77 F.3d 682 (2d Cir. 1996) (same).

46. *See* Geders v. United States, 425 U.S. 80 (1976) (trial court violated right to counsel by prohibiting defense counsel from communicating with defendant during overnight recess of trial); *but cf.* Perry v. Leeke, 488 U.S. 272 (1989) (no Sixth Amendment violation when trial court prohibited defense counsel from communicating with client during fifteen-minute recess of trial).

47. *See, e.g.*, Frazer v. United States, 18 F.3d 778, 785 (9th Cir. 1994); *but cf.* Commonwealth v. Washington, 880 A.2d 536, 543–45 (Pa. 2005) (applying *Strickland* rather than *Cronic* to claim that defense attorney had tremendous animosity toward defendant). As noted above, in *Buck v. Davis*, 137 S. Ct. 759 (2017), the Court applied *Strickland* to such a claim. However, the Court did not reject *Cronic*'s application. The argument apparently was not made by the petitioner's attorney.

48. *See, e.g.*, Mitchell v. Mason, 325 F.3d 732 (6th Cir. 2003) (defense counsel's total failure to discuss the case with client prior to trial); Quintero v. Bell, 368 F.3d 892 (6th Cir. 2004) (attorney's total failure to act as a meaningful advocate for defendant during voir dire); Appel v. Horn, 250 F.3d 203 (3d Cir. 2001) (attorney's total failure to act as an advocate for defendant during a competency hearing); Rickman v. Bell, 131 F.3d 1150 (6th Cir. 1997) (defense counsel was openly hostile toward client in front of jury and did not act as an advocate); Childress v. Johnson, 103 F.3d 1221 (5th Cir. 1997) (defense attorney was a "potted plant" at defendant's guilty plea proceeding, having entirely failed to consult with client at or before plea); Tucker v. Day, 969 F.2d 155 (5th Cir. 1992) (attorney's total failure to act as an advocate for defendant at sentencing hearing); United States v. Swanson, 943 F.2d 1070 (9th Cir. 1991) (defense counsel, who had a hostile relationship with the defendant, conceded the defendant's guilt to jurors during closing argument).

49. *See* United States v. Novak, 903 F.2d 883 (2d Cir. 1990) (citing decisions of various lower courts); *see generally* Bruce A. Green, *Lethal Fiction: The Meaning of "Counsel" in the Sixth Amendment*, 78 IOWA L. REV. 433 (March 1993); Jay M. Zitter, *Criminal Defendant's Representation by Person Not Licensed to Practice Law as Violation of Right to Counsel*, 19 A.L.R. 5th 351 (1994).

50. *See, e.g.*, Berry v. King, 765 F.2d 451 (5th Cir. 1985); People v. Garrison, 765 P.2d 419 (Cal. 1989).

51. *See, e.g.*, Dows v. Wood, 211 F.3d 480 (9th Cir. 2000); Johnson v. Norris, 207 F.3d 515 (8th Cir. 2000).

52. *See* Scarpa v. DuBois, 38 F.3d 1, 13 (1st Cir. 1994) (citing cases).

eligible to practice law (such as an attorney whose license was temporarily suspended for failure to pay bar dues).[53]

The Supreme Court's discussions of the line between *Cronic* and *Strickland* claims in *Florida v. Nixon*[54] and *Bell v. Cone*[55] suggest that a meritorious *Cronic* claim will be the very rare exception to *Strickland*'s rule. In *Nixon*, the Court held that *Cronic* did not apply to a claim that a defense attorney caused a breakdown in the adversary system when he conceded his clearly guilty client's guilt at a capital murder trial to increase the defendant's chance of avoiding the death penalty at the subsequent punishment phase, at least when the defendant had not objected to the proposed strategy (although he had not consented to it either).[56] Subsequently, in *McCoy v. Louisiana*,[57] without relying on *Cronic* but explicitly distinguishing *Nixon*, the Court found a Sixth Amendment violation when a defense attorney conceded his client's guilt at trial over the objection of the client.[58]

In *Bell*, the Court held that an attorney who failed to make any closing argument at a capital sentencing phase and who failed to offer the mitigating evidence promised in his opening statement—but who cross-examined the prosecution's witnesses and who opted not to make a closing argument to prevent an anticipated vigorous closing argument by a veteran prosecutor—did not cause a breakdown in the adversary system within the meaning of *Cronic*.[59]

In *Weaver v. Massachusetts*,[60] the Court held that a defense attorney's deficient performance that results in a "structural error"—within the meaning of the Court's appellate-review jurisprudence—does not rise to the level of a *Cronic* claim and, thus, the defendant must demonstrate *Strickland* "prejudice" to prevail.

13.1.3 Conflict-of-Interest Claims[61]

The third type of IAC claim alleges that defense counsel labored under an impermissible conflict of interest vis-à-vis the defendant. The Supreme Court's decision

---

53. *See, e.g.*, Reese v. Peters, 926 F.2d 668 (7th Cir. 1991) (citing decisions from various jurisdictions); State v. Green, 643 A.2d 18 (N.J. Super. Ct. App. Div. 1994).

54. Florida v. Nixon, 543 U.S. 175 (2004).

55. Bell v. Cone, 535 U.S. 685 (2002).

56. *Nixon*, 543 U.S. at 190–91; *but cf.* State v. Cooke, 977 A.2d 803 (Del. 2009) (finding a *Cronic* violation and presuming prejudice where defendant clearly objected to his trial attorney's admission of defendant's guilt to the jury).

57. McCoy v. Louisiana, 138 S. Ct. 1500 (2018).

58. Oddly, the Court stated: "Because a client's autonomy, not counsel's competence, is in issue, we do not apply our ineffective-assistance-of-counsel jurisprudence, Strickland v. Washington, 466 U.S. 668 (1984), or United States v. Cronic, 466 U.S. 648 (1984), to McCoy's claim." *McCoy*, 138 S. Ct. at 1510–11.

59. *Bell*, 535 U.S. at 696–98.

60. Weaver v. Massachusetts, 137 S. Ct. 1899 (2017).

61. For a related discussion of prosecutors' motions to disqualify defense counsel based on conflicts of interest, *see* Chapter Four.

in *Mickens v. Taylor*[62]—both its holding and dicta—altered the conflict-of-interest jurisprudence followed by most lower courts before *Mickens*.[63]

The Court in *Mickens* discussed three types of conflicts: multiple representation conflicts, successive representation conflicts, and other types of conflicts.[64] A "multiple representation" conflict stems from an attorney's concurrent representation of two or more codefendants charged with the same offense (whether in a joint trial or in separate trials). A "successive representation" conflict stems from an attorney's representation of a defendant in a case in which a former client is an actual or potential witness in the case. The final class includes all other types of conflicts, but usually involves an attorney's personal or financial interests that conflict with the defendant's interests (such as a situation where the attorney should withdraw as the defendant's counsel and become a defense witness).[65] For purposes of determining whether a conflict of interest exists, most courts have imputed a conflict by one member of a law firm to another member of the same law firm.[66]

13.1.3.1 "Multiple Representation" Conflicts

In multiple representation scenarios, the applicable legal standard depends on whether the defendant or defense counsel raised a timely objection to the alleged conflict and whether the trial court adequately dealt with the alleged conflict. If there was an objection to the conflict at the time that it first was apparent and the trial court did not take appropriate corrective action (appoint new counsel, for example, or secure a valid waiver[67] of the right to conflict-free counsel from the

---

62. Mickens v. Taylor, 535 U.S. 162 (2002).

63. *See* Mark W. Shiner, *Conflicts of Interest Challenges Post* Mickens v. Taylor: *Redefining the Defendant's Burden in Concurrent, Successive, and Personal Interest Conflicts*, 60 WASH. & LEE L. REV. 965 (Summer 2003). The Court's specific holdings in *Mickens* were: 1) the "automatic reversal" rule announced in Holloway v. Arkansas, 435 U.S. 475 (1978), only applies to "multiple representation" conflicts; and 2) even in multiple representation situations, *Holloway* only applies if the defense objected in a timely manner to the conflict and the trial court failed to take appropriate corrective action. The Court also suggested in dicta that its decision in Cuyler v. Sullivan, 446 U.S. 335 (1980), may not apply to any type of conflict except a multiple representation conflict (but reserved that question for resolution in a future case). *See Mickens*, 535 U.S. at 166–76.

64. *Mickens*, 535 U.S. at 167–75.

65. *See id.*

66. *See* Austin v. State, 609 A.2d 728, 731–33 & nn.2–3 (Md. 1992) (citing cases from various jurisdictions). In *Burger v. Kemp*, 483 U.S. 776 (1987), the Supreme Court assumed, without deciding, that the conflict of one member of a law firm should be imputed to another member. *Id.* at 783. A more difficult question—which has divided the lower courts—is whether the conflict of one member of a large public defender's office should be imputed to another member of the same office when the conflicted attorney has not assisted in any manner in the defense of the client. *See Austin*, 609 A.2d at 732 n.3 (citing cases).

67. For a discussion of what is required for a valid waiver of the right to conflict-free counsel, *see, e.g.,* Belmontes v. Wood, 350 F.3d 861, 884–85 (9th Cir. 2003); Alessi v. State, 969 So. 2d 430, 440 (Fla. 2007); Tyson v. District Court, 891 P.2d 984, 990–92 & nn.1–2 (Colo. 1995). Essentially, for a waiver to be valid it must be knowing, voluntary, and intelligent—meaning that the defendant must

defendant), then a reversal of the defendant's conviction is automatic without a showing of any prejudice to the defendant.[68]

Conversely, if an objection to the conflict was voiced only after a defendant was convicted—even if the defendant was unaware of the conflict until then (which is usually the case)—the conviction will be reversed only if the defendant shows 1) an actual (as opposed to hypothetical) conflict of interest and 2) such an actual conflict had an adverse effect on counsel's representation of the defendant.[69] Under *Cuyler v. Sullivan*, an actual conflict is one that results from an attorney who "actively represented [the] competing interests" of multiple clients at the same time, as opposed to a hypothetical conflict where a court must speculate about whether an attorney had divided loyalties.[70] A classic example of an actual conflict of interest that adversely affects a defendant involves a single attorney who represents both a husband and wife at a joint trial at which a plausible defense for one or both spouses was to shift blame to the other.[71] Not all multiple representation situations pose actual conflicts that adversely affect one or more of the codefendants represented by a single attorney.[72]

An adverse effect under *Cuyler* is not the same as prejudice under *Strickland*. Rather, the defendant only needs to show a "plausible" or "reasonable" alternative strategy that was not pursued by the conflicted defense attorney because of the conflict of interest—even if there is not a "reasonable probability" that the alternative strategy would have resulted in a different outcome.[73]

---

be informed of the specific nature of the conflict and fully understand how it could adversely affect their representation by the conflicted attorney. *Belmontes*, 350 F.3d at 884–85.

68. *See* Holloway v. Arkansas, 435 U.S. 475 (1978); *see also* Atley v. Ault, 191 F.3d 865 (8th Cir. 1999) (explaining *Holloway*). The scenario in which a timely objection is made almost always involves a court-appointed lawyer who is assigned to represent codefendants who are unwilling to waive an actual or potential conflict.

69. Cuyler v. Sullivan, 446 U.S. 335 (1980).

70. *Burger*, 483 U.S. at 783–84; *see also* United States v. Johnson, 569 F.2d 269, 270–71 (5th Cir. 1978) (an actual conflict exists "whenever one defendant stands to gain significantly by counsel adducing probative evidence or advancing plausible arguments that are damaging to a co-defendant whom counsel is also representing") (citation and internal quotation marks omitted). For an actual conflict to exist, the attorney in question must be aware of the circumstances giving rise to the alleged conflict. United States v. Hopkins, 43 F.3d 1116, 1118–19 (6th Cir. 1995).

71. *See, e.g.*, United States v. Pinc, 452 F.2d 507 (5th Cir. 1971).

72. *See, e.g.*, Woods v. State, 573 S.E.2d 394 (Ga. 2002) (holding that an attorney's representation of two codefendants at their joint murder trial did not involve an actual conflict of interest that adversely affected the defendants).

73. *See, e.g.*, United States v. Feyrer, 333 F.3d 110, 116 (2d Cir. 2003); Reynolds v. Chapman, 253 F.3d 1337, 1343 (11th Cir. 2001); Perillo v. Johnson, 205 F.3d 775, 806 (5th Cir. 2000); State v. Martinez-Serna, 803 P.2d 416, 418 (Ariz. 1990). The majority of lower courts have held that a defendant need only show that the alternative defense strategy that was not pursued would have been "plausible," *see, e.g.*, *Feyrer*, 333 F.3d at 116, or "reasonable," *see, e.g.*, *Reynolds*, 253 F.3d at 1343. Most lower courts additionally require a showing of a link between the actual conflict and the decision to forgo the alternative defensive strategy. *See* Allesi v. State, 969 So. 2d 430, 438–39 (Fla. 2007) (citing cases). At least one lower court, however, has held that to establish an adverse effect, a

13.1.3.2 "Successive Representation" Conflicts

In *Mickens*, the Supreme Court overruled a large number of lower court decisions by holding that only multiple representation conflicts are subject to *Holloway*'s automatic reversal rule when there was a timely objection by the defense and no corrective action by the trial court.[74] The Court also held that it is an "open question" which standard should apply to successive representation conflicts—*Cuyler* or *Strickland*.[75] Since *Mickens*, the lower courts have split over which standard to apply based on a "successive representation." Some courts have applied the *Cuyler* adverse effect standard, while others have applied the more rigorous *Strickland* prejudice standard.[76]

13.1.3.3 Other Types of Conflicts

As noted, *Mickens* limited *Holloway*'s automatic reversal rule to multiple representation conflicts. Thus, even when a timely objection was made to another type of conflict, such as one between an attorney's personal interests and the interests of the defendant, at most the *Cuyler* standard applies. Prior to *Mickens*, the lower courts were divided about whether the *Cuyler* standard applied to conflicts other than multiple or successive representation conflicts, even when a timely objection was made.[77] Since *Mickens*, the lower courts remain divided on this issue, with a majority apparently applying *Strickland* rather than *Cuyler*.[78]

13.2 Extra-Record Claims of Prosecutorial Misconduct

There are two main types of extra-record claims of prosecutorial misconduct[79] that are commonly litigated in motions for new trial as well as in habeas corpus petitions: 1) the prosecution's nondisclosure of evidence favorable to the defense (*Brady* claims[80]); and 2) the prosecution's knowing presentation of perjured

---

defendant must show that a conflicted attorney's failure to pursue the alternative strategy was "not part of a legitimate strategy," McFarland v. Yukins, 356 F.3d 688, 706–07 (6th Cir. 2004), thus applying the *Strickland* deficiency standard to *Cuyler*'s adverse effect prong.

74. Mickens v. Taylor, 535 U.S. 162, 167–68 (2002); *see also McFarland*, 356 F.3d at 700–01.

75. *Mickens*, 535 U.S. at 174–76.

76. *Compare, e.g.*, Hovey v. Ayers, 458 F.3d 892, 908 (9th Cir. 2006) (applying *Cuyler*), *with* Stewart v. Wolfenbarger, 468 F.3d 338, 351 (6th Cir. 2006) (applying *Strickland*); *see also* Scott A. Levin, *An Open Question? The Effect of* Cuyler v. Sullivan *on Successive Representation After* Mickens v. Taylor, 40 No. 1 CRIM. L. BULL. 3 (Jan. 2004).

77. *Compare, e.g.*, Spreitzer v. Peters, 114 F.3d 1435, 1451 n.7 (7th Cir. 1997) (applying *Cuyler* to all types of conflicts), *with* Beets v. Scott, 65 F.3d 1258 (5th Cir. 1995) (en banc) (applying *Strickland* to conflicts other than multiple or successive representation conflicts).

78. *Compare, e.g.*, Rubin v. Gee, 292 F.3d 396, 401–02 (4th Cir. 2002) (applying *Cuyler*), *with* Echols v. State, 127 S.W.3d 486, 493–95 (Ark. 2003) (applying *Strickland*).

79. "Record" claims of prosecutorial misconduct—such as comments on a defendant's Fifth Amendment right to silence during a jury trial—are discussed in Chapter Eight.

80. Brady v. Maryland, 373 U.S. 83 (1963).

testimony or knowing failure to correct such perjured testimony (perjury claims). Both types of claims are rooted in the Due Process Clause.[81]

13.2.1 Brady *Claims*

The first type of claim alleges that some member of the prosecution team—including prosecutors as well as law enforcement officers who worked on a case[82]—failed to timely disclose evidence to the defense that was exculpatory (i.e., was probative of the defendant's innocence or would refute the prosecution's evidence of guilt), could have been used to impeach a prosecution witness or was mitigating for sentencing purposes.[83] To prevail on such a claim, a defendant must show that the nondisclosed evidence not only was favorable to the defendant, but also was material.[84] "Materiality" under *Brady* places the burden on the defendant to show a reasonable probability that if timely disclosure of the evidence in question had been made, the result of the proceeding would have been different.[85] Just as with prejudice in the *Strickland* context, materiality in the *Brady* context does not require a showing of a different outcome by a preponderance of the evidence; rather, it requires a lesser showing, although one that undermines a court's confidence in the verdict.[86] In assessing whether nondisclosed evidence was material, a court considers all of the nondisclosed evidence cumulatively as opposed to considering each item of nondisclosed evidence discretely.[87]

To prevail under *Brady*, the defendant does not need to show that the evidence was intentionally or recklessly suppressed—the good faith (or bad faith) of the prosecutor or other member of the prosecution team in failing to disclose the evidence

---

81. Although the Due Process Clause is the source of the constitutional requirements that prosecutors disclose exculpatory evidence and not knowingly present perjured testimony or evidence, the legal rules of ethics have the same requirements. *See, e.g.*, People v. Mucklow, 35 P.3d 527 (Colo. 2000). Indeed, the legal rules of ethics require disclosure of any evidence tending to negate the defendant's guilt, whether or not it is material evidence under the constitutional standard set forth in *Brady* and *United States v. Bagley*, 473 U.S. 667 (1985). The vast majority of courts will refuse to reverse a defendant's conviction based on a violation of this ethical rule by the prosecution unless it also rises to the level of a constitutional violation. However, prosecutors who violate this ethical rule are subject to professional discipline even if the defendant's conviction is not reversed. *See Mucklow*, 35 P.3d 527.

82. United States v. Morris, 80 F.3d 1151, 1169–70 (7th Cir. 1996).

83. *See Bagley*, 473 U.S. at 676–84 (refining *Brady*'s constitutional standard related to prosecution's failure to disclose favorable evidence to the defense prior to trial); *see also* Turner v. United States, 137 S. Ct. 1885 (2017); Smith v. Cain, 566 U.S. 73 (2012); Cone v. Bell, 556 U.S. 449 (2009); Banks v. Dretke, 540 U.S. 668 (2004).

84. "Materiality" is synonymous here with "harm" or "prejudice." *See* Strickler v. Greene, 527 U.S. 263, 280–82 (1999).

85. Kyles v. Whitley, 514 U.S. 419, 433–34 (1995) (noting that the *Brady* "materiality" standard is essentially the same as the *Strickland* "prejudice" standard applicable to claims of ineffective assistance of counsel).

86. *Kyles*, 514 U.S. at 433–354.

87. *Id.* at 437–38.

is irrelevant.[88] Furthermore, the defense need not have requested the nondisclosed evidence from the prosecution before or during trial. The prosecution's duty to disclose favorable material evidence in the possession of any member of the prosecution team is automatic.[89] However, a defendant cannot complain of the nondisclosure when, through the exercise of reasonable diligence, the defense could have obtained the same evidence before or during trial from a third-party source.[90]

13.2.2 Perjury Claims

The Supreme Court has long held that it violates due process for the prosecution knowingly or recklessly[91] to present false testimony or evidence or knowingly or recklessly fail to correct false testimony from a prosecution witness during the course of the trial even if the trial prosecutor did not elicit it.[92] However, a "mere recantation" by a prosecution witness after a conviction is obtained does not necessarily violate the defendant's constitutional rights if no member of the prosecution team knew of the perjury at the time of trial.[93] A majority of the Supreme Court has never addressed the issue of whether due process is violated by keeping a conviction intact when there has been a "credible recantation" by a non-governmental

---

88. *Id.*
89. *Bagley*, 473 U.S. at 682.
90. *See, e.g.*, United States v. Fallon, 348 F.3d 248, 252–53 (7th Cir. 2003); United States v. Prior, 546 F.2d 1254, 1259 (5th Cir. 1977); Stewart v. State, 801 So. 2d 59, 70 (Fla. 2001).
91. Virtually all courts treat the prosecution's reckless presentation of false testimony or evidence as tantamount to the knowing presentation of perjury. *See, e.g.*, Smith v. Massey, 235 F.3d 1259, 1271 n.6 (10th Cir. 2000). A minority of courts have held that the negligent presentation of false testimony or evidence—i.e., the prosecutor subjectively was unaware of the false nature of the testimony or evidence, but "should have known" of it—violates due process. *See, e.g.*, United States v. Duke, 50 F.3d 571, 577–78 (8th Cir. 1995); United States v. Biberfeld, 957 F.2d 98, 102–03 (3d Cir. 1992). Courts that have found negligence to be sufficient to make out a due process perjury claim have relied on *United States v. Agurs*, 427 U.S. 97 (1976), in which the Court stated in dicta that the prosecution violates due process by presenting testimony or evidence that it "knew, or should have known" was false. *Id.* at 103. A majority of lower courts have held that this dicta did not mean that mere negligence is sufficient to make out a due process violation. *See, e.g.*, Drake v. Portuondo, 321 F.3d 338, 345 (2d Cir. 2003); Smith v. Black, 904 F.2d 950, 961–62 (5th Cir. 1990), *vacated on other grounds*, 503 U.S. 930 (1992).
92. *See, e.g.*, Napue v. Illinois, 360 U.S. 264 (1959); Alcorta v. Texas, 355 U.S. 28 (1957); Pyle v. Kansas, 317 U.S. 213 (1942); Mooney v. Holohan, 294 U.S. 103 (1935). The lower courts are divided over whether it violates due process for a prosecutor who knows that a prosecution witness committed perjury on cross-examination by defense counsel to allow the perjury to go uncorrected. *Compare, e.g.*, United States v. O'Keefe, 128 F.3d 885, 894 (5th Cir. 1997) (no duty to correct perjury elicited by defense counsel on cross-examination of a prosecution witness), *with* United States v. Bantowski, 865 F.2d 129, 133–34 (7th Cir. 1989) (duty to correct false testimony elicited on cross-examination). The Supreme Court has never explicitly addressed this issue; however, Giglio v. United States, 405 U.S. 150 (1972), involved perjury elicited on cross-examination by defense counsel. *See id.* at 151–52. Yet, in that case, the prosecutor also knowingly relied on the false fact in their closing argument. *Id.* at 152.
93. Hysler v. Florida, 315 U.S. 411, 413 (1942).

prosecution witness after trial;[94] the lower courts are divided on this question.[95] Similarly, and unlike its decisions in the *Brady* context, the Supreme Court in the perjury context has not yet imputed to a trial prosecutor the knowledge possessed by all other members of the "prosecution team."[96] The lower courts have taken divergent approaches concerning the imputation of the knowledge of a member of the prosecution team to the trial prosecutor.[97]

Unlike the type of materiality that must be shown to prevail on a *Brady* claim, the type of materiality required to prevail on a perjury claim is considerably more favorable to a defendant.[98] The perjury materiality standard is equivalent to the *Chapman* harmless-error standard applied to constitutional "trial errors" addressed by appellate courts on direct appeal.[99] That is, it requires the prosecution to prove beyond a reasonable doubt that the false testimony or evidence did not "contribute to the verdict."[100] Unlike a *Brady* claim, which places the burden on the defendant

---

94. *See* Durley v. Mayo, 351 U.S. 277, 290–91 (1956) (Douglas, J., dissenting, joined by Warren, C.J., Black, & Clark, JJ.); *see also* Jacobs v. Scott, 513 U.S. 1067 (1995) (Stevens, J., joined by Ginsburg, J., dissenting from denial of stay of execution).

95. *Compare, e.g.*, Sanders v. Sullivan, 863 F.2d 218, 226 (2d Cir. 1988) (finding due process violation when credible recantation of material trial testimony occurs and prosecution leaves conviction intact); Ex parte Chabot, 300 S.W.3d 768 (Tex. Crim. App. 2009) (citing *Sanders*), *with* Reddick v. Haws, 120 F.3d 714, 718 (7th Cir. 1997) (disagreeing with *Sanders*); People v. Brown, 660 N.E.2d 964, 969–70 (Ill. 1995) (same; citing conflicting cases).

96. *See* Briscoe v. LaHue, 460 U.S. 325, 326 n.1 (1983) (noting that the Court had never addressed whether false testimony of police officer at trial would be imputed to the prosecution); *but cf.* Giglio v. United States, 405 U.S. 150 (1972). In *Giglio*, the Court imputed one prosecutor's knowledge that a witness had entered into a plea bargain with the government to another prosecutor in the same office. *Id.* at 151–52. In *Giglio*, the first prosecutor (who struck the plea bargain) did not participate in the trial, and the second prosecutor had been unaware of the deal when he solicited false testimony from the witness that there was no plea bargain. *Id.*

97. *Compare* Ex parte Castellano, 863 S.W.2d 476, 481–86 (Tex. Crim. App. 1993) (imputing knowledge of "any member of the prosecution team" to trial prosecutor with respect to perjury claim); Boyd v. French, 147 F.3d 319, 329 (4th Cir. 1998) (holding that "knowingly false or misleading testimony by a law enforcement officer is imputed to the prosecution"); Schneider v. Estelle, 552 F.2d 593, 595 (5th Cir. 1977) (same); United States v. Morell, 524 F.2d 550, 555 (2d Cir. 1975) (imputing law enforcement officer's knowledge of prosecution witness's perjury where the officer was a key member of the prosecution team and sat at counsel's table during the trial); *with* United States v. Diaz, 176 F.3d 52, 106–07 (2d Cir. 1999) (refusing to impute knowledge of a law enforcement officer who was not a significant member of the prosecution team to trial prosecutor); Smith v. Sec. of New Mex. D.O.C., 50 F.3d 801, 830–31 (10th Cir. 1995) (same); United States v. Stewart, 323 F. Supp. 2d 606, 617–18 (S.D.N.Y. 2004) (refusing to impute false testimony of expert witness offered by prosecution at trial to prosecutors where no showing of prosecutors' knowledge of expert witness's perjury); People v. Rish, 802 N.E.2d 826, 835 (Ill. App. Ct. 2003) (refusing to follow a per se rule concerning whether to impute a police officer's knowledge to a prosecutor for purposes of a perjury claim).

98. Kirkpatrick v. Whitley, 992 F.2d 491, 497 (5th Cir. 1993).

99. *See* United States v. Bagley, 473 U.S. 667, 680 (1985) (citing Chapman v. California, 386 U.S. 18 (1967)). The *Chapman* standard is discussed in Chapter Fourteen.

100. *Id.* The lower courts are divided on the issue of whether the more stringent harmless-error standard applicable to "trial errors" on habeas corpus review, *Brecht v. Abrahamson*, 507 U.S. 619

---

to demonstrate materiality, a perjury claim does not require a defendant to show that there is a reasonable probability that the result of the proceeding would have been different "but for" the perjury. Rather, the prosecution has the burden under a *Chapman*-type standard once a defendant proves that a knowing presentation of perjury occurred.[101] Although the Supreme Court has never addressed the issue, many lower courts have held that, in deciding materiality for a perjury claim, a reviewing court must counterfactually ask what the effect on the verdict would have been if the perjury had been revealed to the jury.[102]

13.3 Extra-Record Claims of Jury Misconduct

Occasionally, after a jury has returned a guilty verdict,[103] defense counsel will discover that one or more jurors engaged in conduct—or were exposed to some type of outside influence—during voir dire, the trial, or jury deliberations that calls into question their impartiality. Recurring examples of such alleged juror misconduct include: 1) one or more jurors visited the scene of the crime on their own time; 2) one or more jurors consulted law books, dictionaries, the Bible, or the Internet to research some legal or factual issue in the case; 3) jurors discussed the merits of the case with each other prior to deliberations or a juror discussed the merits of the case with an outside party (e.g., a spouse) before the verdict was returned; 4) one or more jurors engaged in ex parte communication about the case with a witness, one of the attorneys, or the judge in the case; 5) a juror lied about, or failed to disclose, a material matter during voir dire (the juror's prior relationship with one of the

---

(1993), applies to perjury claims raised on habeas corpus review (as opposed to in a motion for a new trial or on direct appeal). *See* Rosencrantz v. Lafler, 586 F.3d 577, 589–90 (6th Cir. 2009) (applying *Brecht*); Ex parte Fierro, 934 S.W.2d 370 (Tex. Crim. App. 1996) (same); *but see* Hayes v. Brown, 399 F.3d 972, 984–85 (9th Cir. 2005) (en banc) (refusing to apply *Brecht*). The Supreme Court's analogous decision in *Kyles v. Whitley*, 514 U.S. 419, 435–36 (1995) (holding that application of the *Brecht* harmless-error standard to a *Brady* claim once materiality is established is erroneous), appears to contradict these lower court decisions applying *Brecht* to perjury claims. In other words, once *Chapman*-type "materiality" is shown, a defendant raising a perjury claim need not also show harm under *Brecht*. *See Hayes*, 399 F.3d at 984–85. The *Brecht* standard is discussed in Chapter Fifteen.
101. *Bagley*, 473 U.S. at 679–80.
102. *See, e.g.*, United States v. Wallach, 935 F.2d 445, 457 (2d Cir. 1991) ("It was one thing for the jury to learn that Guariglia had a history of improprieties; it would have been an entirely different matter for them to learn that after having taken an oath to speak the truth he made a conscious decision to lie."); Jackson v. Brown, 513 F.3d 1057, 1077 (9th Cir. 2008) ("The State argues that the *Napue* violations were immaterial, because even if the prosecutor had corrected the false testimony, the truth would have done little to impeach the informants' credibility. . . The State underestimates the impeachment value that the prosecutor's correction of McFarland's testimony could have served.").
103. Sometimes information concerning juror bias or a prejudicial outside influence on the jury may surface either during the voir dire process, *see* Chapter Seven, or during the trial itself, *see* Chapter Eight. If that occurs, the issue is initially litigated at that juncture rather than for the first time in a postconviction motion or petition.

parties or lawyers, for example); or 6) one or more jurors slept or were intoxicated during trial or jury deliberations.[104]

Under the Sixth Amendment to the Constitution, a jury must be impartial and a defendant is entitled to a trial and jury deliberations free of prejudicial extraneous influences or jurors.[105] A defendant's right to an impartial jury is violated if even a single member of the jury was biased.[106] The Supreme Court has held that ordinarily, if a trial court conducts a full and fair evidentiary hearing on the issue of juror bias and concludes that a juror was not biased (typically based on the juror's claim not to have been biased), the procedural protection afforded by such a hearing is constitutionally sufficient to protect a defendant's right to an impartial jury.[107]

A juror may be either biased in fact or conclusively presumed to be biased as a matter of law.[108] The former is referred to as "actual bias;" the latter is referred to as "implied bias."[109] A juror with actual bias is one who is found to have some definite animus toward a party in a litigation to the extent that the bias affected the juror's ability to be fair and impartial. Such bias ordinarily may be determined to exist—or not to exist—as a factual matter during an evidentiary hearing in which the parties are permitted to question the juror and the trial court is permitted to hear the juror's answers and observe their demeanor.[110] Conversely, in certain extreme or exceptional cases of jurors with implied bias, such bias is established where specific facts show "a close connection to the circumstances" of the defendant's case.[111] In the latter situation, irrespective of whether the juror claims to have been unbiased and irrespective of whether the trial court found that the juror was actually unbiased, the extreme circumstances of the case require a reviewing court to "imply" bias "as a matter of law."[112]

---

104. *See, e.g.*, Rushen v. Spain, 464 U.S. 114 (1983) (per curiam); Smith v. Phillips, 455 U.S. 209 (1982); Turner v. Louisiana, 379 U.S. 466 (1965); *see generally* Nancy J. King, *Juror Delinquency in Criminal Trials in America, 1796–1996*, 94 MICH. L. REV. 2673, 2708–51 (Aug. 1996).

105. *See* Irvin v. Dowd, 366 U.S. 717 (1961).

106. Dyer v. Calderon, 151 F.3d 970, 973 (9th Cir. 1998) (en banc).

107. *See Smith*, 455 U.S. at 215–18.

108. *Id.* at 221–24 (1982) (O'Connor, J., concurring).

109. *Id.* at 221 (O'Connor, J., concurring) (recognizing the implied bias doctrine in exceptional situations); *see also* McDonough Power Equip., Inc. v. Greenwood, 464 U.S. 548, 558 (1984) (Brennan, J., concurring in the judgment, joined by Marshall, J.) (following Justice O'Connor's concurring opinion in Smith); *id.* at 556–57 (Blackmun, J., concurring, joined by Stevens & O'Connor, JJ.) (same). As is apparent, Justice O'Connor's concurring opinion in *Smith* later garnered a majority of the Supreme Court in *McDonough Power Equip. See* Brooks v. Dretke, 444 F.3d 328, 329 & n.5 (5th Cir. 2006).

110. *Smith*, 455 U.S. at 222 (O'Connor, J., concurring); *see also* Solis v. Cockrell, 342 F.3d 392, 397 (5th Cir. 2003); Hunley v. Godinez, 975 F.2d 316, 318–20 (7th Cir. 1992); Burton v. Johnson, 948 F.2d 1150, 1158–59 (10th Cir. 1991); Tinsley v. Borg, 895 F.2d 520, 528–30 (9th Cir. 1990).

111. United States v. Scott, 854 F.2d 697, 699 (5th Cir. 1988) (citation and internal quotation marks omitted); Gonzales v. Thomas, 99 F.3d 978, 987 (10th Cir. 1996); State v. Fletcher, 596 N.W.2d 770 (Wis. 1999).

112. *Smith*, 455 U.S. at 222 (O'Connor, J., concurring); *see also* United States v. Bishop, 264 F.3d 535, 554 (5th Cir. 2001).

Proving juror misconduct can be difficult for the defense. The rules of evidence in almost all jurisdictions prohibit jurors from "impeaching their verdict" or testifying about what went on during jury deliberations.[113] An important exception to this general rule is that jurors may testify about extraneous influences.[114] Often there is a dispute about what qualifies as an "extraneous"—as opposed to an "internal"—influence. For example, in *Tanner v. United States,* a closely divided Supreme Court concluded that testimony from jurors that they were intoxicated and sleeping during deliberations as a result of drug and alcohol use was inadmissible because it concerned an internal rather than an extraneous matter.[115]

Even if the defense proves that some extraneous factor was introduced to jurors, courts will not reverse the defendant's conviction or sentence unless the extraneous matter actually or (in extreme cases) presumptively prejudiced the defendant in some manner.[116] In deciding whether to presume prejudice under these circumstances, most courts apply an objective test—namely, how the extraneous factor would have influenced a hypothetical average juror rather than rely on a juror's subjective claim not to have been unduly influenced.[117]

In cases in which there has been an extraneous influence on jurors, the lower courts are divided over which party—the defendant or the prosecution—has the burden of persuasion to show prejudice or a lack thereof. Some courts place the burden on the defense to prove prejudice, and other courts place the burden on the prosecution to disprove presumptive prejudice.[118] The Supreme Court has spoken inconsistently on this issue (without resolving the conflict).[119]

Furthermore, those lower courts that place the burden on the defense are divided over what type of showing must be made by a defendant; some courts require a showing of a "reasonable probability" that the extraneous factor affected the jurors'

---

113. *See, e.g.,* FED. R. EVID. 606(b); TEX. R. EVID. 606(b); *see generally* Warger v. Shauers, 574 U.S. 40 (2014).

114. Tanner v. United States, 483 U.S. 107, 121 (1987); United States v. Rutherford, 371 F.3d 634 (9th Cir. 2004) (permitting judicial inquiry into extraneous influence but refusing inquiry into internal influence on jurors).

115. *Compare Tanner,* 483 U.S. at 122–23 (majority), *with id.* at 140–41 (dissent).

116. *See, e.g.,* United States v. DiSalvo, 34 F.3d 1204, 1223 (3d Cir. 1994); United States v. Boylan, 898 F.2d 230, 262 (1st Cir. 1990); United States v. Calbas, 821 F.2d 887, 896 (2d Cir. 1987); State v. Faucher, 596 N.W.2d 770, 783 (Wis. 1999); State v. Hartley, 656 A.2d 954, 962 (R.I. 1995).

117. *See, e.g.,* Calbas, 821 F.2d at 896.

118. *Compare, e.g.,* United States v. Pennell, 737 F.2d 521, 532 (6th Cir. 1984) (burden on defense), *with* State v. King, 460 N.E.2d 1383, 1388 (Ohio Ct. App. 1983) (burden on prosecution).

119. *Compare* Remmer v. United States, 347 U.S. 227, 229–30 (1954) (placing burden on the prosecution in a case involving alleged jury tampering), *with* Smith v. Phillips, 455 U.S. 209, 215 (1982) (placing the burden on the defense in the case of a juror who had applied to work for the prosecutor's office at the time of trial). *See* United States v. Gartmon, 146 F.3d 1015, 1028 (D.C. Cir. 1998) (noting that some, but not all lower courts have concluded that *Smith* overruled *Remmer*).

---

ability to render a fair verdict, while other courts only require a lesser showing of a "reasonable possibility."[120]

In *Pena-Rodriguez v. Colorado*,[121] the Supreme Court held that one type of non-extraneous factor during jury deliberations—racial animus of one or more jurors—is subject to judicial review as a result of the Sixth Amendment right to an impartial jury. However, for a court to inquire about such animus, the defendant must offer proof that "one or more jurors made statements exhibiting overt racial bias that cast serious doubt on the fairness and impartiality of the jury's deliberations and resulting verdict."[122]

> To qualify, the statement must tend to show that racial animus was a significant motivating factor in the juror's vote to convict. Whether that threshold showing has been satisfied is a matter committed to the substantial discretion of the trial court in light of all the circumstances, including the content and timing of the alleged statements and the reliability of the proffered evidence.[123]

13.4 Leading Supreme Court Decisions Concerning Extra-Record Postconviction Claims

- *Napue v. Illinois*, 360 U.S. 264 (1959) (prosecution's "knowing" presentation of, or failure to correct, perjured testimony or false evidence offered by prosecution violates due process if such perjury or false evidence is "material"; perjury or false evidence is "material" unless prosecution proves beyond a reasonable doubt that it did not contribute to the verdict).

- *Holloway v. Arkansas*, 435 U.S. 475 (1978) (defendant's constitutional right to conflict-free counsel under the Sixth Amendment is violated when the defendant or defense counsel objects in a timely manner to counsel's concurrent representation of two codefendants and the trial court fails to take appropriate corrective action in response to such an objection; automatic reversal of defendant's conviction on appeal if trial court failed to do so).

- *Cuyler v. Sullivan*, 446 U.S. 335 (1980) (if no such timely objection is made and instead an objection to the alleged conflict is raised only after a defendant has been convicted, then *Holloway*'s rule of automatic reversal does not apply; rather, to prevail on such a claim, a defendant must show

---

120. *See Hartley*, 656 A.2d at 962 (discussing the division among the lower courts).
121. Pena-Rodriguez v. Colorado, 137 S. Ct. 855 (2017).
122. *Id.* at 869.
123. *Id.*

1) "actual conflict of interest" whereby counsel's loyalties were actually divided, and 2) an "adverse effect" resulted from the actual conflict).

- *Smith v. Phillips*, 455 U.S. 209 (1982) (leading decision on substantive and procedural requirements concerning constitutional claim of a biased juror); *id.* at 221–24 (O'Connor, J., concurring) (discussing the difference between claims of actual bias and implied bias).

- *Strickland v. Washington*, 466 U.S. 668 (1984) (setting forth the two-part standard governing the vast majority of claims of ineffective assistance of counsel (IAC): 1) "deficient" performance by counsel; and 2) prejudice resulting from the deficient performance; "prejudice" is defined as a "reasonable probability" that but for counsel's deficiency, the result of the proceeding would have been different).

- *United States v. Cronic*, 466 U.S. 648 (1984) (holding that in certain extreme cases of deficient performance, amounting to a "breakdown in the adversary system" or a "constructive denial in the assistance of counsel," prejudice is irrebuttably presumed and a defendant need not establish "actual prejudice" under *Strickland*).

- *United States v. Bagley*, 473 U.S. 667 (1985) (refining constitutional standard of *Brady v. Maryland*, 373 U.S. 83 (1963), applicable to claims that the prosecution failed to disclose "material" exculpatory, impeachment, or mitigating evidence before or during trial; adopting *Strickland*'s "reasonable probability" standard as the *Brady* "materiality" standard; contrasting the lesser degree of "materiality" required in perjury context).

- *Kyles v. Whitley*, 514 U.S. 419 (1995) (in evaluating *Brady* claims, reviewing courts must analyze the cumulative effect of all undisclosed evidence in deciding whether the evidence was "material" under *Bagley*).

- *Mickens v. Taylor*, 535 U.S. 162 (2002) (holding that if there was no timely objection to an alleged conflict of interest, the *Cuyler* two-part standard rather than *Holloway*'s rule of automatic reversal applies to "multiple representation" conflict-of-interest IAC claims, even if the trial judge "should have known" of the existence of conflict; further stating that the threshold issue of whether *Cuyler* even applies to a claim of a conflict of interest other than one of concurrent representation of multiple codefendants is an open question in the Court's IAC jurisprudence and suggesting that the *Strickland* standard may apply to other types of conflicts).

- *Wiggins v. Smith*, 539 U.S. 510 (2003) (holding that although deference is due to "strategic" decisions of defense counsel in determining whether counsel performed "deficiently" within the meaning of *Strickland*, reviewing courts must take a hard look at whether purportedly "strategic" decisions actually were based on reasonable determinations by counsel concerning available options).

- *Padilla v. Kentucky*, 130 S. Ct. 1473 (2010) (criminal defense counsel performs deficiently under *Strickland* by failing to advise a noncitizen defendant of the immigration consequences of their guilty plea); *Lafler v. Cooper*, 566 U.S. 156 (2012) (plea bargaining phase of a criminal case is a "critical stage" of the prosecution under the Sixth Amendment and, thus, defense counsel has an obligation to properly advise a defendant whether to accept a plea bargain offer made by the prosecution).

- *Missouri v. Frye*, 566 U.S. 134 (2012) (criminal defense attorney has a constitutional obligation under the Sixth Amendment to convey prosecution's plea offer to the defendant).

- *Pena-Rodriguez v. Colorado*, 137 S. Ct. 855 (2017) (the Sixth Amendment right to an impartial jury requires an exception to the general rule that non-external factors may not be used to impeach a jury's verdict when the defendant proves that one or more jurors displayed "racial animus" during jury deliberations).

- *Buck v. Davis*, 137 S. Ct. 759 (2017) (defense counsel's injection of racial bias against his client during trial was deficient performance under *Strickland* that prejudiced his client).

- *Weaver v. Massachusetts*, 137 S. Ct. 1899 (2017) (a defense attorney's deficient performance that results in a "structural error"—within the meaning of the Court's appellate-review jurisprudence—does not rise to the level of a *Cronic* claim and, thus, the defendant must demonstrate *Strickland* "prejudice" to prevail).

- *McCoy v.* Louiaiana, 138 S. Ct. 1500 (2018) (defense counsel who conceded his client's guilt at trial over the client's objection violated the Sixth Amendment right to counsel).

CHAPTER FOURTEEN

DIRECT APPEALS

After defendants have been convicted and sentenced at the trial court level, many choose to appeal their convictions and/or sentences to an appellate court.[1] There are two main types of appeals, as that term is popularly understood. The first, which is discussed in this chapter, is referred to as a "direct appeal" or "direct review" of a conviction or sentence. The second, which is discussed in the next chapter, is referred to as a "habeas corpus" appeal or "collateral review" of a conviction or sentence.[2] On a direct appeal, a defendant may raise only "record" claims, meaning ones that were factually developed in the existing record (such as a claim that the trial court erred by denying a pretrial motion to suppress evidence seized without a search warrant). Habeas corpus appeals, which can involve new factual development, often involve "record" as well as "extra-record" claims (such as an ineffective assistance of counsel claim raised only after the direct appeal process is completed). Both the direct review and habeas corpus processes often involve appeals through several "layers" of appeals courts (usually an initial appeal to an intermediate state appeals court, followed by a discretionary appeal to the state's supreme court and concluding with a discretionary appeal to the U.S. Supreme Court by the filing of a petition for writ of certiorari).

Although there is no constitutional right to appeal a criminal conviction or sentence,[3] if a particular jurisdiction affords a defendant the right to appeal by

---

1. Some defendants, however, are not permitted to appeal because they waived their right to appeal as part of a plea agreement. Courts generally enforce such waivers as long as a defendant waived their right to appeal in a knowing and voluntary manner. *See, e.g.*, United States v. Marin, 961 F.2d 493 (4th Cir. 1992).

2. A specific type of collateral challenge to a prior conviction—on the specific ground that a prior conviction was obtained in violation of the Sixth Amendment right to counsel—is discussed in Chapter Three. The term "collateral review" is being used here more broadly to mean a postconviction challenge to a conviction or sentence that typically occurs after a direct appeal and is most commonly called a habeas corpus appeal. *Compare* Custis v. United States, 511 U.S. 485 (1994) (specific type of "collateral" challenge to prior uncounseled convictions at sentencing phase of subsequent case), *with* Teague v. Lane, 489 U.S. 288, 300–01 (1989) (broader use of term collateral review as being synonymous with habeas corpus); *see also* Brecht v. Abrahamson, 507 U.S. 619, 633–34 (1993) (noting the difference between "direct review" and "collateral review" in criminal cases).

3. McKane v. Durston, 153 U.S. 684, 687–88 (1894); Hatch v. Oklahoma, 58 F.3d 1447, 1460–61 (10th Cir. 1995).

statute—as the vast majority of states and the federal government do in virtually all types of criminal cases—then certain constitutional protections apply (such as the right to counsel on the first appeal as a matter of right, as discussed below).[4] There are numerous constitutional issues concerning appellate practice and procedure that arise on direct appeal; the most common of those issues will be discussed below.

14.1 Error Preservation and Procedural Default[5]

During the past three decades, state and federal appellate courts, led by the Supreme Court, increasingly have required the parties in criminal cases to raise legal issues in a timely and specific manner in trial and appellate courts to "preserve" the issues for review on a subsequent round of appeal.[6] If a defendant fails to preserve a claim by "procedurally defaulting" it—that is, not complying with the procedural requirements for properly raising a legal issue—then very likely the defendant's conviction and sentence will be left intact even if the record shows that a constitutional violation occurred. At the trial court level, the most common procedural default is a defendant's failure to lodge a "contemporaneous objection,"—an objection at the first available opportunity.[7] At the appellate level, the most common procedural default is failure to raise an issue in an appellate brief filed on the initial round of appeal.[8] In the vast majority of jurisdictions, procedural default rules apply equally to constitutional and nonconstitutional claims.[9] Although criminal defendants file the overwhelming majority of appeals in criminal cases, the procedural default doctrine applies equally to the prosecution if it raises an unpreserved error on appeal.[10] In many jurisdictions, a party's procedural default must be called to the attention of the appeals court by the opposing party or the court will address the merits of the unpreserved claim as if there were no default.[11] Many courts, though, may exercise discretion to invoke procedural bars sua sponte.[12]

The Supreme Court's error-preservation doctrine applies in three different contexts in criminal cases. First, on direct or collateral review of a state or federal criminal conviction and sentence, the defendant initially must have raised an issue

---

4. Likewise, a jurisdiction may afford the prosecution the right to appeal certain matters in a criminal case (e.g., a trial court's order suppressing evidence). *See, e.g.*, 18 U.S.C. § 3731.

5. Much of the following discussion is equally applicable to habeas corpus appeals. Procedural default is further discussed in Chapter Fifteen in the context of habeas corpus review.

6. *See, e.g.*, O'Sullivan v. Boerckel, 526 U.S. 838 (1999); United States v. Olano, 507 U.S. 725 (1993); United States v. Frady, 456 U.S. 152 (1982); Wainwright v. Sykes, 433 U.S. 72 (1977); Costarelli v. Massachusetts, 421 U.S. 193 (1975).

7. *See, e.g.*, Engle v. Isaac, 456 U.S. 107 (1982).

8. Murray v. Carrier, 477 U.S. 478 (1986).

9. *See, e.g.*, People v. Carines, 597 N.W.2d 130, 138–39 (Mich. 1999).

10. *See, e.g.*, United States v. Castillo, 386 F.3d 632 (5th Cir. 2004).

11. *See, e.g.*, Cupit v. Whitley, 28 F.3d 532, 534–36 (5th Cir. 1994).

12. *See, e.g.*, Rosario v. United States, 164 F.3d 729, 732 (2d Cir. 1998).

in the trial court to receive plenary review of the merits of the claim on appeal (unless, as discussed below, an appeals court does not invoke the procedural default).[13] Second, on the Supreme Court's direct review of a state conviction or sentence or on any federal court's collateral review of a state criminal conviction or sentence, the Supreme Court requires a federal constitutional claim to have been raised previously on appeal to the highest state appellate court in which appellate review could be had.[14] Third, to be raised on collateral review of a federal conviction or sentence, a claim generally first must have been raised on direct appeal to a federal appellate court; the exception to this rule concerns claims that could not have been raised on direct appeal (such as an ineffective assistance of counsel claim that could not have been factually developed before the direct appeal process began).[15]

To preserve a legal issue for review by a higher court, a defendant or defense counsel must make a legal argument "which is ample and timely [so as] to bring the alleged [constitutional] error to the attention of the . . . court and enable it to take appropriate corrective action."[16] Although the Court has not gone so far as to hold that a criminal defendant can preserve a constitutional claim "only by citing book and verse on the federal [C]onstitution,"[17] the Court has required the substance of a particular constitutional claim to be fairly asserted in the written or oral submissions made by the defense in a criminal case.[18] Although error-preservation rules that are based on legitimate state interests will be respected on appeal—meaning a defendant's noncompliance with such requirements may result in an appellate court refusing to address the merits of a particular constitutional claim—the Supreme Court has refused to "force resort to an arid ritual of meaningless form."[19] Therefore, a defendant's noncompliance with a procedural requirement that does not have a rational basis or promote a valid state interest will not foreclose review of the merits of a constitutional claim on appeal.[20] In a related vein, the Court has said that a lower court's "exorbitant" application of an "otherwise sound" procedural rule will not bar a higher court's consideration of the merits of a purportedly procedurally defaulted claim that was brought to the lower court's attention in a sufficient manner.[21]

---

13. *See Olano*, 507 U.S. 725; Osborne v. Ohio, 495 U.S. 103, 123–25 (1990); *Frady*, 456 U.S. 152; *Sykes*, 433 U.S. 72.
14. *See O'Sullivan*, 526 U.S. 838; *Costarelli*, 421 U.S. 193.
15. *See* Bousley v. United States, 523 U.S. 614 (1998); *see also* United States v. Massaro, 538 U.S. 500 (2004) (ineffective assistance of counsel claim may be raised for the first time in a federal habeas corpus petition and need not be raised on direct appeal because ordinarily the factual record supporting such a claim will not have been adequately developed by the time of the direct appeal).
16. *Osborne*, 495 U.S. at 125 (citation and internal quotation marks omitted).
17. Picard v. Connor, 404 U.S. 270, 277–78 (1971) (citation and internal quotation marks omitted).
18. *Id.*; *see also Osborne*, 495 U.S. at 125.
19. James v. Kentucky, 466 U.S. 341, 349 (1984) (citation and internal quotation marks omitted).
20. *Id.*
21. Lee v. Kemna, 534 U.S. 362, 376 (2002).

Certain exceptions to the procedural default doctrine exist. First, on direct appeal of a federal conviction or sentence, a federal appeals court possesses discretion to address the merits of a procedurally defaulted claim under the "plain error" standard.[22] Some states also employ a "plain error" or "fundamental error" standard; as long as a state appeals court addressed the merits of an otherwise procedurally defaulted federal claim (under such an exception or for any other reason) and did not do so only in the alternative, the Supreme Court (on direct review) and any federal court (on habeas corpus review) will address the merits as well.[23] Second, if a state court has inconsistently applied an established procedural rule in past cases or applies a new procedural rule without fair warning to a particular defendant, a defendant's noncompliance with the rule will not prevent the Supreme Court (on direct review) or any federal court (on collateral review) from addressing the merits of the claim.[24] Third, at least on collateral review of a state or federal conviction or sentence, a defendant can circumvent a procedural default by showing adequate "cause" for the default and "prejudice" resulting from application of the procedural bar[25] or by showing that they are actually innocent of the charged offense.[26]

---

22. *See Olano*, 507 U.S. at 732 (setting forth a four-prong standard: there must be an error that is (2) "plain," which (3) affected the "substantial rights" of the appellant, and (4) not reversing district court's judgment would "seriously affect[] the fairness, integrity, or public reputation of the judicial proceedings"). The fourth prong is discretionary, meaning a reversal of district court's judgment is not automatic even if there is plain error that affected the substantial rights of an appellant. *Id.* Even if an error was not plain at time of the trial, if it becomes plain based on intervening law applicable to the case while pending on appeal, courts can apply the plain error standard to a procedurally defaulted claim. *See* Henderson v. United States, 568 U.S. 266 (2013); Johnson v. United States, 520 U.S. 461 (1997). It should be noted that this federal plain error standard applies only to forfeited claims (i.e., issues not properly raised in a lower court) as opposed to waived claims (i.e., issues that a defendant knowingly and voluntarily abandoned on the record in the lower court). *Olano*, 507 U.S. at 733 (distinguishing "waiver" from "forfeiture"). Many lower courts use the terms waiver and forfeiture synonymously in the procedural default context, but the two concepts have different meanings.

23. *See* Ake v. Oklahoma, 470 U.S. 68, 74–75 (1985); *see also* Harris v. Reed, 489 U.S. 255 (1989); Michigan v. Long, 463 U.S. 1032 (1983).

24. *See, e.g.*, Johnson v. Mississippi, 486 U.S. 578, 586 (1988); Ford v. Georgia, 498 U.S. 411 (1991); Bennett v. Mueller, 322 F.3d 573, 583–84 (9th Cir. 2003). In such a situation, the state court's procedural bar is not an "independent and adequate state law ground" that forecloses federal review of the state defendant's constitutional claim. *Johnson*, 486 U.S. at 586. In *Beard v. Kindler*, 558 U.S. 53 (2009), the Supreme Court held that merely because a state procedural default rule is "discretionary"—meaning it is applied in some but not all cases by a state appellate court exercising its discretion—does not automatically render the procedural rule an inadequate state law ground.

25. Examples of adequate cause include: 1) a showing that the claim that was procedurally defaulted was "novel" at the time of the default and only had a reasonable basis in the law by the time of the subsequent appeal, *see* Reed v. Ross, 468 U.S. 1 (1984); and 2) a showing that defense counsel who failed to preserve the claim provided ineffective assistance of counsel by failing to do so, *see* Dretke v. Haley, 541 U.S. 386, 394–95 (2004).

26. *See, e.g.*, Bousley v. United States, 523 U.S. 614, 621 (1998); Schlup v. Delo, 513 U.S. 298 (1995); Coleman v. Thompson, 501 U.S. 722 (1991).

14.2 Harmless-Error Analysis on Direct Appeal[27]

Relatively few constitutional errors result in "automatic reversal" of a conviction or sentence on appeal—that is, reversal without consideration of whether the defendant was harmed or prejudiced in any manner by the error. Those that do are referred to as "structural errors" and are limited to such constitutional violations as racial discrimination in the selection of a grand jury or petit jury; a biased judge or jury; the denial of a right to a public trial; an unconstitutional definition of "reasonable doubt" in jury instructions; the denial of a defendant's right to represent themself at trial; and the actual or constructive denial of the assistance of counsel.[28] The Supreme Court has reasoned that these types of error are "structural defects in the constitution of the trial mechanism" that always render the proceeding unfair and are not amenable to a case-by-case harmless-error analysis.[29] The Court has been careful to note that such structural errors are the exception to the general rule and are a "very limited class" of constitutional errors.[30]

Conversely, the vast majority of constitutional errors—e.g., Fourth Amendment violations, Fifth Amendment right-to-silence violations, Confrontation Clause violations, and most types of jury instruction errors—are subject to harmless-error analysis.[31] Under *Chapman v. California*,[32] an appellate court must reverse a defendant's conviction or sentence on direct appeal unless the prosecution proves that such a nonstructural constitutional error is "harmless beyond a reasonable doubt." Such *Chapman* harmless-error analysis is not concerned with whether "but for" the constitutional error there is sufficient evidence to support a conviction or sentence. Rather, it asks whether the error contributed to the verdict or sentence. "To say that an error did not contribute to the verdict is . . . to find that error unimportant in relation to everything else that the [judge or] jury considered on the issue in

---

27. The harmless-error doctrine is also applied on habeas corpus review and is discussed in that context in Chapter Fifteen.

28. Sullivan v. Louisiana, 508 U.S. 275 (1993); Arizona v. Fulminante, 499 U.S. 279 (1991).

29. *Fulminante,* 499 U.S. at 309–10.

30. Neder v. United States, 527 U.S. 1, 8 (1999); *see also* Hedgpeth v. Pulido, 555 U.S. 57 (2008) (per curiam).

31. Two types of constitutional violations—the prosecution's failure to disclose evidence, Brady v. Maryland, 373 U.S. 83 (1963), and most instances of ineffective assistance of counsel, Strickland v. Washington, 466 U.S. 668 (1984)—have a "built-in" harm or prejudice requirement and, thus, are not subject to any independent harmless-error analysis. Unless there is a "reasonable probability" that but for an incompetent defense counsel's acts or omissions or the prosecution's nondisclosure of evidence, the "result of the proceeding would have been different," there is no constitutional violation in either situation. Kyles v. Whitley, 514 U.S. 419, 434–36 (1995). *See* Chapter Thirteen (discussing *Brady* claims and ineffectiveness claims). A third type of constitutional violation, the prosecution's knowing presentation of perjured testimony, also has a built-in harm standard, which is identical to the *Chapman* standard. *See* Chapter Thirteen.

32. 386 U.S. 18 (1967). Harmless-error analysis of nonconstitutional errors on appeal is not governed by *Chapman,* but instead is governed by a less-generous standard for defendants. *See* United States v. Powell, 334 F.3d 42, 45 (D.C. Cir. 2003).

question, as revealed by the record."[33] "Harmless-error review [under Chapman] looks . . . to the basis on which the jury actually rested its verdict . . . . The inquiry, in other words, is not whether, in a trial that occurred without the error, a guilty verdict surely would have been rendered, but whether the guilty verdict in *this* trial was surely unattributable to the error."[34]

14.3 Retroactive Application of "New Rules" of Constitutional Criminal Procedure to Defendants on Direct Appeal

Particularly during the Warren Court era, and from time to time since then, the U.S. Supreme Court and lower appeals courts have announced "new rules" of constitutional criminal procedure. A "new rule" is one that from an objective viewpoint "was not dictated by existing precedent" at the time that an appellate court first applied it in a particular case.[35] A classic example of a new rule of constitutional criminal procedure is *Miranda v. Arizona*.[36] During the Warren Court era, when such new rules were being handed down on a very frequent basis, the Supreme Court eschewed a bright-line approach and instead followed an unpredictable, issue-specific approach to whether a particular new rule of constitutional criminal procedure should be given application to any other defendants besides the one in whose case the new rule was announced.[37]

In 1987, however, in *Griffith v. Kentucky*,[38] the Supreme Court changed its approach regarding retroactivity by drawing a line between defendants whose convictions were "final" and those whose convictions were not "final" at the time that a particular new constitutional rule was announced.[39] Under *Griffith*, any defendant whose conviction is not final at the time a new constitutional rule is announced in another case is entitled to rely on the new rule.[40] The test for "finality" under *Griffith* is whether at the time of the new rule a particular defendant's case was still pending at any point at trial or in the direct appeal process (including pending on petition for writ of certiorari filed with the U.S. Supreme Court).[41] If a conviction was already final at the time of the new rule's announcement, then the defendant may not benefit from the new rule unless the defendant falls within rarely applied exceptions,[42] which are discussed in the next chapter. Merely because a defendant's case was pending on direct appeal at the time the new rule was announced does not

---

33. Yates v. Evatt, 500 U.S. 391, 403–04 (1991).
34. *Sullivan*, 508 U.S. at 279 (internal quotes and cites omitted).
35. Teague v. Lane, 489 U.S. 288, 301 (1989).
36. 384 U.S. 436 (1966); *see* Johnson v. New Jersey, 384 U.S. 719 (1966).
37. *See, e.g., Johnson*, 384 U.S. at 732; Linkletter v. Walker, 381 U.S. 618 (1965).
38. 479 U.S. 314 (1987).
39. *Id.* at 326–27.
40. *Id.*; *see also* Powell v. Nevada, 511 U.S. 79, 84 (1994); *Teague*, 489 U.S. at 300–10.
41. *Griffith*, 479 U.S. at 321 n.6, 326–27.
42. *See Teague*, 489 U.S. at 301, 310.

automatically mean that they will benefit from the new rule, even if their case raises the same issue addressed by the decision announcing the new rule. As a general matter, the defendant also must have preserved the issue for appeal and the error alleged must not be harmless.[43]

Griffith, which is rooted in the equal protection principle that "similarly situated" litigants should be treated equally,[44] also appears to require a state appellate court that announces a new rule of federal constitutional dimension to apply the new rule to defendants whose convictions were not yet final at the time of the new rule's announcement.[45] A state appellate court that announces a new rule based solely on state law—and not based in any manner on federal constitutional law—is not required under *Griffith* to apply the rule to all defendants whose convictions were not final at the time that the new rule was announced.[46] However, if a state court were to apply a new state law rule in an unequal manner to similarly situated defendants (e.g., applying a new rule announced in one case to a defendant in another case pending on direct appeal, but refusing to apply it to a third defendant pending on direct appeal at the same time), then arguably there would be an equal protection violation.[47]

14.4 The Right to Counsel on Direct Appeal

The Supreme Court in *Douglas v. California*[48] held that as a matter of due process and equal protection the right to counsel—including appointed counsel for indigent defendants—applies during a state or federal criminal defendant's "first appeal as a matter of right"[49] in cases in which the right to counsel existed in the trial

---

43. *See* United States v. Booker, 543 U.S. 220, 267–68 (2005).

44. *Griffith*, 479 U.S. at 323, 327.

45. Although the U.S. Supreme Court has not yet addressed this issue, *see* Lego v. Illinois, 488 U.S. 902 (1988) (Marshall, J., joined by Brennan, J., dissenting from the denial of certiorari), all state supreme courts that have addressed the issue have held that *Griffith* requires a state appellate court to apply its own new rule based on federal constitutional principles to all defendants whose convictions were not final at the time of the rule's announcement. *See, e.g.*, People v. Shields, 575 N.E.2d 538, 542–43 (Ill. 1991); Farbotnik v. State, 850 P.2d 594, 602 (Wyo. 1993); *but cf.* Robinson v. Ponte, 933 F.2d 101, 103–04 (1st Cir. 1991) (in a federal habeas corpus case, refusing to apply *Griffith*'s retroactivity doctrine to a state court's new rule based in part on federal constitutional principles that had been announced before the habeas petitioner's conviction became final).

46. *See, e.g.*, Murtishaw v. Woodford, 255 F.3d 926, 956 (9th Cir. 2001); Lackey v. Scott, 28 F.3d 486, 491 (5th Cir. 1994); People v. Sexton, 580 N.W.2d 404, 410–11 (Mich. 1998). An exception to this rule is if a state appeals court interprets a state penal statute in a manner that renders a previously convicted defendant's conduct noncriminal; if the court holds that its interpretation of the statute is a statement of what the law always should have been, then even the defendants whose convictions are final must receive the benefit of the court's ruling. Fiore v. White, 531 U.S. 225 (2001) (per curiam).

47. Myers v. Ylst, 897 F.2d 417 (9th Cir. 1990).

48. Douglas v. California, 372 U.S. 353 (1963).

49. *Id.* at 358.

court.[50] In *Halbert v. Michigan*,[51] the Court extended *Douglas* to any first-round appeal, whether discretionary (in the sense that the appellate court has discretion to refuse to allow the defendant leave to appeal) or one "as a matter of right." However, the right does not apply to any subsequent round of appeals, whether on direct or habeas corpus review.[52] In most criminal cases, a first-round appeal is heard by a state or federal "intermediate" appellate court—referred to as a "court of appeals" in most jurisdictions—which usually consists of a three-judge panel. Unlike a defendant proceeding in the trial court, a defendant proceeding on appeal does not have a corresponding constitutional right to proceed pro se.[53] Therefore, a criminal defendant wishing to appeal may be required to accept the services of a court-appointed appellate lawyer.

Unlike defense counsel at the trial court level, who always must act as a defendant's advocate, appellate counsel for a criminal defendant need not always act as an advocate throughout the appeals process. If there are no "nonfrivolous" issues to raise in an appellate brief, then counsel is ethically obligated to move to withdraw as appellate counsel and may not file a "merits brief"; appellate counsel may do so without violating the defendant's constitutional right to counsel.[54] However, the Supreme Court in a series of cases culminating in *Smith v. Robbins* has held that an appellate lawyer may not move to withdraw without first reviewing the entire record and making a good-faith determination that there are no "nonfrivolous" issues apparent from the record.[55] The appellate court thereafter must engage in an "independent review" of the record before determining that there are no nonfrivolous issues on appeal and allowing the attorney to withdraw without filing a merits brief.[56] An issue is "frivolous" only if it is "squarely foreclosed" by statute or controlling judicial precedent and, furthermore, if such statute or judicial precedent is not subject to reconsideration based on contrary precedent.[57] Put another way, if a "reasonable jurist" (even one in another jurisdiction) could agree that a particular

---

50. *See* People v. Wong, 155 Cal. Rptr. 453 (Cal. Ct. App. 1979).

51. Halbert v. Michigan, 545 U.S. 605 (2005).

52. Ross v. Moffitt, 417 U.S. 600 (1974); Pennsylvania v. Finley, 481 U.S. 551 (1987).

53. *Compare* Martinez v. Court of App. for Cal., 4th App. Dist., 528 U.S. 152 (2000) (no constitutional right to self-representation on appeal), *with* Faretta v. California, 422 U.S. 806 (1975) (constitutional right to self-representation in the trial court).

54. Smith v. Robbins, 528 U.S. 259 (2000); McCoy v. Court of Appeals of Wis., Dist. 1, 486 U.S. 429 (1988); Penson v. Ohio, 488 U.S. 75 (1988); Anders v. California, 386 U.S. 738 (1967).

55. *Smith*, 528 U.S. at 278–81. Prior to *Smith*, in *Anders*, 386 U.S. 738, the Supreme Court appeared to require a more elaborate procedure for appellate attorneys seeking to withdraw based on a perception that there were no nonfrivolous issues to raise. The "*Anders* brief" procedure required attorneys to file a brief that explicitly discussed why there are no nonfrivolous issues and mention any issues with any arguable merit. *Anders*, 386 U.S. at 744. Although the filing of such *Anders* briefs is no longer constitutionally required after *Smith*, federal appeals courts still generally follow the *Anders* procedures. *See, e.g.*, United States v. Marvin, 211 F.3d 778 (3d Cir. 2000).

56. *Smith*, 528 U.S. at 278–81.

57. *See* Barefoot v. Estelle, 463 U.S. 880, 893–94 & n.4 (1983); *see also* McKnight v. General Motors Corp., 511 U.S. 659, 659–60 (1994) (per curiam).

legal argument has merit—notwithstanding that the appeals court hearing the defendant's appeal has already rejected the argument in a prior appeal—the issue is nonfrivolous and appellate counsel should not file a motion to withdraw.[58]

In *Evitts v. Lucey*,[59] the Supreme Court held that a lawyer representing a defendant on their first appeal must provide "effective assistance of counsel."[60] There are many types of claims of ineffective assistance of appellate counsel, each of which if meritorious would entitle a defendant to a new appeal with competent appellate counsel.[61]

First, if an appellate lawyer is permitted to withdraw without following a procedure that is constitutionally sufficient under *Smith v. Robbins*—namely, requiring the appellate lawyer first to examine the entire record and make a good-faith determination that there are no nonfrivolous issues on appeal—then there is a constructive denial of the assistance of counsel and prejudice is presumed (i.e., the defendant need not identify any meritorious issues that they would have raised in a brief).[62] This same presumptive prejudice rule applies to appellate counsel who did not file a merits brief, but who also did not move to withdraw (resulting in the appellate court's dismissal of the appeal for lack of prosecution).[63] The second type of ineffective assistance of appellate counsel occurs when a defendant's appellate counsel complied with *Smith* and withdrew without filing a merits brief, yet a defendant can identify at least one nonfrivolous issue that existed on appeal. In that situation, there is not presumptive prejudice; rather, a defendant must show a "reasonable probability" that had the attorney filed a merits brief raising the omitted issue, the appeals court would have reversed the conviction or sentence.[64] Third, if an appellate lawyer filed a merits brief, but omitted a particular nonfrivolous claim, a defendant likewise must show a "reasonable probability" that had the attorney raised the omitted claim, the appeals court would have reversed the conviction or sentence.[65] Finally, if appellate counsel fails to obtain an available portion of the appellate record or fails to review a portion of the existing record before filing a brief—as opposed to failing to obtain or review the entire record—the defendant

---

58. *Barefoot*, 463 U.S. at 893 n.4; *see also* United States v. Hauersperger, 27 F. App'x 684, 685 (7th Cir. 2001) ("a circuit split normally would present a non-frivolous issue for review," thus foreclosing the filing of a motion to withdraw by appellate counsel).

59. Evitts v. Lucey, 469 U.S. 387 (1985).

60. *Id.* at 396–97.

61. See generally Gregory G. Sarno, *Adequacy of Defense Counsel's Representation of Criminal Clients Regarding Appellate and Post-Conviction Remedies*, 15 A.L.R. 4th 582 (1982 and supplement).

62. *Penson*, 488 U.S. at 85–89 (citing United States v. Cronic, 466 U.S. 648 (1984)).

63. *See, e.g.*, Cannon v. Berry, 727 F.2d 1020 (11th Cir. 1989).

64. *Smith*, 528 U.S. at 284–89 (citing Strickland v. Washington, 466 U.S. 668 (1984)).

65. *Id.*; *see also* Eagle v. Linahan, 279 F.3d 926 (11th Cir. 2001); *but cf.* Jones v. Barnes, 463 U.S. 745, 751 (1983) (defendant possesses no constitutional right to have appellate counsel press nonfrivolous points in a merits brief, even if the defendant requests it).

must show a "reasonable probability" that had counsel utilized the entire record, the appeals court would have reversed their conviction or sentence.[66]

In other situations, it is not an appellate attorney, but instead trial counsel who denied a defendant their right to counsel on the first appeal. First, if a defendant asked their counsel in the trial court to file a notice of appeal after the sentence was imposed and the trial counsel either refused or negligently failed to do so (thus foreclosing an appeal), the trial counsel's omission violated the defendant's constitutional right to counsel, and the defendant is entitled to an out-of-time appeal without any showing of prejudice (meaning the defendant need not show that they would prevail on appeal).[67] Defense counsel must file a notice of appeal at the direction of a client even if the client waived the right to appeal in a plea agreement.[68]

Second, if trial counsel failed to consult with the defendant concerning whether they wished to file an appeal when there was an objective basis for believing that the defendant would have wanted to appeal, a defendant is entitled to an out-of-time appeal upon showing a "reasonable probability" that they would have pursued an appeal if trial counsel had consulted with them.[69] Finally, although the Supreme Court has never addressed the issue, some lower courts have held that trial counsel, whether appointed or retained, has a constitutional duty to advise the defendant of their right to the assistance of counsel on first appeal, including appointed appellate counsel if the defendant cannot afford to pay for retained appellate counsel. Failure to do so will result in an out-of-time appeal if the defendant did not know of this right to appellate counsel and furthermore if the defendant shows a "reasonable probability" that they would have pursued an appeal if so advised.[70]

14.5 Constitutional Right to Proceed In Forma Pauperis on Appeal

A defendant appealing conviction or sentence—whether a felony or misdemeanor, including petty misdemeanors where the only punishment was a fine[71]—who

---

66. *See, e.g.,* Bransford v. Brown, 806 F.2d 83, 86–87 (6th Cir. 1986). If an appellate attorney failed to obtain (or review) all or the vast majority of the record on appeal before filing a brief, such incomplete representation on appeal arguably would amount to a constructive denial of appellate counsel under *Cronic,* 466 U.S. 48.

67. Roe v. Flores-Ortega, 528 U.S. 470, 477 (2000).

68. Garza v. Idaho, 139 S. Ct. 738 (2019).

69. *Id.* at 478–83.

70. *See, e.g.,* Martin v. State of Texas, 737 F.2d 460, 462 (5th Cir. 1984).

71. Mayer v. City of Chicago, 404 U.S. 189 (1971); Williams v. Oklahoma City, 395 U.S. 458 (1969) (per curiam). *Mayer,* which involved a defendant convicted of a petty misdemeanor offense that carried a maximum punishment of a monetary fine, appears to be in tension with Scott v. Illinois, 440 U.S. 367 (1979), which held that a defendant convicted of a misdemeanor and sentenced to a fine only does not have a constitutional right to counsel in the trial court proceedings. *See* M.L.B. v. S.L.J., 519 U.S. 102, 140–41 (1996) (Scalia, J., joined by Thomas, J., dissenting).

is unable to pay the cost of filing fees or a court reporter's transcription of the relevant proceedings in the trial court may proceed in forma pauperis and ordinarily is constitutionally entitled to these free of cost.[72] The Supreme Court has held that in some instances, an adequate substitute for transcripts, such as a stipulation of the relevant facts by the parties or sufficiently detailed "minutes" by the trial judge or a clerk, will suffice.[73] Unlike the right to appointed counsel on appeal, which is limited to the defendant's first appeal, the constitutional right to free transcripts and a waiver of other costs of an appeal extends, to some extent, to discretionary appeals and habeas corpus appeals.[74]

A related issue arises when the record of a trial is lost or unavailable by the time of the appeal. If, for reasons that are no fault of the court or prosecution, a record of the trial is unavailable by the time of an appeal (e.g., the court reporter lost their notes or died leaving no notes that can be transcribed), there is no constitutional violation resulting from the absence of the record on appeal,[75] although as a matter of statutory law many jurisdictions will reverse a defendant's conviction.[76] Similarly, if a defendant was required under a jurisdiction's law to request a court reporter to record the relevant proceedings in the trial court and failed to do so (at least when then represented by counsel), absence of a transcription of the proceedings on appeal would not be a constitutional violation.[77]

---

72. Griffin v. Illinois, 351 U.S. 12 (1956) (plurality); *see also Mayer*, 404 U.S. at 193–94.

73. Draper v. Washington, 372 U.S. 487, 495 (1963); *see also* Britt v. North Carolina, 404 U.S. 226 (1971).

74. *See* Smith v. Bennett, 365 U.S. 708 (1961) (indigent prisoner is entitled to file a habeas corpus petition without paying the filing fee); Long v. Dist. Ct. of Iowa, 385 U.S. 192 (1966) (per curiam) (right to free transcription of state habeas corpus evidentiary hearing to be used on appeal in state court system); Gardner v. California, 393 U.S. 367 (1969) (right to free transcript of state habeas evidentiary hearing where state law prohibited appeal of denial of habeas corpus relief, but allowed petition to be refiled in an appellate court); *but cf.* United States v. MacCollom, 426 U.S. 317 (1976) (holding that it does not violate the Constitution to require a federal habeas corpus petitioner who did not file a direct appeal to show that their claims are nonfrivolous before affording them a free transcription of the trial proceedings). Therefore, while a habeas petitioner does not possess a constitutional right to free transcripts before filing a habeas corpus petition, if he thereafter files a petition and an evidentiary hearing is conducted, but habeas corpus relief is denied, the petitioner does have a right to free transcripts for the appeal. *Compare MacCollom*, 426 U.S. 317, *with Long*, 385 U.S. 192; *see also* Thompson v. Wainwright, 741 F.2d 213 (8th Cir. 1984).

75. *See* Norvell v. Illinois, 373 U.S. 420 (1963); *see also* Hemsley v. Warden, 236 A.2d 302 (Md. 1967). A different result would occur if a defendant was denied their constitutional right to counsel on a first appeal and the court reporter's notes were destroyed during the delay occasioned by the defendant's successful litigation over their right to counsel claim. *Cf.* Commonwealth v. De Simone, 290 A.2d 93 (Pa. 1972). In such a scenario, the loss of the record would be attributable to the violation of the right to counsel.

76. *See, e.g.*, United States v. Upshaw, 448 F.2d 1218, 1223 (5th Cir. 1971); Dunn v. State, 733 S.W.2d 212 (Tex. Crim. App. 1987).

77. *See, e.g.*, State v. Jones, 563 P.2d 1021, 1025 (Kan. 1977).

14.6 Standards of Review on Appeal

The "standard of review" applied by an appellate court to a particular issue raised on appeal is often as important as the underlying merits of the particular issue.[78] "A standard of review indicates to the reviewing court the degree of deference that it is to give to the actions and decisions under review. In other words, it is a statement of the power not only of the appellate court, but also of the tribunal below, measured by the hesitation of the appellate court to overturn the lower court's decision."[79]

The most common standards of review are: 1) the "de novo" or "plenary review" standard; 2) a deferential standard (such as the "abuse of discretion" standard); and 3) the "clear error" standard.[80] De novo review means that an appellate court gives no deference to the lower court's resolution of a particular issue (almost always a "legal" issue) and engages in an entirely independent consideration of the issue, while an abuse-of-discretion standard affords deference to the lower court's resolution of an issue, thus making a reversal more difficult than under a de novo standard.[81] A clear error standard applies to the lower court's factual findings and requires the appellate court to accept a factual finding as correct unless no rational factfinder could conclude otherwise based on the evidence introduced in the lower court.[82] Whether an issue is deemed a "factual" issue or a "legal" issue generally will dictate the level of appellate scrutiny given to the issue.[83]

Certain issues, however, are considered "mixed questions of law and fact" or issues of "constitutional fact," which has led courts to grapple over whether such issues should receive de novo or clear error review.[84] The Supreme Court's jurisprudence on such "mixed question" or issues of "constitutional fact" has been inconsistent.[85] For instance, the Court has held that the constitutional issues of whether a defendant's confession was involuntary,[86] whether a defendant was "in custody" for purposes of *Miranda*,[87] and whether probable cause or reasonable suspicion existed

---

78. *See* Mary M. Schroeder, *Appellate Justice Today: Fairness or Formulas*, 1994 WIS. L. REV. 9, 19 (1994).

79. Martha S. Davis, *Standards of Review: Judicial Review of Discretionary Decisionmaking*, 2 J. APP. PRAC. & PROCESS 47, 47–48 (Winter 2000).

80. *See generally* STEVEN ALAN CHILDRESS & MARTHA S. DAVIS, FEDERAL STANDARDS OF REVIEW (3d ed. 1999). A "standard of review" should be contrasted with "harmless-error review," which is discussed above. A standard of review factors in the appellate court's initial determination of whether a legal or factual error occurred in the proceedings in the lower court. Conversely, harmless-error review occurs (as a remedial issue) only after an appellate court has determined that there was error.

81. Ornelas v. United States, 517 U.S. 690, 694–700 & n.3 (1996).

82. Hernandez v. New York, 500 U.S. 352, 369–70 (1991) (plurality); *see also* Anderson v. Bessemer City, 470 U.S. 564, 573–75 (1985).

83. *See Hernandez*, 500 U.S. at 369–70; Miller v. Fenton, 474 U.S. 104, 113–14 (1985); *see also* Henry P. Monaghan, *Constitutional Fact Review*, 85 COLUM. L. REV. 229 (March 1985).

84. *Miller*, 474 U.S. at 113–14.

85. *Id.* at 110–14 (discussing cases).

86. *Id.* at 110–11; Beckwith v. United States, 425 U.S. 341, 348 (1976).

87. Thompson v. Keohane, 516 U.S. 99 (1995).

to support a search or seizure are "mixed questions" of law and fact that should be given de novo review on appeal.[88] Conversely, the Court has held that the issue of whether a defendant's consent to search given to a police officer was involuntary is a "factual" issue,[89] which has led the vast majority of lower courts to review the issue for "clear error" on appeal.[90] Another example of a factual issue of constitutional dimension—subject to clearly erroneous review on appeal—is whether a prosecutor or defense lawyer exercised a peremptory challenge in a discriminatory manner.[91] To add to the confusion, the Supreme Court has indicated that some constitutional issues may be reviewed in a de novo manner as "mixed questions" of fact and law on direct appeal, but must be treated as "factual" issues on habeas corpus review subject to tremendous deference to the trial court's findings.[92] As a general matter, an issue that has a constitutional component and is not determined solely by assessing a witness's credibility is a "mixed question" and receives de novo review on appeal, at least with respect to the legal component of the issue.[93]

A different type of standard of review applies to a trial court's jury instructions that are challenged on appeal as being unconstitutional in some respect (e.g., an unconstitutional definition of "reasonable doubt"). According to the Supreme Court, an appellate court must ask "whether there is a reasonable likelihood that the jury has applied the challenged instruction in a way that violates the Constitution."[94] The fact that a reasonable juror "could" or "might" have done so is insuf-

---

88. *Ornelas*, 517 U.S. at 694–700.

89. Ohio v. Robinette, 519 U.S. 33, 40 (1996) (citing Schneckloth v. Bustamonte, 412 U.S. 218, 227 (1973)).

90. *See, e.g.*, United States v. Erwin, 155 F.3d 818, 822 (6th Cir. 1998) (en banc); United States v. Tompkins, 130 F.3d 117, 120–21 & n.11 (5th Cir. 1997).

91. Hernandez v. New York, 500 U.S. 352, 367 (1991) (plurality); *id.* at 372–73 (O'Connor, J., joined by Scalia, J., concurring).

92. *See, e.g.*, Greene v. Georgia, 519 U.S. 145 (1996) (per curiam) (holding that state appellate court is not bound by Supreme Court's prior decision holding that question of whether a juror can set aside anti-death penalty views and fairly serve on a capital sentencing jury is a "factual" question subject to limited judicial review on federal habeas corpus).

　　For instance, in *Drope v. Missouri*, 420 U.S. 162, 174–75 & n.10 (1975), a direct appeal, the Court stated that although "factual" in nature, the issue of a defendant's mental competency was nevertheless a constitutional matter to be reviewed with some degree of independence by the Court. However, in two subsequent per curiam decisions decided in federal habeas corpus cases, the Court treated a defendant's mental competency as a question of fact—to be determined by a trial court— and subject to extremely limited appellate review. *See* Maggio v. Fulford, 462 U.S. 111 (1983) (per curiam); Demosthenes v. Baal, 495 U.S. 731 (1990) (per curiam); *but see* Maggio, 462 U.S. at 118–19 (White, J., concurring in judgment) (stating that competency is a mixed question of fact and law); *see also* Washington v. Johnson, 90 F.3d 945, 951 & n.4 (5th Cir. 1996) (discussing the apparent conflict in the Court's competency cases).

93. *See, e.g.*, United States v. McConney, 728 F.2d 1195, 1200–03 (9th Cir. 1984) (en banc).

94. Estelle v. McGuire, 502 U.S. 62, 72–73 & n.4 (1991); Boyde v. California, 494 U.S. 370, 380–81 (1990). The "reasonable likelihood" standard is essentially the same as the "reasonable probability" standard used in *Strickland v. Washington*, 466 U.S. 668, 694 (1984). *See Boyde*, 494 U.S. at 380 n.4.

ficient to warrant a reversal on appeal.[95] If an appellate court finds an instruction unconstitutional under this standard, the court still must determine whether the error was harmless.[96]

14.7 Sufficiency-of-the-Evidence Review on Appeal

One special type of standard of review concerns an appellate court's review of the sufficiency of the evidence offered in support of the jury's verdict. As discussed in Chapter Nine, under the Due Process Clause, a defendant cannot be convicted of the charged offense unless a "rational jury" could find all of the elements of the offense beyond a reasonable doubt. In *Jackson v. Virginia*,[97] the Supreme Court held that an appellate court reviewing a jury's guilty verdict thus must reverse the conviction when a rational jury could not have found each element of the charged offense beyond a reasonable doubt based on the evidence offered at the trial. When engaging in such "sufficiency review," an appellate court must consider the evidence "in a light most favorable to the prosecution"[98]—resolving reasonably disputed facts in the prosecution's favor—but cannot consider any evidence not offered at the trial itself, even if it is contained elsewhere in the record.[99] If an appeals court reverses a conviction after finding constitutionally insufficient evidence under the *Jackson* standard, the Double Jeopardy Clause prevents a retrial of the defendant.[100]

An open question that has divided the lower courts[101] is whether an appellate court may find sufficient evidence in a case in which the defendant testified at trial, when the remaining evidence would not prove the defendant's guilt beyond a reasonable doubt, based on the supposition that jurors discredited the defendant's exculpatory testimony and inferred the opposite to be true.[102]

---

95. *Boyde*, 494 U.S. at 380–81.

96. *See* Calderon v. Coleman, 525 U.S. 141, 146–47 (1998) (per curiam) (*Boyde* standard of review and harmless-error doctrine are separate types of analysis that each must be applied on appeal).

97. Jackson v. Virginia, 443 U.S. 307 (1979).

98. *Id.* at 319.

99. Young v. Guste, 849 F.2d 970, 973 n.2 (5th Cir. 1988).

100. Burks v. United States, 437 U.S. 1 (1978).

101. *Compare, e.g.*, United States v. Zeigler, 994 F.2d 845, 845–46 (D.C. Cir. 1993) (holding that an appellate court may not find sufficient evidence based on the supposition that jurors found the defendant's exculpatory testimony incredible and found the opposite to be true), *with* United States v. Zafiro, 945 F.2d 881, 888 (7th Cir. 1991) (finding sufficient evidence based on such a supposition); *see also* Stallings v. Tansy, 28 F.3d 1018, 1023–24 (10th Cir. 1994) (discussing the differing approaches of the Second, Fifth, Seventh, Ninth, Eleventh, and D.C. Circuits in criminal appeals).

102. Although three members of the Supreme Court have addressed the issue, *see* Wright v. West, 505 U.S. 277, 295–96 (1992) (plurality opinion of Thomas, J., joined by Rehnquist, C.J., & Scalia, J.) (stating that an appellate court may find sufficient evidence based on the supposition that jurors found the defendant's exculpatory testimony to be incredible), a majority of the Court has never addressed the issue in a criminal case. In civil cases, the Court has stated that "[n]ormally the discredited testimony [of a witness] is not considered a sufficient basis for drawing a contrary

14.8 Leading Supreme Court Decisions Concerning Direct Appeal Practice

- *McKane v. Durston*, 153 U.S. 684 (1894) (no constitutional right to appeal in a criminal case, at least in noncapital case).

- *Griffin v. Illinois*, 351 U.S. 12 (1956) (if a particular jurisdiction affords a direct appeal process in criminal cases, as the vast majority have done, due process and equal protection require the jurisdiction to supply free transcripts or an adequate substitute to indigent appellants and must waive filing fee for indigents as well).

- *Douglas v. California*, 372 U.S. 353 (1963) (if a particular jurisdiction provides a direct appeal process in criminal cases, as the vast majority have done, due process and equal protection require the jurisdiction to afford indigent appellants appointed counsel on "the first appeal as a matter of right" in direct appeal process).

- *Chapman v. California*, 386 U.S. 18 (1967) (setting forth "harmless-error" standard applicable to the vast majority of constitutional claims raised on direct appeal; prosecution has the burden to prove "beyond a reasonable doubt" that such constitutional error did not contribute to the verdict or sentence).

- *Ross v. Moffitt*, 417 U.S. 600 (1974) (holding that there is no constitutional right to appellate counsel for discretionary appeals beyond the "first appeal as a matter of right" in the direct review process).

- *Jackson v. Virginia*, 443 U.S. 307 (1979) (holding that an appellate court must reverse a criminal conviction if a "rational jury" could not have found each element of the charged offense beyond a reasonable doubt based on the evidence offered at trial).

- *Griffith v. Kentucky*, 479 U.S. 314 (1987) (a "new rule" of constitutional criminal procedure is applicable to all cases not yet "final" at the time the new rule was announced; "finality" defined as a conclusion of direct appeal process or, if no direct appeal was filed, the last date on which a notice of appeal could have been timely filed).

- *Osborne v. Ohio*, 495 U.S. 103 (1990) (discussing the requirement of error preservation in the trial court, i.e., the "contemporaneous objection rule"; if defense reasonably and timely raised a specific issue in a manner that

---

conclusion." Bose Corp. v. Consumers Union of United States, Inc., 466 U.S. 485, 512 (1984); *see also* Moore v. Chesapeake & Ohio R. Co., 340 U.S. 573, 576 (1951) ("disbelief of [a witness's] testimony would not supply a want of proof ").

called an alleged error to trial court's attention, appellate court should address merits of claim rather than procedurally default it).

- *Boyde v. California*, 494 U.S. 370 (1990) (in determining whether a trial court's jury instructions were erroneous in some manner, an appellate court asks whether there was a "reasonable likelihood" that jurors interpreted the instructions in the allegedly erroneous manner).

- *Sullivan v. Louisiana*, 508 U.S. 275 (1993) ("structural" errors not subject to harmless-error analysis under *Chapman*; specifically holding that an unconstitutional definition of reasonable doubt in jury instructions is such a structural error warranting automatic reversal of conviction on appeal).

- *Ornelas v. United States*, 517 U.S. 690 (1996) (discussing the difference between de novo and deferential standards of appellate review of constitutional issues).

- *Smith v. Robbins*, 528 U.S. 259 (2000) (leading modern decision concerning the right to the effective assistance of counsel on direct appeal; also holding that an "*Anders* brief" need not comply with precise requirements of *Anders v. California*, 386 U.S. 738 (1967)).

- *Halbert v. Michigan*, 545 U.S. 605 (2005) (extending right to counsel on appeal first announced in *Douglas v. California* to all first-round appeals, whether discretionary or as a matter of right).

- *Garza v. Idaho*, 139 S. Ct. 738 (2019) (defense counsel deprives a defendant of the Sixth Amendment right to effective assistance of counsel by refusing to file a notice of appeal even if the defendant waived their right to appeal in a plea agreement).

CHAPTER FIFTEEN

POSTCONVICTION HABEAS CORPUS REVIEW

After the direct appeal process has been completed, a criminal defendant may file a "collateral" challenge to a conviction and/or sentence.[1] Such collateral review—most commonly referred to as "habeas corpus"[2]—is a separate quasi-civil proceeding, typically filed with the original trial court, and is not a continuation of the "direct" review process.[3] Postconviction habeas corpus review should be distinguished from preconviction habeas corpus actions, which may be filed in federal court under 28 U.S.C. § 2241 when a defendant wishes to challenge a state's right to proceed on criminal charges as a violation of the Double Jeopardy Clause.[4] Certain jurisdictions also permit preconviction habeas corpus actions to challenge "excessive" bail amounts or outright denials of bail.[5] In the vast majority of jurisdictions, to file any type of habeas corpus action, a criminal defendant must be in custody at the time that the habeas corpus petition is filed, although that term has been liberally construed in this context (e.g., being released on bond, parole, or probation generally qualifies as "custody").[6]

---

1. Occasionally, defendants who did not file a direct appeal will file a habeas corpus petition alleging claims that could not have been raised on direct appeal (e.g., ineffective assistance of counsel or *Brady* claims).
2. "Habeas corpus" is Latin for "you have the body" and historically was a directive to a warden with custody over a prisoner to bring them to court. BLACK'S LAW DICTIONARY 728 (8th ed. 2004).
3. For a discussion of the difference between direct and collateral review, see Chapter Fourteen.
4. *See, e.g.*, Arizona v. Washington, 434 U.S. 497 (1978). Such a preconviction federal habeas corpus action theoretically could be based on other types of constitutional claims where there are special circumstances permitting such a pretrial challenge to a state's right to prosecute a defendant (e.g., a defendant can show that a state criminal prosecution is being brought in bad faith without any legitimate basis in law or fact). *See* Carden v. Montana, 626 F.2d 82, 83–84 (9th Cir. 1980). In reality, however, preconviction federal habeas petitions filed by state inmates are almost always limited to double jeopardy claims, which may be litigated in an interlocutory manner prior to a trial in a successive prosecution. *See* Justices of Boston Municipal Court v. Lydon, 466 U.S. 294, 302–03 (1984). For a discussion of successive prosecution double jeopardy claims, *see* Chapter Four.
5. *See, e.g.*, Ex parte Shumake, 953 S.W.2d 842, 843 n.3 (Tex. App. 1997); Rainwater v. Langley, 587 S.E.2d 18 (Ga. 2003).
6. *See, e.g.*, Maleng v. Cook, 490 U.S. 488 (1989) (per curiam); Mendez v. Superior Court, 104 Cal. Rptr. 2d 839, 841–42 (Cal. Ct. App. 2001).

Criminal defendants convicted in the state courts have the opportunity to file two types of postconviction habeas corpus actions—the first in the state court system and a subsequent action in the federal court system under 28 U.S.C. § 2254.[7] Both "record" and "extra-record" claims may be litigated in a habeas corpus action, although in most jurisdictions, a record claim usually may not be litigated on habeas corpus review if it could have been raised on direct appeal, but was not so raised.[8] Furthermore, with limited exceptions in both the state and federal court systems, only constitutional claims are "cognizable" on habeas corpus review; the vast majority of nonconstitutional claims may not be litigated on collateral review.[9] The most common types of "extra-record" claims are those alleging ineffective assistance of counsel, prosecutorial and police misconduct, and jury misconduct.[10]

A related, but distinct (and rarely used) federal postconviction remedy available to convicted federal defendants[11] is a "writ of coram nobis." Coram nobis is an attack on a prior conviction when a defendant is no longer in any type of "custody." Coram nobis relief is available only for "extraordinary" errors that were not apparent at the time of trial and resulted in a fundamental miscarriage of justice, causing serious prejudice to a defendant after being released from custody (e.g., significant civil disabilities). In addition, to prevail, a defendant must show good cause for failing to have challenged the conviction on direct or habeas corpus review.[12]

15.1 State Habeas Corpus Review

Although the Supreme Court has held that a criminal defendant does not possess a constitutional right to a direct appeal, the Court has not yet held that a state defendant possesses no constitutional right to some type of state court collateral review of federal constitutional challenges to their conviction or sentence,[13] but it

---

7. Unlike state prisoners, who may seek habeas corpus relief from both the state and federal courts, federal prisoners challenging their federal convictions or sentences have no ability to obtain habeas corpus relief from state courts and instead are limited to seeking relief from the federal courts. *See, e.g.*, Ableman v. Booth, 62 U.S. 506 (1858).

8. Bousley v. United States, 523 U.S. 614 (1998); Lockett v. State, 644 So. 2d 34 (Ala. 1994). A record claim may be raised in a federal habeas corpus action as long as it was first raised or ruled on in the state court system. Rose v. Lundy, 455 U.S. 509 (1982).

9. *See, e.g.*, Smith v. Phillips, 455 U.S. 209, 221 (1982); Ex parte Sanchez, 918 S.W.2d 526, 527 (Tex. Crim. App. 1996); *but cf.* Stone v. Powell, 428 U.S. 465 (1976) (Fourth Amendment claims not cognizable on federal habeas corpus review).

10. *See* Chapter Thirteen.

11. The federal writ of coram nobis is unavailable to state defendants seeking relief from a federal court. *See, e.g.*, Sinclair v. Louisiana, 679 F.2d 513, 514–15 (5th Cir. 1982). Certain states, however, allow for an equivalent coram nobis remedy. *See, e.g.*, Larimore v. State, 938 S.W.2d 818, 822 (Ark. 1997).

12. *See* United States v. Morgan, 346 U.S. 502 (1954); *see also* United States v. Esogbue, 357 F.3d 532, 535 (5th Cir. 2004).

13. *See* Case v. Nebraska, 381 U.S. 336 (1965) (per curiam) (granting certiorari to decide "whether the Fourteenth Amendment requires the States to afford state prisoners some adequate corrective

did make such a statement in dicta.[14] It is clear, however, that if a state provides a habeas corpus or other collateral remedy, as all states do in most criminal cases, then the state courts must afford defendants procedures that comport with basic due process.[15] In addition, if a state court addresses the merits of a federal constitutional claim raised in a state collateral appeal and does not rest its decision on an "independent and adequate state law ground" (for example, a procedural default), then the Supreme Court has jurisdiction to review the state court's judgment on collateral review.[16]

Notably, the Supreme Court has remanded state habeas corpus cases to the state courts to conduct evidentiary hearings when the state courts initially denied a hearing in spite of a defendant's allegations in a state habeas corpus petition that if true, would entitle the defendant to relief.[17] Traditionally, however, the Supreme Court defers consideration of otherwise "cert-worthy" issues to permit the lower federal courts the opportunity to address the issues on subsequent federal habeas corpus review.[18] In view of the many procedural and substantive hurdles that a state prisoner faces on federal habeas corpus review, the Supreme Court increasingly has granted review—and ultimately granted relief—in situations in which the prisoner would lose on federal habeas review but has raised a meritorious constitutional claim.[19]

---

process for the hearing and determination of claims of violation of federal constitutional guarantees," *id.* at 337, but refusing to address the issue because the state legislature provided for such review after certiorari was granted); *see also* Kyles v. Whitley, 498 U.S. 931, 932 (1990) (Stevens, J., concurring in the denial of a stay of execution) (noting that "the scope of a State's obligation to provide collateral review is shrouded in so much uncertainty").

14. *See* Pennsylvania v. Finley, 481 U.S. 551, 557 (1987).

15. *See* Long v. Dist. Ct. of Iowa, 385 U.S. 192 (1966) (per curiam) (state prisoner has constitutional right to free court reporter's transcription of state habeas corpus evidentiary hearing for purpose of appeal in state court system); *cf.* Ohio Adult Parole Authority v. Woodard, 523 U.S. 272, 288–90 (1998) (O'Connor, J., joined by Souter, Ginsburg, & Breyer, JJ., concurring in judgment) (basic due process protections apply in postconviction clemency process); *id.* at 291–92 (Stevens, J., dissenting); Ford v. Wainwright, 477 U.S. 399, 418–27 (1986) (Powell, J., concurring in judgment) (basic due process protections apply in postconviction process to determine the competency of death row inmate to be executed).

16. *See, e.g.,* Smith v. Texas, 543 U.S. 37 (2004) (per curiam).

17. *See, e.g.,* Wilde v. Wyoming, 362 U.S. 607 (1960) (per curiam); Pennsylvania ex rel. Herman v. Claudy, 350 U.S. 116 (1956); *cf.* Giles v. Maryland, 386 U.S. 66 (1967) (plurality) (remanding to state courts for reconsideration of a federal constitutional claim based on police reports first made part of the record in front of the U.S. Supreme Court).

18. *Kyles,* 498 U.S. at 932 (Stevens, J., concurring in the denial of a stay of execution); *see also* Spencer v. Georgia, 500 U.S. 960, 960 (1991) (Kennedy, J., concurring in the denial of certiorari).

19. *See, e.g.,* Madison v. Alabama, 139 S. Ct. 718, 726 (2019) (granting relief on the merits of a state prisoner's Eighth Amendment claim that the Court had previously rejected on federal habeas review without actually addressing the merits); *see also* Z. Payvand Ahdout, *Direct Collateral Review,* 121 COLUM. L. REV. 159 (2021) (discussing the Supreme Court's increasing tendency to grant certiorari and review state courts' decisions issued on state habeas corpus review).

As discussed below, two major procedural hurdles that prisoners face on federal habeas corpus review are the *Teague* nonretroactivity doctrine concerning "new rules" of constitutional criminal procedure[20] and the *Brecht* harmless-error doctrine.[21] The Supreme Court has not yet addressed whether *Brecht* applies to state habeas corpus cases, and the state courts are divided.[22] In *Danforth v. Minnesota*,[23] the Supreme Court held that state courts possess discretion whether to follow *Teague*'s retroactivity framework on state collateral review for "new rules" of constitutional law. However, in *Montgomery v. Louisiana*,[24] the Court held that state courts must apply "substantive" new rules retroactively on state collateral review.

15.2 Federal Postconviction Habeas Corpus Actions[25]

Article I, Section 9 of the Constitution, commonly referred to as the "Habeas Corpus Suspension Clause," provides: "The Privilege of the Writ of Habeas Corpus shall not be suspended, unless when in Cases of Rebellion or Invasion, the public Safety may require it."[26] The Supreme Court has held that Congress may not totally "suspend" the federal habeas corpus remedy except for the reasons set forth in the text of the Constitution, but may impose reasonable restrictions on the scope of the remedy (such as denying a prisoner the opportunity to file multiple habeas corpus actions without showing good cause for doing so).[27]

Starting with *Brown v. Allen*,[28] a case decided shortly before Chief Justice Earl Warren's tenure on the Supreme Court began in 1953, and continuing through the early 1970s, federal habeas corpus review was the vehicle for numerous major decisions affecting constitutional criminal procedure.[29] Beginning in the mid-1970s, and culminating with the Antiterrorism and Effective Death Penalty Act of 1996 (AEDPA),[30] the Supreme Court and Congress erected numerous procedural (and a few substantive) hurdles over which prisoners—particularly state prisoners—must

---

20. Teague v. Lane, 489 U.S. 288 (1989).

21. Brecht v. Abrahamson, 507 U.S. 619 (1993).

22. *Compare, e.g.*, Hill v. State, 615 N.W.2d 135, 140–41 (N.D. 2000) (refusing to apply *Brecht* on state habeas corpus review), *with* Ex parte Fierro, 934 S.W.2d 370, 371–72 (Tex. Crim. App. 1996) (applying *Brecht* on state habeas corpus review).

23. Danforth v. Minnesota, 552 U.S. 264 (2008).

24. Montgomery v. Louisiana, 136 S. Ct. 718 (2016).

25. Any practitioner handling a federal habeas corpus case should consult the extremely comprehensive treatise by JAMES S. LIEBMAN AND RANDY HERTZ, FEDERAL HABEAS CORPUS PRACTICE & PROCEDURE (7th ed. 2016).

26. U.S. CONST. art. I, § 9 (capitalization in original).

27. Felker v. Turpin, 518 U.S. 651, 663–64 (1996).

28. Brown v. Allen, 344 U.S. 443 (1953).

29. *See, e.g.*, Barker v. Wingo, 407 U.S. 514 (1972); Stovall v. Denno, 388 U.S. 293 (1967); Pate v. Robinson, 383 U.S. 375 (1966); Townsend v. Sain, 372 U.S. 293 (1963).

30. 104 Pub. L. No. 132, 110 Stat. 1214 (Apr. 24, 1996).

now jump before the federal courts can grant them relief based on a federal constitutional violation affecting their convictions or sentences.

Despite such hurdles, which are discussed below, the federal writ of habeas corpus still is a viable remedy for federal constitutional violations in many cases.[31] Certain types of claims—ineffective assistance of counsel claims, prosecutorial and police misconduct claims, and claims based on intervening watershed interpretations of the "substantive" penal law[32]—typically are discovered only well after sentencing and thus are raised on habeas corpus review rather than on direct review.

15.2.1 Differences Among 28 U.S.C. §§ 2241, 2254, and 2255 Actions

There are three different types of federal habeas corpus remedies. The two most common are set forth in 28 U.S.C. § 2254 and 28 U.S.C. § 2255. Section 2254 permits defendants convicted in state court to challenge their convictions or sentences in federal court on constitutional grounds after unsuccessfully litigated their constitutional claims through the state court system (on direct appeal or state habeas corpus review). Section 2255 is the analog of § 2254 for federal prisoners who wish to attack their federal convictions or sentences. Although the plain language of § 2255 speaks of a "motion attacking sentence," the courts have construed § 2255 as a vehicle to challenge a federal defendant's conviction as well as sentence.[33] Ordinary nonconstitutional claims (such as a state trial court's violation of state law or a federal sentencing court's misapplication of the U.S. Sentencing Guidelines) generally are not cognizable in a § 2254 or § 2255 case.[34] An open question is whether a convicted capital defendant's claim of "actual innocence"—based on "truly persuasive" evidence discovered after the death sentence was imposed—is cognizable in a federal habeas corpus action and if shown to have merit would require federal courts to prevent the inmate's execution from occurring.[35]

Section 2241 permits a postconviction challenge by an inmate who alleges a defect in the implementation of their sentence as opposed to a constitutional defect in the underlying conviction or sentence—such as loss of "good-time credit" for

---

31. *See, e.g.*, Smith v. Cain, 565 U.S. 73 (2012); Abdul-Kabir v. Quarterman, 550 U.S. 233 (2007); Banks v. Dretke, 540 U.S. 668 (2004); Wiggins v. Smith, 539 U.S. 510 (2003); Penry v. Johnson, 532 U.S. 782 (2001).
32. *See, e.g.*, Bailey v. United States, 516 U.S. 137 (1995).
33. *See, e.g.*, United States v. Hayman, 342 U.S. 205 (1952).
34. *See, e.g.*, Estelle v. McGuire, 502 U.S. 62 (1991); United States v. Timmreck, 441 U.S. 780 (1979); *but see* Peguero v. United States, 526 U.S. 23 (1999) (federal district court's failure to advise a federal criminal defendant of his statutory right to appeal is cognizable in a § 2255 case if the defendant was prejudiced thereby).
35. *See* Herrera v. Collins, 506 U.S. 390, 417 (1993) (assuming, without deciding, that the execution of an innocent person would be unconstitutional and thus a showing of actual innocence would be a basis for federal habeas corpus relief); *id.* at 419 (O'Connor, J., joined by Kennedy, concurring) (execution of innocent person would be unconstitutional); *id.* at 429 (White, J., concurring in judgment) (same).

invalid reasons or a wrongful revocation of parole.[36] The federal courts of appeals are divided over whether § 2241 (as opposed to § 2254) is the proper vehicle for such a challenge to the implementation of a sentence by a state prisoner.[37] Section 2241 also is a vehicle for persons alleging that they are being illegally detained in immigration custody[38] and in military custody.[39] Finally, the Supreme Court has held that it possesses jurisdiction under § 2241 to grant an "original" writ of habeas corpus to state or federal prisoners in exceptional cases when there are procedural or jurisdictional obstacles under §§ 2254 or 2255,[40] although the Court has never done so in the modern era.[41]

There are significant differences regarding venue for § 2241 cases and §§ 2254 or 2255 cases. With the exception of original writs filed directly with the U.S. Supreme Court, prisoners may bring a § 2241 action only in the federal district where they are in custody.[42] A state defendant may bring a § 2254 action in either the district of incarceration or the district where the inmate was convicted,[43] although a court in the district of incarceration is empowered to transfer the case to the district of conviction if it is more convenient for the parties and witnesses.[44] A federal prisoner must bring a § 2255 action in the district of conviction, and the case ordinarily is assigned to the judge who sentenced the defendant.[45]

15.2.2 *Judicially Created Hurdles*

Long before Congress erected numerous hurdles to federal habeas corpus relief in the AEDPA (discussed below), the Supreme Court created some of its own barriers.

---

36. *See, e.g.*, United States v. Cleto, 956 F.2d 83, 84 (5th Cir. 1992).

37. *Compare, e.g.*, Wadsworth v. Johnson, 235 F.3d 959 (5th Cir. 2000) (§ 2254 is the exclusive remedy for state prisoners), *with* Montez v. McKinna, 208 F.3d 862, 865 (10th Cir. 2000) (§ 2241 is an appropriate vehicle for state prisoners challenging the "execution" of their sentences). Whether § 2241 is available for state prisoners is important in a practical sense, as some of the hurdles facing § 2254 petitioners are not present in a § 2241 case. *See* White v. Lambert, 370 F.3d 1002, 1008 (9th Cir. 2004).

38. *See, e.g.*, Zadvydas v. Davis, 533 U.S. 678 (2001).

39. *See, e.g.*, Rumsfeld v. Padilla, 542 U.S. 426 (2004).

40. Felker v. Turpin, 518 U.S. 651, 660, 664–65 (1996). The writ is considered an original writ because it is filed with the Supreme Court in the first instance (rather than being filed in the lower federal courts and appealed to the Supreme Court), although the Court exercises its appellate (rather than its original) jurisdiction in such cases. *Id.* at 667 n.1 (Souter, J., concurring).

41. *See, e.g.*, In re Stanford, 537 U.S. 968 (2002) (per curiam) (5-4 decision); Breard v. Greene, 523 U.S. 371 (1998) (per curiam); In re McDonald, 489 U.S. 180, 184–85 (1989) (per curiam).

42. *Rumsfeld*, 542 U.S. at 433–451.

43. *See Wadsworth*, 235 F.3d at 961.

44. *See, e.g.*, Pracht v. Beard, 2004 U.S. Dist. LEXIS 19621 (E.D. Pa. Sept. 23, 2004). Some federal districts have local rules requiring the petition to be litigated in the district of conviction. *See, e.g.*, E.D.CAL. L.R. 81–191(g).

45. United States v. Hayman, 342 U.S. 205 (1952).

15.2.2.1 Procedural Default[46]

If the defense failed to object to a violation of the defendant's rights in the trial court or failed to raise a claim on direct appeal (even if it was raised in the trial court), ordinarily the defendant's claim will be "procedurally defaulted" or "procedurally barred" on federal habeas corpus review.[47] Unless one of the exceptions applies (discussed below), a federal court may not grant habeas corpus relief, even if the claim has merit.

Procedural default is an "affirmative defense," which means that ordinarily the prosecution waives the right to invoke a procedural bar on federal habeas corpus review unless it raises the bar in a timely manner in federal district court.[48] The lower federal courts are divided over whether a federal court on habeas corpus review—including a federal appellate court in the first instance—may raise a procedural bar sua sponte.[49] It is clear, however, in a § 2254 case that unless state courts make a "plain statement" about the defense, they are procedurally defaulting a claim presented for review; neither the prosecution nor the federal courts may rely on the petitioner's failure to comply with the state procedural rule; and the federal courts must address the merits of a federal constitutional claim.[50]

In a § 2254 case, a procedural default also does not preclude federal court review if the state's procedural rule is not an "independent and adequate state law ground."[51] A state procedural rule is not "independent" if its operation requires the application of federal constitutional law.[52] A state procedural bar is not "adequate" if the state court has not consistently and regularly applied the procedural rule to similarly situated defendants.[53] Likewise, a novel application of a state procedural

---

46. Procedural default in the context of both direct appeal and habeas corpus appeals is discussed in Chapter Fourteen. It is further discussed in this chapter in the specific context of federal habeas corpus review.

47. *See* Wainwright v. Sykes, 433 U.S. 72 (1977); Frady v. United States, 456 U.S. 152 (1982); Bousley v. United States, 523 U.S. 614 (1998).

48. Gray v. Netherland, 518 U.S. 152, 165–66 (1996).

49. *See* Trest v. Cain, 522 U.S. 87, 90 (1997) (noting a circuit split on the issue, but declining to resolve it in that case); *see also* Jeffrey C. Metzcar, *Raising the Defense of Procedural Default Sua Sponte: Who Will Enforce the Great Writ of Liberty?*, 50 CASE W. RES. L. REV. 869 (Summer 2000).

50. Harris v. Reed, 489 U.S. 255 (1989); *see also* Lewis v. Sternes, 390 F.3d 1019, 1029–30 (7th Cir. 2004).

51. *See* Catherine T. Struve, *Direct and Collateral Federal Court Review of the Adequacy of State Procedural Rules*, 103 COLUM. L. REV. 243 (March 2003).

52. *See* Ake v. Oklahoma, 470 U.S. 68, 75 (1985) (in determining whether error would be addressed on direct appeal notwithstanding defendant's failure to object in court below, state appellate court sought to determine whether error was of federal constitutional magnitude; Supreme Court held that state court's procedural bar was thus not "independent"); *but cf.* Stewart v. Smith, 536 U.S. 856 (2002) (per curiam) (state court's procedural default rule did not require court to consider the "merits" of a defaulted constitutional claim, and thus the default was an "independent" state law ground).

53. Dugger v. Adams, 489 U.S. 401, 409–10 (1989). However, in *Beard v. Kindler*, 558 U.S. 53 (2009), the Supreme Court held that merely because a state procedural default rule is discretionary—

---

rule to a defendant where there was no fair warning of the procedural rule is not adequate.[54] In addition, if a state inequitably applies a generally sound procedural rule in an "exorbitant" manner, then the procedural bar will not be adequate.[55]

There are two primary exceptions to the application of an otherwise valid procedural bar. First, if a habeas petitioner shows both cause for the procedural default and prejudice resulting from application of the procedural bar, then a federal court must address the merits of the otherwise defaulted claim.[56] "Cause" usually means some objective factor external to the defense that prevented compliance with the state procedural rule[57] or a showing of ineffective assistance of counsel (within the meaning of *Strickland v. Washington*[58]) in failing to preserve the issue at trial or on direct appeal.[59] The fact that it would have been futile to raise a particular claim in the face of adverse appellate precedent at the time of default is not sufficient cause.[60] Conversely, if a claim was truly novel at the time of the default—in that no existing precedent reasonably supported the claim and no reasonable lawyer would have thought to raise the claim—then such novelty does constitute sufficient cause.[61] "Prejudice" means not merely the possibility of prejudice, but that the error "worked to [the defendant's] *actual* and substantial disadvantage, infecting their entire trial [or sentencing] with an error of constitutional dimensions."[62]

With respect to cause resulting from ineffectiveness by a federal habeas corpus petitioner's prior state court attorney, the Supreme Court has held that ordinarily, such cause exists only when the ineffectiveness occurred at a point when the Sixth Amendment guaranteed the right to the assistance of counsel—in trial or sentencing proceedings or on the first round of the direct appeal (and not on subsequent

---

meaning it is applied in some, but not all cases by a state appellate court exercising its discretion—does not automatically render the procedural rule an inadequate state law ground.

54. Ford v. Georgia, 498 U.S. 411 (1991).

55. Lee v. Kemna, 534 U.S. 362, 375 (2002).

56. *See* Coleman v. Thompson, 501 U.S. 722, 730 (1991).

57. Amadeo v. Zant, 486 U.S. 214 (1988) (concluding that the belated discovery of relevant evidence by the defense resulting from the prosecution's intentional suppression of such evidence was cause).

58. Strickland v. Washington, 466 U.S. 668 (1984). Ineffective assistance of counsel issues are discussed in Chapter Thirteen.

59. *See* Murray v. Carrier, 477 U.S. 478 (1986).

60. Engle v. Isaac, 456 U.S. 107 (1982). It is arguable, however, that failure to raise an issue in a lower court that is squarely foreclosed by a higher court's precedent would constitute sufficient cause. *See* Brent E. Newton, *An Argument for Reviving the Actual Futility Exception to the Supreme Court's Procedural Default Doctrine*, 4 J. APP. PRAC. & PROCESS 521 (2002) (discussing conflicting decisions in the Supreme Court's jurisprudence regarding the futility of objecting in view of a higher court's precedent).

61. Reed v. Ross, 468 U.S. 1 (1984). However, if the claim lost its novelty only after the defendant's conviction became final on direct appeal, then *Teague v. Lane*, 489 U.S. 288 (1989), would likely preclude habeas corpus relief on the ground that the claim relied on a new rule of law. The *Teague* doctrine is discussed below.

62. Frady v. United States, 456 U.S. 152, 170 (1982).

appeals, including state habeas corpus review).[63] The Court has recognized two exceptions to this general rule. First, if an attorney in state court proceedings beyond the first appeal entirely abandoned their client without notice—resulting in a procedural default—then such abandonment can constitute cause.[64]

Second, although ordinarily the mere negligence of a state habeas corpus attorney will not serve as cause for a procedural default—insofar as the Sixth Amendment did not provide the right to counsel at the point when the default occurred—the Supreme Court has made a limited exception for a defaulted Sixth Amendment claim of ineffective assistance of counsel.[65] If an attorney representing a state prisoner on an initial state habeas corpus review failed to raise a claim of ineffectiveness concerning the prisoner's trial or direct appeal attorney and the state court thereafter procedurally defaulted that claim for that reason, the prisoner thereafter may raise that claim on federal habeas corpus review by establishing that the prior state attorney was ineffective and failed to raise the ineffectiveness claim.[66] Similarly, a state court's failure to provide appointed counsel to an indigent state prisoner on their initial state habeas corpus appeal also constitutes cause for the pro se prisoner's failure to raise an ineffectiveness claim at that juncture.[67]

In addition to showing cause and prejudice, a federal habeas petitioner can circumvent a procedural bar with a showing by a preponderance of the evidence that but for the unpreserved constitutional error, the defendant would not have been found guilty of the offense of conviction.[68] In capital cases, a defendant also may circumvent a procedural bar by showing by clear and convincing evidence that but for the unpreserved constitutional error, no rational judge or jury would have found them eligible for the death penalty.[69] The lower courts are divided over whether this exception applies to procedural bars related to constitutional challenges to noncapital sentences.[70]

In a § 2254 case, if a lower state court procedurally defaulted a claim, but a higher state appellate court disregarded the lower court's procedural default ruling and instead addressed the merits of the claim, the federal courts may not rely on the procedural default and must address the merits of the claim.[71] However, if a lower

---

63. Coleman v. Thompson, 501 U.S. 722 (1991).
64. Maples v. Thomas, 565 U.S. 266 (2012).
65. Martinez v. Ryan, 566 U.S. 1 (2012).
66. *Id.* at 7–15.
67. *Id.* at 16; *see also* Trevino v. Thayler, 569 U.S. 413 (2013); *but cf.* Davila v. Davis, 137 S. Ct. 2058 (2017) (federal habeas court is not allowed to hear procedurally defaulted claim of ineffective assistance of direct appeal counsel based on the fact that the petitioner's state postconviction counsel provided ineffective assistance by failing to raise that claim).
68. Schlup v. Delo, 513 U.S. 298 (1995).
69. Sawyer v. Whitley, 505 U.S. 333, 336 (1992).
70. Dretke v. Haley, 541 U.S. 386, 392 (2004) (noting the division among the lower federal courts on this issue, but declining to resolve the split in that case); *see also* Lindsey v. United States, 615 F.3d 998, 1001 (8th Cir. 2010) (noting persistent circuit split).
71. Harris v. Reed, 489 U.S. 255 (1989).

state court procedurally defaulted a claim and the state appellate court denied relief without written order (thus without affirming or rejecting the lower court's procedural ruling), federal habeas courts must presume that the state appellate court adopted the lower court's procedural default ruling.[72]

15.2.2.2   *Teague* Nonretroactivity Doctrine[73]

In *Teague v. Lane*,[74] the Supreme Court held that with limited exceptions (discussed below), a state or federal defendant on federal habeas corpus review is not entitled to have a new rule of constitutional criminal procedure applied to them unless the rule was logically dictated by existing precedent at the time that the petitioner's conviction became final on direct appeal (when the Supreme Court denied certiorari or at the point in the direct review process when a defendant ceased pursuing discretionary appeals). If no direct appeal was filed, a conviction became final for purposes of *Teague* when the time for filing a notice of appeal expired.[75] The *Teague* bar ordinarily is raised by the prosecution; if it is not raised by the prosecution, a federal court (including a federal appellate court) has discretion to raise the *Teague* bar sua sponte.[76]

Teague applies both to situations where a federal habeas corpus petitioner seeks to rely on a "new rule" announced in another case (decided after the petitioner's conviction became final) and to situations where a petitioner raises a claim that itself proposes a new rule not yet announced in any prior case. *Teague* does not bar the application of a preexisting general rule to a novel set of facts when the general rule logically dictates the outcome.[77] "Existing precedent" for *Teague* purposes appears to include Supreme Court precedent as well as decisions of the lower courts (at least where there is a consensus or clear majority among the lower courts that addressed the issue when the Supreme Court had not yet done so).[78]

---

72. Ylst v. Nunnemaker, 501 U.S. 797 (1991).

73. Retroactivity of "new rules" to cases on direct appeal is discussed in Chapter Fourteen.

74. Teague v. Lane, 489 U.S. 288 (1989) (plurality). Justice O'Connor's plurality opinion in *Teague* was adopted by a majority of the Supreme Court in numerous subsequent cases. *See, e.g.*, Beard v. Banks, 542 U.S. 406 (2004); Caspari v. Bohlen, 510 U.S. 383 (1994).

75. *See, e.g.,* Ferguson v. United States, 911 F. Supp. 424, 428 (C.D. Cal. 1995).

76. *See Caspari*, 510 U.S. at 389.

77. *See* Wright v. West, 505 U.S. 277, 304 (1992) (O'Connor, J., concurring); *id.* at 308 (Kennedy, J., concurring); *see also* Williams v. Taylor, 529 U.S. 362, 382 (2000) (opinion of Stevens, J.).

78. *See Williams*, 529 U.S. at 412 (opinion of O'Connor, J., for a majority of the Court) (stating in dicta that the AEDPA goes further than *Teague* by "restrict[ing] the source of clearly established law to this Court's jurisprudence"); *see also id.* at 380–82 (opinion of Stevens, J., for four members of the Court) (same, in dicta); *see also* Carey v. Musladin, 549 U.S. 70 (2006); *cf. Caspari*, 510 U.S. at 394–95 (in engaging in analysis of whether a rule was "new" under *Teague*, the Court examined the decisions of federal circuit courts and state supreme courts); *but see* Soffar v. Cockrell, 300 F.3d 588, 597–98 (5th Cir. 2002) (en banc) (contending that "existing precedent" for *Teague* purposes refers only to Supreme Court decisions, not lower federal court decisions).

The Supreme Court originally recognized two exceptions to *Teague's* nonret-roactivity doctrine. The first was that, if the new rule was a truly fundamental or "watershed" rule of criminal procedure, the petitioner was entitled to benefit from the rule, despite its newness.[79] Second, the Court held that *Teague* does not apply to a claim that does not rely on a new rule of criminal procedure, but instead relies on a new rule of substantive law (such as a constitutional prohibition on criminal punishment for certain types of activity or a judicial determination that certain conduct is not in violation of a penal statute).[80] In 2021, in *Edwards v. Vannoy*,[81] the Court abolished the first exception after observing that the Court never had, and never would, apply that exception to any newly-created constitutional rule of criminal procedure. Therefore, only the second exception still exists in the Supreme Court's habeas corpus jurisprudence. At least one federal court of appeals has recognized an additional exception to *Teague*: when the claim asserted on federal habeas corpus review could not have been raised on direct appeal and instead could only have been raised for the first time on collateral review.[82]

15.2.2.3 *Brecht* Harmless-Error Doctrine

As discussed in the preceding chapter, if a defendant's constitutional rights were violated at trial or at sentencing, an appellate court on direct appeal generally must determine whether the error was "harmless beyond a reasonable doubt."[83] Conversely, on federal habeas corpus review, this *Chapman* standard generally is inapplicable, and instead, a habeas petitioner faces a considerably less favorable harmless-error standard.[84] Unlike the *Chapman* standard, which places the burden on the prosecution to show beyond a reasonable doubt that the error did not affect or contribute to the guilty verdict or sentence, the *Brecht* standard places a lower burden on the prosecution to show that the error did not have a "substantial and injurious effect" on the verdict or sentence.[85] The *Brecht* standard applies on federal habeas corpus review even if the state courts wrongly failed to apply the *Chapman* standard (because they erroneously found no error as a threshold matter) or unreasonably applied the *Chapman* standard.[86] If an error is "structural" in nature, then reversal is automatic, either on direct appeal or on federal habeas corpus review.[87]

---

79. *Banks*, 542 U.S. at 416–17.
80. Schriro v. Summerlin, 542 U.S. 348, 352 & n.4 (2004). For examples of cases in which the Supreme Court determined that new rules were "substantive" and thus applied retroactively, *see* Welch v. United States, 136 S. Ct. 1257 (2016), *and* Montgomery v. Louisiana, 136 S. Ct. 718 (2016).
81. 141 S. Ct. 1547 (2021).
82. *See* Jackson v. Johnson, 217 F.3d 360, 364 (5th Cir. 2000).
83. Chapman v. California, 386 U.S. 18, 24 (1967).
84. *See* Brecht v. Abrahamson, 507 U.S. 619 (1993); *see also* O'Neal v. McAninch, 513 U.S. 432 (1995).
85. *Brecht*, 507 U.S. at 631.
86. *See* Fry v. Pliler, 551 U.S. 112 (2007).
87. *See* California v. Roy, 519 U.S. 2 (1997) (per curiam). Structural errors are discussed in Chapter Fourteen.

15.2.2.4   *Stone v. Powell* Bar to Fourth Amendment Claims

In *Stone v. Powell*,[88] the Supreme Court held that Fourth Amendment exclusionary rule claims based on an illegal search or seizure are not cognizable on federal habeas corpus review as long as the habeas petitioner had a full and fair opportunity to litigate the claim both at trial and on direct appeal (whether or not the claim was raised in the state courts).[89] The Supreme Court has never clarified precisely what constitutes a "full and fair opportunity," and the federal courts of appeals take divergent approaches to the meaning of the phrase.[90] The Court has held that a Sixth Amendment claim of ineffective assistance of counsel based on prior counsel's failure to raise a Fourth Amendment claim in the trial court or on appeal is cognizable on federal habeas corpus review.[91] The Court to date has refused to extend *Stone* to other types of constitutional claims (such as *Miranda* claims).[92]

15.2.3 *Statutory Hurdles*

The Antiterrorism and Effective Death Penalty Act of 1996[93] created certain new hurdles that did not previously exist (e.g., the statute of limitations; deference to state courts' legal rulings) while supplanting some prior judicially created hurdles with more stringent hurdles (e.g., "successive petition" provisions); and it left in place certain judicial hurdles not addressed in the AEDPA (e.g., *Teague*, procedural default, and harmless-error doctrines). The AEDPA also created special procedures—with even higher hurdles for petitioners—in § 2254 capital habeas corpus cases when states "opt in" by meeting rigorous standards concerning the appointment of counsel in state habeas corpus proceedings.[94] However, with one possible exception, to date no state with capital punishment has qualified for opt-in status under the AEDPA.[95]

---

88. Stone v. Powell, 428 U.S. 465 (1976).

89. *Id.* at 494 & n.37; *see also* United States v. Ishmael, 343 F.3d 741 (5th Cir. 2003) (noting that the lower federal courts have applied *Stone* in § 2255 cases).

90. *See* Shoemaker v. Riley, 459 U.S. 948, 948–49 (1982) (White, J., dissenting from the denial of certiorari) (discussing divergent approaches taken by various federal circuit courts); *see also* Janet B. Jones, *What Constitutes "An Opportunity for Full and Fair Litigation" in State Court Precluding Habeas Corpus Review Under 28 U.S.C. § 2254 in Federal Court of State Prisoner's Fourth Amendment Claims*, 75 A.L.R. FED. 9 (1985 with 2004 updates).

91. Kimmelman v. Morrison, 477 U.S. 365 (1986).

92. *See, e.g.,* Withrow v. Williams, 507 U.S. 680 (1993).

93. The AEDPA only applies to federal habeas corpus petitions filed on or after its effective date, i.e., April 24, 1996. *See* Lindh v. Murphy, 521 U.S. 320 (1997).

94. *See* 28 U.S.C. §§ 2261–2266. The U.S. Attorney General is charged with determining whether a particular death penalty state qualifies under the "opt in" provision. *See* 28 U.S.C. §§ 2261(b)(1) & 2265.

95. *See* Cristina Stummer, *To Be or Not to Be: Opt-in Status Under the Antiterrorism and Effective Death Penalty Act*, 25 VT. L. REV. 603, 608 & n.31 (Winter 2001).

15.2.3.1   One-Year Statute of Limitations

Under 28 U.S.C. §§ 2244(d)(1) and 2255, state and federal prisoners ordinarily have one year from the date that their convictions became "final" to file a habeas corpus petition. The definition of "finality" is adopted from the *Teague* context, i.e., the date that the Supreme Court denied certiorari on direct appeal or, if no certiorari petition was filed, the point when a defendant ceased pursuing discretionary appeals on direct review.[96] However, if no appeal was filed after the defendant was sentenced, the one-year clock starts to run from the date on which the notice of appeal was due.[97]

In certain other situations, the statute of limitations runs from the latest of three different dates (if any of the three is later than the "finality" date): 1) the date that an impediment to filing caused by governmental action was removed; 2) the date on which a new rule relied on by a petitioner was announced by the Supreme Court "if the right has been . . . made retroactively applicable to cases on collateral review"; or 3) the date on which the factual predicate of the claim raised by the petitioner "could have been discovered through the exercise of due diligence."[98]

Of these three triggering situations, the one that has generated the most controversy is when a new rule is announced by the Supreme Court and then made retroactively applicable to cases on collateral review. In *Dodd v. United States*,[99] the Supreme Court held that the date on which the Court announces a new rule starts the limitations clock running, rather than the date on which the rule is applied retroactively (unless both events occur on the same date). The lower federal courts are in agreement that a lower court's decision that a prior Supreme Court decision (that announced a new rule) is retroactively applicable to cases on collateral review permits a habeas petitioner to receive the benefit of the statute of limitations' date extension.[100] Thus, if the Supreme Court announces a new rule, a habeas petitioner whose conviction and sentence already have become final on direct appeal has one year in which to attempt to convince a lower federal court to retroactively apply the new rule.

In § 2254 cases, § 2244(d)(2) provides that the time during which a "properly filed application for state post-conviction or other collateral review" is pending is tolled for purposes of the federal statute of limitations if the state litigation concerned the same criminal judgment or sentence being challenged in the federal litigation (whether or not the state litigation actually concerned the same claims

---

96. Clay v. United States, 537 U.S. 522 (2003); *see also* Gonzalez v. Thaler, 565 U.S. 134, 149–51 (2012).
97. *See, e.g.*, Egerton v. Cockrell, 334 F.3d 433, 435 (5th Cir. 2003).
98. 28 U.S.C. §§ 2244(d)(1)(A)–(D) & 2255.
99. Dodd v. United States, 545 U.S. 353 (2005).
100. *See* United States v. Thomas, 627 F.3d 534, 536–37 (4th Cir. 2010) (citing decisions).

later raised in the federal case).[101] "Properly filed" simply means that the petitioner filed their state petition in accordance with state rules for filing; the fact that a state court dismissed the state petition on procedural default grounds (other than under a state statute of limitations) is irrelevant.[102] Under § 2244(d)(2), the statute of limitations is not tolled during the time that a state prisoner litigated a previous federal habeas petition that ultimately was dismissed for failure to exhaust state remedies.[103] Thus, if the petitioner refiles a federal petition after exhausting state remedies, the time spent in federal court in connection with the initial, unexhausted federal petition did not toll the limitations period.

In *Holland v. Florida*, the Supreme Court recognized the doctrine of "equitable tolling" of the AEDPA's statute of limitations in rare cases involving exceptional circumstances beyond the petitioner's control, such as a court-appointed counsel's grossly negligent failure to file a habeas corpus petition in a timely manner despite the petitioner's repeated demands or an unrepresented inmate who was insane during the entire limitations period.[104] The Supreme Court also has recognized that a showing of "actual innocence" by a federal habeas petitioner is an equitable exception to the statute of limitations.[105]

The Supreme Court has held that a federal court ordinarily has discretion to sua sponte raise a statute of limitations bar not raised by the respondent.[106] A court lacks that power, however, when the respondent had intentionally abandoned the limitations defense.[107]

15.2.3.2   Exhaustion of State Court Remedies

The AEDPA includes a requirement that a state prisoner who files a § 2254 habeas petition must have exhausted available state court remedies with respect to every claim raised in the federal petition (on direct appeal and/or on state habeas corpus review).[108] The AEDPA is similar to the prior statutory requirement of exhaustion,[109] although it now provides exhaustion cannot be waived by the state unless expressly waived.[110] Under prior law, the state could implicitly waive ex-

---

101. *See, e.g.*, Ford v. Moore, 296 F.3d 1035 (11th Cir. 2002); Tillema v. Long, 253 F.3d 494 (9th Cir. 2001).
102. Artuz v. Bennett, 531 U.S. 4 (2000); *see also* Allen v. Siebert, 552 U.S. 3 (2007); Pace v. Diguglielmo, 544 U.S. 408 (2005); Carey v. Saffold, 536 U.S. 214 (2002).
103. *See* Duncan v. Walker, 533 U.S. 167 (2001).
104. Holland v. Florida, 560 U.S. 631 (2010); *see also* Calderon v. United States Dist. Ct., 163 F.3d 530 (9th Cir. 1998) (en banc); United States v. Patterson, 211 F.3d 927, 931–32 (5th Cir. 2000).
105. McQuiggin v. Perkins, 569 U.S. 383 (2013).
106. Day v. McDonough, 547 U.S. 198 (2006).
107. Wood v. Milyard, 565 U.S. 463 (2012).
108. 28 U.S.C. § 2254(b)(1).
109. Rose v. Lundy, 455 U.S. 509 (1982).
110. 28 U.S.C. § 2254(b)(3).

haustion by failing to assert non-exhaustion in a timely manner.[111] Filing a federal petition with even a single unexhausted claim (called a "mixed petition") will require dismissal of the entire petition, unless the petitioner chooses to delete the unexhausted claims from the petition or unless the federal court proceeds to deny the unexhausted claim(s) on the merits.[112] The Supreme Court has held that federal district courts have limited discretion to hold a federal habeas corpus petition in abeyance, pending the petitioner's return to the state courts to exhaust an unexhausted claim(s) to prevent the petition from being dismissed under the statute of limitations.[113]

To exhaust state remedies, a state prisoner must have "fairly presented" both the legal and factual bases of all claims to the state courts that the petitioner later raises on federal habeas corpus review.[114] Each claim must be framed as a federal constitutional claim—raising an analogous state law claim is insufficient to exhaust it for federal review.[115] In addition, a state prisoner must raise the claim on a discretionary appeal to the state's highest court, if such a discretionary appeal is available under state law,[116] in addition to raising the claim on the first appeal as a matter of right to a state's intermediate appellate court.[117] As long as a state defendant fairly presented a claim to the state appellate courts, the claim is considered exhausted; if the state courts ignored the claim, the claim will be deemed exhausted.[118] "Factual" exhaustion issues often turn on whether the supposedly "new" facts offered in the federal proceeding "fundamentally alter the legal claim already considered by the state courts."[119] If they do not do so, then the claim will not be dismissed.[120]

---

111. Gordon v. Nagle, 2 F.3d 385, 386 n.3 (11th Cir. 1993).

112. *Rose*, 455 U.S. at 522; *see also* 28 U.S.C. § 2254(b)(2).

113. Rhines v. Weber, 544 U.S. 269 (2005).

114. *See, e.g.*, Frederickson v. Wood, 87 F.3d 244, 245 (8th Cir. 1996).

115. *See* Duncan v. Henry, 513 U.S. 364 (1995) (per curiam); *see also* Baldwin v. Reese, 541 U.S. 27 (2004).

116. O'Sullivan v. Boerckel, 526 U.S. 838 (1999). A state may effectively opt out of this requirement by providing that under state law such a discretionary appeal to the state's highest court is not required in order to exhaust judicial review in the state court system. *See, e.g.*, Randolph v. Kemna, 276 F.3d 401, 404–05 (8th Cir. 2002). There is a similar, judicially created "administrative" exhaustion requirement for prisoners who file § 2241 habeas petitions challenging the manner in which their sentences were executed. Such a prisoner must first seek relief from an administrative body, if one is available. *See* United States v. Cleto, 956 F.2d 83, 84 (5th Cir. 1992).

117. Castille v. Peoples, 489 U.S. 346 (1989).

118. Smith v. Digmon, 434 U.S. 332 (1978) (per curiam).

119. Vasquez v. Hillery, 474 U.S. 254, 260 (1986).

120. *Id.* (finding that supplemental facts offered in federal habeas corpus proceeding did not fundamentally alter the claim previously litigated in the state courts); *see also* Weaver v. Thompson, 197 F.3d 359, 364 (9th Cir. 1999).

15.2.3.3   Abuse of the Writ/Successive Petitions

The AEDPA includes new provisions drastically limiting second or "successive" federal habeas corpus petitions.[121] The new law places greater limits on successive petitions than the prior, judicially created "abuse-of-the-writ" doctrine (as set forth in *McCleskey v. Zant*[122]).

The AEDPA provides that "a claim presented in a second or successive habeas corpus application under § 2254 that was presented in a prior [federal petition] shall be dismissed."[123] There are no exceptions here.[124] Under prior law, in certain circumstances a claim previously raised could be raised again in a successive § 2254 habeas corpus appeal based on intervening legal developments or newly available facts.[125] There is no equivalent absolute ban on raising the same claim again in a successive § 2255 petition; rather, such claims are subject to the general limits on successive petitions described below.

With respect to claims not raised in a prior federal habeas petition, but included in a subsequent petition, the AEDPA provides, in both §§ 2254 and 2255 cases, that such claims are permitted only under two narrow circumstances: 1) the petitioner relies on a "new rule of constitutional law made retroactive to cases on collateral review by the Supreme Court that was previously unavailable"; or 2) the petitioner raises a claim based on newly discovered evidence that establishes by clear and convincing evidence that but for the constitutional error, no rational jury would have found the petitioner guilty of the underlying offense.[126]

Under the AEDPA, a petitioner who wishes to file a successive petition in federal district court, in either a § 2244 or § 2255 case, must receive permission to file the petition from a three-judge panel of a federal court of appeals. No rehearing petition or certiorari petition is permitted if the panel denies such permission.[127] The Supreme Court has stated, however, that in an exceptional case, an original writ of habeas corpus can be filed in the U.S. Supreme Court in the first instance pursuant to 28 U.S.C. § 2241 after a panel refuses permission to file a successive petition.[128]

With respect to the new rule exception to the bar on successive petitions, such a rule must be both announced and retroactively applied by the Supreme Court for

---

121. *See* 28 U.S.C. §§ 2244(b) & 2255.
122. McClesky v. Zant, 499 U.S. 467 (1991).
123. 28 U.S.C. § 2244(b)(1).
124. Tyler v. Cain, 533 U.S. 656, 661 (2001).
125. Lackey v. Scott, 885 F. Supp. 958, 969 (W.D. Tex. 1995).
126. 28 U.S.C. §§ 2244(b)(2) & 2255 (last paragraph).
127. 28 U.S.C. §§ 2244(b)(3) & 2255 (last paragraph).
128. *See* Felker v. Turpin, 518 U.S. 651 (1996); *see also* In re Davis, 557 U.S. 952 (2009) (exercising jurisdiction over such an original writ of habeas corpus; transferring to the federal district court for an evidentiary hearing).

the exception to apply.[129] This appears to differ from the new rule exception to the statute of limitations, whereby, according to a majority of lower federal courts, a petitioner may rely on a lower court decision that has retroactively applied a new rule announced by the Supreme Court.[130]

When § 2255 bars a successive petition for federal prisoners, 28 U.S.C. § 2241 may still provide a vehicle for federal inmates to file a successive petition in district court.[131] Such a successive petition may be filed only when there has been a judicial decision interpreting the scope of a federal penal statute that compels the conclusion that the defendant's conduct was not criminal and the defendant could not have prevailed on that claim (based on then-extant law) in their original § 2255 action.[132]

15.2.3.4   Deference to State Court Adjudications "on the Merits"

Under pre-AEDPA law, federal courts on habeas corpus review engaged in independent, de novo review of legal claims previously adjudicated by a state court, subject only to the *Teague* doctrine's limits on new rules.[133] Conversely, under the AEDPA, a federal court generally must afford a large degree of deference to the state courts when the federal court reviews a claim previously rejected on the merits by a state court.[134] This deferential "standard of review" (for lack of a better term) precludes federal habeas corpus relief with respect to any claim that was adjudicated on the merits in State court proceedings unless the state court's adjudication 1) "resulted in a decision that was contrary to, or involved an unreasonable application of, clearly established Federal law, as determined by the Supreme Court of the United States"; or 2) "resulted in a decision that was based on an unreasonable determination of the facts in light of the evidence presented in the state court proceeding."[135]

In *Williams v. Taylor*,[136] the Supreme Court interpreted this new standard of review. The Court held that under the "contrary to" clause, a federal habeas court may grant the writ if the state court arrives at a conclusion opposite to that reached by the Court on a question of law or if the state court decides a case differently than the Court has on a set of materially indistinguishable facts. Alternatively, "[u]nder the 'unreasonable application' clause, a federal habeas court may grant the writ if the state court identifies the correct governing legal principle from this Court's decisions but unreasonably applies that principle to the facts of the prisoner's case."[137]

---

129. *Tyler*, 533 U.S. at 664–68.
130. United States v. Thomas, 627 F.3d 534, 536–37 (4th Cir. 2010) (citing cases).
131. *See, e.g.*, Reyes-Requena v. United States, 243 F.3d 893 (5th Cir. 2001).
132. *See id.*; *see also* In re Dorsainvil, 119 F.3d 245 (3d Cir. 1997).
133. *See* Wright v. West, 505 U.S. 277 (1992); Brown v. Allen, 344 U.S. 443 (1953).
134. 28 U.S.C. § 2254(d).
135. 28 U.S.C. § 2254(d)(1) & (2); *see also* Panetti v. Quarterman, 551 U.S. 930, 953–54 (2007).
136. Williams v. Taylor, 529 U.S. 362 (2000).
137. *Id.* at 412–13.

In dozens of cases since the AEDPA was enacted, the Supreme Court has ruled that a state court's adjudication of a federal constitutional claim was "not unreasonable" in view of existing Supreme Court precedent.[138]

The new standard of review is superficially similar to the *Teague* doctrine, but differs in four important respects: 1) *Teague*'s "old rules" could have been found in lower court precedent, while under the AEDPA, "clearly established federal law" refers solely to U.S. Supreme Court decisions;[139] 2) under *Teague*, as long as an "old" rule was involved, a state court's incorrect application of the old rule was sufficient to permit a federal court to find that *Teague* did not preclude federal habeas corpus relief, while under the AEDPA a state court's misapplication of the old rule must not only be incorrect, but also be objectively unreasonable for federal habeas corpus relief to be granted;[140] 3) under *Teague*, the relevant date for looking at existing precedent is the date that the petitioner's conviction and sentence became final in the direct appeal process, whereas under the AEDPA the relevant date is the date that the last state court adjudicated a constitutional claim on the merits;[141] and 4) a state could waive *Teague* if it failed to invoke it (although a court could invoke it sua sponte), while the AEDPA's standard of review is mandatory.[142]

In addition, the AEDPA changed the manner in which a federal habeas court reviews the factual predicate of a constitutional claim adjudicated in state court in terms of deciding whether the legal ruling warrants deference (based on the relevant facts). The Supreme Court, in interpreting various provisions in the AEDPA, has held that a federal court's determination of whether a state court's adjudication of a claim was "contrary to" or an "unreasonable application" of Supreme Court precedent must be based solely on the evidence before the state court (and not also on new evidence offered for the first time in a federal habeas corpus proceeding).[143] Thus, even more so than under *Teague*, the state court's adjudication of a federal constitutional claim is very difficult (although not impossible) to challenge in federal court.[144]

An "adjudication on the merits" by a state court means that the state court rejected the claim based on the merits—even if in a summary manner without providing any reasons[145]—as opposed to finding the claim procedurally defaulted (and,

---

138. *See, e.g.*, White v. Woodall, 572 U.S. 415 (2014); Burt v. Titlow, 571 U.S. 12 (2013).

139. *See* Carey v. Musladin, 549 U.S. 70, 74 (2006).

140. *Id.* at 77.

141. Greene v. Fisher, 565 U.S. 34 (2011).

142. Goeke v. Branch, 514 U.S. 115 (1995).

143. *See* Cullen v. Pinholster, 563 U.S. 170 (2011).

144. *See, e.g.*, Shoop v. Hill, 139 S. Ct. 504 (2019) (per curiam); Sexton v. Beadreaux, 138 S. Ct. 2555 (2018) (per curiam); Dunn v. Madison, 138 S. Ct. 9 (2017) (per curiam).

145. *See* Harrington v. Richter, 562 U.S. 86, 98–100 (2011). If a state appellate court rejected a constitutional claim without offering any reasons—including by apparently ignoring a claim entirely—a federal court ordinarily must "look through" that summary opinion to any lower state court offering reasons in its adjudication of the claim on the merits and apply the AEDPA's deference to that opinion instead. Wilson v. Sellers, 138 S. Ct. 1188, 1192 (2018).

thus, not addressing the merits, not even in the alternative).[146] In other words, if a state court's order simply denied a prisoner's appeal without offering any reasons, a federal court should presume the state court rejected all federal constitutional claims raised "on the merits." Only if the state court record indicates that the state court refused to address the merits of a claim that was fairly presented may a federal court then engage in de novo review under the AEDPA, subject only to the *Teague* doctrine.[147]

15.2.3.5   Deference to State Court Findings of Fact

Under the pre-AEDPA law, although federal courts on habeas corpus review generally had to defer to factual findings previously made by state courts, there were numerous exceptions to such a "presumption of correctness."[148] Frequently under the prior law, a state court's factual findings were rejected by the federal courts on the ground that the state court hearing in which the facts were developed was not "full" and "fair" in some respect.[149] Under the AEDPA, however, it is very difficult for a federal court to disregard a state court's factual findings.[150] Despite these new statutory provisions requiring great deference to a state court's factual findings, the Supreme Court has stated that "[d]eference does not by definition preclude [federal habeas corpus] relief."[151] If a state court's factual findings are "objectively unreasonable" based on the evidence presented in the state court proceeding, then no federal court deference is required.[152] A federal habeas corpus petitioner may not challenge the correctness of a state court's factual findings by offering new evidence that was not offered in the state court proceeding and, instead, is limited to challenging a state court's factual finding as unreasonable based on the evidence offered in the state court proceeding.[153]

---

146. *Richter*, 562 U.S. at 99–100.
147. *See* Fisher v. Texas, 169 F.3d 295, 300 (5th Cir. 1999).
148. *See* Sumner v. Mata, 455 U.S. 591, 592 & n.1 (1982) (per curiam); *cf.* Townsend v. Sain, 372 U.S. 293 (1963).
149. *See, e.g.*, Hakeem v. Beyer, 990 F.2d 750, 770–71 (3d Cir. 1993).
150. *See* 28 U.S.C. § 2254(e)(1) ("a determination of a factual issue by a state court shall be presumed correct [and] [t]he applicant shall have the burden of rebutting the presumption of correctness by clear and convincing evidence"); *see also* § 2254(d)(2) (permitting federal habeas corpus relief when the state court decision "resulted in a decision that was based on an unreasonable determination of the facts in light of the evidence presented in the state court proceeding").
151. Miller-El v. Cockrell, 537 U.S. 322, 340–41 (2003); *see also* Miller-El v. Dretke, 545 U.S. 231 (2005); Brumfield v. Cain, 576 U.S. 305 (2015); Tharpe v. Sellers, 138 S. Ct. 545 (2018) (per curiam).
152. *Cockrell*, 537 U.S. at 340–41 (citing 28 U.S.C. § 2254(d)(2)). It should be noted that in the very rare case where state factual findings help rather than hurt a federal habeas corpus petitioner, those findings still bind the federal courts. *See* Burden v. Zant, 498 U.S. 433 (1991) (per curiam).
153. Cullen v. Pinholster, 563 U.S. 170 (2011); *see also* Stokley v. Ryan, 659 F.3d 802, 807–08 (9th Cir. 2011). An open question, which has divided the federal circuit courts, is whether 28 U.S.C. § 2254(e)(1) requires a federal habeas corpus petitioner to show by "clear and convincing" evidence that the state court's adjudication of a constitutional claim was "based on an unreasonable determination of the facts" (within the meaning of 28 U.S.C. § 2254(d)(2)) in light of the evidence

15.2.3.6   Limitations on Federal Evidentiary Hearings

Under the pre-AEDPA law, a federal habeas petitioner who, given the opportunity, failed to present material evidence in the state court proceedings was procedurally barred from developing such evidence in the federal proceedings unless they could show cause and prejudice or, alternatively, their actual innocence.[154] The AEDPA partially modified this rule.[155] Section 2254(e)(2) now states that:

> If the applicant has failed to develop the factual basis of a claim in state court proceedings, the [federal] court shall not hold an evidentiary hearing on the claim unless the applicant shows that—(A) the claim relies on (i) a new rule of constitutional law, made retroactive to cases on collateral review by the Supreme Court, that was previously unavailable; or (ii) a factual predicate that could not have been previously discovered through the exercise of due diligence; and (B) the facts underlying the claim would be sufficient to show by clear and convincing evidence that but for constitutional error, no reasonable factfinder would have found the applicant guilty of the underlying offense.[156]

Therefore, the AEDPA is much stricter than pre-AEDPA law in that a petitioner's failure to develop facts in the state court precludes any further development. The phrase "failed to develop" in § 2254(e)(2) means that the petitioner or their state lawyer was to blame (as a result of neglect or failure to exercise due diligence).[157] Section 2254(e)(2) does not foreclose a federal evidentiary hearing in a case in which the lack of factual development in the state courts was not attributable to the petitioner or their counsel.[158]

15.2.4 *Appeals in Federal Habeas Corpus Cases*[159]

Because all types of federal habeas corpus actions are deemed civil cases for purposes of Federal Rule of Appellate Procedure 4(a), petitioners (as well as

---

before the state court (when no new evidence has been offered in the federal court proceeding. The Supreme Court has noted the circuit split but has not resolved it yet. *See* Wood v. Allen, 558 U.S. 290, 299–300 & n.1 (2010) (citing lower court cases).

154. *See* Keeney v. Tamayo-Reyes, 504 U.S. 1 (1992).

155. *See* 28 U.S.C. § 2254(e)(2).

156. *Id.*

157. Williams v. Taylor, 529 U.S. 420 (2000).

158. *Id.*

159. A federal habeas corpus petitioner may apply for release on bond pending an appeal of a district court's judgment granting or denying federal habeas corpus relief. *See* FED. R. APP. P. 23(b) & (c); *see also* Hilton v. Braunskill, 481 U.S. 770 (1987). A federal district court also possesses equitable authority in "extraordinary" situations to grant a habeas petitioner (including a state prisoner) release on bond while a habeas corpus petition is pending before the district court. *See, e.g.*, Landano v. Rafferty, 970 F.2d 1230, 1239–40 (3d Cir. 1992). However, the petitioner must have a high probability of success in order to be released on bond. *Id.*

respondents) in §§ 2241 and 2254 cases have thirty days to file a notice of appeal under Rule 4(a)(1)(A) and sixty days in § 2255 cases under Rule 4(a)(1)(B). At the same time or shortly after a notice of appeal is filed, a habeas petitioner also must file an application for a certificate of appealability (COA) under 28 U.S.C. § 2253 and Federal Rule of Appellate Procedure 22 to proceed with an appeal. If a district court denies a COA, then the petitioner may reapply for a COA from the court of appeals. If the court of appeals denies a COA, then a certiorari petition may be filed with the Supreme Court from the court of appeals' denial[160] or the petitioner may reapply for a COA from a Circuit Justice (although such applications are almost never granted).[161]

To obtain a COA, a petitioner who lost in federal district court must make a "substantial showing" of a denial of a constitutional right regarding each claim for habeas corpus relief sought to be appealed.[162] A COA is essentially the equivalent of the former certificate of probable cause (CPC) in § 2254 cases[163] and merely codifies the old standard for a CPC set forth in *Barefoot v. Estelle*.[164] A COA, unlike the former CPC, is issue-specific—that is, an appeal is authorized only on those issues specifically certified by a court that grants a COA.[165] The Supreme Court has characterized the COA requirement as "non-jurisdictional" in nature.[166]

The *Barefoot* "substantial showing" standard requires only that the issue sought to be raised on appeal be "debatable among jurists of reason; that a court could resolve the issues [in a different manner than the district court]; or that the questions are adequate to deserve encouragement to proceed further."[167] A petitioner must only show that "reasonable jurists" would find their claim "debatable," not that a reasonable jurist would find the claim meritorious.[168] If a federal district court denied relief on threshold procedural grounds (e.g., refused to address the merits of claim on procedural default grounds), a petitioner need only show that the district court's procedural ruling was debatable among reasonable jurists and that the petition simply "state[d] a valid claim" for relief.[169] If a petitioner's argument finds direct support in another court's precedent, then the petitioner necessarily is

---

160. Hohn v. United States, 524 U.S. 236 (1998).
161. *See* Brent E. Newton, *Applications for Certificates of Appealability and the Supreme Court's "Obligatory" Jurisdiction*, 5 J. App. Prac. & Process 177 (2003).
162. 28 U.S.C. § 2253(c)(2).
163. *See* Miller-El v. Cockrell, 537 U.S. 322, 335–38 (2003); *see also* Barefoot v. Estelle, 463 U.S. 880 (1983).
164. *Cockrell*, 537 U.S. at 337–38.
165. 28 U.S.C. § 2253(c)(3).
166. Gonzalez v. Thaler, 565 U.S. 134 (2012).
167. *Barefoot*, 463 U.S. at 893 & n.4 (citations and internal quotations omitted; bracketed language in original).
168. *Cockrell*, 537 U.S. at 337–38.
169. Slack v. McDaniel, 529 U.S. 473, 484 (2000).

entitled to a COA under the *Barefoot* standard.[170] The *Barefoot* standard also governs a federal court's decision of whether to grant a stay of execution in a capital habeas case.[171]

15.3 Leading Supreme Court Decisions Concerning Federal Habeas

- *Stone v. Powell*, 428 U.S. 465 (1976) (a Fourth Amendment claim is not cognizable on federal habeas corpus review if the defendant had a full and fair opportunity to raise the claim at trial and on direct appeal).

- *Wainwright v. Sykes*, 433 U.S. 72 (1977) (§ 2254 federal habeas corpus review of merits of a constitutional claim that was "procedurally defaulted" during state court appeals process ordinarily is precluded unless petitioner shows "cause" and "prejudice" for procedural default).

- *Rose v. Lundy*, 455 U.S. 509 (1982) ("mixed" federal habeas corpus petition—i.e., one containing both exhausted and nonexhausted claims—must be dismissed or the petitioner must dismiss the nonexhausted claims).

- *Engle v. Isaac*, 456 U.S. 107 (1982) (mere fact that it would have been futile to raise a legal claim in a particular court based on that court's then-extant adverse precedent is not cause for the default since the court theoretically could have reconsidered its precedent and granted relief).

- *Frady v. United States*, 456 U.S. 152 (1982) (applying *Sykes* "cause and prejudice" standard to claims raised for the first time in a § 2255 postconviction proceeding that could have been raised at trial but were not so raised).

- *Barefoot v. Estelle*, 463 U.S. 880 (1983) (setting forth the reasonably debatable standard governing a certificate of probable cause (CPC) to appeal in a federal habeas corpus case), *reaff'd* in *Miller-El v. Cockrell*, 537 U.S. 322 (2003) (adopting the *Barefoot* standard for renamed certificate of appealability (COA) under the AEDPA).

- *Reed v. Ross*, 468 U.S. 1 (1984) (novelty of a constitutional claim at the time of a procedural default constitutes cause for the default).

- *Vasquez v. Hillery*, 474 U.S. 254 (1986) (state defendant must exhaust factual as well as legal bases of federal constitutional claims in state courts before such claims may be litigated on federal habeas corpus review).

---

170. *See* Lozada v. Deeds, 498 U.S. 430 (1991) (per curiam).
171. Delo v. Stokes, 495 U.S. 320 (1990) (per curiam); *see also* Barnard v. Collins, 13 F.3d 871, 875 (5th Cir. 1994).

- *Murray v. Carrier*, 477 U.S. 478 (1986) (ineffective assistance of counsel under *Strickland v. Washington*, 466 U.S. 668 (1984), resulting in procedural default is cause for the procedural bar as long as the ineffectiveness occurred during a time when a defendant had a constitutional right to the assistance of counsel).

- *Amadeo v. Zant*, 486 U.S. 214 (1988) (prosecution or police officers' suppression of evidence is cause for procedural default of a claim related to such evidence, so long as evidence was not reasonably available to defendant at time of default).

- *Harris v. Reed*, 489 U.S. 255 (1989) (unless last state court offering a reasoned analysis of a constitutional claim issued a "plain statement" that the claim was procedurally defaulted under state law, a federal court must address merits of claim and cannot invoke a procedural bar as a basis for refusing to address merits of the claim).

- *Teague v. Lane*, 489 U.S. 288 (1989) (holding that new rule of constitutional criminal procedure ordinarily is not retroactively applicable to cases that were final at the time of the new rule's announcement; two narrow exceptions to this nonretroactivity doctrine: 1) new rules that render a defendant ineligible for criminal liability or punishment, and 2) bedrock rules of criminal procedure that are truly fundamental in nature, such as the right to counsel).

- *Dugger v. Adams*, 489 U.S. 401 (1989) (state procedural default rule that has not been consistently and regularly applied by the state courts in other cases is not an adequate state law ground barring federal habeas corpus review of a constitutional claim that was subject to this procedural default rule).

- *Coleman v. Thompson*, 501 U.S. 722 (1991) (incompetence of state habeas corpus counsel in failing to properly exhaust federal constitutional claim is not cause for state court's application of a procedural bar to the claim because there is no constitutional right to counsel on state habeas corpus review; federal courts may not address merits of such a procedurally defaulted claim).

- *Brecht v. Abrahamson*, 507 U.S. 619 (1993) (refusing to apply *Chapman* direct appeal, harmless-error standard to cases on federal habeas corpus review; constitutional error is harmless on federal habeas review only if it had a "substantial and injurious effect or influence" on the defendant's conviction or sentence, i.e., actual prejudice occurred).

- *Schlup v. Delo*, 513 U.S. 298 (1995) (federal habeas petitioner's actual innocence, if proven by a preponderance of the evidence, will excuse a procedural default of a claim related to the evidence of innocence).

- *Duncan v. Henry*, 513 U.S. 364 (1995) (per curiam) (to exhaust a federal constitutional claim in the state court system, a defendant must fairly present the claim as a federal claim and not merely as a related state-law claim).

- *O'Neal v. McAninch*, 513 U.S. 432 (1995) (placing burden on prosecution with respect to *Brecht* standard, i.e., for constitutional error to be deemed harmless on federal habeas corpus review, prosecution must show that the error did not have a "substantial and injurious effect or influence" on the defendant's conviction or sentence).

- *Bousley v. United States*, 523 U.S. 614 (1998) (holding that in a § 2255 case, a claim that was not raised on direct appeal but could have been so raised, is procedurally defaulted subject to the "cause and prejudice" and "actual innocence" exceptions).

- *Williams v. Taylor*, 529 U.S. 362 (2000) (opinion of O'Connor, J., for a majority of the Court) (leading decision discussing the standard of review under the AEDPA).

- *Williams v. Taylor*, 529 U.S. 420 (2000) (under AEDPA, the lack of factual development during the state court proceedings does not foreclose a federal habeas corpus evidentiary hearing if the failure to develop facts was not attributable to the petitioner or their counsel in the state court system).

- *Duncan v. Walker*, 533 U.S. 167 (2001) (holding that AEDPA's one-year statute of limitations is not "tolled" during the time that a § 2254 petitioner spent pending in federal court on an initial petition that ultimately was dismissed on nonexhaustion grounds).

- *Tyler v. Cain*, 533 U.S. 656 (2001) (under AEDPA, for a claim based on a new rule to be raised in a successive federal habeas corpus petition, the U.S. Supreme Court, as opposed to a lower federal court, must declare that the new rule applies retroactively to cases on collateral review).

- *Stewart v. Smith*, 536 U.S. 856 (2002) (per curiam) (state procedural default rule that requires, as a threshold matter, the state court's resolution of the merits of a federal constitutional issue is not an independent state law ground barring federal habeas corpus review of the issue).

- *Massaro v. United States*, 538 U.S. 500 (2003) (creating an exception to *Bousley*'s procedural default rule for claims of ineffective assistance of trial counsel in § 2255 actions; ordinarily such claims need not be raised on direct appeal in a federal case and, instead, may be raised for the first time in a § 2255 action).

- *Carey v. Musladin*, 549 U.S. 70 (2006) (a state court does not unreasonably apply clearly established Supreme Court precedent under the AEDPA unless the state court's decision was contrary to a specific holding in a prior case decided by the Supreme Court; open questions in the Supreme Court's jurisprudence necessarily are not subject to being resolved by federal habeas courts applying the AEDPA).

- *Holland v. Florida*, 560 U.S. 631 (2010) ("equitable tolling" doctrine applies to AEDPA's statute of limitations if "extraordinary circumstances" exist).

- *Cullen v. Pinholster*, 563 U.S. 170 (2011) (under the AEDPA, federal habeas corpus petitioner may not challenge the correctness of a state court's factual findings by offering new evidence that was not offered in the state court proceeding and, instead, is limited to challenging a state court's factual finding as unreasonable based on the evidence offered in the state court proceeding).

- *Maples v. Thomas*, 565 U.S. 266 (2012) (holding that a federal habeas corpus petitioner can establish "cause" for a procedural default on state habeas corpus review if the default resulted from the petitioner's prior state attorney's "abandonment" without notice).

- *Martinez v. Ryan*, 566 U.S. 1 (2012) (holding that a federal habeas corpus petitioner's prior state habeas corpus attorney's ineffectiveness constitutes cause for failing to a raise a claim about trial counsel's alleged ineffectiveness under Sixth Amendment on the initial state habeas corpus appeal).

- *McQuiggin v. Perkins*, 569 U.S. 383 (2013) (creating an "actual innocence" exception to the AEDPA's statute of limitations).

- *Wilson v. Sellers*, 138 S. Ct. 1188 (2018) (if a state appellate court summarily rejected a constitutional claim without offering any reasons, a federal habeas court ordinarily must "look through" the summary opinion to any lower state court offering reasons in its adjudication of the claim on the merits and apply the AEDPA to the lower state court's opinion).

- *Edwards v. Vannoy*, 141 S. Ct. 1547 (2021) (abolishing *Teague*'s original "watershed" rule exception).

INDEX

G

J

L

M

P

T